The Pro-Life Pregnancy
Help Movement

The Pro-Life Pregnancy Help Movement

SERVING WOMEN OR SAVING BABIES?

Laura S. Hussey

University Press of Kansas

Small portions of Chapters 1–8 and Appendices A and B were previously published in or adapted from articles in the journals *American Politics Research* and *Politics & Policy*.

Published by the University Press of Kansas (Lawrence, Kansas 66045), which was organized by the Kansas Board of Regents and is operated and funded by Emporia State University, Fort Hays State University, Kansas State University, Pittsburg State University, the University of Kansas, and Wichita State University.

Library of Congress Cataloging-in-Publication Data

Names: Hussey, Laura S., author.

Title: The pro-life pregnancy help movement : serving women or saving babies? / Laura S. Hussey.

Description: Lawrence, Kansas : University Press of Kansas, [2019] | Includes bibliographical references and index.

Identifiers: LCCN 2019025431

ISBN 9780700629008 (cloth ; alk. paper)

ISBN 9780700629015 (epub)

Subjects: LCSH: Pro-life movement—United States. | Abortion—United States.

Classification: LCC HQ767.5.U5 H87 2019 | DDC 362.1988/800973—dc23

LC record available at https://lccn.loc.gov/2019025431.

British Library Cataloguing-in-Publication Data is available.

Printed in the United States of America

10 9 8 7 6 5 4 3 2 1

The paper used in this publication is recycled and contains 30 percent postconsumer waste. It is acid free and meets the minimum requirements of the American National Standard for Permanence of Paper for Printed Library Materials Z39.48-1992.

Contents

Figures and Tables

Tables

Preface and Acknowledgments

As this book goes to press, I harbor conflicting emotions. On the one hand, I am excited to share with scholars and members of the public the findings and insights of a research project that has been an important part of my life for the past several years. This project has intrigued, challenged, humbled, and rewarded me, intellectually and in other ways; I feel grateful and honored to have had the opportunities to design, conduct, and publish it, especially as part of my job. This research enabled me to engage the same long-standing fascination with the strategies that people and policy makers use—or could use—to solve social problems that sparked my interest in a career in political science. For this book, the relevant "problems" (in quotation marks to recognize that not every reader will see them as problems) were abortion and the socioeconomic challenges that carrying an unintended pregnancy might pose for women's lives. Although I do not offer my own solutions in this book because my goals in writing it have always been empirical rather than normative, I do describe and analyze some aspects of the solutions offered by participants in the social movement I have studied. I look forward to the thoughtful and constructive conversations that I hope the book will inspire.

On the other hand, I am a little anxious. This is because these are times of greatly polarized and uncivil politics, in which the realm of the "political" has expanded to all kinds of business and social interactions, and in which the most vocal participants in politics often seem to conflate disagreement about a position with judgment of a person. I am conscious that in writing a book that has something to do with abortion, I am wading into an issue that ranks as one of the most polarizing of all and that can strike a personal chord. Indeed, I sometimes feel nervous when people ask me the subject of my book. My concern is that when I reveal it, my conversation partners will draw on well-established negative stereotypes to make assumptions (many of them likely false) about my motives, values, and character—and worse, that they will anticipate judgment from me, damaging our relationship. I am also bracing myself for the possibility that in this political climate, some readers might evaluate my book based on ideology rather than on its social-scientific merits.

Such anxiety might well be irrational, self-centered, and unfair. Thankfully, I cannot recall a time in my career or collegiate education in which anyone treated me or my work unfairly, or withheld their advice, talent, respect, friendship, or support, because of what they knew or suspected about my position on abortion or other issues. I approach my roles as a researcher, teacher, mentor, and member of various communities in the same way, proud of the commitments to scientific integrity, excellence, collegiality, inclusion, and care for people that we maintain at my institution, the University of Maryland–Baltimore County (UMBC), and its Department of Political Science, and that I have encountered elsewhere in my field. I personally find it quite easy—perhaps sometimes too easy—to detach myself from my own beliefs about issues. I am troubled, however, about how our political culture seems to be losing its will and capacity for sincere discussion and even social relations among people with different political beliefs or identities. So I would like to reach out specifically to any readers who might be active in the abortion conflict: I want to thank you for opening my book and ask you for understanding and an open mind. This book represents my good-faith effort to do sound empirical research and make a relevant contribution to debates about social issues. Although the book is unlikely to satisfy all readers, I have tried my best to examine a sensitive issue fairly and communicate my findings diplomatically to a politically diverse audience.

That said, I appreciate that you and other readers might want to be aware of my position on abortion and other issues engaged by this book, so out of respect I will break with typical practice of empirically oriented researchers to share them. I believe that the right to life is and ought to be recognized as a universal human right, held regardless of age, size, location, condition of dependency, or virtually any other characteristic one could imagine. I like to think of myself as consistently pro-life rather than antiabortion. My worldview has been greatly shaped by exposure to Catholic social thought as well as stories of human suffering in the world associated with material poverty, social marginalization, political oppression, and other ills. Among other things, I support robust antipoverty policies and programs, condemn the death penalty, and celebrate women's empowerment. I empathize greatly with women who are pregnant and do not want to be. I regret (and sometimes also resent) the consequences it can mean for their lives. If I could control the world, I would design our culture and our socioeconomic structures very differently, in the hopes of preventing or mitigating those situations and their accompanying hardships—and even though I cannot, I think reforms are worth pursuing. So is anything else we can do now to support women carrying pregnancies and raising children in difficult circumstances, along with helping their families.

I will also disclose that I have had some past involvement in the pro-life movement. This was mostly confined to my youth and largely petered out as I progressed in graduate school, as responsibilities toward work, study, and my children escalated. I also felt a need to distance the research I was doing then from any influence, or appearance of influence, related to abortion politics. Among other activities, I belonged to student pro-life clubs, attended some Marches for Life, tracked policy, and interned and worked for a major pro-life advocacy group. I believe it was through my undergraduate right-to-life group that I first learned about pregnancy centers. I was immediately intrigued and inspired by what I saw in the women who staffed the pregnancy center near my campus. They seemed so radically compassionate, nonjudgmental, and practical and demonstrated keen, perhaps even "progressive," awareness of the perspectives and socioeconomic contexts of women thinking about or choosing abortion. During my senior year, I trained as a volunteer and spent a few hours a week staffing the pregnancy center's waiting room and helping with various chores from clerical tasks to organizing donated goods. My experience there and in the larger pro-life movement is not part of this research—I did not even start thinking about writing a book on pregnancy centers until more than a decade after my volunteer experience—but it is part of the background that led me to ask the research questions I eventually did. Although I do not know for sure, it might have also helped me gain the access I did to the organizations and activists this book concerns.

I did not start this research intending to write a book on the pro-life pregnancy help movement. My original interest was in the politics and substance of what the pro-life movement was doing (or not) about poverty, given that many people believe this is an important factor in abortions. I wanted to explore the nature, correlates, and consequences of the pro-life movement's approach to this issue, but I also thought there was an interesting story to be told about the antipoverty work going on at pregnancy centers, such as the one near my college campus. Having done some previous research on ideological cross pressures and political behavior, I started wondering whether there were any links between the ongoing ideological polarization of US politics and the fact that the pro-life movement's most substantive work to aid pregnant women and the poor was happening outside of political arenas. Meanwhile, the more time I spent reading others' studies on the pro-life movement, the more I came to appreciate how understudied pregnancy centers and related pro-life service providers were. I recognized that there was more I ought to learn about that form of pro-life activism and that my experience with the pregnancy center near my undergraduate campus might not be typical of the movement in other locations or at the present time. Pregnancy centers were gaining political attention, so the scope of my research on the pregnancy help movement grew and became the centerpiece of the project.

Completing this book was harder and took far longer than I anticipated, something I am hardly the first academic to say. It required many drafts and a lot of good advice from others for me to produce a version that I could be proud of and that did not sound overly wonky. I made things harder on myself by stubbornly persisting for a while in trying to write two books in one despite one early proposal reviewer's prophetic warning. My role at work also changed greatly while this book was in progress, as promotions to associate professor and director of a scholarship program ushered in some rewarding and welcome new responsibilities but drastically reduced the time I could devote to research. However, on the positive side, writing this book also availed me of the wisdom, support, and assistance of others, whom I want to acknowledge here.

I am mightily grateful to the anonymous peer reviewers and my editor, David Congdon, at the University Press of Kansas. They offered critical ideas for how to reframe and reorganize my book that improved its focus and enabled retention of some material on my previous poverty-related research question. This book benefitted in countless other ways from the reviewers' extraordinarily careful and constructive comments. It also benefitted from the comments and interest of peer reviewers and editors elsewhere.

Several UMBC students provided valuable research assistance. Laszlo Korossy, Kristin Shields, Lauren Shores, and Jacqueline Winning helped with various aspects of the data collection, entry, analysis, and presentation. Though some of that material was tied to the earlier version of my research question and eventually had to be removed or reduced for the sake of focus, the students' work was truly excellent. At the end, Shaheen Reid provided critical help with clerical tasks. To all those students, I want to say thank you. It was such a gift to be able to count on you, and working with you was a pleasure.

My UMBC colleagues have been blessings in my life and to this book. Art Johnson and George LaNoue provided early advice as I began planning to write a book. Carolyn Forestiere supported me and this project in so many small ways, including taking tasks off my plate, sharing research funds, giving me an inspirational book, ensuring that I took care of myself, and providing encouragement and true friendship. My former dean, John Jeffries, funded course releases that were invaluable as I collected data. My staff at the Sondheim Program, especially Jessica Cook, so very ably kept things running smoothly during stretches when I needed to focus disproportionately on this book. I am so thankful to all of the political science faculty and staff for various forms of advice and support. They looked out for me during a rough stretch of my life while this book was in progress and have created the kind of culture in which it feels good to come to work each day and where everyone is valued.

This research would not have been possible without the cooperation of its subjects. Special thanks go to Jor-El Godsey at Heartbeat International, Tom Glessner at the National Institute of Family and Life Advocates, and especially Cindy Hopkins at Care Net for their willingness to work with me when I first reached out with a request to survey their affiliates. I also appreciate how they welcomed me into their organizations and provided the documents and opportunities to facilitate this research. I am also so very grateful to everyone in the pro-life pregnancy help movement who shared themselves with me in surveys or interviews or who otherwise opened their organizations to me.

Many others also helped me, directly or indirectly, in writing this book. Many former professors or research mentors, although not involved in this project, contributed greatly to my development as a scholar and encouraged me toward a future in research. These include especially Jennifer Warlick, Christina Wolbrecht, Jim Gimpel, Mark Lopez, and Randy O'Bannon. My mother, Diane; my brother, Brian; my husband, Pat; and my friend Holly read and commented on chapter drafts from the perspective of non-PhDs. My father, Bernie; my mother-in-law, Diane; and others gave prayer support. I also want to thank God for providing me interesting and fulfilling work and wonderful people to share it with, for giving me ability and opportunity, and for sustaining me when it would have been easy to get discouraged.

1. The Puzzle of Pregnancy Help Activism

"Pregnant? New Mom?"

From a storefront across the street from the Department of Social Services, next to a corner liquor store, on a heavily trafficked commercial strip in a working-class neighborhood just outside the boundaries of central Baltimore, the Center for Pregnancy Concerns beckons women with the questions above and a list of free services available within:

- Sonograms
- Pregnancy Tests
- Material Assistance
- Classes in Parenting Life Skills and More
- Post-Abortion Counseling

Inside, natural light illumines a small waiting area and receptionist's counter. A pale, sterile-looking hallway, not unlike what one might encounter in a doctor's office, leads to rooms used for ultrasound exams, conversations with counselors, client resource storage, and staff offices. What stood out the most when I visited, however, was the spacious front room visible from the street and through glass in the waiting room walls, a baby "boutique" featuring colorful collections of new clothing, furniture, and other supplies arranged and displayed with obvious care on racks and in a glass display case. The goods had been purchased by donors and made available to any woman who needed them. This included those new mothers who center staff said they meet virtually every day—mothers who cross the street, often referred by social services personnel for help beyond what the welfare office can provide. The center's director fondly told me that the center will give women who need help affording things for a child "whatever they need," from formula to layettes to a pack-and-play crib.[1] The aid and the classes, as well as the trained counselors and other staff available to help a woman resolve any number of practical problems she might encounter during or after pregnancy, are important pieces of the center's work to fulfill the pledge its website makes to pregnant women:

"We commit to walking with you through the next steps. We will support you with material assistance, referrals, and genuine friendship. All free of charge."[2]

The operation is part of a vast but little-known charitable network associated with the pro-life movement. The Greater Baltimore Center for Pregnancy Concerns (GBCPC) is a typical example of organizations pro-life activists call *pregnancy centers; pregnancy resource centers; pregnancy help centers;* or, to use an older term, *crisis pregnancy centers.* Pregnancy centers are community-based nonprofits that purport to support and empower women in choosing an alternative to abortion. The options counseling GBCPC and other pregnancy centers pair with their pregnancy testing and ultrasound imaging won't endorse or refer for abortion, but it comes with a promise of resources and a relationship the center's staff hopes will persuade women to carry their pregnancies to term. A 2007 feature in *TIME* magazine heralded staff at pregnancy centers as "the new face of an old movement,"[3] and a 2013 front-page article in the *New York Times* portrayed them as rapidly growing, under the radar, in resources and sophistication.[4] Pregnancy centers are the core institution of a larger body of explicitly pro-life service providers—including maternity homes, adoption and general social service agencies, hotlines, support groups, aid networks, and more—activists often call "the pregnancy help movement." This movement, according to one of its leaders, aims to make abortion "unwanted now and unthinkable in future generations,"[5] first and foremost by ensuring "that no woman ever feels forced to have an abortion because of lack of support or practical alternatives."[6]

This kind of work is arguably not what most people think of when they think about the pro-life movement. Based on patterns in academic and journalistic coverage of the movement, the US public is instead likely to associate pro-life activism with bombings and disruptive protests at abortion clinics and with lobbying for legislation and the election of politicians who would restrict abortion rights and access.[7] Further, the movement has never enjoyed much of a reputation for concern about women's well-being.[8] Political discourse about the abortion conflict often portrays it as a contest between the rights of women and the rights of the unborn and places pro-life activists squarely on the side of the latter.[9] For much of their history, scholars assert, abortion opponents portrayed the pregnant woman as a perpetrator of violence if she had an abortion, if they paid her much attention at all,[10] and showed little concern for how unintended pregnancy could affect a woman's life.[11] Various commentators have charged politicians and activists who oppose abortion with inappropriately calling themselves "pro-life," given failure to back policies that would aid children, their mothers, and the poor.[12] In doing so, pro-life activists allegedly neglect what *Newsweek*'s Kurt Eichenwald argues is an obvious and compassionate alternative path to substantially reducing abortions: paying to support the many women who cite financial need as a reason for their abortions.[13]

Yet the form of pro-life activism known as pregnancy help is not new, and it is far more common and extensive than probably popularly believed. Recognizing this activity as one of four "streams"—the "individual outreach stream"—of the US pro-life movement, sociologist Ziad Munson contends that it draws more people, volunteer hours, and organizations than any other tactic the pro-life movement employs.[14] Although this claim is difficult to verify with national statistics, the scale of the pro-life pregnancy help movement is indeed substantial. As of July 2018, the Worldwide Directory of Pregnancy Help maintained by Heartbeat International, a membership association of pro-life pregnancy help service providers, listed 2,740 pregnancy centers and 4,201 service providers total for the United States.[15] According to a "pregnancy center service report" produced by Charlotte Lozier Institute (CLI), a research organization linked to a pro-life political advocacy group, the Susan B. Anthony List, 67,400 individuals volunteered at US pregnancy centers in 2017. The report further states that in 2017, these centers met with nearly 900,000 new clients.[16] By comparison, in 2014, the most recent year for which data are available, 1,671 clinics, hospitals, or physicians' offices performed an estimated 926,200 abortions in the United States.[17]

Despite its scale, direct service to women remains the least well known or understood of the pro-life movement's tactics.[18] Its existence receives passing mention in many academic works on the pro-life movement, but little focused attention. Munson and Ginsburg interview activists in this stream, representing five cities between them, as part of broader studies of pro-life activism.[19] Research by sociologist Kimberly Kelly represents an exception and an important advance.[20] Kelly offers an overview of pregnancy centers' activities, a rich discussion of their philosophies, and an exploration of how their work reflects activists' religious and gender-related identities and ideas. The data Kelly collected are relatively limited in scope, however, consisting of document review and ethnographic work at a pregnancy center she later learned was atypical, augmented by some additional interviews and brief observations at several other pregnancy centers. Further, although offering some clues, this work also leaves largely untouched several bigger-picture questions about how and why the pregnancy help movement emerged, evolved, and expanded, and how it fits into the rest of the pro-life movement's better-known efforts to end abortion.

In this book I demystify the pregnancy help movement by presenting a focused, in-depth study of its history, identity, work, impact, and relation to the larger pro-life movement. As I argue later in this chapter, key features of pregnancy help organizations' approach to fighting abortion present intriguing puzzles for those who wish to understand the US pro-life movement and the tactics of social movements more broadly. A compelling case for studying the pregnancy help movement also arises from important, recent shifts in the political and policy context surrounding pregnancy centers.

DEFINING PRO-LIFE PREGNANCY HELP:
THE POLITICAL STAKES

Ripening the case for their study, pro-life pregnancy centers have increasingly entered the public sphere. There, their work and motives have become subjects of political contestation. Beginning in the 1990s, some key pro-life movement leaders have pushed to highlight pregnancy centers more prominently in their public communications, in order to combat perceptions that the movement did not care about women.[21] Movement representatives often point to pregnancy centers' and other pregnancy help organizations' work when challenged over what the movement is doing to help women with children or to cope with the social problems often linked to unwanted pregnancies. The advocacy group National Right to Life, for example, praises the "real solutions" it says pregnancy centers offer to the underlying issues that make pregnancy a problem. Through them, the pro-life movement extends "assistance that respects the dignity of both mother and child."[22] The group's newsletters also often praise pregnancy centers' "saintly volunteers" and characterize them as working on "a shoestring budget relying entirely on the graciousness and generosity of people who will never know the babies whose lives they have helped save."[23]

Pro-choice activists have long argued that pregnancy centers are not the nonjudgmental, compassionate service providers they claim to be. Instead, they describe the centers as places where antiabortion ideologues masquerade as abortion clinics or promise help to draw women inside, only to subject them to pressure, shame, and more lies regarding their pregnancy options, delaying their abortions in the process. Leading pro-choice advocacy group NARAL Pro-Choice America claims, "While some CPCs [crisis pregnancy centers] may provide appropriate support and information to women facing unintended pregnancies, many do not."[24] Instead, what they offer is an "ideologically motivated staff" relying primarily on "lies and coercion" to accomplish their "sole purpose of preventing women from accessing abortion."[25] Planned Parenthood charges, "These fake health centers go to outrageous lengths to lure them [pregnant women] away from the real doctors and clinicians at Planned Parenthood and other quality providers" and in doing so pose a clear and present danger to women's well-being.[26]

Since at least the 1980s, pro-choice activists have waged a public relations campaign geared toward exposing a range of unethical and unprofessional practices they attribute to pregnancy centers. They have also lobbied public officials to investigate and more tightly regulate pregnancy centers.[27] Pro-choice activists have also targeted campaigns at private companies such as Google to persuade them to stop running, or tightly restrict the circumstances under which they will run, advertisements for pregnancy centers.[28]

In recent years, battles over public policy affecting pregnancy centers have intensified. Fighting back against pro-choice activists' claims, pro-life political advocacy groups have worked with pregnancy centers to secure legislative resolutions honoring pregnancy centers; at least nineteen states had enacted such resolutions as of 2018.[29] At least fourteen states reportedly directed public funding to pregnancy centers in 2018, typically under the auspices of state programs promoting abortion alternatives or from the sale of "Choose Life" license plates.[30] Meanwhile, pro-choice advocates have scored victories in a different set of states and localities. Between 2009 and 2018, several localities and at least three states enacted legislation regulating pregnancy centers' advertising or signage, typically by mandating that they include specific disclaimers. The first and best known of the state laws is California's Reproductive Freedom, Accountability, Comprehensive Care, and Transparency (FACT) Act, which requires pregnancy centers to provide information on how to access abortion. Pregnancy centers and their allies have challenged these laws in federal courts, mostly successfully, as politically motivated infringements on their freedom of speech. In 2018, the US Supreme Court agreed, striking down the Reproductive FACT Act by a five-to-four margin in *NIFLA v. Becerra,* a case that could further escalate the visibility of pregnancy centers and the political controversy surrounding them.

DEFINING PRO-LIFE PREGNANCY HELP:
SCHOLARS' PERSPECTIVES

Elements of these competing political narratives about the nature of pregnancy centers also appear in scholarship on the pro-life movement, although scholars' portrayals of pregnancy centers exhibit much less polarization. A small number of studies of pro-life activism, none of which involve the authors' own empirical study of pregnancy centers or discuss pregnancy centers in much depth, situate pregnancy centers within a narrative of antiabortion radicalism. Attributing to them "deceptive tactics," Blanchard groups pregnancy centers under what he calls the "Turn to Radicalism" in the antiabortion movement.[31] In doing so, he associates them with what had been the movement's increasingly aggressive efforts to shut down abortion clinics through blockades, vandalism, harassment, arson, and violence.[32] Risen and Thomas, although offering little further discussion of pregnancy centers, note that a future abortion clinic bomber was instrumental in starting one and that Randall Terry of the direct-action group Operation Rescue based his operations in a pregnancy center.[33] Joshua Wilson suggests that activists from the pro-life movement's direct-action stream retreated into pregnancy centers in order to continue their efforts to shut down abortion clinics after legal changes made it more difficult for them to continue protesting in front of them.[34]

A much larger and somewhat more recent body of literature, however—that has involved some primary data collection on pregnancy centers through interviews, site visits, and document review—alternatively describes pregnancy help activists' work in relatively benign, though not always uncritical, terms. Although some of these works acknowledge the controversy associated with pregnancy centers, there is something close to a consensus in recognition of pregnancy centers as providers of a substantial array of goods and services. Alesha Doan states plainly, "The outreach branch concentrates its efforts on aiding women who are facing unplanned and unwanted pregnancies. Crisis pregnancy centers offer services to help pregnant women and encourage them to keep their children or place them up for adoption."[35] Kimberly Kelly observes that centers disproportionately serve low-income women and that most pregnancy center clients do not plan to have abortions.[36]

Much of this scholarship situates pregnancy help organizations as representing a nurturing, woman-focused side of the pro-life movement and thus perhaps a counterstereotypical departure from the pro-life movement's usual rhetoric and methods. "Much of the antiabortion movement remains focused on changing laws," wrote journalist Nancy Gibbs in a 2007 *TIME* magazine feature, contrasting that with pregnancy centers' aims at "changing hearts."[37] Similarly, according to Sara Diamond, whereas other pro-life and Christian Right activists operate by "demonizing" those who undergo or perform abortions and seek to end abortion through coercion, activists at pregnancy centers rely on "persuasion" and "see women, to some degree, as decisionmaking agents" and "*victims:* of abortion doctors, of bad information, of pressure from husbands and boyfriends."[38] Academics who have interviewed pregnancy center staff members cast them as more emotionally if not also ideologically moderate than the typical pro-life activist.[39] Sociologist James Kelly presents pregnancy centers as an example of the "transformative" and consistently "pro-life" elements within what he otherwise characterizes as a "reactionary counter-movement" too closely wedded to the Republican Party and too blind to the poor.[40] Kimberly Kelly, although criticizing aspects of the pregnancy center movement and disagreeing with its opposition to abortion, concludes, "The CPC movement represents far more than a conservative movement bent on interfering in women's reproductive autonomy. This collection of national and local organizations embodies a significant social force dedicated to a feminized, religious response to crisis pregnancy and abortion."[41] In contrast to the worldview of a male-dominated, public, pro-life movement, Kelly elaborates, pregnancy center activists "asserted that material needs and a lack of support from significant others were systemic among women, and therefore abortion required sustained efforts toward meeting women's needs."[42] In doing so, she argues, pregnancy centers effectively employ the pro-choice movement's frames and take advantage of its weakness at advancing poor women's rights *not* to have abortions.[43]

Such claims make the existence and recent growth of pro-life pregnancy help service provision a fascinating case to explain. In particular, three features of pregnancy help activists' approach to fighting abortion stand out. First, to borrow terms from the literature on political campaigns, pregnancy help activists "trespass" on an issue arguably "owned" by the pro-choice movement and its Democratic political allies: women's well-being. Issue owners enjoy a superior reputation for their handling of an issue, whereas trespassers adapt owners' positions, contesting owners' advantage on the issue.[44] Second, pregnancy help activists pursue social change outside of formal political processes and venues, targeting nonstate actors (pregnant women and, to some extent, the culture) and using as their primary means direct service and what they hope will be transformative information. Third, pro-life individual outreach is believed to be growing in resources and influence, suggesting that its privatized and counterstereotypical approach to fighting abortion might be increasing in its appeal to pro-life citizens.

Because pregnancy help activism exhibits these features—also observed at various times in other social movements—its study can potentially illuminate several active areas of inquiry concerning the forms social action takes. Social movement scholarship has shown increasing interest in tactical diversity and activity that does not target the state.[45] The literature on civic participation has called attention to an increasing variety of ways in which individuals address public problems.[46] Scholars specifically have demonstrated curiosity and sometimes concern about the possibility that US citizens have been increasingly substituting volunteer service for traditional political participation.[47] They also express perceptions that people go to some lengths to define volunteer and even activist work as something other than "politics."[48] Recognizing the blurriness of the boundaries between "service" and "activism," scholars have coined such terms as "border activists," "servant-activists," and "social movement-borne nonprofits."[49] The first two terms describe volunteers who, despite working for groups that embrace a social change mission as part of their service to vulnerable populations, refuse to acknowledge that their work is "political" or "activism." The third term differentiates service providers linked to social movements (as pregnancy help organizations arguably are to the pro-life movement) from the larger universe of nonprofit service providers. Similarly, Nancy Davis and Robert Robinson illustrate a movement-level phenomenon, which they call "bypassing the state," with the cases of four social movements in the United States and abroad. As part of projects to transform the culture, Davis and Robinson argue, these movements minimize political advocacy while investing heavily in their own service-providing institutions and activist networks.[50] Social scientists worry that such retreats from politics might signal that a critical and growing mass of US citizens view government and politics as overly polarized, ineffective, unrepresentative of or unresponsive to their interests, or irrelevant to their lives.[51]

Pro-life pregnancy help organizations and the activists who staff them are potentially instances of such phenomena. In this book, therefore, I consider some specific questions as I strive to account for the rise of the pregnancy help movement: To what extent does service replace more overtly political action geared toward protecting the unborn, helping pregnant women, or both? If such a substitution effect is at work, why? How has this tactic fared at advancing the goals of the pregnancy help movement and the wider pro-life movement? My exploration of the pregnancy help movement's origins, development, and growth presents an opportunity to understand how, why, and to what effect activists use service to work for social change.

THEORIZING PREGNANCY HELP ACTIVISM

Why would the pro-life movement develop a response to abortion such as the pregnancy help movement, which relies on service rather state-directed action in its quest for change and does so using arguments and activities "owned" by its political opponents? And why is it growing in popularity? Existing literature and theory pertaining to social movements generally, and the pro-life movement specifically, suggest some explanations.

The Conventional Wisdom: The Role of Political Opportunity

No scholarly work to date has examined the origins of pro-life pregnancy help activism. Several scholars who have acknowledged this form of pro-life activism, however, have treated it as a tactical innovation by the pro-life movement that emerged or increased greatly in its appeal as activists' attempts to end abortion through other strategies—direct action to stop abortions at particular clinics along with legislative and legal advocacy—produced failure and frustration.[52] For example, in telling how the major pro-life political group in Fargo, North Dakota, came to open a pregnancy center, Faye Ginsburg says, "LIFE Coalition, recognizing that it was not succeeding in the political arena, began to shift its focus from the [campaign to close the local abortion] clinic per se to its clientele through a program of 'sidewalk counseling' and plans for a 'problem pregnancy center.'"[53] Also inspiring this strategy change was a concern about the pro-life movement's reputation and "a new emphasis in national pro-life strategy to promote 'alternatives to abortion.'"[54] Scholars' tendency to highlight political frustration in framing the rise of pregnancy centers is consistent with how scholarship commonly frames the rise of the pro-life movement's much more extensively studied street-level, confrontational, direct-action stream.[55]

This view implies that many pro-life activists believe the means matters little relative to the goal, which Rose asserts "has always been to stop abortions, irrespective of the circumstances that prompt women to seek them."[56] It also implies a view of the pro-life movement as possessing relatively flexible and fungible resources. As eloquently phrased by political scientist Joshua Wilson, based on how he says the pro-life movement adapted to the rising costs of clinic protest, "Like flowing water that hits an obstruction, efforts in the conflict were merely diverted to a different course."[57] This was enabled by "a combination of passionate, able activists and available resources. The former creates the will and aptitude to develop new strategies in the face of defeat, while the latter provides the means to persist."[58]

This assumption about what motivates pro-life activists' interest in service reflects in part the enduring (even if contested) influence of a perspective known as "political process theory" in social movement scholarship. Political process theory is a parsimonious explanation of social movement mobilization that posits it as a function of resources, "mobilizing frames" (the narratives used to inspire action), and the opportunities the political system provides for activists to push their causes.[59] Political opportunities, the key contribution of this theory's advocates, encompass practical access to formal political institutions, the likelihood of an imminent realignment in elite political and party coalitions, closeness to sympathetic political elites, and the likelihood that the state would try to quash the movement.[60] Movements need some minimal degree of resources, mobilizing frames, and political opportunities to form in the first place, and from there the abundance, diversity, and specific content of these three ingredients shape and constrain the forms their actions take.

The political process tradition assumes that activists opt for the most direct path available to achieving the change they seek.[61] The power concentrated within the modern state thus renders it the "default target of contentious claims making."[62] Deviation from this pattern is explained by the related assumption that movements press their claims against targets and in those venues that offer them the best prospects for achieving the change they seek.[63] Movements' action outside of state channels, then, might signal that activists lack savvy about or access to the political system, doubt the capacity of political institutions to deliver the change they seek, or have limited tolerance for policy making anticipated to proceed incrementally over the long term.[64] Because the state's coercive power, resources, and experience as a target of social activism give it tools to regulate, insulate itself from, and contain the impact of movements' action, activists might anticipate greater success at achieving the social change they would have sought through policy if they can set their sights on more vulnerable targets, such as individual pregnant women.[65] This is just what Doan argues has been at work in the pro-life movement's adoption of direct-action tactics.[66]

Pregnancy Help Activism in the Context of the Pro-Life Movement

Scholars—and some prominent pro-life activists—do indeed interpret much of the pro-life movement's history as a series of failures and frustrations. More than forty-five years after the Supreme Court declared a constitutional right to abortion in *Roe v. Wade* (1973), the US pro-life movement has yet to achieve its central political goal, enshrinement of a fetal right to life in the nation's law, much less its ultimate goal of ending abortion. The outcome of *Roe* and a companion case, *Doe v. Bolton* (1973), surprised many pro-life leaders. Soon after the movement began to mobilize in the mid- to late 1960s, victories in several state legislatures and some promising court decisions pertaining to fetal rights offered hope that activists would be able to arrest or even reverse a nascent trend in state liberalization of long-standing prohibitions on abortion. Many expressed faith that the Supreme Court would affirm their side in *Roe* and *Doe*. The rulings in those cases, however, felled the abortion laws of forty-six states, far exceeding the extent of abortion law liberalization that had occurred in the typical state legislature.[67] Though *Roe's* language permitted states to ban abortion in the third trimester of pregnancy, provided they allowed exceptions to preserve the life and health of the pregnant woman, the broad definition of "health" laid out in *Doe* virtually ensured that women's right to abortion would apply through all nine months of pregnancy.

Pro-life activists mounted a multipronged political and legislative response to *Roe* but seemed to find themselves thwarted at nearly every turn. Many in the rapidly growing movement worked with their state legislatures to resist updating their laws in accordance with *Roe*. Several states passed legislation designed to limit abortion access, such as bills requiring parental permission for minors' abortions or allowing only those procedures doctors deemed "medically necessary."[68] Federal courts struck down most of these early abortion restrictions.[69] In Congress, although pro-life forces succeeded in limiting federal funding of abortion through the Hyde Amendment, a proposed human life amendment to the US Constitution met considerable resistance. Pro-lifers' increasing involvement in election campaigns yielded growing numbers of pro-life Congress members and a president, Ronald Reagan, who pledged to support their cause. Still, their quest for a human life amendment was frustrated by many leading Democrats' conversion to a pro-choice position as well as disagreements within the pro-life coalition over the proposed amendment's language.[70] The return of abortion rights cases to a Supreme Court altered by appointees of Reagan and his converted pro-life successor, George H. W. Bush, inspired hope in many pro-life activists that *Roe* might be finally overturned. Yet *Webster v. Reproductive Health Services* (1989) and *Planned Parenthood v. Casey* (1992), although widening states' berth to regulate abortion, left the constitutional right to abortion untouched. *Casey,* in fact, specifically affirmed that right with the votes of three of the five Reagan and Bush appointees.[71] Later that year, an avowedly pro-choice president, Bill Clinton, was elected along with a large Democratic majority in both chambers of Congress. A leading political scientist credited Clinton's election to pro-choice enthusiasm.[72]

Since that time, even as the cast of characters in Washington, DC, has changed with respect to support of or opposition to abortion, scholars generally describe federal abortion policy as persisting in a state of stalemate. Doan argues that, as long as *Roe* remains law, pro-life activists will never be able to get what they want in politics. Political process theory would predict that the pro-life movement would be expected to alter its tactics, focus its attention in alternative venues, and direct its efforts to stop abortion at new targets, including those outside the state.[73]

However, there are also important reasons to question how strongly pro-life activists' experiences with other tactics, especially conventional political advocacy, drove the movement's interest in service provision. Not only did the origins of some pregnancy centers predate the nationwide legalization of abortion in *Roe* but also individual outreach played a salient role in the earliest wave of US antiabortion activism, according to Kerry Jacoby and Daniel Williams, as pro-life citizens responded to the liberalization of state abortion laws in the late 1960s and early 1970s.[74] That enthusiasm for pregnancy help activism shows little sign of abatement even as the pro-life movement at the time of this writing appears to enjoy unprecedented political power further diminishes the case that the political opportunity structure drives the movement's involvement in service.[75] Indeed, as Williams points out, more than forty years after *Roe,* assessment of the pro-life movement's success or failure is subjective.

Abortion remains legal, but its incidence has fallen to the levels observed in the early 1970s. Abortion provider supply has been rapidly declining; states have alarmed pro-choice activists with their increasingly aggressive regulation of abortion; and though the pro-life movement may have lost the Democrats, the Republican Party maintains a strong antiabortion position and has greatly increased its national political power since *Roe*.[76]

The need for an alternative account of the US pro-life movement's service provision becomes more apparent in light of important and intriguing observations Munson has made about the structure of the movement. Although scholars and journalists tend to treat the pro-life movement as a monolithic actor, Munson argues that it is not. He instead describes the contemporary movement as comprising four independent "streams"—politics, direct action, public outreach, and individual outreach—defined by the main tactic activists employ to try to end abortion and the ideas that justify each tactical approach. The politics stream aims to change abortion law through legislation and elections. The direct-action stream aims to stop abortions from taking place at specific clinics, affecting access to abortion. The public outreach stream educates in order to move public opinion against abortion. The individual outreach stream tries to reduce demand for abortion, primarily through changing the minds of pregnant women. It extends counseling and direct service to those women, mostly at pregnancy centers. Participants in the different streams share the common goal of ending abortion, but they lack a central leader. They also often question the merits of each other's activities.[77]

To understand the pro-life movement, Munson suggests, one must understand its individual streams. He argues, "Streams define the very structure of the movement and as such define both the possibilities and the limits for movement recruitment, coordination, and impact."[78] Table 1.1 compares and contrasts the approaches of these streams in terms of their primary targets, venues, tactics, and rationales.

The four-stream structure of the US pro-life movement presents a number of interesting questions to students of social action that I address in this book: How do individuals choose which stream, or form of activism, in which to participate? Do the fortunes of activists in one stream influence the extent to which activists and donors invest time, capital, and other resources into other streams? Did some of the streams indeed grow out of others, or did they develop independently? How do these different streams of the movement relate to and influence each other today?

Table 1.1 Strategic Approaches of Pro-Life Movement Streams

Stream	Primary Target(s)	Venue(s)	Tactic(s)	Rationale
Politics	State	Three branches of government; political parties and election campaigns	Legal and legislative advocacy; election of pro-life officials	Regulating abortion provision and procurement and ultimately restoring legal protection of the unborn will reduce the availability and acceptability of abortion
Direct action	Abortion providers	Abortion facilities and public property surrounding them	Public protest ranging from peaceful to violent; dialogue with or harassment of abortion clinic staff; "rescue" (blockades); destruction of clinic property; "sidewalk counseling" of women entering abortion clinics	Curtailing access to and supply of abortion at specific locations will directly stop abortion
Public outreach	US public	Media, schools, and other informational venues	Advertisement of the pro-life message; education about abortion from a pro-life perspective	Providing information about fetal development and other aspects of the abortion issue will change minds on the issue and therefore votes, pregnancy decisions, and other relevant behavior, contributing to a "culture of life"
Individual outreach	Pregnant women	Nonprofit pregnancy centers, maternity homes, adoption and social welfare agencies, and other service providers	Provide information, goods, and services geared toward encouraging and supporting childbirth over abortion	Addressing circumstances in individual women's lives that lead them to contemplate abortion will reduce demand for abortion

Source: Author's analysis based on description in: Ziad Munson, *The Making of Pro-Life Activists: How Social Movement Mobilization Works* (Chicago: University of Chicago Press, 2008).

Munson's research offers answers to some of these questions. Based on interviews with pro-life activists in four US cities, Munson concludes that the stream in which pro-life activists participate is largely an accident of social encounters that occur in a period of personal transition, when an individual is "available" for activism. Individuals do not set out purposively to contribute to the pro-life movement and then choose rationally among its streams; surprisingly, Munson finds, many activists begin participating in the movement *before* forming their pro-life beliefs, much less more elaborate ideas about the best way in which the movement should address abortion. Ideas regarding which form of activism is best, he argues, develop later as activists are socialized into a particular stream.

Munson explicitly challenges a view of movement resources as fungible across tactics and overall observes little interaction across movement streams. At the individual level, activists tend to stay in the stream through which they first encountered the movement, he observes, and are more likely to leave the movement entirely than to switch from one stream to another. Meanwhile, at the macro level, the pro-life movement lacks a central authority that coordinates movement strategy. Tactical innovations develop and diffuse within single streams of the movement, not across them.

This combination Munson observes of movement fragmentation and the lack of savvy exhibited by new activists suggests that knowledge about the beliefs, methods, experiences, and strategic outlook of activists in the pro-life movement's better-known streams might be limited in their usefulness for understanding the rise and work of pro-life individual outreach. It does not mean that these factors are irrelevant. Munson himself remarks that an "undercurrent of frustration with the ineffectiveness of legislative and legal strategies runs throughout the conversations I had with activists in other streams of the movement."[79] Because Munson's research focuses on mostly rank-and-file activists working locally, long after establishment of the pro-life movement's four-stream structure, it cannot show much about how the ideas that define the streams developed and gained acceptance. This design might also lead him to underestimate the extent to which the streams of the pro-life movement act in strategic and coordinated fashion because this kind of work would be disproportionately likely to involve leaders of national organizations. Further, historical patterns such as the one perceived by Jacoby, in which the locus of the pro-life movement's energy has shifted among its streams over time, can unfold without any transfer of resources among streams.[80] This can happen, for example, when one stream experiences an influx of new activists or other resources or when a tactical innovation attracts fresh attention to the stream.

Clearly, the pregnancy help movement needs further study in its own right. Although it is important to consider pregnancy help activism in the context of the larger pro-life movement's fight against abortion, it might also be useful to view pro-life pregnancy help organizations through a different lens. This is because some important scholarship on social movements and advocacy has minimized the role of liberal/conservative political ideology in grassroots organizations' tactics and practices, uncovering many similarities in their forms and the factors that shape them.[81] Research on the pro-life movement's direct-action stream, for example, often notes that its earliest activists borrowed from, and often brought personal experience with, the direct-action branches of the civil rights and peace movements.[82] Scholars might therefore enrich their theoretical perspective by considering the pregnancy help movement as a case of a social movement using service as its primary route to change.

Direct Service and Tactical Choice in Social Movement Scholarship

Theory explaining social movements' engagement in service provision is not presently well developed. A helpful starting point for anticipating its determinants, however, might be the considerable existing scholarship that offers general insights on factors shaping the strategies of social movements and their constituent organizations. One might complement these by drawing lessons from case studies of service-providing organizations encompassed by social movements, including those representing racial and ethnic minorities; women and victims of gender-based violence; people with AIDS; lesbian, gay, and transgender individuals; sex workers; and homeless and poor people.[83] From these examples, the one that might most closely resemble pro-life pregnancy centers' change-oriented service provision is the network of rape crisis centers established by the feminist movement in the 1970s. Initially run mostly by female volunteers, such centers were founded as feminist organizations that would provide practical assistance to rape victims *and* pursue the cultural change their staff and volunteers believed was required to end all rape.[84]

First looking at generic factors shaping social movement organization (SMO) action, the literature recognizes multiple instrumental considerations beyond activists' analysis of the political opportunity structure. One important insight is that social movements might choose targets, venues, and tactics in order to counter the activities of an opposing movement.[85] Even when political circumstances have not changed, activists might change their strategies to draw fresh attention to their issues.[86] Strategy is often governed by "political logics," which Elizabeth Armstrong identifies as "background sets of assumptions about how society works, the goals of political action, and appropriate strategies to pursue desired ends." These have cultural roots and are constrained by conventions of the arenas in which activists operate.[87]

Social action might serve expressive as well as instrumental goals. Avoidance of the state can signal activists' alienation from it.[88] Activists' political or social ideologies and worldviews might steer them toward or away from particular targets, venues, or tactics.[89] They might act in a way that models the social change they seek, even when reason exists to believe other tactics would be more effective.[90] Movements' activities might also reflect collective emotion as well as cognition. Gould suggests that some emotions, such as compassion, pride, and anger, channel themselves more naturally into some forms of social action rather than others.[91]

SMOs' activity often shows sensitivity to social context and reflects the identities of activists as part of a group embedded in that context. Activists might take cues from "reference groups," defined as other social groups or institutions with which they might identify,[92] or from prevailing norms in the "fields," or arenas, in which they operate.[93] The forms of their action might represent the actions they deem "appropriate for 'groups like them.'"[94] Similarly, argue Taylor and Van Dyke, activists "choose options that conform to their ideological visions, are congruent with their collective identities, and embody the cultural schemas that provide meanings, motives, and templates for action."[95] In short, tactics must "resonate" with activists themselves.[96]

The influences of many of these factors, as well as political opportunity constraint, are discernible in the multiple cases of movement-linked service provision, though there appears to be no single common factor or set of factors that unites the cases. For example, Debra Minkoff and Elisabeth Clemens argue that political disenfranchisement and exclusion prompted movements of women and racial and ethnic minorities to invest in service-providing institutions.[97] Minkoff calls service provision the dominant "social change strategy" for these groups prior to the 1960s.[98] Yet these institutions continued their work, and new ones were founded, even after the political opportunity structure changed in ways that encouraged the proliferation of movement-linked political advocacy groups. Minkoff finds that advocacy groups did not crowd out service-providing groups, and that startups and failures of service-providing institutions were unrelated to the party of the president.[99] Conversely, however, in the more recent case of a (much smaller) movement representing sex workers, the founding of service-providing nonprofits represented a deliberate shift of resources away from state-directed political action because activists grew pessimistic about their prospects for policy change and recognized that they lacked the resources to try to change their political opportunity structure.[100] Case studies suggest that the establishment of movement-linked rape crisis centers, AIDS service organizations, and hospitality houses for the homeless and poor reflected alienation from the state, including distrust in the state's willingness or capacity to appropriately serve target populations.[101] By contrast, in cases involving food pantries, homeless shelters, employment assistance projects, and other social service agencies run by religious as well as transgender advocacy movements, scholars perceived not alienation from the state but efforts to model actions desired from government or other citizens or to imitate or signal what the public should expect should the movement ever get to wield the power of the state.[102] Gould posits that the formation of AIDS service organizations expressed a collective identity of the gay community as one that takes care of its own.[103]

Some of the cases suggest particular types of political logistics, ideologies, or identities that especially encourage direct service. Armstrong recognizes service provision to people suffering from or at risk of AIDS as operating according to a "logic of responding to an epidemic," which she describes as entailing large-scale, intensive investments of labor, expertise, emotional energy, and other resources into direct care for people and other projects.[104] Others have similarly rested service provision on a theory of change, perhaps with ideological correlates, that prescribes direct, personal engagement with an afflicted group.[105] For religious fundamentalist movements in diverse cultures that have heavily invested in social service provision, Davis and Robinson argue that a communitarian ideology—one that unites cultural conservatism and economic egalitarianism under a mandate of concern for neighbors—undergirds the effort.[106] Meanwhile, studies of the people staffing movement-linked service-providing organizations suggest that female identity might contribute to participation in activist activities that involve and are constructed as service, given cultural norms that tend to link women to caregiving rather than the more aggressively constructed activity of pressing claims upon the state.[107]

Cases of movement-linked service also suggest additional factors that might attract SMOs and activists to this form of social action. One acknowledged or implied almost universally across the cases is the reality or perception of problematic conditions such as poverty, domestic violence, and disease, closely linked to movements' grievances and urgently threatening human well-being. Activists' most direct motives are humanitarian: they seek, within their locus of control, to provide some immediate relief, reflecting the care for people and concern about problems that some scholars put at the root of both political "activism" and seemingly nonpolitical "volunteer work."[108] Similar to the theories of market and government failure often invoked to explain the formation of nonprofit organizations, activists recognize need that other social institutions generally are not meeting and move to meet it themselves, often out of empathy for and a sense of social solidarity with those affected.[109]

Another theme is that service-providing SMOs sometimes rationalize their humanitarian efforts as complementing and facilitating long-term social change campaigns directed at the state. The logic is that service-providing institutions can mobilize their target groups into the movement. They do so by organizing and physically or emotionally strengthening people and also by instructing service beneficiaries into practical skills and new ways of thinking about their situations and their capacities. Movement-linked service providers often bundle this education with their aid.[110] Some activists suggest that visibly serving a marginalized group, such as AIDS patients or sex workers, can make a powerful political statement about that group's worth.[111]

A third notable insight from cases of movement-linked service provision is that creating and working through institutions activists control ensures that services can be provided in ways that reflect a movement's values. Some activists construct this as helping, empowering, and respecting the dignity of their target population.[112] Davis and Robinson add that alternative service-providing institutions, especially if established on a large scale and opened broadly to the public, can offer platforms through which a movement can proclaim and spread its values, potentially enabling it to "bypass the state" to achieve the change it seeks in the culture.[113]

Alternative Factors in Pregnancy Help Service Provision

Some recent scholarship on the pro-life movement has indeed looked beyond political opportunity constraints to assert that some of the other motives mentioned above inspired or helped to sustain pro-life activists' investment in pregnancy centers and other service-providing nonprofits. Williams's brief discussion of the founding of the first association of pro-life pregnancy centers,

Birthright, credits it to the perspective pro-life women brought to the movement's response to legalized abortion. He also describes the central activity in which those first pregnancy centers engaged—providing material aid to young and poor mothers—as being consistent with the political ideologies and identities predominant among the earliest pro-life activists. These early activists tended to be Catholics and Democrats who held liberal views on social welfare issues and who envisioned the expansion of public aid to families as an important part of their long-term, pro-life agenda.[114] Although focusing on contemporary pregnancy center activists, whom she characterizes as disproportionately evangelical and conservative, Kelly highlights gender and evangelical gender ideologies as keys to understanding activists' investment in pregnancy centers and the nature of pregnancy centers' service. By her account, pregnancy center activists' religious beliefs, refined by their identities and experiences as women, influence their support of the centers' woman-centered approach to abortion. Their activism is confined to pregnancy centers because of patriarchal ideologies within evangelical Christianity that assign men and women to separate spheres and limit the real influence women can exercise in their churches and the pro-life movement. Pregnancy center activists largely accept these ideologies, Kelly suggests, but the virtually women-only space of the pregnancy center enables them to address abortion on their own terms. In doing so, they subtly challenge and set boundaries on the authority of evangelical men, whom Kelly portrays as critical of activists' efforts to help and empower women.[115]

Still, no one has attempted to systematically assess the roles these and other factors identified by social movement theory have played in the origins, evolution, and growth of this woman-focused yet privatized form of pro-life activism. There has, in fact, been little work in broader social movement scholarship to assess the comparative importance of various potential factors in shaping movements' use of service; one exception is Debra Minkoff's research, which considers variables relating to politics, resources, and organizational characteristics.[116] While deepening people's understanding of the US pro-life pregnancy help movement, in this book I also aspire to do just that.

DATA

My study of the pregnancy help movement, on which this book is based, approaches it from multiple perspectives and comprises multiple methods of data collection and analysis. I look at the movement in the aggregate as well as from the perspectives of organizations and individual activists at the national and local levels. I gathered quantitative and qualitative data. When I let activists speak for themselves, I draw from what they say to different audiences, including the public; clients; each other; potential supporters; and me, the researcher. In exploring movement motives, I address both the "why-did-it-start" and "what-makes-it-tick" questions.[117]

The most important data sources are two national surveys I conducted—one on the characteristics of pregnancy centers and the other on the characteristics of the people who staffed them—and semistructured interviews of twenty-two individuals who by role or reputation were considered leaders in the national movement or in a local pregnancy help community, the central Maryland region, spanning the Baltimore and Washington, DC, metropolitan areas. These data were gathered in 2012. Brief descriptions of these and other data sources follow, and Appendix A contains additional methodological detail.

The first, the Pregnancy Center Director Survey, was administered online via a link emailed to pregnancy centers affiliated with the three largest umbrella organizations for US pregnancy centers: Care Net, Heartbeat International, and the National Association of Family and Life Advocates (NIFLA). The questions covered pregnancy centers' structures, services, staffing, clientele characteristics, political activities, and ties to outside organizations. The Pregnancy Center Director Survey was completed by 510 respondents on behalf of 734 pregnancy center locations (some "centers" are local chains). Its data therefore covered 37 percent of the pregnancy center locations affiliated with Care Net, Heartbeat International, or NIFLA as of 2010.

The second one, the Pregnancy Center Staff Survey, was a self-administered, anonymous paper survey offered at thirty-one pregnancy center office locations in twenty states and returned via postal mail. It covered the demographic characteristics, backgrounds, political and abortion-related attitudes, and activism history of adult employees and volunteers. The Pregnancy Center Staff Survey was completed and returned by 272 individuals, accounting for nearly 49 percent of the number of employees and volunteers pregnancy center directors reported having at their centers during the time the survey was in the field.

Leader interviews aimed at understanding subjects' perspectives on their movement and its development. Questions dealt with leaders' entry into the pregnancy help movement, notable growth and change at their organizations, their differentiation of the pregnancy help movement's worldview from that of the rest of the pro-life movement, their perceptions of their relationships with other pro-life organizations, and their views about the importance and effectiveness of the material aid and social services pregnancy help organizations offer. I interviewed the presidents of the three largest US pregnancy center umbrella groups (as of 2012), plus the US division head and the president, respectively, of two other major umbrella groups, Birthright and 1st Way Pregnancy Centers. I also interviewed the president of another national pregnancy help organization, the Nurturing Network, and some other individuals holding past or present national-level leadership positions in the largest pregnancy center umbrella groups. At the local level, I approached directors of pregnancy centers and other pregnancy help service providers with an eye toward representing salient organizations as well as diversity in terms of geography, core services and clientele, and national affiliations. My list of interviewees later grew to include a few other individuals whom other interviewees identified as significant to the national or local pregnancy help movement; these included three people who contributed to leadership of the pregnancy help movement in ways other than leading a service-providing organization. No interview request was declined. I conducted the majority of interviews in person, nearly all at the leaders' workplaces; the rest I conducted by telephone. Appendix A lists interviewees and their roles at the time of data collection (2012). All interviewees chose to be identified by name.

In the book, I also use other data sources. I read key publications of the pregnancy help movement, including books and articles authored by its leaders, manuals used to train pregnancy center volunteers, and reports produced by or on behalf of major pregnancy center associations. I attended Care Net's 2011 national pregnancy center conference and made observations about pregnancy centers' physical appearances during visits for interviews. I subscribed to email lists and monitored news coverage of pregnancy centers in mainstream and pro-life news outlets. Not all of this information played a direct role in the research, but it did help to inform the questions I asked my research subjects and to check and enrich interpretation of my main data. I also used an online pregnancy center directory to assemble datasets linking centers and other service providers to their political, demographic, and socioeconomic contexts, including the locations of abortion clinics from another dataset I assembled using online directories. I introduce additional information about these and other minor data sources when these sources appear in the book.

PLAN OF THE BOOK

Chapter 2 shows what pro-life pregnancy help service provision looks like and how participants in this work understand it as a tactic advancing the goals of the pro-life movement. This overview of the contemporary pregnancy help movement covers its goals, structure, organizational characteristics, and key ideas about abortion, with which activists rationalize their approach and differentiate it from that of other pro-life activists. It also describes the goods, services, and other tools pregnancy centers and other service providers use to promote and support abortion alternatives. The chapter establishes empirically that pregnancy help activists identity with the pro-life movement, target women and the culture rather than the state, operate in relatively privatized venues, employ direct service on a large scale, and use frames and tactics popularly associated with liberal and pro-choice politics.

Chapters 3 and 4 present a narrative of the origins and evolution of the pro-life pregnancy help movement. Chapter 3 focuses on how direct service to women emerged as a tactic of the pro-life movement. Chapter 4 discusses tactical innovation and resource growth in the pro-life movement's direct-service stream, exploring their nature and the factors appearing to drive them.

Chapters 5 and 6 investigate sources of the present-day appeal of service provision as a form of pro-life activism. In doing so, they shed further light on the characteristics of the organizations and individuals this movement stream encompasses and how they relate to the larger pro-life movement. In Chapter 5 I infer lessons about such matters by observing patterns in the locations of pro-life pregnancy centers. The chapter reveals where in the United States the pro-life movement is most actively engaged in direct service and how these patterns correspond to factors in the literature on movement-linked service provision. Individual activists' perspectives are the focus of Chapter 6. The chapter analyzes data on pregnancy help activists' attitudes about and experiences with politics and pro-life activism and identifies other themes in activists' mobilization into the individual outreach stream. Picking up questions of interest to civic participation scholars, the chapter addresses the extent to which one can understand pregnancy help service as a substitute for political action and, if so, why.

Chapters 7 and 8 extend and conclude my study. Chapter 7 engages pragmatic questions that critics inside and outside the pregnancy help movement have posed, or that this research might invite, about the impact and future of its work. The discussion highlights potential impacts on abortion incidence and women's well-being, sketching foundations of some answers and setting an agenda for future research. It also explores how likely the movement might be to abandon some of the distinguishing features of its strategy in the future. Chapter 8 synthesizes key findings about the nature of the pro-life pregnancy help movement and the factors that have shaped the development of this service-providing stream of pro-life activism. It elaborates on the emergent role of religious faith in the worldview with which activists frame many aspects of their movement. The chapter concludes by clarifying its contributions to understanding US pro-life activism and the forms social action takes.

ARGUMENTS

In this book I make several key arguments about pro-life pregnancy help activism. I weigh in on competing political narratives about what pro-life pregnancy centers are by documenting the perhaps surprising extent of help they make available to a perhaps surprisingly diverse cast of women, including pregnant women not considering abortion and financially needy mothers who had not previously been pregnancy center clients. Although the research ultimately does not enter the counseling room to test pro-choice activists' claims about the accuracy of information or the extent of emotional coercion delivered there, it reveals some patterns of behavior consistent with pregnancy help activists' claim that they focus on serving women, not necessarily stopping abortions, or to speak in pro-life movement parlance, "saving babies." To some extent, my book challenges conventional wisdom that the US pro-life movement devotes little attention to the circumstances that prompt women to choose abortion and the concrete implications of "choosing life" for women's lives. I also acknowledge, however, ways in which tension between the goals of serving women and saving babies has surfaced in the pregnancy help movement's history, arising in strategic debates, contributing to tactical innovation, and coloring evaluations of the movement's effectiveness. I further recognize that some of what activists offer in service to women might not necessarily be congruent with what their targets want to receive.

In accounting for why pro-life activists have invested so heavily in service and seemingly embraced it with extra enthusiasm in recent years, I argue that these phenomena are better understood with regard to the rich variety of factors the social movements literature has identified as drawing activists *to* service as they seek social change, rather than from the narrower political opportunity framework, which highlights failures and frustrations activists have experienced in fighting abortion with more state-directed, confrontational, and fetus-centered tactics. Likewise, the appeal of pro-life individual outreach does not appear to arise in any substantial way from a phenomenon in which negative views about politics and the state are prompting a retreat to service—though these considerations are not irrelevant to how some individual activists explain the appeal of pregnancy help work or to the lack of participation in other forms of pro-life activism I observe in some of their ranks.

In particular, there is evidence that service to pregnant and parenting women carries inherent appeal to those activists who engage in it. After they are exposed to this form of pro-life activism, some individuals sense that it resonates with their identities, beliefs, personalities, emotions, experiences, and/or lifestyles. Although not necessarily opposed to public policies that involve the state in saving babies *or* serving women, activists in the pregnancy help movement express a drive to be personally involved in the lives of pregnant and parenting women in their communities—to promote what they understand to be their well-being, and for other reasons that go beyond achievement of the pro-life movement's goal of ending abortion. Socialization into the pregnancy help movement, through which activists acquire a worldview and set of learning experiences, appears to activate and strengthen this conviction and infuse it with spiritual significance.

What glues together the pregnancy help movement's diverse and perhaps ideologically cross-cutting activities, underlies its other strategic choices, frames its relations to a larger body of pro-life activists, and gives the movement its present energy is not a traditional political ideology, a clearly feminist or antifeminist worldview, or a zealous opposition to abortion. Instead, it appears to be a brand of religious faith stressing a love of one's neighbor inseparable from the love of a God who redeems, guides, provides, and calls diverse people to play different roles in a larger "body of Christ." It is humanitarian, pragmatic, and relational in its implications. It motivates, constrains, and at times works in tension with activists' strategic engagement with their abortion-providing countermovement. In their view, its most authentic expression requires that they establish and work from within alternative institutions that facilitate formation of relationships. These they see as the building blocks for a "culture of life" entailing much more than absence of abortion.

Service to pregnant women has been part of the mainstream pro-life movement's repertoire for nearly its entire history. It did not grow in any meaningful way out of the politics or direct-action stream. No significant transfer of resources across the movement fueled its growth. What Munson observed in the present also characterizes the past: the individual outreach stream has largely developed and operated independently of other pro-life movement streams. Activists also tend to voice belief in the moral and tactical superiority of their approach. However, Munson might somewhat overstate the extent of rivalry and fragmentation in the movement. Not unlike members of a family, pregnancy help activists might sometimes criticize their counterparts in other movement streams or keep busy with their own affairs, but they also tend to express some solidarity, perceive that they are supported, contribute to their work in their private lives, and even occasionally collaborate.

2. Overview of the Pregnancy Help Movement

The pregnancy help movement aims to make abortion "unwanted now and unthinkable in future generations."[1] Although its leaders do not oppose laws that would restrict access to legal abortion, the movement's path to an "abortion-free America"[2] (and for some of the transnational organizations it encompasses, an abortion-free globe) is a path on which individual pregnant women freely reject abortion. Leaders describe their movement as "committed to providing alternatives to abortion" and as "empowering . . . women to choose life."[3] The intention of those working in the pregnancy help movement, Heartbeat International President Margaret "Peggy" Hartshorn writes, "is that no woman ever feels forced to have an abortion because of lack of support or practical alternatives."[4]

In this chapter I address how the pro-life pregnancy help movement, as of the writing of this book, attempts to fulfill these lofty goals. It also explores how the movement frames this work, especially as it relates to the pro-life movement and the goal of ending abortion. I first describe the types of organizations the pregnancy help movement comprises and salient characteristics of the people who staff them. Next, I discuss key ideas about abortion that define the pregnancy help movement and rationalize the actions of that movement, and the philosophies and general strategic approaches pro-life activists identify as guiding their work. I describe how activists' efforts to persuade, support, and empower women to choose an alternative to abortion translate into concrete goods, services, and programming. In the chapter I also provide data on pregnancy help organizations' funding and clientele.

ORGANIZATIONS AND STRUCTURE

The pregnancy help movement is a network of pro-life service providers that promote and support alternatives to abortion. Providers are typically incorporated under the US tax code as 501(c)(3) nonprofits. These are organizations established for charitable, religious, or educational purposes.

Women who encounter the pro-life pregnancy help movement are likely to do so first through a community-based "pregnancy center" such as the one I described at the start of Chapter 1 or through one of several telephone or internet-based pregnancy help hotlines that eventually steer callers to pregnancy centers for follow-up services and care. Pregnancy centers advertise their services through phone books, billboards, online search engines such as Google, and other media. By offering free pregnancy tests; information; counseling; material help; and, increasingly, free ultrasound imaging to confirm and date pregnancies, pregnancy centers aim to provide the initial "crisis intervention" that inspires women experiencing an unintended or problem pregnancy to carry the pregnancy to term. The typical pregnancy center follows this with ongoing support during pregnancy and parenting. Many also offer programs not geared toward direct avoidance of abortion but at changing cultural conditions that activists believe contribute to abortion. These programs deal with topics such as abstinence and postabortion support. Nearly 3,000 pregnancy centers—2,740, according to Heartbeat International's "Worldwide Directory of Pregnancy Help" as of July 2018—dot the US landscape.[5] Because pregnancy centers are the most numerous and controversial type of pregnancy help service provider, and because of the gateway role they play in the pregnancy help movement, they receive the most attention in my book.

Most pregnancy centers are rooted in a particular local area, seeing clients at a single office (69 percent on the Pregnancy Center Director Survey) or out of a few locations in neighboring communities.[6] Although the median number of offices reported by multilocation pregnancy centers on the 2012 Pregnancy Center Director Survey was two, some local chains are much larger and have been growing since the time the survey was fielded. Among the nine local pregnancy centers whose leaders I interviewed, one had recently opened its third location, and two others were in the process of opening their third and fourth locations, respectively. One interviewee identified this kind of expansion of local pregnancy centers as an important, ongoing trend in the movement's growth.[7] The pregnancy center that claims to be "the largest, most successful pregnancy resource center in America," the Women's Care Center, has proliferated so extensively that it is no longer strictly local. It originated in South Bend, Indiana, in 1984 and as of 2018 operated twenty-nine locations in ten states, stretching from Florida to North Dakota.[8] Some pregnancy centers operate vans, buses, or recreational vehicles that they have fitted in order to offer some of their core services, especially pregnancy testing, counseling, and ultrasound imaging, in a wider range of neighborhoods than they might otherwise serve. Heartbeat International's "Worldwide Directory of Pregnancy Help" listed 104 mobile units as of September 2018.[9]

Most pregnancy centers affiliate with one or more national or international associations that provide various services to their members.[10] The largest of these associations in the United States are Care Net, Heartbeat International, and the National Institute of Family and Life Advocates (NIFLA). According to a pregnancy center "service report" produced on these networks' behalf by the conservative group Family Research Council, 1,969 centers affiliated with one or more of these associations as of 2010.[11] Other well-established national associations include Birthright, which claimed at least 265 US centers as of 2012, and 1st Way Pregnancy Centers, an offshoot of Birthright that claimed "about" 25.[12]

The three largest national associations offer consulting, legal audits, training, credentialing, networking opportunities, newsletters, and other services to their affiliates but require them to undergo training and adhere to their "Commitment of Care and Competence."[13] Care Net and Heartbeat International can assist centers with virtually all aspects of their work, from the time that founders first explore starting a center. They also directly interact with women by operating national pregnancy assistance hotlines; Heartbeat International's is called Option Line and Care Net's is called the Pregnancy Decision Line. The most important differences between the two organizations include their religious identities, their guidelines about the role of religion in their affiliated centers, and the number of conditions required for affiliation. Care Net is an evangelical Protestant organization that requires its center staff to adhere to a statement of faith and calls them to share their faith with clients. Heartbeat International, though founded by Catholics, did not formally adopt a religious identity ("Christian," later revised to "Christ-centered") until the 1990s. Its individual centers may decide whether to openly evangelize. Care Net's national office asks its affiliates to adhere to more detailed expectations than Heartbeat International does with respect to different aspects of operations.[14] NIFLA provides more specialized assistance to established centers, most importantly legal services and advice, training and technical assistance to centers wishing to become licensed medical clinics. Birthright and 1st Way Pregnancy Centers are much smaller and more informal than Care Net, Heartbeat International, and NIFLA and offer fewer services to members, emphasizing branding instead. Birthright governs its local centers by a strict charter that among other things requires they use the Birthright name, limits the types of services they can provide, and prevents them from collaborating with other organizations.[15] 1st Way Pregnancy Centers emerged from a schism within Birthright; its head said in an interview that it still uses an older version of the Birthright charter. She differentiated her association from Care Net for its policies against evangelizing and recruiting volunteers through clergy, and from both Care Net and Heartbeat International for its resistance to the professionalization and other stylistic changes I will describe in Chapter 4. Though Birthright and 1st Way Pregnancy Centers are officially secular, they have been traditionally associated with Catholics.[16]

The pro-life pregnancy help movement also encompasses service providers other than "pregnancy centers." The "Worldwide Directory of Pregnancy Help," maintained by Heartbeat International, listed 1,461 of them as of July 2018.[17] Examples include adoption agencies, maternity homes, organizations offering support for women who regret a prior abortion, and general social service agencies that offer pregnancy-related assistance from a pro-life perspective, such as local Catholic Charities organizations. They also include church-based pregnancy aid ministries and groups that deliver services through networks of volunteers and donors rather than brick-and-mortar facilities. Some of these organizations do their own direct outreach to women, whereas others maintain relationships of varying formality with local pregnancy centers and receive many of their clients via referrals from pregnancy centers.

The twenty-two leaders I interviewed included three who represented service providers other than pregnancy centers. One of these service providers, the Nurturing Network (TNN), aims to meet the practical needs of pregnant women whose college or employment situations present barriers to pregnancy and parenthood. The California-based organization claimed as of 2012 to serve women throughout the United States and in thirty-three other countries. A woman connects with the organization through a hotline, and then staff members develop help tailored to her situation. An important part of this help involves connecting the woman to local networks of citizens who have pledged to provide women contacting TNN with jobs, medical care, legal assistance, a home, or other financial or material aid. TNN claims to have relationships with about a thousand universities that have agreed to accept immediate transfers of pregnant students to their campuses and to work with them to make college compatible with their situations. TNN staff members sometimes also offer to intervene in situations at the woman's current university, such as when a college threatens her scholarship.[18]

Providing a different type of assistance, but through a similar local network-based delivery system, is the Gabriel Project, "a network of church communities throughout the United States committed to offering immediate and practical help to any woman faced with a crisis pregnancy."[19] As of 2014, the organization's website identified affiliates in multiple cities of nineteen states plus Washington, DC. In Maryland, the organization's signs advertising help for pregnant women are prominently posted on the grounds of many Catholic churches. Though the national Gabriel Project began as an outreach of the Catholic Church in Texas, the director of Maryland's affiliate, Anthony DiIulio, said in his interview with me that in practice his organization now involves many non-Catholic churches, volunteers, and staff. The Maryland affiliate, called the Gabriel Network, operates a pregnancy help hotline and two main programs. Its "Angel Friend" program connects pregnant women to female volunteers who pledge emotional support, mentorship, and help for women to obtain relevant practical resources offered through the volunteer's church or other networks, including assistance with housing and employment. The network also provides shelter and social services through the three maternity homes it operates, two serving women during pregnancy and one serving women after delivery.[20] The organization's mission statement says that it "provides a supportive Christian environment and help with basic needs to pregnant women facing poverty and homelessness, empowering them to embrace motherhood and choose life."[21]

An example of a pro-life pregnancy aid program provided through a general social service agency is the Sanctuaries for Life program run by the Catholic Charities affiliate serving Washington, DC, and its Maryland suburbs. Originally founded and operated by the Catholic Archdiocese of Washington, as program director Michelle Williams explained in her interview, the program pays prenatal care and delivery expenses for low-income pregnant women lacking adequate health insurance. If the woman has some financial resources, she is asked to contribute whatever she can toward the cost, however small, but otherwise all services are free. Sanctuaries for Life also links program participants to Catholic Charities' wider range of charitable aid, including food, clothing, and assistance with payments for rent and utilities.[22]

HUMAN RESOURCES

Pregnancy help work is a people-intensive enterprise. Though most pregnancy service providers now appear to employ at least some paid staff, the movement relies heavily on volunteer labor. The extent ranges across organizations. Sanctuaries for Life, for example, is administered by a regular Catholic Charities employee, and local Catholic hospitals deliver clients' medical care through financial arrangements with the program. Meanwhile, Birthright and its pregnancy centers are so heavily volunteer oriented that the woman concurrently directing its US operations and its Atlanta center as of the time of her interview was reported to have spent her forty-five years with the organization without pay.[23] TNN's network members are also volunteers—numbering 50,000 as of 2010, according to the group—who have signed up to offer resources and help to pregnant women.[24]

Care Net, Heartbeat International, and NIFLA-affiliated pregnancy centers, from whom I gathered quantitative staffing data, also lean heavily, though not exclusively, on volunteers. They reported to the Pregnancy Center Director Survey for 2011 a mean of 39.6 volunteers per center and totals ranging from 0 to 500. Volunteers completing the Pregnancy Center Staff Survey reported contributing an average of 4.8 hours per week and a mean of 4.7 years since they first started volunteering at a pregnancy center.[25] Across the sample, weekly hours volunteered ranged from 1 to 25, and years since first involvement at a pregnancy center ranged from less than 1 year to 31 years. Volunteers play various roles for the centers, including serving as "peer" pregnancy counselors, teaching classes on parenting or other topics, answering telephones, performing clerical work, sorting and managing donated goods, and delivering professional services. Particularly important forms of volunteer professional service delivery at pregnancy centers are the contributions of physicians in providing or supervising onsite nurses' provision of medical services to clients.

Nearly all (98 percent) Care Net, Heartbeat International, and/or NIFLA-affiliated centers employed paid staff in 2011. The number of employees per center ranged from 0 to 95, with a mean of 5.7 and a median of 4. Employees responding to the Pregnancy Center Staff Survey averaged 27.9 hours of work per week and 7.3 years since they first became involved with a pregnancy center. Employee years since first involvement at a pregnancy center ranged from less than 1 year to 26. The experience of leaders I interviewed suggests that many employees begin as volunteers.[26]

Care Net, Heartbeat International, and NIFLA center staff—volunteers and employees alike—stand out notably from the general US adult population for three characteristics measured by my Pregnancy Center Staff Survey. First, nearly all of them (97 percent) are female. Second, nearly all (93 percent) report attending religious services at least once per week. Third, respondents overwhelmingly identified as evangelical or born-again Christians (83 percent). Most of the remaining respondents (13 percent) were Catholics. The sample likely overrepresents the ratio of evangelicals to Catholics among the staff of pregnancy centers because of better response rates from Care Net centers relative to Heartbeat International centers and because Birthright centers, which have been traditionally affiliated with Catholics, were not included in the survey. Among respondents at Heartbeat International centers that did not also affiliate with Care Net, 40 percent of respondents identified as Catholic. Appendix A includes additional demographic statistics on Care Net, Heartbeat International, and NIFLA pregnancy center staff.

Women's predominance in the pregnancy center movement has been noted by others as a defining feature, and it appears at all levels of the movement with only a little bit of falloff.[27] On my Pregnancy Center Staff Survey, women constituted 88 percent of employees and volunteers reporting that they held a graduate degree or equivalent, something likely to mark the doctors, lawyers, social workers, and others contributing professional services to the pregnancy center movement. Of the centers responding to the Pregnancy Center Director Survey, 92 percent reported that a woman served as executive director or chair of their board of directors. In the year I fielded these surveys, 2012, women held the top leadership position in four of the five national pregnancy center umbrella organizations included in my study, although in what might or might not be a notable development, by 2018 the presidencies of Care Net and Heartbeat International had passed to men.

THE PROBLEM OF ABORTION: PREGNANCY HELP ORGANIZATIONS' APPROACH

Theory of Abortion

The pregnancy help movement's theory of abortion features the idea that lack of support, other circumstantial pressures, and the perception of having no other choice drive most women's abortion decisions. Care Net's volunteer training manual (used by 61 percent of the Pregnancy Center Director Survey sample) provides statistics indicating that women cite "overwhelmingly circumstantial pressures" as reasons for having an abortion and that the vast majority of "clients" would "have kept their babies under better circum-stances."[28] Says Heartbeat International, "So many times clients and patients will say or imply, 'I have no choice.'"[29] Its volunteer training manual (used by 20 percent of the Pregnancy Center Director Survey sample) portrays abor-tion as an "act of despair" that conflicts with most women's consciences and "maternal instincts."[30] Women "choose against their conscience because of pressure from others and their circumstances. They choose abortion out of fear—fear of not being able to raise a child, fear of losing their partner if they do not have an abortion, fear of losing control over their lives, etc."[31] Declares pro-life freelance writer Frederica Mathewes-Green, in a book endorsed by many of the top pregnancy help movement leaders and cited in Heartbeat International's volunteer training manual, "No one wants an abortion as she wants an ice-cream cone or a Porsche. She wants an abortion as an animal, caught in a trap, wants to gnaw off its own leg."[32]

These ideas appear widely accepted by the employees and volunteers of local pregnancy centers and by the leaders of other pregnancy help orga-nizations. Women's contemplation of abortion is usually "based on lack of something," whether support from a boyfriend, employment, or a steady in-come, said the director of Sanctuaries of Life, a Washington, DC, area Cath-olic Charities program that provides medical care and other aid for indigent pregnant women. Some women have had "diabolical things" done to them, a Maryland pregnancy center director said, in the context of discussing her cen-ter's counseling work and the particularly challenging situations, such as rape and incest, that some women bring to their pregnancy decision making. On the Pregnancy Center Staff Survey, 86.1 percent of volunteers and employees agreed (nearly half of them, strongly) that, "Most women who have abortions are pushed by others or their circumstances." Less than 5 percent disagreed.

Among the various circumstantial pressures they say face women with un-planned pregnancies, pregnancy center theory especially elevates those associ-ated with relationships.[33] This thought portrays women as turning to abortion because a partner, parents, or peers might fail to support her in continuing the pregnancy or explicitly press her to have an abortion. Based largely on "listen-ing sessions" conducted at pregnancy centers around the country with women who had obtained abortions, Mathewes-Green concluded, "In nearly every case, the abortion was undertaken to fulfill a felt obligation to another person, a parent or boyfriend. . . . The woman considering abortion doesn't feel auton-omous, but enmeshed in relationships which bind and constrain her decision, now this way, now that."[34] "Many women lack support from their families and loved ones," states Heartbeat International.[35] Care Net tells its volunteers, "You may be one of the few people who are dependable, who believe in her, and who offer her help in attaining her goals."[36]

Sometimes a woman's sense that she would be unsupported in carrying a pregnancy to term is constructed as stemming from emotional damage inflicted by longer-term relationship problems. Both the Care Net and Heartbeat International training manuals state that women experiencing problem pregnancies are more likely than the general population to come from homes with divorced or never-married parents.[37] Women contemplating or undergoing abortions, one longtime Maryland pregnancy center director asserted, have a "brokenness" in their lives that she said pro-life activists outside of pregnancy centers generally do not appreciate.[38] Another local center leader shared her perception that many of her center's clients had been used by men for much of their lives and had never been shown true love.[39] Multiple leaders and documents portrayed the unintentionally pregnant woman as lacking the self-esteem, self-love, and self-confidence the leaders saw as key to choosing to continue a pregnancy despite pressures to choose abortion.[40]

Pregnancy help movement discourse on why women have abortions also identifies the wider culture as an important source of pressure. As women cope with difficult circumstances, some center leaders said, abortion providers and the culture lead them to believe abortion is the only feasible and proper response to their unplanned pregnancy, reinforcing their sense of powerlessness. Society, according to Cookie Harris, board chair of a Maryland pregnancy center, tells women to get abortions; it fails to tell women they have an alternative and fails to back up that alternative with resources. Care Net's volunteer training manual laments:

> Our culture seems to consider a woman to lack good judgment if she carries to term, in spite of difficulties, embarrassment, or inconvenience. She often has to go against the tide of popular opinion about the meaning of abortion and what is happening within her. She must also overcome the mass media, which brings messages into her living room showing powerful, beautiful, and intelligent people supporting abortion as the answer to women in unplanned pregnancies.[41]

Pregnancy center theory also places economic pressures among the factors pushing women toward abortion. These take the form of budget constraints as well as opportunity costs associated with the difficulty pregnancy and child-bearing can pose for a woman as she tries to advance and support herself in school or the workplace. Care Net's training manual teaches, "Often, the differences between the joy of pregnancy and the crisis of pregnancy are matters of circumstance. How will I stay employed? Can I stay in school? Will he leave me? These circumstances cannot be trivialized since they can be real impediments to her well-being."[42] The Gabriel Network asserts, "Many women who want to choose life are facing poverty, homelessness, or even abandonment. In these cases, abortion can appear to be the only reasonable option."[43] An undated Heartbeat International fund-raising letter I received in 2014 warned potential donors, "There can be no question that our weak economy is driving abortion-vulnerable women to Planned Parenthood and the hellish world of abortion."

Leader interviews likewise revealed widespread acknowledgement of financial hardship as one of many complex factors involved in women's contemplation of abortion and as a reality in many clients' lives. Two leaders who emphasized most the economic aspects of abortion decision making said their organizations served large shares of immigrants. "It's real," one local pregnancy help program director I interviewed stated, citing examples of economically desperate women she had encountered who thought abortion was their only choice. A former Maryland pregnancy center director elaborated on the circumstances of the Latina immigrants that she said had been her center's core clients. Despite the word "abortion" being a cultural taboo, she said, Hispanic women are told "that everybody does it here [in the United States] and that's the only way you're gonna get ahead." Before coming to the United States, she explained, immigrants do not always know just how high the cost of living is. It is enough of a struggle for an immigrant to pay her basic expenses on the meager wage she is likely to make, and she also often wants to fulfill a pledge to send money home. Then add pregnancy and her need for child care, and things look "impossible." As a result, the "temptation to solve it quickly" through abortion is difficult to resist. Financial need, in this leader's experience, was "usually the number one reason" women seek abortions.[44] Both leaders cited the high cost of delivery—not covered for most immigrants by private or public insurance—relative to abortion as an especially salient economic factor in women's decision making.

The logical consequence of an understanding of abortion that emphasizes pressures on women is that it is potentially largely preventable through changing society in a way that makes it friendlier to motherhood. The founder of Birthright wrote optimistically in 1973, "The crux of the abortion problem is the unwanted child; and yet it is our society which has created the conditions that make a child unwanted. So these conditions can be changed! We do not have to accept them." She suggested that "correct[ing] our socio-economic failures and shortcomings" was the preferable alternative to "eliminating the children before they come into our midst."[45] States Care Net, "Peer counselors at pregnancy centers have a great opportunity to provide alternative help to many women who may choose life for their unborn child if the pressures are understood and addressed."[46] The training manual later continues, "The key factor in whether or not clients choose to carry and parent will be the quality of the support systems available to them."[47]

Though they emphasize circumstantial pressures, leaders of the contemporary pregnancy help movement stop far short of arguing that changing the short-term conditions surrounding a pregnant woman will suffice in most cases to change her plans about abortion, as if her own preferences and vision for her life do not matter. Care Net, for example, concedes that unintended pregnancy tends to produce negative emotions for most women, one of which is said to include anger over "the blocking of many goals by the potential or actual pregnancy."[48] The Heartbeat International manual explains that women "think of abortion as life saving for themselves. That is, if they continue the pregnancy, their life as they know it will end. Abortion is almost self-defense ... abortion is the *least* of three evils" of abortion, adoption, and parenthood.[49] A Maryland center director whose work included counseling clients described the clients' initial and dominant mind-set simply: they typically just want the pregnancy to go away. In interviews, movement leaders treated these as understandable sentiments.[50]

The statements above signal what has been a gradually increasing acceptance in the pregnancy help movement of the idea that women contemplating abortions do not want to be mothers at a particular time, regardless of what financial and other help is extended to them. According to one key leader, pregnancy center activists evolved over time from holding naïve faith that an offer of support provided in a single visit would change a woman's mind against abortion to one of greater awareness of the magnitude and complexity of the forces they were up against. She cites this growing awareness in explaining the attention contemporary centers give to a number of what observers might call "morality" or "lifestyle" issues, on top of the practical help and personal affirmation they extend to women feeling pressured to choose abortion.[51]

Heartbeat International now tells its volunteers that pregnancy center clients tend to "have very complex problems." It offers a "tornado" as a metaphor for the typical client's life, constructing the client as "on a whirlwind course of destruction," propelled in part by her immoral choices but also by breakdowns in the important relationships in her life, past traumas, low self-esteem, and the deleterious consequences of her choices. It notes that her "attitudes have been shaped in a culture that places great value on expediency and little value on human life," and it also describes her as "suffering."[52]

Serving Women, Not (Necessarily) Saving Babies

Pregnancy help organizations describe themselves as "woman-centered" or "woman-focused" enterprises. Volunteer training documents and other writing by movement leaders heavily emphasize this point, and the idea repeatedly surfaced in leaders' answers to an interview question about how the philosophy, ideology, or worldview of pregnancy help organizations differs from those of the rest of the pro-life movement. To be "woman-centered," according to Heartbeat International, means: "You care about her, not just about her baby . . . you care about her physical, emotional, intellectual, social, and spiritual well-being."[53] As a former center director put it, a woman-centered approach to pregnancy counseling is "about you and what you need." "We help you form a plan that fits in with your life," Birthright's website promises to women, "a plan that works best for you and your pregnancy."[54]

Mary Cunningham Agee, founder and president of TNN, explains the rationale for a woman-centered approach to abortion and admonishes readers of a Catholic pro-life publication:

> In essence, we must remember that it is the mother in crisis—not the unborn child, no matter how infinitely valuable his or her life truly is—who has the power and responsibility to make a life and death decision. We cannot afford to overlook the fact that it is the mother who is being asked to accept the economic hardship, social embarrassment, and physical sacrifice of her unplanned pregnancy. It is the mother in crisis, far more than anyone else, who must hear compassionate words and credible offers of assistance if she is to persevere on the lonely path of protecting the life of her unborn child.[55]

Care Net's training manual discusses the difference between "woman-focused" and "baby-focused" ministries at some length, calling baby-saving "a misplaced goal."[56] It tells volunteers, "Our role is to minister to the client's needs, recognizing that it is she who must make the ultimate choices. When we choose instead to focus our efforts on saving babies, we can easily lose sight of this role of ministry to the client."[57] Care Net further states:

> We should not allow our desire to prevent abortion to lead us to assume that God somehow thinks more highly of the client's baby than He does of her. . . . Of course, this [focusing on the woman rather than the baby] does not mean that every baby will be saved from abortion. But it does mean that you will have respected the woman as a person made in God's image.[58]

Care Net and Heartbeat International volunteer training manuals both emphasize listening skills and empathy as desirable qualities for peer counselors. They teach that meetings with clients should begin with an intake process that involves learning about the client's situation, feelings, and perceived needs.[59]

This ability to adopt the pregnant woman's perspective and to identify with her was incorporated in the idea of being "woman-centered" and constituted a second important, related contrast pregnancy help leaders drew between their movement and the rest of the pro-life movement. This included the ability to understand why a pregnant woman would have, or be inclined to have, an abortion. Leaders such as Williams of Sanctuaries for Life said of the woman that they tried to "look through her lens" and learn what was important to her. The response to abortion that pregnancy centers offered, a Care Net national consultant and Connecticut center director said, was "the compassionate response . . . reaching out with the practical help." It involved full awareness of what "choosing life . . . really means" for the pregnant woman, including coping with many practical issues and "standing up to" a lot of people who think she should be choosing abortion. It is "hard to be single and pregnant," Birthright's then US director, Terry Weaver, stated frankly.

To several leaders, being woman-centered or woman-focused required abandonment of the baby-saving orientation they believed characterized other pro-lifers, including in the way they framed their own missions. Birthright's Weaver said of her organization, "Are we fighting abortion? No, we're helping pregnant women." Care Net stated, similarly, "Pregnancy center ministry is not about changing laws, nor is it even ultimately about saving babies. Pregnancy center ministry addresses the needs of individual women."[60] The

Care Net and Heartbeat International volunteer training manuals deny that saving babies is something their counselors can do. Instead they portray it as something that only the babies' mothers can do, and that they hope will be the fruit of their work.[61] Saving a baby could be a pregnancy counselor's desire, some suggested, but it could not be her goal. Stated former Maryland center director and Heartbeat board member Mary Hamm, "The higher goal is to meet that person where they're at and give them compassion and care." Local center director Mariana Vera shared that her center did not even like to call itself a "pregnancy center" because such a term called attention to the baby and away from the woman, while failing to adequately capture the range of services the center provided to women.

Volunteer screening and training processes, some leaders said, aim to catch the many people who come to their movement with what Care Net vice president Cindy Hopkins called "an agenda" that is not "right."[62] That agenda was one focused on babies rather than women, and one, Heartbeat International's president Peggy Hartshorn added in her interview, whose holder sees in pregnancy centers the opportunity to convince women not to get abortions. Hartshorn said that in trainings she personally conducted, she would make it clear to such prospective volunteers that pregnancy center work was not about debating the woman but loving her and standing by her.[63] Hopkins added that the baby-savers in her centers' ranks would consistently drop out or change their views.

In addition to identifying reasons they believed that being woman-centered was the moral way to approach decisions about abortion, some leaders added their belief that baby-centered strategies would be ineffective when it came to changing women's minds about abortion. For several years, said interviewee Mathewes-Green, a Maryland writer who has extensively promoted pregnancy centers while playing various roles in the pro-life movement, the rest of the pro-life movement separated the woman and her baby, taking the baby's side. They viewed the woman "as an aggressor and murderer," a strategy that eventually "backfired."[64]

Pregnancy help movement leaders have long treated it as normative that a pro-life position in words must be backed up with deeds. Birthright founder Louise Summerhill wrote in 1973:

> Generally speaking, if a girl keeps her child . . . she must also be able to support
> him, with perhaps some subsidizing, and here, I believe, is where our Welfare

System should be changed. I know I have been criticized for helping girls to have babies who may have to be supported by welfare. Nevertheless, our greatest asset, and our hope for the future of our country, is in our people. . . . Therefore, we should be happy to invest in the welfare of our future citizens by giving help to mothers.[65]

At various times, pregnancy help leaders have taken such a message—although typically directing it at a pro-life and Christian "we" rather than at the government—to wider audiences. In a 1984 book, Care Net leader Melinda Delahoyde repeatedly challenges readers, in addition to endorsing government aid to people with disabilities, to do more personally to help families bearing children, especially children with disabilities, under difficult circumstances: "It is not enough to tell a parent that you must choose life and then walk away. Our words mean nothing if we do not back them up with loving support for that family."[66] Wrote another leader to Catholics, "It simply is not enough for any Christian to say that we are 'for life' unless we are willing to provide the practical means to support it."[67] Anyone objecting to a problem has to be ready to solve that problem, 1st Way Pregnancy Centers director Denise Cocciolone insisted in an interview, so that pregnancy centers would be that answer to the problem of abortion. In that way, she said of activists protesting legal abortion, "we validate their movement. . . . Without us, they make no sense."[68]

Leaders frequently conveyed an understanding of the term *pro-life* that encompassed not just opposition to abortion but a host of activities that facilitate human well-being. The director of a Maryland pregnancy center, for example, noted that when discussing positive pregnancy test results with clients not interested in abortion, counselors ask a number of questions to ensure that the woman is en route to a healthy pregnancy and able to get the medical attention she needs. "That's just to be pro-life," she said. Proclaimed pastor Tony Evans in a keynote address at Care Net's 2011 conference, while celebrating the impact of pregnancy centers such as his church's on women's lives, "We offer whole life, not term!"[69]

"Empowering" Women

Leaders portray the pregnancy help movement as empowering the women it serves. They identify multiple ways in which they do this. They say they empower women with information—about abortion, pregnancy, the availability of help, and other matters. They say they try to get women to think in terms of their "power to make a choice that can help bring good out of" the "evil" that might have been associated with their crisis pregnancies.[70] Some participants in the pregnancy help movement also aim to counter what they say is a widely held belief that having an unintended child out of wedlock necessarily dooms a woman and her child to a life of unhappiness and failure. Although pregnant women might be understandably worried about their futures and the challenges ahead, the "woman-centered" counseling a former director said her center provided was "about showing them the light at the end of the tunnel . . . show[ing] them a picture of a successful single mother." In the pregnancy help movement, empowerment also means helping the client "so that she truly can act on the positive options that you have opened up to her."[71] Pregnancy centers say they do this, among other things, by providing economic assistance; medical care; referrals to community resources; and classes on parenting, health, and other topics. Said TNN's Agee in summing up what her organization did for women, "They're going to be empowered to do what their heart calls them to do . . . to make a choice they can be proud of."

Activists at various times claim that it is their movement, rather than that of abortion providers and advocates, that truly empowers women and offers them "real" choices and solutions to the issues that make pregnancy a problem. No one has told the women "they can do it," Maryland's pregnancy center leader Harris claimed in her interview. "Women are very strong," she said, but abortion clinics are not telling them that. Leaders also stress pregnancy centers' financial disinterest in women's decisions. "While abortion clinics typically demand cash or a major credit card before services will be performed, PRCs offer all services free," NIFLA president Tom Glessner writes.[72] An undated fund-raising letter from Heartbeat International that I received in 2014 alleged, "The abortion clinics are not interested in 'giving women a choice.' They are interested in turning a profit. That's why *91% of pregnant women who go to Planned Parenthood have an abortion!*"

Despite the volunteer training manuals and other statements urging restraint in the work of baby-saving, the leadership of the pregnancy help movement treats abortion as unequivocally bad—not just for the unborn but for the women choosing it. Some leaders argue that case in social terms: a culture that legalizes abortion and sells it as the best or most responsible way for women to cope with a problem pregnancy can make the exercise of "choice" much more difficult for women who do not want to have abortions and pro-vide society an excuse to do little to support them. "Making abortion available forecloses women's other choices," argued Mathewes-Green in her interview, because then women repeatedly hear that abortion is the choice they should make.[73] Women "do 'deserve better' than abortion," wrote another leader, in-voking a Feminists for Life slogan.[74]

Still more commonly, leaders when describing abortion as disempowering invoke risks they say it poses to patients' physical and psychological health. Pregnancy centers were claiming the harmful effects of abortion on women, based on the stories from postabortion support networks that formed there, well before such "woman-protective" arguments diffused into mainstream an-tiabortion discourse.[75] Early on, Summerhill claimed that having an abortion could afflict a woman with an "ineradicable and crushing" feeling of guilt.[76] Today—based, they say, on research and the testimonials of clients and other women—pregnancy help activists associate abortion with a broader array of risks. Citing academic journals and other medical sources, a Care Net brochure directed at pregnant women lists immediate risks of abortion procedures as including heavy bleeding, infection, and organ damage and identifies future preterm births and a heightened risk of breast cancer as long-term risks.[77] Heartbeat International's volunteer training manual reproduces a lengthy fact sheet by a pro-life research group, the Elliot Institute, that also heavily cites academic journal articles in linking abortion to suicide, depression, eating dis-orders, substance abuse, relationship problems, symptoms of post-traumatic stress disorder, and other psychological risks.[78] Findings of such studies are disputed (see Chapter 7).

Some activists charge that abortion advocates and providers hide those risks from women. Sandy Christiansen, an obstetrician-gynecologist whose roles in the pregnancy help movement include service as medical director for a local pregnancy center and as a consultant for Care Net affiliates re-garding medical issues, cited women's personal stories about their abortion experiences as an important motivation for her movement.[79] Those stories, she argued, exposed the "seedy underbelly" of abortion and how it is "not health-promoting." Those working in pregnancy centers "have seen the devas-tation," especially psychological, that comes with having an abortion and were responding by warning women about abortion's risks and caring for those women coping with the consequences of a past abortion.[80] Similarly, TNN's Agee writes, women's voices expose "the falsehoods lurking behind the 'choice' rhetoric" and the "broken hearts" abortion leaves behind.[81] For women who have had abortions, the director of a Maryland pregnancy center said, "that heaviness, that brokenness, is just huge." "The thing that keeps me going is the women who are still being hurt," professed another center director, who shared that she herself had undergone an abortion.

Pregnancy centers' treatment of the health risks associated with abortion provokes strong criticism from pro-choice advocates, who allege such information is misleading or false.[82] My study was not designed to adjudicate the competing claims of activists on the risks of abortion but does elaborate on this debate in Chapter 7.

Seeking Social Change

Pro-life pregnancy help organizations rarely make claims upon the state. They maintain consciously apolitical identities as service providers and "ministries," and a few interviewees explicitly defined their work as something other than "activism." Care Net's training manual tells its staff, "Christians must continue to pray and to act to change the morally bankrupt laws that leave our unborn children without protection. . . . But pregnancy center ministry transcends these political solutions."[83]

Though federal law allows charities to spend a limited portion of their resources on nonelectioneering political activities, such as policy advocacy and get-out-the-vote efforts, statistics from the Pregnancy Center Director Survey suggest that centers do not often use these rights. Two-thirds of centers reported no political activity in the previous two years, and another 6 percent was not sure if anyone had represented their center in political activity. Of those who reported any political activity, most (two-thirds) answered on a follow-up question that this activity concerned only legislation or regulation pertaining directly to pregnancy centers rather than general abortion policy or other public policy questions. Centers also handle other forms of pro-life activism with caution. Of those surveyed, 55 percent reported having an explicit policy against staff participation in "sidewalk counseling" (a practice linked to the direct-action stream in which pro-life activists try to intercept women on their way into an abortion clinic and talk them out of that decision) and protests in front of abortion clinics. Many other centers added in space for clarifying comments that although the center did not explicitly ban this activity, it was strongly discouraged or just not done. Pregnancy centers have "one thing: service," said Birthright's Weaver, in differentiating them from the rest of the pro-life movement.

This reluctance to embrace identities as "activists" coexists with bold statements some leaders make about social change. In interviews and their public writing, several leaders framed their movement as seeking justice for the unborn and for vulnerable women. The cover of Care Net's 2011 conference program featured the Biblical instructions: "Learn to do right! Seek justice, encourage the oppressed. Defend the cause of the fatherless, plead the case of the widow.—Isaiah 1:17." Heartbeat International explained its motivations on its website in similar justice-oriented, and also Biblical, terms: "Altogether, the pregnancy help movement is passionate about faithfully answering the call to 'Give justice to the weak and the fatherless; maintain the right of the afflicted and the destitute. Rescue the weak and the needy; deliver them from the hand of the wicked' (Psalm 82:3–4)." Summerhill, Canada's founder of Birthright whose vision is supposed to guide the organization even today, derived her organization's name from children's "right to be born."[84] Meanwhile, she incorporated women's rights in defining Birthright's "creed and philosophy": "to uphold, at all times, that any pregnant girl or woman has the right to whatever help she may need to carry her child to term, and to foster respect for human life at all stages of development."[85] The pregnancy center movement, according to longtime Birthright/1st Way leader Cocciolone, is a "grassroots endeavor" striving "to halt the behemoth of abortion and provide a peaceful and dignified future to mothers and babies."[86]

Leaders not infrequently aligned their work with that of other great movements on behalf of disadvantaged populations. NIFLA president Glessner, in a book, portrays pregnancy centers as the cornerstones of a larger movement to achieve a "sanctity-of-life ethic" and calls for those in the movement to take inspiration from British abolitionist William Wilberforce. In fighting slavery, Glessner argues, Wilberforce "combated an entrenched institution that, like abortion, dehumanized, exploited, and killed other human beings."[87] Care Net national consultant and Connecticut pregnancy center director Linda Cochrane wrapped pregnancy centers' fight against abortion in an historical narrative of fights against injustices such as slavery and child labor. She also compared pregnancy centers' efforts to institutionalize support for pregnant women to Dorothy Day's movement to institutionalize care for the poor. Cochrane opined, "It is a pioneer movement. I don't think there was pregnancy care in any other time in history that there is today." Pregnancy centers might encounter resistance from outside and sometimes even within the pro-life movement, she suggested, but predicted that as with Day's movement, centers would eventually be recognized as mainstream, necessary institutions.[88] A Maryland pregnancy center director, citing a speech in which Catholic cardinal Timothy Dolan had linked the plights of downtrodden and socially marginalized groups differentially favored by the political left and right, said that in her pregnancy center work she was living out a personal calling to serve "the uns." Dolan's speech, delivered at New York's 2012 Al Smith Dinner, identified these *uns* as: "the *un*-employed . . . the *un*-insured . . . the *un*-wanted . . . the *un*-wed mother, and her innocent, fragile *un*-born baby in her womb . . . the *un*-documented . . . the *un*-housed . . . the *un*-healthy . . . the *un*-fed . . . the *under*-educated."[89]

Part of the social change the pregnancy help movement advocates involves how society, including people who call themselves Christian or pro-life, treats unmarried and other women who carry an unintended pregnancy to term. Some of my interviewees bristled at the way they believed the pregnant woman had been ignored or otherwise constructed by other pro-life activists in the past or even the present. Birthright's charter has included the following among the goals that its affiliates must pursue: "to create and maintain in society an awareness of the needs of pregnant girls and women, to remove the social stigma associated with the unwed mother and her child, and to encourage a more humane understanding of her and her problems."[90] National pregnancy help movement leaders have used their public platforms to recast women who carry problem pregnancies to term as heroes and "profiles in courage."[91]

Some leaders claimed to seek nothing less than total cultural transformation: the development of what one national leader called "a Culture of Life around the world" and what another described as the triumph of a "sanctity-of-life ethic" over the "quality-of-life ethic" seen as increasingly governing US culture.[92] The reformed culture these leaders envision recognizes that all human life is inherently and equally valuable because God created it in His own image. Such a culture manifests that recognition not just in its laws but in the ways people support, love, and respect each other in their daily living.

Movement participants do not envision change unfurling in sweeping, top-down fashion. They direct their talk of justice and rights at society, not at the state. They imagine change created from the bottom up, person by person, community by community. As Susan Hoffman, director of a small network of

Maryland and Pennsylvania pregnancy centers phrased it, the centers work at "changing policy in their neighborhood."[93] The theory of social change suggested by pregnancy help movement discourse is one in which justice can be achieved in part through individual acts of compassion. These acts gradually transform the receiver, the giver, and perhaps the bystander as well. As they multiply, they eventually transform the entire culture.

Part of the Pro-Life Movement?

Given the terms with which pregnancy center activists describe their work and differentiate it from that of other pro-lifers, including the fact that they have named their endeavor a "movement," one might be tempted to question whether they identify as part of the pro-life movement at all. Activists' words and behavior, however, especially at the national leadership level, show clearly that they do. Care Net's Hopkins, Heartbeat International's Hartshorn, and 1st Way Pregnancy Centers' Cocciolone, respectively, described pregnancy centers as one of the movement's "three pillars" (the "compassion" pillar, with the others being the political and direct-action pillars), the pro-life movement's "service arm," and the "serving end of the movement." National Right to Life's daily news emails, to which I subscribed, regularly carried stories about pregnancy centers. Speakers at the rally preceding the annual Washington, DC, March for Life typically include representatives of pregnancy help service providers.[94] At pro-life movement leaders' 2013 Rose Dinner, an event linked to the annual March for Life and coinciding with the fortieth anniversary of the *Roe* decision, the president of Heartbeat International delivered the keynote address.

Although associating themselves with the pro-life movement, leaders' descriptions of their organizations also often linked pregnancy centers to different "reference groups," that is, those social or professional enterprises after which activists models themselves or consider themselves most like.[95] Groups invoked by pregnancy help leaders included their churches and the professional fields of social services, medicine, and education. Borrowing from Elizabeth Armstrong's conceptualization of social movements, pro-life pregnancy help looks like a "field" (an arena of social action, comprising its own set of actors, goals, norms, and strategic logic) nested within other fields, one of which is the wider pro-life movement.[96]

PROMOTION AND SUPPORT OF ALTERNATIVES TO ABORTION

How do pregnancy centers go about persuading pregnant women to "choose life"? What do they and other pregnancy help service providers do, concretely, to act on their pledges to support and empower the women who make this choice? Competing political narratives surrounding pregnancy centers' work differ about the extent to which pregnancy centers actually do provide meaningful aid and service to women, as opposed to (or in addition to) deception and emotional coercion designed to save babies from abortion. Although my research did not follow pregnant women into the counseling rooms and therefore cannot verify what pregnancy center counselors actually say to them there, I did look at key counselor training materials and collect data on the goods and services pregnancy centers and their partners offer to support alternatives to abortion.

Pregnancy Tests, Options Counseling, and Ultrasounds

From the start, pregnancy centers have advertised themselves as places where a woman could receive free pregnancy tests, information about her options, a listening ear, and nonjudgmental support. These offers appear to still draw clients today. Heartbeat International's website, as of 2018, claims that its Option Line receives more than a thousand contacts per day via telephone, text message, email, or live chat and that it has received more than three million contacts since it began in 2003.[97] Meanwhile, brick-and-mortar pregnancy centers performed 679,600 free pregnancy tests in 2017, according to a "pregnancy center service report" produced for national pregnancy center umbrella organizations by Charlotte Lozier Institute (CLI), a conservative pro-life think tank.[98]

Volunteer training manuals produced by Care Net and Heartbeat International provide detailed guidance and training exercises regarding the general structure of a pregnancy test client's visit and other aspects of peer counselors' interactions with clients. Prior to administration of the pregnancy test, counselors are prompted to have a conversation with the client about her situation, guided by an intake form the counselor completes. Heartbeat International's sample form asks about marital status; education; income; employment; religious preference; pregnancy symptoms; recent use of medication, drugs, alcohol, or tobacco; pregnancy history; pregnancy intention; contraceptive use; relationship with the potential father; the possibility that she has been a victim of abuse; and what she is seeking from the center visit. Conversation resumes after the test, covering test results and the client's reaction to those results, presentation of information and discussion of options, referrals to further resources, and an attempt to schedule a follow-up contact. Training manuals prepare counselors to discuss pregnancy options with extensive information about fetal development and the progression of a pregnancy, abortion procedures and risks, and considerations involved with decisions between single parenting, married parenting, and adoption.

Counseling at pregnancy centers is supposed to follow the woman-centered approach outlined earlier in this chapter. Heartbeat International teaches a four-step approach to counseling that it dubs "The LOVE Approach," in which L = "listen and learn," O = "open options," V = "vision and values," and E = "extend and empower."[99] Substantively, this means that pregnancy center staff members first should "listen to the client or patient and learn who she is, her story, her thoughts, confusion, beliefs, and more. Next, help her discover a clearer understanding of her options, introducing her to a new vision of herself: who she is created to be and can become with the grace of God. Then extend and empower her to make a dramatic life change—perhaps one small step at a time."[100] Care Net states that a qualified volunteer counselor will exhibit four key qualities exemplified by Jesus Christ: sincerity, "unconditional acceptance and love" for everyone, genuine humility, and both intellectual and emotional empathy for the client.[101] It tells volunteers to conceive of themselves as servants and let go of their own agendas, including as they relate to the pregnant woman. "When we act humbly, with a servant's heart, we do not seek to control others," Care Net instructs.[102]

The national networks place this effort to form a caring personal relationship with the client at the heart of pregnancy center counseling as well as the whole of pregnancy center work. "If we are going to have a life-saving and life-changing impact, we must start by forming a relationship.... The relationship we aim for must be one of unconditional love that sees warts and all and still conveys love," Heartbeat's training manual says.[103] Some centers do this with less formality than others, especially in the Birthright and 1st Way wing of the movement. Writes a longtime 1st Way pregnancy center director, Terry Ianora, of these centers' counseling training and philosophy, "We learned all that we could, but in the end counseling women is about loving the mother and child and getting out of God's way as He speaks to them through us. . . . If there is one word to sum up and describe crisis pregnancy counseling such as 1st Way offers, it is this, personal."[104]

National networks articulate counseling guidelines that implicitly address some of the negative tactics others have attributed to pregnancy centers. Birthright International's website as of 2018 prominently promoted the organization as "A Safe Place for All." It pledged that women would encounter "no pressures, scare tactics, lectures, or judgment. Whatever the circumstances may be, we support all women who are pregnant or think they may be."[105] Birthright prohibits its centers from using graphic pictures of abortion. The goal, said its US national director, is to "love them [pregnant women] to life, not scare them to life." She said also that her center's counselors do not ask for last names or personal data and that the center does not refer women to agencies where they would encounter religious pressure. Centers in the other major networks have also generally rejected use of graphic abortion pictures.[106]

Care Net and Heartbeat International volunteer training manuals go to some pains to spell out the ethical standards expected of staff. For example, "always be truthful," Care Net commands its volunteers. "Answer all questions directly. . . . Deceiving clients in any way does not represent Christ and undermines the ability of the center to serve clients."[107] Heartbeat instructs, "Know as much about each option as possible and make sure your information is accurate. . . . Use only center- or clinic-approved materials." It continues, "Do not use overly emotional terminology. . . . Ask if you can share information with her on abortion or fetal development, especially if it is graphic, before you begin."[108] If a woman wants to leave the center at any time, even while still intending to have an abortion, Care Net tells its volunteers to respectfully let her go: "Your client has the freedom and legal right to choose abortion. If God, being all powerful, can allow her to choose abortion, then we must show the same respect for her as a person. You have prayed for her to come to the center, people are praying while she is at the center, and you must pray for her when she leaves, trusting God with the outcome."[109]

Increasingly, pregnancy centers have been acquiring the capacity to offer medical services, a phenomenon I discuss in more detail in Chapter 4. By far the most widespread of these services—and presently at some "medical" pregnancy centers, the only service—is ultrasound confirmation of pregnancy. Women are shown the image of the fetus, under the logic that this visual will help the woman and anyone she brings with her to embrace what they see on the screen as their unborn child, activating their protective instincts. The ultrasound scans are typically performed by a nurse working under the supervision of an on- or offsite physician who serves as the center's medical director and whose medical license is the basis for the center's authority to offer such a service. As of 2012, 59 percent of Care Net, Heartbeat International, and NIFLA centers responding to the Pregnancy Center Director Survey reported offering medical services, such as ultrasound, beyond pregnancy testing. As of 2017, considering the wider universe of pregnancy centers including those with national networks less enthusiastic about adding medical services, more than 70 percent of US pregnancy centers offered ultrasound. This was according to the pregnancy center service report compiled for the national networks by CLI, which also said these pregnancy centers performed 400,100 free ultrasounds in 2017.[110]

Material Aid and Social Services

Pregnancy centers and other pregnancy help service providers devote substantial attention to helping families reduce their baby-related expenses and meet other basic needs such as food, clothing, shelter, and medical care. This work also consumes substantial physical space, as I observed when visiting Maryland pregnancy centers to interview leaders. When asked about the importance of material assistance and social services to their organizations' mission and work, leaders tended to use words such as "very integral," "very important," "vital," and "huge." With such terms, leaders referenced both the practical needs these helped to fill as well as less tangible goals that they perceived the aid accomplished. Perhaps most importantly, leaders professed that paying attention to a client's material needs signaled to her that she was a person of great worth, for whom others cared deeply. This message, they hoped, would prepare clients to receive counselors' messages about abortion. Williams explained, "I often think about Christ." As Jesus did, it makes sense to "meet the need first. When you meet the need, you get her attention." In doing that, "you're showing her you care about her first" and are not just thinking of her as an "object" carrying a baby: "If you listen to her heart, hear what her needs are, then she'll listen to you. . . . Then she can begin to bond with that child and listen to your suggestions." "Symbolically, it is important," said a former Care Net executive, Curtis Young, of the centers' material aid. It "meets a practical need" for the woman, and it constitutes a "strong statement of affirmation" of her. "It gives them hope," said Care Net's Cochrane, also noting the practical importance of economic assistance and its ability to help women with unintended pregnancies have some of the "nest-building" experiences enjoyed by women with planned pregnancies. Tangible material assistance, some suggested, enhanced the authenticity of centers' pro-life messages and the credibility of their pledges to support the women. As Mathewes-Green said, it demonstrates that "we put our money where our mouth is."

Provision of free baby-related goods, and often other aid as well, is a staple of pregnancy center offerings across umbrella organizations. Cocciolone of the National Life Center/1st Way Pregnancy Centers reported that the local pregnancy center she simultaneously ran generally kept diapers, infant formula, and clothing on hand and was prepared to help women purchase new furniture. As for anything else a pregnant woman or mother might need, the center would provide it if it could or else find another community organization that might be able to help. Birthright's Weaver downplayed the scope of the economic assistance offered, noting her preference for helping women navigate the array of resources available in the community to meet their specific needs. Her organization avoided a set array of services because "you don't know what you're going to do until you find out what the need is." She said clothing was generally available at her Atlanta center, however, and her center presented gift layettes to clients after childbirth. At a Maryland Birthright center I visited during the research, children's and maternity clothing, diapers, sheets, baby bouncer seats, and miscellaneous supplies that would be included in gift layettes filled two rooms.

My Pregnancy Center Director Survey collected more extensive information about material aid and social services from pregnancy centers affiliated with Care Net, Heartbeat International, and NIFLA. Figure 2.1 presents these centers' responses about the availability of 19 different types of goods or services a financially needy family might seek.[111] For each item, directors were asked to specify whether their center "a) Provides this assistance, either at the center or through affiliated individuals and organizations that have pledged to serve your center's clients; b) Refers clients to specific, unaffiliated individuals or organizations that can provide this assistance; or c) Neither provides nor refers for this aid." Question wording specified that it concerned only "NON-GOVERNMENTAL resources" offered to families "for little or no cost." As of 2012, centers provided a mean number of 5.8 of those goods and services, ranging from 0 (at five centers) to 17 (at two centers).

Figure 2.1 Pregnancy Centers' Provision of Material Aid and Social Services

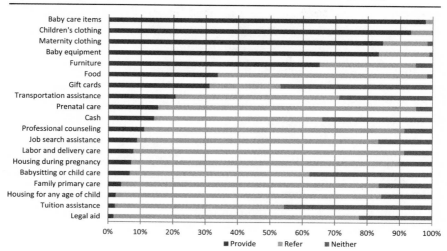

Source: Pregnancy Center Director Survey. N = 471–493.

Nearly every Care Net, Heartbeat International, and NIFLA center reported providing baby-related goods, including diapers and formula (98 percent); baby clothes (93 percent); maternity clothes (85 percent); and baby equipment such as strollers, car seats, and highchairs (83 percent). Most (65 percent) also reported providing larger furniture items such as cribs, beds, or dressers. No other community organization was offering such goods, a Baltimore interviewee claimed, a perception mostly consistent with a front-page local news feature that ran a few years later on low-income families' difficulties affording and accessing diapers.[112]

Smaller shares of pregnancy centers reported extending other forms of economic aid, including emergency cash (14 percent); food (34 percent); transportation assistance (21 percent); job search assistance (9 percent); housing (7 percent); and free or low-cost prenatal (15 percent), labor and delivery (8 percent), or family primary (4 percent) medical care. Most centers that did not offer these latter goods and services reported referring clients to other nongovernmental organizations or individuals that could. Earlier in this chapter, I described some examples of pregnancy help service providers that have sprouted to meet some of these specific needs, such as the Gabriel Network's maternity homes for housing, Catholic Charities' Sanctuaries for Life program for health care, and TNN's efforts to help pregnant and parenting women stay in college or employed. An additional Pregnancy Center Director Survey question asked whether centers kept on hand "information for clients on laws regarding maternity leave and/or pregnancy-related employment discrimination." One-quarter of respondents said they did.

Multiple leaders volunteered that a shortage of affordable housing presented an especially important concern for their clients; one Maryland center director even called finding solutions to that problem an important weakness of her center. Though likely insufficient in scale to meet the need, a segment of the pregnancy help movement is devoted to providing housing. Heartbeat International's "Worldwide Directory of Pregnancy Help" listed 377 pro-life US organizations providing housing as of September 2018.[113] The most common type of housing provided is a *maternity home*, a place where women can live during pregnancy and for some time after birth, typically in a group setting. The institutions are not specific to the pro-life movement, and they have a long and sometimes controversial history in the United States—but others have recognized the pro-life movement as being disproportionately interested in and involved in the operation of such homes in the post-*Roe* era.[114]

Although not disaggregated by maternity homes' alignment with the pro-life movement, data analysis by Mathematica Policy Research provides a snapshot of modern ones. As of the early 2000s, these homes served a mean of eleven women and their families; few homes housed more than twenty women. Homes that reported time limits on top of age restrictions for residence most commonly reported a two-year limit. Nearly all homes offered parenting and life skills classes, and most extended other supportive services such as transportation, child care, and employment training and counseling. Some homes boasted larger arrays of educational, mental health, and medical services. Most homes are staffed around the clock, some by shift workers and others by live-in directors. Homes typically bind their residents to rules regarding chores; drug and alcohol use; curfews; visitors; and participation in in-house programming, school, or employment. Teenagers, especially those coming from socioeconomically disadvantaged backgrounds, tend to be the main clientele, but some maternity homes, including some linked to the pro-life movement, target older, especially homeless, women. Some offer that housing in apartment settings that enable older women to live more independently than teenage clients.[115]

Whether the need is housing, medical care, or something else, pregnancy centers also help women identify and access resources available through gov-

Figure 2.2 Pregnancy Centers' Public Social Welfare Referral Activity

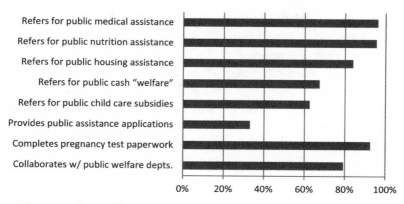

Source: Pregnancy Center Director Survey. N = 474–484.

ernment and other community organizations. As seen in Figure 2.2, nearly every Care Net, Heartbeat International, and NIFLA pregnancy center refers clients to public medical and nutrition assistance programs, and large majorities also refer clients for public cash, child care, and housing assistance programs. Nearly every center (93 percent) reports completing the paperwork documenting a positive pregnancy test that women typically need to qualify for public assistance. A third of centers provided public assistance applications in-house. Nearly 80 percent reported formal or informal collaborations with public departments of health or social services geared toward "help[ing] clients apply or qualify for public assistance programs." Meanwhile, in interviews, some leaders expressed pride in the relationships they had built with other social service providers in their communities and in the efforts their centers had devoted to developing inventories of community resources, upon which they drew to point clients where to go for free or low-cost help with needs as diverse as creditor mediation, domestic violence recovery, and medical care for nonpregnant clients.

Pregnancy centers provide their in-house material aid to virtually any family that seeks it. This includes, according to the Pregnancy Center Director Survey, cases in which the woman does not consider abortion (98 percent), families who did not receive pregnancy services at the center (84 percent), and families with children aged past infancy (79 percent offer goods appropriate for children aged one and older, whereas 20 percent offer goods appropriate for children older than five).[116] All but about 10 percent of Care Net, Heartbeat International, and NIFLA centers, however, said that they ask something of clients in order to receive some (65 percent) or all (25 percent) of their material aid. Over time, many pregnancy centers affiliated with these networks have instituted systems in which they require clients to "earn" some of their baby items, especially more expensive goods like cribs and strollers, through their participation in parenting or other classes. At other centers, as gleaned from interviews, movement documents, and some information volunteered in space for clarifying comments on the survey, centers might ask that clients complete intake forms, have a conversation with a staff member, or have a history of keeping appointments, especially if a client is coming regularly for aid. One center director defended the practice of asking clients who made frequent trips for aid to talk with a counselor as an expression of concern about the family's well-being and an opportunity to learn about and perhaps help with underlying conditions, such as unemployment or illness, that might be driving the need.

A Supportive Person

Pregnancy help movement rhetoric especially elevates one other resource: the availability of a supportive person willing to accompany the woman on her journey through pregnancy and parenthood, to provide companionship and to work with her to resolve whatever practical problems she might encounter along the way. This could include mediating difficult conversations with parents or a partner, driving or accompanying women to medical appointments or the hospital, or looking for an affordable way to access some specific resource. A woman just finding out about an unintended pregnancy, Weaver reasoned in her interview, "feel[s] very much alone," as if standing in the middle of an unmarked map. "The best alternative to abortion is another person," Heartbeat International's website proclaims.[117] Interviewees described her as "someone to believe in them," someone with whom a woman could just "cry it all out" without feeling as if she were burdening a close acquaintance, and an affectionate friend that affirmed the woman for making a "bold choice." The pregnancy center volunteer, according to Weaver, was also to deliver a message that she said left many women "awestruck" because they were not hearing it elsewhere: "It's okay for you to have this baby."

Parenting and Life Skills Programs

Many pregnancy centers—87 percent as of 2018, according to CLI—offer free classes on pregnancy health, childbirth, parenting, "life skills," and other topics.[118] All of the seven Maryland centers I visited except for the one affiliated with Birthright offer classes of some sort, and most of these have meeting space dedicated for that purpose. Pregnancy help activists often frame classes as part of their "empowerment" work. They also tout their potential to prevent poverty among the low-income, single mothers who make up a disproportionate share of pregnancy center clients. Leaders project that clients who participate in this programming over the long term will gain self-confidence, larger social support networks, and practical knowledge and skills. Advocates further argue that such parenting education will improve child well-being and strengthen families. CLI claimed that 295,900 individuals participated in centers' parenting or prenatal education programs in 2017.[119]

Although some pregnancy centers design their own classes, most now appear to implement preexisting curricula. One of these programs, Earn While You Learn (EWYL), claimed as of 2013 to have been adopted by almost a thousand pregnancy centers.[120] Another popular program, associated with Heartbeat International, is called Bridges. Both of these programs were designed by individual pregnancy centers and then spread. Both programs say they promote valuable bonding between instructors or mentors and students. Both also involve arrangements in which participants earn new baby items, or some unit of exchange that they can accumulate and trade for new items, as they reach certain milestones in the programs. Topics covered by EWYL's "main curriculum" include care for self and baby during pregnancy and after birth, fetal and infant development, childbirth, adoption, breastfeeding, parent-child bonding, discipline, child safety, first aid, returning to work after birth, and child-care arrangements.[121] Additional curricula concern parenting toddlers, studying the Bible, lessons targeting fathers, and "life skills." The "life skills" curriculum begins with lessons on the importance of abstinence and then covers economic topics including money management, credit, savings, home rental, auto purchases, time management, tight budgets, job searches, job interviews, and success in the workplace.[122] Bridges features instruction on childbirth, parenting, and life skills, plus individual mentorship by "Christian men and women" for mothers and fathers. Outside activities such as employment, schooling, and "spiritual or personal growth activities" can add to participants' earnings. The program calls for every session to foster "friendship," "fellowship," and "mentoring" and to involve sharing a meal prepared by volunteers.[123]

As I mentioned in the description of maternity homes, these institutions also typically offer and require participation in educational programming. At the homes run by one of my local interviewees' organizations, the Gabriel Network, the director said clients met weekly with a licensed social worker who addressed such topics as eligibility for public programs and job searches. Clients took classes on parenting and first aid and engaged in other "formative activities" such as field trips and instruction intended to help them make an informed decision between parenting and adoption. They could receive counseling if desired. The three to four women residing at each of the organization's homes at any given time shared meals and prayers and provided valuable friendship and support for each other.

CLIENTS

CLI's pregnancy center service report credited US pregnancy centers with serving 883,700 new clients in 2017; it did not estimate how many repeat or ongoing clients these organizations also served.[124] On a per-center basis, for 2011, Pregnancy Center Director Survey respondents reported client totals ranging from 0 (centers newly opened in 2012) to 19,000. This worked out to a sample mean of 1,062 clients and a median of 550 clients.

Pregnancy Center Director Survey respondents reported what might be some surprising statistics about clients of Care Net, Heartbeat International, and NIFLA-affiliated pregnancy centers. These are summarized in Figure 2.3. They are based on multiple-choice questions asking directors to estimate the percentage of their clients with a given characteristic. For each characteristic, the stacked bars show the percentage of responding centers choosing each of the five percentage ranges.

Consistent with the diversity of pregnancy centers' programming, many pregnancy centers' clients come to them for something other than a pregnancy test. The median range estimated on the Pregnancy Center Director Survey for this clientele share was 26–50 percent. A large share of those clients visiting the center for something other than a pregnancy test appear to be seeking material assistance for children already born. On the Pregnancy Center Director Survey, the median range chosen for those clients as a share of *all* clients

Figure 2.3 Pregnancy Center Client Characteristics

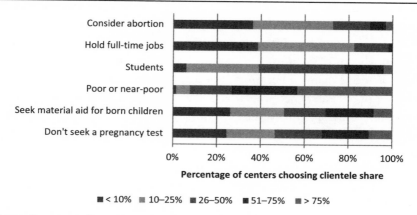

Percentage of centers choosing clientele share

■ < 10% ■ 10–25% ■ 26–50% ■ 51–75% ■ > 75%

Source: Pregnancy Center Director Survey. N = 429–452.

seeking services at the center in 2011 was 10–25 percent. The full distribution of responses in Figure 2.3 shows that 30 percent of centers estimated that material assistance clients formed the majority of their 2011 client totals; that is, they fell into the 51–75 percent or > 75 percent categories for this clientele characteristic.

Continuing with Figure 2.3, Pregnancy Center Director Survey respondents perceived that financially strained women made up a large share of their clientele. For 2011, the median center chose the 51–75 percent range as its estimate of the share of its clients appearing to be "poor or near poor."[125] Just 8 percent of centers reported that a quarter or less appeared to be poor or near poor, whereas 43 percent of centers reported that poor or near-poor clients made up three-quarters or more of their 2011 clientele. The median center estimated that 26–50 percent of its clients were students and that 10–25 percent held full-time paying jobs.

Notably, and as Kimberly Kelly has also observed with different data, the typical pregnancy test client at most centers does not intend to have and does not even appear to staff members to be considering an abortion.[126] When the Pregnancy Center Director Survey asked respondents to estimate the percentage of pregnancy test clients who "indicate that they are considering abortion," the median response was the 10–25 percent range. Of respondent centers, 73 percent selected the "less than 10 percent" or the "10–25 percent" ranges, and just 10 percent selected the 51–75 percent or the 75–100 percent ranges. As of 2011, nationally, 21.2 percent of pregnancies (excluding miscarriages and stillbirths) were estimated to have ended in abortion.[127]

I did not seek client data from other types of pregnancy help organizations. During interviews, however, the Gabriel Network's director volunteered that most of his organization's maternity home residents did not want to have abortions and that they disproportionately included homeless, poor, and immigrant women. The director of Catholic Charities' Sanctuaries for Life program identified many of her program's clients as immigrants who are not eligible for public safety net programs. She also included poor women, women at risk for abortion, and women enduring medically high-risk pregnancies among the primary clientele.

PROGRAMMING SUPPORTING A CULTURE CHANGE MISSION

Some pregnancy centers' work includes activities indirectly tied to the prevention of abortion, at most. These activities promote changes in individual lives as part of the cultural change mission that Care Net, Heartbeat International, and NIFLA have increasingly embraced. Their proponents also frame them as advancing the well-being of the women they serve. According to the "vision" statement Care Net articulated as of 2018, "Care Net envisions a culture where women and men faced with pregnancy decisions are transformed by the gospel of Jesus Christ and empowered to choose life for their unborn children and abundant life for their families." The organization defines "abundant life" as "not only saving the life of the unborn child, but having that child raised in a loving Christ-centered family, ideally with a mom and a dad that are married."[128] Heartbeat International says, "Our goal is to save lives in a life-changing way."[129]

Along with aspects of the centers' parenting education programs, which serve multiple aspects of centers' missions, the most important and commonly practiced of these activities are postabortion support, sexuality education, and Christian evangelization. Though these efforts were not the focus of my research, some description of them is helpful for understanding the movement's identity and work and how these vary across the national networks.

Postabortion Support

Pregnancy centers commonly offer counseling, support groups, Bible studies, or other programming to women who regret a previous abortion, as do some specialized pregnancy help organizations. As I discussed earlier in this chapter, the idea that abortion harms women—emotionally, psychologically, socially, and spiritually, if not also physically—is a critical part of the pregnancy help movement's worldview. So, too, is the belief that women troubled by their abortions can be, and ought to be, healed. The CLI pregnancy center service report stated that three-quarters of centers offer "abortion recovery" programming, serving more than 24,100 clients in 2017.[130]

Contemporary pregnancy help leaders highly value this work. Care Net's Christiansen, the medical consultant, pronounced postabortion healing ministry one of the "most amazing" parts of the pregnancy center world, and another interviewee emphasized this work in contrasting the pregnancy help movement with other forms of pro-life activism. As further evidence of this value, recipients of Care Net's annual award for lifetime achievements that advance the pro-life cause include a pregnancy center director best known for authoring an abortion-recovery Bible study used widely around the world.[131] The Care Net honoree's program, entitled *Forgiven and Set Free,* aims to lead women out of the bitterness and depression that it says can follow an abortion through recognition and acceptance of God's love, forgiveness, and call to live joyfully.[132]

One interviewee, a fund-raising specialist who had also formerly administered a pregnancy center network associated with the Southern Baptist Convention, explicitly connected abortion-recovery programs to a larger Christian mission she understood pregnancy centers to be advancing. In her view, widespread experience of abortion even among churchgoers—and the emotional and spiritual damage she attributed to it—was harming women and holding back the church from being all that it could be. "Women sitting in the churches need to hear that healing message" that God loves them, and they will never be broken from Him, she opined. If Christians can be healed of their abortion experiences, she reasoned, they can be freed and will be more enthusiastic about their own "salvation" and about sharing the gospel with others.[133]

Sexuality Education

Part of the pregnancy help movement's work toward making abortion "unwanted and unthinkable" involves what one interviewee called "go[ing] upstream"—trying to influence the sexual norms and behaviors that activists believe contribute to the likelihood of unintended pregnancy and the temptation to resolve it with abortion. Care Net and Heartbeat International volunteer training manuals thus encourage peer counselors to initiate conversations with individual clients, especially those with negative pregnancy tests, about alternative sexual lifestyles if the counselors discern in the course of conversation that "the client is open to the message."[134] Pregnancy centers are also involved in more formal abstinence-only education. They offer some in-house programs but appear to more commonly share their vision with outside groups, such as making staff available to give presentations at schools, churches, and other settings. CLI reported that 41 percent of pregnancy centers delivered such outside "sexual risk avoidance" presentations in 2017, reaching 1,102,200 students.[135]

Leaders justify these efforts, however, with more than their desire to prevent abortion. A former center director and Heartbeat International board member I interviewed, for example, attributed some of the movement's interest in teaching abstinence to the recognition that when unmarried, pregnant clients "choose life," as pregnancy center personnel hope they will do, their lives as single parents are likely to be stressful, and there is a credible risk for continuation of a cycle of broken families and emotional damage. Leaders and movement documents also frequently articulate a conviction that sex outside of marriage, especially with multiple partners, both results from and then compounds low self-esteem, poses health risks, and is ultimately not what most girls and women really desire. They also often construct their clients' sexual choices as having roots in insufficiently loving family backgrounds or abusive relationships, including past sexual traumas, and as products of a materialistic, sex-saturated culture. Sexually active, unmarried clients, Care Net says, "often admit that they have been looking for love in a relationship that has failed to provide the intimacy and commitment they so deeply desire."[136] A lifestyle inconsistent with what Heartbeat International calls "God's Plan for Our Sexuality" wounds rather than empowers and, when scaled up, wreaks devastating social consequences.[137] The organizations describe their counseling and programming in this area as geared toward education regarding healthy relationships and the health risks of sex outside of a loving marriage, helping to heal the hurt in clients' pasts, and bolstering clients' sense of self-worth so as to strengthen them to resist cultural pressure while they hold out for the kind of relationship they deserve. The organizations might also include an effort to help clients develop a relationship with Jesus Christ, which they suggest can help to satisfy natural human needs for intimate relationships characterized by unconditional love.

In describing the vision they teach, contemporary pregnancy centers often eschew the term *abstinence* in favor of alternatives such as "sexual integrity" and "sexual risk avoidance." To Heartbeat International, "sexual integrity" represents an idea supposed to be more holistic that communicates a more positive view of sex than "abstinence." Whereas abstinence "is limited to not doing something," sexual integrity "is a way of life, based on our identity as created by God, male and female, made in His image, and intended by Him to be joined together in love, cooperating with God in bringing His creation, the next generation, into the world."[138] A key component of the "sexual integrity" programming designed by Heartbeat International is presentation of an alternative vision of femininity and fertility that treat them as concepts of wonder and worth.[139] As implemented by one Maryland center whose director I interviewed, in a ten-session in-house sexual integrity program called "Girls Talk: Live in Purpose," moderated discussions among young women were said to address not just the consequences of a sexually active lifestyle but also careers, fashion, and other issues. One goal was to inspire participants to plan for their futures and build confidence in their capacity to achieve. If a young woman is having sex, especially with multiple partners, the director theorized, "clearly, she doesn't love herself enough. . . . She's been beaten and broken and hurt." In light of this, "it makes no sense to talk about abstinence" alone. Although much of pregnancy centers' programming has been developed with their traditional clients, women, in mind, some in the pregnancy center movement have shown interest in reaching men with messages designed to inspire chaste living.[140]

Sharing the Gospel

Care Net specifically calls its centers to share the gospel of Jesus Christ with their clients. It frames this as the duty of Christians as well as a gift to clients that, if accepted, will ultimately promote their welfare and happiness. A relationship with Jesus Christ, it promises, will fulfill her "deep need to feel loved and secure."[141] Care Net impresses on its staff, "The client needs to be aware that God loves her, and that He offers her the opportunity to enter into an eternal and personal relationship that can never be broken."[142]

Statements by leaders and in the volunteer training manual acknowledge that many clients might be unreceptive to these efforts, that some volunteers might feel uncomfortable initiating conversations about religion, and that in all cases any such conversation should proceed with sensitivity. The Care Net training manual warns, "Young people are not looking for a lecture about salvation; they are looking to see whether our lives, the way we speak, and the way we listen, reflect the compassion and love of Christ."[143] It recommends that counselors first listen to a client's story, and it suggests ways for counselors to identify openings to share the "good news" of the salvation secured by Jesus Christ, along with personal testimony. Staff members understand themselves to be the "hands and feet and mouthpiece of Jesus," one local Care Net–affiliated center director, Carol Clews, claimed. Just as Jesus never forced himself on others, they were to do the same and to stop discussion of religion if the women "shut down." However, she said that all women visiting the center for whatever reason sat down with a counselor for a substantive conversation that would include discussion of her relationship with the Lord. The center would help women find a church, if desired, and give all of them a Bible. Care Net has produced its own Bible for distribution to pregnancy center clients. Titled *Beautiful Everyday*, it is prefaced with a letter written by a former pregnancy center client assuring her peers of God's love and inviting them to hope in God's wonderful plans for their lives.[144]

To different degrees and with different methods, other national pregnancy center organizations include evangelization among their aims. Heartbeat International allows affiliated centers to choose how they wish to handle evangelization, whether with words or by simply "being Christ" through the goodness shown to others. It encourages the latter strategy, citing the example of Catholic St. Francis of Assisi: "Perhaps we can serve our clients and patients in such a Christ-like way with such joy that they experience the love of Jesus simply through who we are and how we serve them."[145] Birthright specifically prohibits evangelization. Instead, its then US director said clients should be able to tell there is something different about Birthright volunteers by the way they behave. 1st Way centers claim a similar philosophy.[146]

FUNDING

Movement documents and the comments of leaders I interviewed portray pregnancy centers as heavily dependent on individual donations. Many pregnancy help organizations actively fund-raise by holding banquets, walks, races, and other activities. They also commonly benefit from church-based collections of money or baby items.

Some pregnancy centers receive federal or state government funding, though the availability of and movement's reliance on this money appears relatively limited. Using data provided by pregnancy centers, CLI claims that only 14 percent of pregnancy centers, or 364, receive any federal or state funds and that these funds constitute less than 10 percent of all pregnancy centers' revenue.[147] An unsympathetic congressional report on pregnancy centers identifies "more than 50" as having received federal funds between 2001 and 2005, largely through abstinence education grants.[148] Rewire.News, a reproductive health issues news site that describes pregnancy centers as "fake clinics," reported that the federal government awarded at least $3.1 million in grants to pregnancy centers in 2017, all from pots dedicated to abstinence-only education.[149] It counted fourteen states as having provided any funding to pregnancy centers as of 2018.[150]

In addition to the abstinence education grants, some of which are routed through states, there are two other major channels for state funding of pregnancy centers. One is the state sharing a portion of revenue generated from its sales of "Choose Life" license plates. As of 2017, according to the pro-choice Guttmacher Institute, seventeen states directed such money to specific pregnancy centers or other organizations that oppose abortion.[151] Another is through state programming to support alternatives to abortion, which states typically fund with grant money linked to the Temporary Assistance to Needy Families (TANF) program, that is, the "welfare" program that replaced Aid to Families with Dependent Children (AFDC) in 1997. According to progressive news site ThinkProgress, another organization critical of pregnancy centers, seven states funded pregnancy centers in this manner as of 2016, supplying about $30 million to pregnancy centers over a four-year period.[152]

CONCLUSION

The pro-life pregnancy help movement practices a form of antiabortion activism that targets pregnant women and the culture instead of the state; relies on direct-service provision; and in its largely sympathetic, woman-centered frames and substantial attention to the hardships poor women and others would face by forgoing abortion, arguably "trespasses" on—co-opts—concerns and values associated with its political opponents.

There are still ways in which much of the pregnancy help movement appears to fulfill stereotypes associated with antiabortion activists, such as in the faith-based character and concerns about sexual morality expressed by some movement actors. The critical reader might challenge the accuracy of pregnancy help activists' construction of the abortion-seeking woman, which arguably highlights her victimhood. She might also question the sufficiency of what the pregnancy help movement offers to poor women relative to the magnitude of parenthood's socioeconomic consequences. Kelly, for example, discerns in the pregnancy center movement an "inability to see structural forces at play in clients' lives."[153] By choosing the targets it has, the movement has done little to empower the activists in its ranks who do show this awareness.

Nonetheless, the scale of the pregnancy help movement's charitable aid is substantial, as is its cultural advocacy on behalf of unwed mothers and women with abortion histories. The pregnancy help movement does not appear to be one of radical antiabortion "rescuers." A key piece of evidence comes from the extensive and forceful extent to which training materials appeal to religion when instructing their ranks to prioritize compassionate and ethical service to a woman over stopping an abortion. It also comes from the enormous resources the movement devotes to providing material aid, social services, and other programming to the large number of clients it encounters for whom an abortion is not at stake.

Although we still have opportunities to deepen our knowledge about the pro-life pregnancy help movement, it presents an interesting puzzle to explain. Thinking about why pregnancy help organizations have adopted this largely humanitarian, yet privatized, approach to antiabortion advocacy invites questions about the role of ideology, political environment, social conditions, and other potential factors that shape forms of social action. I now turn to why pro-life pregnancy help activists have responded to abortion in the way they have, beginning with the story of their movement's origins.

3. Origins and Early Growth

As I discussed in Chapter 1, scholarship and journalism on the pro-life movement casually suggest many different stories about the timing, motives, and circumstances of the pro-life pregnancy help movement's rise. Often, its approach to fighting abortion is portrayed as an innovation pro-life activists developed because it became clear that conventional political action would not soon end abortion. Pregnancy help outreach is sometimes situated within the movement's radical wing. Others cast it as an early, humanitarian response to the pressures women faced when experiencing unplanned pregnancies, including pressure to choose abortion when it became a legal option.

In this chapter I aim to settle that debate by presenting a detailed history of how direct service to women emerged as a tactic of the pro-life movement. The history is based largely on the published writing of past and present leaders of pregnancy help organizations and personal interviews. Although these activists and the organizations they represent have not always been on amicable terms with each other, the stories they tell are quite consistent. Evidence strongly corroborates the view of pregnancy centers as an early and largely humanitarian response to the increasing availability of abortion. Pregnancy centers sprang up rapidly in US communities beginning in the late 1960s. By 1971, two years before the nationwide legalization of abortion in *Roe v. Wade* (1973), two associations of pregnancy centers had formed: Birthright and the organization now known as Heartbeat International.

The concept of a pregnancy center was actually imported from Canada. One might say that the critical encounter inspiring the opening of what appears to have been the first US pregnancy center took place in a women's restroom in Chicago, to which an attendee of a pro-life convention had escaped in order to nurse her infant and met the Canadian who would inspire her. The Canadian would also inspire others, through newsletters and pre-*Roe* pro-life conventions, who would be critical to the spread of pregnancy centers. First, however, this narrative begins with a context other than the fight against abortion that might also be relevant for understanding the emergence of pregnancy centers.

A LONGER HISTORY?

Some participants and observers claim for the pregnancy help movement a longer history than the history of pregnancy centers themselves. Specifically, they situate their work within a tradition of charitable activity by Christian organizations and Christian women toward unwed mothers and poor people.[1] The tradition encompasses maternity homes, adoption agencies, day-care centers, homeless shelters, employment assistance, and various other social service projects as well as informal assistance such as networks in individual Catholic parishes that feminist scholar Kathy Rudy credits with providing social and economic support to unwed mothers long before *Roe v. Wade*.[2]

That history is beyond the scope of this book, but a summary of a slice of it pertaining to service to unwed or poor mothers, drawn largely from academic literature, confirms its existence and illuminates its nature. It also suggests the ageless quality and the multiplicity of ideas about the enterprise in which pro-life pregnancy help organizations are engaged: reconciliation of moral codes with pragmatism and the demands of compassion. Historians and other scholars, for example, are gradually revealing the nuanced history of maternity homes—many of which were run by Catholic and Protestant agencies and religious orders—and other types of pregnancy-related services. This research tells a story considerably more complex than that captured by popular images of the maternity home as a large, mysterious, and punitive institution to which unwed mothers were sent during pregnancy to spare their families from shame.[3] Surely the image has an empirical basis. Reflecting the social stigma attached to unwed motherhood, maternity homes indeed aimed at concealment, often locating in geographically isolated places and steering their clients toward adoption.[4] They also promoted what they understood as the moral reform of their residents.[5]

But historians' narratives of Christian service to unwed mothers also highlight the existence of competing social constructions of the unwed mother and differing ideas and practices regarding how she was to be served. Among other things, these stories involve tension between the merits of parenthood versus adoption and between local service providers who offered homier, faith-based settings and social work professionals attempting to remake them as formal, secular, efficient, and scientifically driven institutions.[6] Historian Maureen Fitzgerald, for example, documents the extensive social service activity of New York's Irish Catholic nuns in the nineteenth and early twentieth centuries. She credits them with pioneering the idea that poor women should be supported in living with their children, regardless of the sexual behavior that might have led the women to bear children they could not support. They designed their residential, day-care, and other charitable programs to relieve poverty, Fitzgerald states, but also with the explicit intention of preventing infanticide and child abandonment. She argues that their efforts should be recognized as important foundations of the modern welfare state. She also describes them as being in tension at the time with Protestant women's groups' practices of facilitating adoptions by affluent Protestant families and with standards promulgated by the emerging social work profession, with which the Protestant groups became increasingly tied.[7] Within the realm of evangelical, Protestant service provision, Kunzel and Morton document in the early 1900s the existence of family-style, evangelizing maternity homes and the popularity of the idea that a mother would be best off spiritually and otherwise if she were not separated from her child by adoption—practices and ideas that would be challenged as proponents of "scientific charity" gained more influence in the leadership of maternity home networks.[8] What had been maternalistic, empathetic, and socially intimate sites of women helping women, Kunzel argues, were transformed into cold, clinical, and intrusive treatment centers no less judgmental about the women's sexual behavior.[9]

The legalization of abortion theoretically changed the context of these older forms of pregnancy assistance. Informal Catholic parish support networks, Rudy argues, gradually withered away as abortion became more broadly available. The cause was disappearing demand because women resolved out-of-wedlock pregnancies through abortion instead.[10] Between that option and changing norms regarding the desirability and acceptability of single parenthood, the number of domestic adoptions plummeted after the legalization of abortion.[11] Maternity homes were closing and demand for space in them decreasing even before *Roe,* a phenomenon attributed to a number of factors including not just the legalization of abortion but also increasing acceptance of unwed parenthood, women's desires to live independently in their communities, and the increasing availability of alternative services that made that lifestyle possible.[12] An innovation in the delivery of pregnancy assistance, the "pregnancy center," emerged from that new context.

FOUNDING OF THE FIRST CENTERS

The first pregnancy center to open in the United States cannot be identified with certainty, although activists involved with the earliest centers reported that organized outreach to pregnant women for help with alternatives to abortion began in the late 1960s. The difficulty in pinning down the first center derives in part from the nature of the movement's origins: it was not an effort organized from the top down by a particular institution but a service initiated independently by citizens in multiple communities. Eventually some of these citizens got to know each other and established formal associations, the first of which in the United States were formed in 1971.[13] A second difficulty with identifying the first pregnancy center is that it depends on what characteristics one considers essential to defining a "pregnancy center." Though they would eventually formally incorporate and occupy office space to which clients would come, many of the first outreach services to pregnant women were informal efforts run out of an individual's home, a doctor's office, or elsewhere.[14]

Often credited with some of the first organized pro-life crisis pregnancy outreach in the era of legal abortion is the Right to Life League of Southern California, which had formed to fight a 1967 state abortion legalization bill. According to an activist, the organization provided help to pregnant women before it launched the physical infrastructure supporting that work in 1971.[15] Similarly, a doctor active in the pro-life movement who opened a Toledo, Ohio, pregnancy center in 1971 had been known previously to have served as a resource for women with crisis pregnancies in the context of his obstetrics practice.[16] The author of a piece in a liberal magazine states that the first pregnancy center was founded in 1967 in Honolulu by Robert Pearson, a controversial figure in the movement.[17] Neither of two published histories of the pregnancy help movement written by its participants mention Pearson's center in their accounts of the movement's origins.[18] Meanwhile, historian Daniel Williams credits Pearson and his wife with financing construction of a maternity home and with making and fulfilling a pledge to pay the delivery costs of women who might otherwise be tempted to choose abortion, but dates the start of this activity to 1970, when Hawai'i broadly legalized abortion.[19] The institution with the strongest claim to be the first US pregnancy center is one that opened in Atlanta in 1969 under the name of Birthright, founded by homemaker and pro-life activist Terry Weaver.[20]

According to activists and confirmed by a new history of the pre-*Roe* pro-life movement, organized pro-life individual outreach emerged as a response to pre-*Roe* events during the campaign to legalize abortion.[21] Specifically, during the 1960s, bills to legalize and regulate abortion began arising on state legislative agendas. The pre-*Roe* state bills enacted into law were generally less permissive than *Roe* would be, but in laying out circumstances under which an abortion could be legally obtained, they constituted an important break from the status quo, in which abortion had been broadly illegal. Beginning with Mississippi, eighteen states liberalized their abortion laws between 1966 and 1972.[22]

One of the early legalizers was California. In 1969, the political movement that had formed to lobby against the legalization bills formally incorporated as the Right to Life League of Southern California and claimed as its purpose "to address the needs of women who were faced with an unplanned pregnancy."[23] In 1971, the league initiated the first known pregnancy help hotline. It saw clients at a physical pregnancy center in Whittier, near Los Angeles.[24]

US Birthright chapters opened first and most extensively in states that legalized abortion early.[25] The opening of the organization's Atlanta center was followed quickly by others—in Minneapolis and Chicago and then in Woodbury, New Jersey, in 1970, according to the Woodbury founder. A Birthright center serving Washington, DC, and its Maryland suburbs, which I visited during my research, also dates itself to this 1969–1970 period.[26]

Founders of the Atlanta (Weaver) and Woodbury (Denise Cocciolone) centers both shared in interviews that they began their involvement in the pro-life movement with state and local groups that formed to fight the abortion legalization bills proposed in their states. Weaver traced her involvement to the early 1960s, when she learned through a mothers' group at her church of a new political movement to legalize abortion in Georgia. She characterized herself and her friends as "busy moms and housewives" who would not have been otherwise inclined toward political activity, but the abortion issue "hit us because it was babies." Working through civic networks in which she was already participating, such as the Georgia La Leche League and "natural childbirth causes," she founded a pro-life group, Concerned Committed Citizens. The group informally gathered to educate the public about abortion legislation and write to legislators and would later change its name to Right to Life when the national movement using that name began. Similarly, Cocciolone recalled learning in 1968 of legislation to legalize abortion in New Jersey. She said that her own desire to stop the spread of abortion had been shaped years earlier by what she had learned from two friends' illegal abortions in high school. Cocciolone's first reaction was to call her local priest and ask why no one appeared to be doing anything about it. She became president of a local right-to-life group and joined the board of directors of New Jersey Right to Life. The first pro-life meeting in her county, she told me, took place in her basement. In practice, however, Cocciolone says that her work in those capacities largely involved "theoretical" matters rather than political activism.

Weaver and Cocciolone were inspired to found pregnancy centers when they learned of the work of Canada's Louise Summerhill. Summerhill had started an organization to assist pregnant women in 1968 and was advocating that other citizens do the same. She called her organization Birthright, in reference to the idea that "children have a right to be born."[27] Birthright was founded at a time when Canada was moving toward legalization of abortion. In 1967, the country's increasingly strong pro-choice movement convinced the Canadian federal government to formally review its prohibition on abortion. The law would officially change in 1969.[28] As this debate proceeded, Summerhill, a Catholic and full-time mother, had been serving as secretary for a pro-life advocacy group when a new idea took root in her mind. As Summerhill wrote in a book designed to share Birthright's history and philosophy and to guide others in setting up such centers, "I was convinced that abortion is entirely destructive, but it is so easy to become deeply and emotionally involved in 'lobbying' against the legalization of abortion in government, and overlook the humane concern of our opponents for the suffering and despair of distraught pregnant women. With me, there came a gradual awakening to a general sense of my responsibility to do something positive within my own radius of action."[29] The plan Summerhill eventually developed was inspired by the model of a British telephone service that helped women obtain clandestine abortions when the procedure was still illegal. Her service would offer, "instead, counsel and positive aid to carry their babies to term, that is alternatives to abortion."[30] Cocciolone learned about Birthright from an article in a Catholic newspaper and contacted Summerhill in response. Weaver met Summerhill personally at a conference of pro-life leaders in Chicago in 1969—in a restroom, where Weaver had gone to nurse her infant son and where Summerhill had retreated to consult her notes before she was scheduled to give a speech. Weaver and Cocciolone would quickly set up their own local Birthright chapters, before the organization had even formalized its status as an association of pregnancy centers. They both would soon serve in Birthright's leadership as centers rapidly proliferated in North America.

Both women emphasized the attractiveness of the idea of pregnancy centers in explaining why they were moved to found them. Weaver suggested that her encounter with Summerhill precipitated a paradigm shift in her thinking about her pro-life work. Summerhill's idea, as Weaver remembers, "knocked my socks off." The idea was, "Instead of saying 'why have an abortion,' let me say 'let me help you have this baby.'" Cocciolone, calling herself "a bottom-liner person," said she was struck by the practicality of Birthright's approach. As Cocciolone saw it at the time, girls and women with unintended pregnancies were "scared to death." Given that, it made sense that the best way to prevent abortions would be to reach those girls and women, find out why they felt they needed abortions, and address those needs.

Meanwhile, other US communities were reaching similar conclusions about the need to reach out with help to pregnant women as abortion became legal and available there. In Ohio, the organization now known as Heartbeat International began with obstetrician-gynecologist John Hillabrand. As Margaret "Peggy" Hartshorn, who served as the group's president from 1993–2016, recounted in her organizational history, by the time states started debating legalization of abortion, Hillabrand was well established in his field and had been building a portfolio as an expert witness and consultant on legal questions pertaining to reproductive health.[31] Hillabrand believed strongly that human life begins at conception and delivered that message to legislatures around the country. He contributed to the effort to organize the pro-life movement on a national and international scale and along the way helped to found the political and legal groups Ohio Right to Life (1968) and Americans United for Life (1971). Meanwhile, in his private practice, Hillabrand noticed more of his patients asking him about abortion and also where they could find practical help for acquaintances with problem pregnancies. Providing information and assistance to women with problem pregnancies soon became such an important part of Hillabrand's practice that he decided to set up another office devoted to that purpose. He requested help in that effort from Lore Maier, a recently widowed patient and survivor of Nazi Germany whose interest in the pro-life cause had been shaped by the evil and death she had witnessed during World War II. Maier had cared for refugees during the war before being forced to become one herself, surviving multiple close brushes with death. After the war, she performed humanitarian and other public service work under the auspices of the United Nations and the new German government before moving to the United States. While involved in the US pro-life movement, she spoke frequently about the important role humanitarian service could play in ending abortion. Hillabrand and Maier's pregnancy center, Heartbeat of Toledo, opened in 1971.

In California, still other important components of the pregnancy help movement were developing. Paula Vandegaer, a Catholic Sister of Social Service and licensed social worker involved with the Right to Life League took responsibility for training volunteer pregnancy counselors. Assisted by other social workers from a Catholic agency, she developed a pregnancy counseling manual that would quickly be shared with and adopted by pregnancy centers around the country. Even before the 1973 *Roe* decision, Vandegaer reportedly traveled extensively to train citizens staffing newly founded pregnancy centers.[32]

Word of these types of pregnancy help responses to legalized abortion began to spread, most commonly through Catholic and professional networks and the newly organizing grassroots right-to-life movement. Catholic priests helped connect activists such as Summerhill, Weaver, Cocciolone, Hillabrand, Maier, Vandegaer, and others and to organize national conferences. One priest credited in two activist histories was Father Paul Marx, a sociology professor at St. John's University in Minnesota.[33] Annually from the mid-1960s to the early 1970s, Marx hosted weeklong "Family Life Seminars," in which an interdisciplinary cast of "internationally prominent faculty" participated.[34] The seminars provided a forum for generating and sharing ideas and for networking; regular attendees at these seminars reportedly contributed to the founding of several pregnancy help and other pro-life organizations. Activists also especially acknowledge the head of the Family Life Bureau of the National Conference of Catholic Bishops, Monsignor James McHugh, for his efforts to connect pregnancy center founders to each other and facilitate their formal organization.[35]

Citizens running pregnancy centers in the United States and Canada held a series of pivotal meetings in 1971 that resulted in the formal birth of two international associations of pregnancy centers, the aforementioned Birthright and Alternatives to Abortion. Early participants attributed the formation of two associations to disagreement over who would lead the movement and how independent individual pregnancy centers would be from each other and their associations. Birthright centers would use the same name and a uniform charter, whereas Alternatives to Abortion was designed as a loose alliance of independent centers.[36] The latter group, which quickly added International to its title (becoming AAI) and since 1993 has gone by the name "Heartbeat International," recognizes Hillabrand, Maier, and Vandegaer as its founders. Maier served as its first executive director.

Pregnancy centers spread rapidly after the founding of AAI and Birthright. AAI promoted itself as a resource for citizens who wanted to start pregnancy centers, and as Hartshorn told it in a 2012 interview, the next few years after its 1971 founding were marked by a "gigantic burst of activity." After it opened, AAI's "phones were ringing off the hook," and its staff "couldn't respond fast enough" to people "getting this vision." This interest coincided with more states loosening their prohibitions on abortion and then with the *Roe v. Wade* decision. Those citizens who wanted to start pregnancy centers were aware of and part of the fight against the legalization of abortion, Hartshorn says. Yet Hartshorn credits the interest to something she believes God added to the pull of these political and social changes: particular individuals were "called out" to be part of the movement to support alternatives to abortion. The first edition of AAI's directory, which attempted to catalog all known pro-life pregnancy help resources in the world, whether affiliated with AAI or not, was released in early 1972 and contained about 130 entries, all but 12 of which were located in the United States.[37]

Many more centers were founded in the wake of *Roe v. Wade*. A pregnancy center history compiled by Terry Ianora, who started a Eugene, Oregon, Birthright center in 1973 and participated in many of the early national conferences of the nascent pro-life and pregnancy help movement, includes the stories of nine Birthright-affiliated centers started during the 1970s, most in the founders' own words.[38] Those centers' origins shared many common threads. In the typical center's story, a woman deeply concerned about the legalization of abortion sought to take action and learned through Catholic newsletters or pro-life conferences of the idea of the pregnancy center. The idea of responding to abortion in this way resonated with the woman: it was consistent with her empathy for pregnant women, it enabled her to contribute to the pro-life cause despite full-time responsibilities caring for her own children, and in many cases she developed a strong sense in her prayers that God was calling her to the work. The woman would turn to her parish and friends for assistance with the project. She would often report receiving donations of money, office space, furniture, labor, and guidance from individual Catholic priests, Catholic social service and fraternal organizations, and other local acquaintances. Ianora claims that the pregnancy center movement was "a direct result and expression of the drive and the vision on the part of ordinary women with nurturing intuition who have stepped up to combat abortion face to face and to help pregnant women to live in peace."[39]

THE CONCEPT OF THE PREGNANCY CENTER: ORIGINAL VISION AND SCOPE

The first pregnancy centers were modest in size and scope. Activists' histories describe most of them as being run out of small, donated office spaces and in some cases out of activists' own homes. Before receiving donated office space, Weaver said, she and her fellow Birthright volunteers would meet with clients at McDonalds, identifying themselves with red roses. Centers were generally staffed by volunteers and supported by donations founders pooled from their personal social and religious networks.

By design, pregnancy centers would be a first point of access for women suspecting a problem pregnancy, a gateway through which women could access a variety of community resources that might be relevant to their needs. Pregnancy centers invited women inside by advertising free pregnancy tests, a significant offer in those days predating the availability of an inexpensive, at-home test. An important part of the centers' work involved ensuring women could meet their basic needs during pregnancy. Center personnel devoted special attention to housing, given that social stigmas attached to unwed pregnancy not uncommonly led young clients to report fear of being forced from their parents' homes or other living arrangements. In addition to referring these girls to shelters and maternity homes, pregnancy center staff relied on local pro-life activists and supporters to house pregnant women in their own homes. In some cases they were able to provide a woman and her children their own apartment. Other priorities included helping women find obstetric medical care, a service often donated by pro-life doctors with whom the pregnancy center had established relationships.

At least as importantly, pregnancy centers were also envisioned as places where pregnant women could encounter everyday human beings, often mothers, who offered themselves as friends, partners, or mentors to the women as they coped with the pregnancies and their consequences. At their root, pregnancy centers aimed to be "an outreach of one caring individual to another."[40]

Summerhill put it similarly: "The essence of the Birthright service is love."[41] In the space they made for the development of authentic personal relationships, pregnancy centers were envisioned differently than professional social service and health-care agencies, even though professionals in social work, medicine, and other fields contributed to the founding and functioning of many centers, especially in the AAI/Heartbeat International branch.

As movement insiders' histories suggested, confirmed in many of the interviews I conducted for this research, pregnancy centers began operating under the assumption that a change in abortion law, coupled with cultural changes pro-life people perceived with regard to sexual mores and the valuation of human life, would place tremendous pressure on women and girls to resolve unintended pregnancies with abortions they did not really want. Heartbeat International's Hartshorn frequently invoked the term "safety net" to describe how some of the founders of the first pregnancy centers understood their organizations' roles.[42] "Crisis intervention" was another frequently used term. As is still the case in today's pregnancy help movement, early founders such as Summerhill saw abortion not just as inherently evil but as an act that would later haunt with guilt the women undergoing it.[43]

There is evidence that early leaders of the pregnancy help movement saw abortion as a more tractable problem than their counterparts seem to do today. Writing of what she understood God to be showing her through her first years at Birthright, Summerhill shared her faith that "there are practical solutions to the problems of distressed pregnant women and that these are found in a positive and loving dedication to women in distress."[44] Wrote Hartshorn, "In the late '60s and '70s, we presumed that these women were in short-term crisis. ... We thought our culture was in a short-term memory lapse and would soon return to its Judeo-Christian values."[45]

RELATIONSHIPS TO OTHER PRO-LIFE ACTORS

Independence from the Political Right-to-Life Movement

Though many early pregnancy center leaders and interviewees with the longest tenures in the movement first entered the pro-life movement through state and local right-to-life groups and sometimes involved themselves simultaneously in pro-life political and service work, this would change. Pregnancy

center personnel and political pro-life activists were working largely independently of each other by 1973. Hartshorn, a former college English professor
who looked to get involved in pro-life activism right after the *Roe* decision, and
found first the political and educational group Columbus [Ohio] Right to Life,
writes that not until 1978 did she learn that "*another* entire army of pro-life
warriors," the pregnancy help movement, existed.[46]

Anecdotal evidence, however, indicates that political right-to-life groups
were not necessarily uninvolved in the issue of alternatives to abortion. Hartshorn reported, for example, that Columbus Right to Life routinely fielded calls
from community members wondering where they could obtain assistance for
themselves or for an acquaintance facing hardship as a result of an unplanned
pregnancy. Like some other members of the group, she and her husband
hosted in their home several young women denied housing because of their
pregnancies. She had been aware of a Birthright office in her community but
perceived that the office lacked the capacity to reach and work with women
not yet committed to carrying a pregnancy to term. Hartshorn said the local
Birthright staff had refused Columbus Right to Life's offer to help them start
and fund a crisis pregnancy hotline, citing constraints in their charter. Against
this background, the logic of AAI pregnancy centers grabbed and stuck with
Hartshorn when she learned about them at a right-to-life conference. Later,
while participating in a couples' retreat weekend organized by Marriage Encounter, a lay Catholic marriage enrichment program, she and her husband
began discerning in their prayers what they understood as a call from God to
start a pregnancy center themselves. Hartshorn reported that many members
of the Columbus Right to Life group and couples involved with the Marriage
Encounter program contributed to the effort; the center opened in 1981.[47]

That after being founded, pregnancy centers would function independently
of pro-life political groups makes some sense. Their tax status as charities
might be one reason. Further, pregnancy center activists have long argued that
being perceived as a political group would damage the centers' credibility with
their clients and limit the willingness of their communities to support them.
For these reasons, Summerhill reported resigning from her work at a political
antiabortion group when she founded Birthright.[48]

Early activists also reported that they lacked the time, and in some cases,
the inclination, to maintain involvement in both the political and outreach
streams of the movement. Weaver, Cocciolone, and Hartshorn all left their positions in their local right-to-life groups after starting their pregnancy centers.

Weaver, in addition to sharing her belief in the value of pregnancy center work, expressed relief at finding a way to contribute to the pro-life movement without having to deal with "political baloney." She said that she and her friends in her pro-life group had quickly familiarized themselves with politics because they had to but "didn't want to be a political group." Weaver found that the schedule she could keep at Birthright was also much more compatible with her role as a stay-at-home mother of several children than lobbying had been. Lacking a babysitter, she said that she would have to bring her children with her when she lobbied. In contrast, Hartshorn recalled in her interview that she had initially expected to return to her right-to-life group after getting the pregnancy center off the ground. However, as the center developed, she said that she felt a "prompting by the Holy Spirit that leads you in a certain direction," "a sense," that she needed to be more involved with the pregnancy center. As she told it, she would eventually discern calls from God to increasingly more intensive involvement with the wider pregnancy help movement. In 1993, she would take leave from her job as a college professor to become president of Heartbeat International.

Independence from the Catholic Church

Early pregnancy center founders and leaders were disproportionately Catholic, but the pregnancy center movement has always been largely independent of the institutional Catholic Church. All of the founders covered by these histories with the exception of Vandegaer, a nun, were laypeople. In some cases, such as Hartshorn's, Summerhill's, and many of the Birthright chapter testimonials, founders described the idea as emerging from their personal prayer life, taking the form of a call.[49] Summerhill went as far as to call God the "Founder" of Birthright.[50] As she told it, the idea was inspired by the Holy Spirit. Despite all the excuses she found herself presenting as to why she should not be the one to implement it, "inwardly, I knew that this was something God was asking of me, personally."[51] She said she discerned this "in prayer," and "through prayer" she found the will to go through with it.[52]

The Catholic Church, though not exclusively the institutional church, did serve as an important facilitator of the movement, providing critical resources for the implementation of these calls and the dissemination of ideas. This was a role few other institutions, at the time, might have been willing and equipped to play. First, the Catholic Church offered a worldview and an institutional culture that lent itself not just to pro-life activism but to activism of the form practiced by pregnancy centers. At the time of *Roe v. Wade,* the Catholic Church stood virtually alone among prominent US religious bodies in its opposition to abortion.[53] The church had also established a track record on poverty and social services as an operator of a large network of social service agencies and as a political advocate.[54] Second, as a large, highly visible, hierarchical, and transnational organization, the Catholic Church was capable of rapidly mobilizing large numbers of people and distributing its ideas. The church's role in facilitating not just the early pregnancy help movement but also the larger pro-life movement illustrates Zald and McCarthy's contention that churches can be potent forces in social movement mobilization.[55]

The development of community-based centers promoting alternatives to abortion appears to have been received warmly by those Catholic bishops active on the abortion issue. One activist credits them with funding the first National Convention of Pregnancy Counseling Services, held in Washington, DC, in 1971.[56] The US Catholic bishops' 1975 Pastoral Plan for Pro-Life Activities, a strategy document, included encouragement of pregnancy centers as well as plans to establish "Respect Life" committees in local dioceses and to continue to work toward restoring legal protection for the unborn.[57] Some early pregnancy help leaders reported receiving proposals to incorporate their centers into official Catholic social service agencies, such as Catholic Charities, or to otherwise bring their centers under control of Catholic dioceses.[58]

Activists refused these overtures from the church. Their reasons for doing so included their beliefs that their centers should be informal, personal, and flexible, rather than mimicking the style of a large, professional, social service agency. Cocciolone said in her interview that she deliberately avoids asking clergy for help recruiting volunteers for her center, including among the reasons her fear of becoming too dependent on a clergy member and thus open to control. Early center leaders also insisted on identifying themselves as nonsectarian and nondenominational. Activists did not want to turn off potential clients or volunteers, and they also perceived that pro-choice activists were eager to paint the pregnancy center movement as a Catholic one to marginalize it.[59] This fear of being too visibly aligned with the Catholic Church was not unique to pregnancy help activism. As the pro-life movement matured, rhetoric making its way into major newspapers evolved in a way consistent with leaders' efforts to "de-catholicize" the movement.[60]

THE MOVEMENT GROWS: ARRIVAL OF THE EVANGELICALS

Pregnancy centers continued to proliferate as the wider pro-life movement mobilized. By 1977, AAI records placed the total number of US pregnancy centers at 782 and the total number of centers abroad at 1,350, including some centers in process of opening.[61] The movement's numbers would grow still further as evangelical Christians entered the pro-life movement en masse.

The Commencement of Evangelical Pro-Life Activism

Though contemporary characterizations of evangelicals in politics frequently highlight their conservatism on cultural issues such as abortion and suggest that those issues motivate their activism in a special way, evangelical leaders hardly presented a clear and unified opposition to abortion when *Roe v. Wade* was decided.[62] That lack of unified opposition to abortion showed up even among the evangelical leaders I interviewed who were old enough to have entered adulthood around the time of *Roe* and who incorporated *Roe* or its immediate aftermath into their accounts of the start of their activism. Melinda Delahoyde, president of Care Net at the time of her 2012 interview, professed that despite being a Christian she had supported abortion rights when she started on her path into the pregnancy center movement as a graduate student in 1977.[63] Thomas Glessner, president of NIFLA and a former president of Care Net, in his interview claimed indifference upon hearing about *Roe* in the news. He had been in law school at the time, and although weakly pro-life and a Christian, he described himself as a child of the 1960s, involved in antiwar activity and the Young Democrats and bent on advancing a political career for himself. He recalled that the news item that had most grabbed his attention (and moved him to sadness) from January 22, 1973, was the death of former president Lyndon B. Johnson; to the *Roe* decision, he said he thought, "Who cares?"[64] In contrast, former Care Net executive director Curtis Young, then a sophomore at the University of Illinois, suggested that he was disturbed by the legalization of abortion. He would soon come into contact with other evangelicals who would draw him into their project to activate Protestant churches for the pro-life cause.

Not only were evangelicals generally uninvolved with the abortion issue in the early 1970s but also by some accounts they were not a particularly active or salient political constituency at all. It was not that evangelicals were uninvolved in politics, for the preachers had long taken interest in public issues such as prohibition of alcohol and the threat presented by communism. They were just not clearly aligned with either of the two major political parties.[65] Others have described and accounted for their path to becoming, by the 2000s, one of the most loyal constituencies in the Republican coalition and a force that grew and transformed the US pro-life movement.[66] In this section, drawing primarily on insider histories provided in interviews or other published documents, I share the pieces of that story most important for understanding evangelicals' entrance into the pregnancy help movement.

As with most of the earliest Catholic activists, the earliest evangelicals' path into the pregnancy help movement passed through the political wing of the pro-life movement but in somewhat different fashion. It began with the 1975 founding of the Christian Action Council (CAC), an advocacy group envisioned as the voice of evangelicals in politics, most centrally on the abortion issue. CAC would later evolve into an association of pregnancy centers and change its name to Care Net.

Though the organization was founded in the home of the Reverend Billy Graham, an evangelical icon, Graham was not actually present at the meeting, and his views against abortion were described by one of my interviewees as "weak."[67] Further, according to accounts described or endorsed by CAC interviewees Young and Glessner and another's written history, the organization itself was the brainchild of Catholics—working with pro-life evangelicals that were concerned about their faith leaders' failures to speak out against abortion—and started with money provided by the Ad Hoc Committee in Defense of Life, a lobbying group and network of Catholic pro-life leaders.[68] Their goal was to prevent the pro-life movement's marginalization as a Catholic cause. Evangelicals, however, took full ownership of the organization and took other actions to rally their colleagues and congregations to become active in pro-life politics.

A pivotal figure in this process was the late Harold O. J. Brown, a professor at Trinity Evangelical Divinity School and Reformed Theological Seminary, a writer for several Christian magazines, a pastor, and a founding member of CAC.[69] A January 1976 article he published in his capacity as contributing editor for the popular *Christianity Today* magazine called Christians to action on the abortion issue and introduced CAC to the evangelical public. A CAC history published online by its first executive director, Robert Case, identifies the piece as what not only prompted him to seek involvement with CAC but also as the "seminal article which began the national evangelical pro-life movement."[70]

Two evangelical leaders I interviewed flagged relationships with Brown as critical to their future involvement in pro-life work. Young, CAC executive director from 1978 to 1987, took a class taught by Brown while in the seminary at Trinity and said that Brown's discussion of abortion interested him in the issue and inspired him to want to get involved in the pro-life cause. Though Young had previously regarded abortion as bad—he said that his first reaction, upon hearing about the *Roe* decision while an undergraduate was, "What a terrible thing for a man to make a woman go through!"—he said that in seminary he began to think more deeply about the issue in the context of his studies of theology and ethics and to see abortion as a profound contradiction of God's word on the sanctity of human life. He began to feel called to pro-life work, and the job as CAC executive director became available as he graduated from seminary. Delahoyde, Care Net president from 2008 to 2013, also got involved with Brown in the 1970s while studying for a master's degree at Trinity's divinity school. This followed her conversion from pro-choice to pro-life, which she said occurred while she was doing abortion-related research for a professor and became exposed to philosophical arguments that abortion had implications for all human life, not just the unborn. Brown invited Delahoyde to serve on CAC's board, and thereafter she would continue to be involved with the organization in various capacities.

CAC initially emphasized political advocacy. A 1976 brochure CAC distributed, "Abortion: What Can I Do?," calls Christians to many forms of action, including the personal extension of help to women, but drives home the point that believers must get involved in the democratic process.[71] The specific policy aim outlined in CAC's "Statement of Purpose" was amending the US Constitution to reverse *Roe v. Wade*. While working to inspire grassroots activism, CAC staff also lobbied Congress directly.

Eventually evangelicals would awaken on abortion. A pivotal event in this process was the 1979 release of the documentary *Whatever Happened to the Human Race?*, produced by evangelical leaders C. Everett Koop (who would later be appointed surgeon general by Ronald Reagan) and Francis Schaeffer, a theologian. The film argued for the humanity of the unborn and assigned abortion a central role in the culture's alleged slide down a slippery slope on which the increased practice of infanticide and euthanasia and the development of other technologies would gravely threaten human life and dignity, especially among the most vulnerable people. As Koop and Schaeffer toured the country screening the film and facilitating discussions at evangelical churches, evangelicals would be galvanized and mobilized to take action against abortion.[72] Other organizations aiming to represent evangelicals in politics also sprouted.[73]

From Politics to Pregnancy Centers

Despite evangelicals' newfound interest in political action, it was not long before CAC would change its tactics. In the late 1970s, Young would be introduced to Hillabrand and Maier's group, AAI. The AAI approach to abortion appealed greatly to Young, who claimed a "theological conviction" that it was "not just enough to say no to abortion."

The AAI approach also resonated with other CAC leaders and members. In her interview, Delahoyde recalled CAC early on received letters from its members asking, "What do we do for women?" In a book she authored on the implications of abortion for children with disabilities, written in part from her personal perspective as the parent of a disabled child, Delahoyde firmly identified herself with an argument that she said then was popular in the pro-life movement: "Fighting against abortion also means caring for children and for the mothers who might otherwise seek an abortion."[74] She proceeded to call out Christians for their personal inaction on the matter, especially when it came to support for families of children with disabilities, arguing, "Our words mean nothing if we do not back them up with loving support. . . . We cannot lightly say to parents or society 'choose life.' In some situations, making that choice will bring years of sacrifice and pain. We must be there to ease that pain and share the burden with them."[75]

Thus, in those early days, there was a sense at CAC of an unmet need for outreach and aid to women experiencing crisis pregnancies. Despite the many fiscal conservatives among politically active evangelical Christians, Young said CAC personnel did not necessarily oppose delivery of some aid through the welfare state. Delahoyde's book proclaimed, "Our government has a responsibility to care for the truly needy in society" and specifically lamented the insufficiency and political vulnerability of public aid for people with disabilities.[76] Young said he realized that when it came to helping pregnant women,

"Government isn't going to do it. Churches need to." His rationale for that conclusion cited Planned Parenthood's "overwhelmingly dominant" influence on the federal government. Young also suggested, not unlike Summerhill had done in differentiating Birthright from social service agencies, that CAC's vision for how pregnant women should be helped could not be implemented by a secular, bureaucratic state. CAC "approached centers as ministries, not social services," he explained, because its leaders were concerned not just with pregnant women's social and material welfare but also with their spiritual well-being.

In AAI pregnancy centers, Young recalled, he encountered a "workable model" for providing aid to pregnant women. Intrigued by the possibility of getting CAC involved in pregnancy center work, Young sought guidance from AAI and soon accepted an invitation to serve on the organization's board of directors. CAC began to spread the word about pregnancy centers to its own membership, encouraging them and their churches to start pregnancy centers and offering them guidance in doing so. The first CAC-affiliated pregnancy center opened in Baltimore in 1981—the Greater Baltimore Center for Pregnancy Concerns, which I introduced in Chapter 1.

The pregnancy center concept spread through evangelical networks much like it had through Catholic networks a decade earlier. The evangelicals' political awakening on social issues buoyed their interest in the movement, Delahoyde suggested. CAC's efforts to get the word out later received a boost when James Dobson, a pediatric psychologist and founder of the Christian organization Focus on the Family, began promoting pregnancy centers on his popular radio broadcasts. One of Care Net's vice presidents I interviewed for this research professed that she "got the bug" for pregnancy centers from Dobson and believed his encouragement was an important reason for a surge in CAC centers that executives say were founded between the mid-1980s and early 1990s. Dobson's primary audience was believed to be women outside the workforce, and pregnancy centers were perceived by those women as a place to make a difference on the social issues about which they were increasingly coming to care.

Though CAC's first pregnancy center opened in a highly urban, majority black community, the organization's current executives characterized the *typical* community in which CAC centers opened differently. In a phenomenon Care Net executives explained in terms of the demands involved with opening a center, the typical location was suburban, exurban, or rural and majority white. The typical lead founder was a financially comfortable woman who had finished raising her children; she was also described as a "networker" who would organize her husband and members of her church to support the effort.

Some of CAC's earliest centers were projects of particular congregations. According to the current executive director of CAC's first pregnancy center, based on organizational records she reviewed and summarized in an undated speech to her board of directors that she shared to supplement her interview, the idea for the center arose with "several couples" who watched Schaeffer's documentary in 1979 and came away from it with "an increased desire, not only to testify to the evil of abortion, but also to do something about it that would make a difference." As they prayed and planned, one particular woman "God then brought forth" took the helm of the effort and inspired the Christian church she attended to play an especially important role in the early funding and volunteer support of the center.[77] Members of a Lutheran church initiated another early CAC center included in this research; in its first years, four other churches also contributed to its support. That center, now called The Pregnancy Clinic, opened in May 1982 in Bowie, Maryland, as CAC's thirteenth center. The pastor of that Lutheran congregation was reportedly passionate about abortion, though a firsthand account of the center's founding puts a different factor in the foreground.

Foreshadowing the importance women with abortion histories would come to have in the pregnancy help movement, a woman's abortion experiences would help inspire the Bowie center. According to the center's current executive director, Pam Palumbo, who had been a member of that Lutheran congregation, witnessed events leading to the center's creation, and served as one of its first volunteers, the process of opening the center began when a member of the church shared her experience of having undergone four abortions. The woman told members of the church that she had felt trapped when she had had the abortions and had believed that she had no other options. She appealed for pro-lifers' help in reaching out to pregnant women.[78]

CAC-affiliated centers differed from AAI-affiliated centers most importantly in that they would offer women the gospel (understood to mean the "good news" of Jesus Christ communicated in the Bible) along with the pregnancy tests, counseling, material aid, and social service referrals typically provided at pregnancy centers. When asked about the reasons people who contacted CAC to start pregnancy centers supplied, Young added a third motivation, to "save souls," to Christians' desires to "stop abortion in their towns" and "save babies and help women." Young fondly recalled the period when CAC and local groups of Christians were first founding pregnancy centers as a "form of revival" marked by people's willingness to "make sacrifices, take risks." He underscored that the founding of pregnancy centers was "spiritually motivated, no question about that."

As with those of Birthright and AAI, the earliest CAC centers were relatively informal. CAC and its network of centers, Young opined, "operated like an underground left-wing organization," meaning "on a shoestring, with a lot of youthful zeal." The work was exciting, and Young thought of the people setting up those first centers as "pioneers." Palumbo also described her center as operating for some time on a low-budget, donation-to-donation basis. The center offered only pregnancy tests and material aid. With public assistance for medical care less available than it currently is and with fewer community organizations serving low-income people, Palumbo said the center recruited its own network of doctors and local hospitals that would care for the center's clients on a sliding-fee scale (reducing prices according to clients' ability to pay). She also opined that, in retrospect, the center's attempts to counsel women about their pregnancy options reflected much less understanding of women and the counseling process than she believes her center has today. She cited as an example a slide show of fetal images that her center used to show women, produced by a past president of National Right to Life.

Although CAC's political advocacy continued into the 1980s, according to Young, its sponsorship of pregnancy centers eventually "eclipsed" its lobbying activity. In the 1990s, CAC officially dropped advocacy from its purposes and changed its name to "Care Net." By that time, however, the Washington, DC, area had become populated by a number of other advocacy groups such as the Moral Majority and the Christian Coalition associated with evangelical Christians that voiced opposition to abortion.

CONTINUED PROLIFERATION

Pregnancy centers continued to proliferate long after the initial bursts of activity surrounding the legalization of abortion and the uptake of pregnancy center work by the leading evangelical pro-life organization, CAC. By 1984, Birthright alone reported having 600 North American centers.[79] CAC's Young said that by the time he left his position in 1987, 350 CAC-affiliated centers had opened. These numbers do not include independent centers, those affiliated with AAI, or the smaller chains also founded. Care Net's Delahoyde said she believed the bulk of pregnancy centers that exist today were founded by the early 1990s.

This claim about the timing of the most important phases of pregnancy center diffusion initially seems inconsistent with the statistics reported by Kimberly Kelly, which, though they do not cover approximately the first two decades of pregnancy center history, suggest that massive growth in pregnancy center numbers has been a more recent phenomenon. The number of AAI/ Heartbeat International affiliates grew from 175 in 1994 to 600 in 2000. CAC/ Care Net affiliates grew in number from 425 in 1992 to 500 in 1999. Then, between 1999/2000 and 2008, affiliates of Heartbeat International and Care Net approximately doubled.[80] National association leaders, however, suggested that though new centers certainly were being established, these rising affiliate counts reflect the alignment of existing centers with one or both of these national networks. Heartbeat International's Hartshorn writes that her organization, at the time she assumed the presidency in 1993, had been suffering from internal problems at the national office and had been at a low point in terms of affiliates.[81] Glessner similarly described that association as of the early 1990s as "dying on the vine." The organization then had to turn its attention to affiliate recruitment. Care Net leaders interviewed also attributed important periods of growth the organization experienced in the late 1990s and from 2003 to 2008 to specific affiliate recruitment initiatives, including one associated with the organization's renaming and rebranding of itself from CAC to Care Net and a merger with another pregnancy center network, Sav-a-Life.

Although centers of local leaders I interviewed might not constitute a representative sample of pregnancy centers, the timing of their organizations' origins was roughly consistent with a story in which most of the pregnancy center movement's basic infrastructure had been established by the early 1990s. Nearly all of those leaders' centers had been founded by the late 1980s, with the most recent of the centers represented by my interviewees dating itself to 1992. Some of those centers, however, had since that time opened additional offices in neighboring communities.

Founding stories of my interviewees' centers that had opened after the two initial bursts of activity in the Catholic and evangelical wings of the movement suggested considerable consistency in the basic identities, motivations, and circumstances of the founders. All of their centers were projects of religious networks: a group of Catholic women who sought help from St. Polycarp and their local archdiocese's new Respect Life office, an airline pilot who discerned a call from God and shared it with his men's breakfast prayer group, a steering committee involving Christian pastors and a nurse, parishioners at a particular Catholic parish, and a group recruited by a Catholic priest given their interests and connections to the target community.[82] As interviewees told it, centers grew out of concern about abortion and—in perhaps one departure from the stories of the earliest centers—perception that a center was "needed" in a given community. Of two interviewees who specified the nature of this need, both cited characteristics of the community believed to make women there especially vulnerable to having abortions. In one case, in the early 1990s, a Washington, DC, area priest noticed Spanish-language advertisements for abortion proliferating in local media and, with others, reached the conclusion that the Catholic Church must specifically reach out to Latinas with pregnancy help. In the other, a new office of an existing center just preparing to open in 2012, a priest working closely with the founders said that they were conscious of abortion clinics' attempts to reach the women in their area and that their county did not yet have a pregnancy center, despite its geographically large size and the fact that it was home to two colleges.[83]

DIVERSIFICATION

In addition to the growing number of pregnancy centers, the pregnancy help movement also expanded in the variety of service providers it encompassed. Diversification of organizational types and the resources offered to women began as early as the 1970s. Some of these initiatives involved the reform and repackaging of older models of service provision, such as the maternity home and the adoption agency, to reflect explicitly pro-life identities, respond to abortion's availability as a legal option, and provide what activists suggest is a more personal and compassionate level of service than that offered by older agencies. Other initiatives were new.

Some interviewees, others in the pro-life movement, and even former president Reagan recognized Jim and Anne Pierson as leaders in the revival of maternity homes under the auspices of the pro-life movement.[84] In the early 1970s, they founded the House of His Creation maternity home. The home claims to be the first in the country to follow a "family model," in that the

Piersons and their family lived in the house with the women and served as "Houseparents" rather than employing external staff for shift work.[85] Others followed. One that gained national visibility was the Liberty Godparent Home, an initiative of the Reverend Jerry Falwell of the Moral Majority, a Christian conservative lobby. Falwell allegedly acted in response to a reporter's challenge regarding what he was doing to end abortion other than trying to outlaw it and founded the home in 1982.[86] By 1989, the pro-life movement's sponsorship of maternity homes had grown extensive enough to merit a front-page article in the *New York Times*.[87]

The Nurturing Network (TNN), the organization I described in Chapter 2 that works to help pregnant women continue with college or careers, began in 1985. TNN was founded by Mary Cunningham Agee, a Catholic who had gained recognition for being one of the rare women in senior management at two Fortune 100 companies. Political content in Agee's founding story is limited to her opinion that opposing abortion without taking practical action to help pregnant women is callous and unproductive. More than this political element, however, TNN's founder emphasizes circumstances in her personal life that inspired TNN: it was in her prayer over the grief of a late-term miscarriage that Agee says she discerned a call from God to start her outreach to women with crisis pregnancies.[88]

The Gabriel Project, another pregnancy help initiative with a national reach (see Chapter 2), began formally in 1990 in Texas but had longer, informal roots in signs placed outside a small number of Catholic parishes that advertised help for women facing crisis pregnancies.[89] The effort gradually expanded over time. The project's Maryland affiliate, represented in my interview research, emerged in the wake of the 1992 elections—specifically from an unsuccessful 1992 referendum campaign targeting a recently enacted Maryland law that had liberalized abortion regulations. Pro-life activists had mobilized to repeal the law under the banner of the Vote kNOw Coalition, spearheaded by the Maryland Catholic Conference and involving others such as the Catholic Archdiocese of Washington and the Protestant group Pastors for Life.[90] The Gabriel Network's executive director told me in a secondhand history that following the election, in which defeat of the coalition's position had been coupled with the election of pro-choice President Bill Clinton and a Democratic Congress, this idea emerged with respect to stopping abortion: "We have to do this ourselves. We have to take the case directly to the women." A participant in the coalition proposed bringing the Gabriel Project to Maryland. In 1993, the coalition spun off a nonprofit educational foundation that would implement the Gabriel Project and other crisis pregnancy outreach.[91] This organization's story is the only one in my research that cited political events or conditions in its founding story, aside from those founded in the immediate wake of the legalization of abortion.

CONCLUSION: WHY DID THE PREGNANCY CENTER MOVEMENT START?

Pro-life pregnancy centers were founded in response to the legalization or the threat of legalization of abortion. They were founded by individuals committed to the view that human life was created by God and sacred; therefore, abortion was wrong and an injustice that must be fought. These early activists largely appeared to understand women's interest in abortion as a function of their anxiety about the economic and especially the social consequences of unintended pregnancy and single parenthood. With abortion being legal, the activists reasoned, pressure placed on women by those who would stand to lose from their pregnancy and motherhood would also surely escalate, resulting in an increase in abortions. In the form of the pregnancy center, activists invented or discovered a way of fighting abortion that enabled them to balance their advocacy for the unborn with their sympathy for pregnant women. To them, the idea of outreach to pregnant women simply made sense. It was also consistent with what some activists perceived God as calling them to do as well as with their personalities and lifestyles. They portray their movement as a pragmatic, humanitarian, and grassroots effort. Though the first pregnancy centers were not founded as religious organizations, many of the early activists saw them as a product of prayer and hoped that in running them they would honor God. Birthright's Summerhill tellingly dedicates her book about her organization to "Mary, the Mother of Our Lord."[92]

Centers were not entirely new animals, for churches, church members, and various social service agencies had long been providing assistance to unwed mothers through maternity homes, adoption agencies, and informal networks. However, pregnancy centers differed from these social service providers in that their work reflected a new social reality in which abortion had been moved from the private to the public realm and whether to carry a pregnancy to term was increasingly a woman's legal choice to make. The logic of at least the older maternity home system, which fed into adoption agencies, was to take unmarried women out of society during their pregnancies.[93] In contrast, pregnancy centers could surround them with support in the community where they lived.

Given that the founding of the first US pregnancy centers predated *Roe*, one cannot attribute the movement's genesis to blocked political opportunities and activist frustrations. Although dim *prospects* about the future of abortion legalization could have been relevant to why activists founded pregnancy centers rather than pouring all of the resources they devoted to the pro-life movement into political work, there is also little reason to believe this was the case. That abortion would be legalized as broadly as it would be in *Roe v. Wade* had not been viewed by the earliest pro-life activists as inevitable; many, for example, reported being caught by surprise by the scope of *Roe*.[94] Heartbeat International's Hartshorn, who joined her local right-to-life group right after the *Roe* decision and eventually became that group's president, recalled in an interview that many people active in her group believed that the new right-to-life movement would be able to quickly undo *Roe* legislatively. She admitted that she herself had been less optimistic but denied that this had anything to do with why she founded a pregnancy center years later.

Contracting political opportunities also appear to have little to do with the rapid spread of pregnancy help organizations across the United States. The most extensive growth in numbers of pregnancy centers and diversity of organizational types appeared to precede the series of political disappointments and setbacks pro-life activists suffered in the late 1980s and early 1990s (see Chapters 1 and 4). Although Staggenborg endorses a view of pregnancy center growth taking off after 1983, following failed efforts to advance a constitutional amendment protecting fetal life, these events did not seem particularly salient to the leaders I interviewed.[95] CAC's Young, who presided over the organization's transition from political to pregnancy center work, explicitly remarked that the opening of CAC's first pregnancy center followed the election of Reagan as president, an event that he said had filled him and his colleagues with hope.

Likewise, ideology—at least in the traditional liberal-conservative sense—and the opportunities the political system offered for activists to push policies consistent with their values offers little traction for understanding the origins and early growth of the pregnancy help movement. Historian Daniel Williams nests the early Birthright pregnancy centers within a narrative about the social welfare liberalism of the first, largely Catholic, wave of pro-life activists.[96] Meanwhile, pregnancy centers also proved attractive to evangelicals, who tended to express more conservative policy views than Catholics and were rapidly moving into the Republican camp at the time CAC was opening its centers.[97] Both groups of pro-life activists enjoyed ideological allies in government at the time they started setting up pregnancy centers. Catholics mobilized at a time when the major parties had not yet sorted themselves out on the abortion issue, so that the nation's political elite included many liberal pro-life Democrats.[98] Evangelicals' mobilization into pregnancy centers in the 1980s overlapped with a period of conservative political ascendancy.

Though aiding pregnant women has been part of the pro-life movement's repertoire virtually since its inception, the contrast between the portrayals of pregnancy centers in this chapter and Chapter 2 shows that pro-life individual outreach has changed in some ways over time. This is especially the case in terms of the movement's scope and style and the complexity of its theory of abortion. Further, though they might be difficult to reconcile with the portrayals of contemporary pregnancy centers in Chapter 2 and the work of other scholars, allegations of unethical practices at pregnancy centers performed in the name of baby-saving (see Chapter 1) raise the possibility that at least some centers might have strayed from the vision of movement founders.[99] Chapter 4 explores the movement's more recent growth and the change in how it has approached the problem of abortion.

4. Strategy Change and Resource Growth

Packed into a ballroom for a morning general session of Care Net's 2011 annual pregnancy center conference, perhaps upward of a thousand pregnancy center personnel listened with rapt attention to the young, tattooed abortion-clinic-director-turned-pro-life-activist pacing the stage. Abby Johnson had been talking about Planned Parenthood, her former employer, and the tactics it used to attract clients. She reminded her audience that they were up against "one of the world's largest industries. And one of the most evil industries."

Then she turned to pregnancy centers: "I walk into some pregnancy centers, and I walk in, and I see mauve on the walls. And I see furniture that looks like it's from my great-grandma's house. And I see, um, every brochure in there has a woman that looks like this." She paused to imitate the facial expression. "And I see ceramic plates hanging on the wall. Or, I see stuffed bunnies on the ground, or I see doilies everywhere, or, I see starched, you know, starched hats, you know. Those are hanging up on the wall. . . . And it makes me laugh because I think to myself, if you were trying to attract the 60-year-old woman that miraculously gets pregnant after menopause, you are right on track!"

Chuckles arose from the audience as Johnson continued her critique. However, the moment of comic relief was just that. Johnson would soon circle back to a larger message that did not sound funny at all. "We are trying to reach the women that are going into the abortion industry, right?" Johnson asked. "We are trying to reach the women that are going into Planned Parenthood."

Johnson elaborated on how pregnancy centers could learn from Planned Parenthood about how to attract their target clientele: "All we have to do is look to them, see what they're doing, and do it better." Johnson was not talking about the deceptive strategies often attributed to pregnancy centers (see Chapter 1). She was talking about making pregnancy centers more appealing to women in their teens and twenties through branding and public outreach and improving the credibility of the ways in which they talked about abortion with clients.

Despite their identity as "ministries," pregnancy centers should also be thinking of themselves as "businesses," Johnson had warned, or else their ministries might have no one to serve. The call to action was clear: "Now is the time to be competing with the abortion industry. . . . It's time to get down to business. It's time to get serious. It's time to start making some changes."[1]

A Care Net–, Heartbeat International–, and NIFLA-affiliated pregnancy center I visited in the summer of 2012 appeared to be on the cutting edge of some of those kinds of reforms. Situated in a newly refurbished house in a mixed residential/commercial neighborhood in Annapolis, Maryland, across a narrow, busy street from a brown office building housing an abortion clinic, it was the recently opened third location of a center called the Pregnancy Clinic. A sign outside advertised preabortion ultrasounds. Inside, cozy-looking furniture and a modest number of brochures dotted a small waiting room. A hallway led past the office manager's station into large front rooms with a desk and computer that could be closed off for overflow counseling or use by volunteers. My tour proceeded into meeting space used for the center's classes, then into the sonography room, where the center's director proudly pointed out the 3D/4D ultrasound machine. The second floor included more office space, a lab area for processing tests, and two counseling rooms. Floors were mostly hardwood, and the decor throughout struck me as stylish and updated—decidedly uncluttered and exuding peace. Counseling rooms were sparsely outfitted with contemporary furniture and earthy color schemes of reds, grays, browns, and dark greens.

Baby-related goods were nowhere in sight. They were stashed instead on the center's upper floor in a storage room accessible through the back of the kitchen, used only by center staff, and what the center kept on hand at that location was a more limited array of aid—mainly diapers and formula—than I had seen at every other center I visited. The center hid the goods, the director explained, because of a belief that it would disrupt the "upscale" appearance that she believed most women sought in a service provider and that her center tried to project. The center did not want to be seen as a place people went to get things for free because that was not the center's primary mission. Its mission instead was more broadly to "care for, support, and empower women to make life-affirming decisions for their pregnancy and themselves."

The Pregnancy Clinic's director proudly told me about ways in which she said the center was meeting more demanding professional standards in health care, counseling, financial management, and other areas than those required by law or the major national pregnancy center associations—and holding itself accountable. Having served as director since soon after the center opened in 1982, she mused during her interview about how far the center had come since its earliest days, when the resources it could offer had been much more limited, when pregnancy tests took an hour to run in a test tube, when it had naively counseled women with a slideshow of fetal imagery, and when its financial situation had been so precarious that a wad of cash a priest once placed on her desk had been a lifeline.

Like the Pregnancy Clinic, the pro-life pregnancy help movement has indeed grown and changed substantially over its history, as I described in these scenes and the contrast in Chapters 2 and 3 of early and modern pregnancy centers. The number of service providers has multiplied. The movement has greatly expanded in scope, both in terms of the diversity of pregnancy help outreach it encompasses and the array of services offered at pregnancy centers. Pregnancy centers have been gradually professionalizing, a change closely intertwined with what might be the most salient change in their history: their increasing emphasis on medical services. Substantial growth in the pregnancy center movement's resources has enabled this latter transformation.

In this chapter I ask: How and why has this tactical innovation and resource growth in the pro-life movement's direct service stream occurred? I tell this story largely from activists' perspectives, as I collected them from interviews and documents, although I check activists' accounts when possible against other sources. As in Chapter 3, I pay special attention to the timing of changes and to activists' framing of those changes when assessing the roles of the explanatory factors proposed in Chapter 1. I begin with a brief account of the expansion of some pregnancy centers—largely those affiliated with Care Net, Heartbeat International, or NIFLA—and proceed into the outreach to groups beyond pregnant women and the programming intended to promote client lifestyle transformation. In most of the rest of the chapter, I focus on pregnancy centers' most salient innovation, conversion to "medical clinics," a change that has contributed to increasing professionalization of the movement. I address how this developed, what it has meant for the pregnancy center movement, and how some activists envision building on it to better compete with abortion providers. Pregnancy center activists' discourse on such matters engages different ideas about their organizations' identities, images, and effectiveness, along with the core services they ought to offer women.

THE EXPANDING SCOPE OF PREGNANCY CENTERS

As I showed in Chapter 2, the work of the typical pregnancy center affiliated with one of the three big networks—Care Net, Heartbeat International, and NIFLA—encompasses far more than crisis pregnancy intervention and follow-up care. Among other things, the centers offer programming promoting abortion "recovery," "sexual integrity" or "sexual risk avoidance," and parenting and other life skills. Many have set up systems of exchange through which clients "earn" new baby clothing, furniture, and other goods through participation in centers' personal development classes. At best, these activities only indirectly "save babies" from abortion. Instead, they aim for individual transformation and cultural reform. The pregnancy center movement's adoption of these practices is also an interesting phenomenon because some of these programs are informed by traditional Christian doctrine, and their logics are consistent with the interest in cultural or lifestyle issues that animated many conservative Christian political activists in the 1980s and beyond. This might cast doubt on a narrative of pregnancy centers as counterstereotypically engaging the political left's issues and raise questions about how distinct the political and service streams of the pro-life movement really are.

Looking at the timing of the expansion of the scope of pregnancy centers' services, there is little reason to believe they were ushered in by a contraction of political opportunities that shifted activists and other resources from conventional political activism into pregnancy centers.

In the case of abortion "recovery" programs, although the visible mobilization of women with abortion histories into the pro-life movement has been an important recent phenomenon, a nascent movement of such women had become intertwined with the pregnancy center movement by the 1980s, if not earlier.[2] According to Siegel, and seconded by some of the leaders I interviewed, pregnancy centers helped connect those women to each other, and the women's experiences greatly influenced pregnancy centers' commitment to woman-focused service and arguments against abortion.[3] Pregnancy centers also claim they were moved to action by the hurt they perceived in the lives of pregnancy-test clients with abortion histories. Early in the pregnancy centers' histories, a prominent movement leader wrote, they began to experiment with counseling programs designed to help women cope with the guilt, emotional distress, and subsequent negative lifestyle choices their personnel believed were associated with abortions. This began even before pro-life researchers began proposing the existence of a "post-abortion syndrome," which they did in the 1980s.[4]

Pregnancy centers' involvement with local schools' abstinence education had also begun by the early 1980s. Even before that, Heartbeat International's then president said, the author of the organization's first counseling manual had encouraged the discussion of abstinence from sex until marriage with clients receiving negative pregnancy-test results. She further claimed that the wider abstinence education movement was "birthed out of" pregnancy centers associated with her network and reported that the pregnancy center she had personally founded was one of a small number to receive new Reagan-era abstinence education grants in the 1980s.[5] A "pregnancy center service report" suggested that the availability of federal funding contributed to pregnancy centers' interest in offering such programs.[6]

These two innovations thus started becoming institutionalized during the early years of the Reagan administration—many scholars regard that as a time when energy and hope ran especially high for activists in the pro-life movement's political stream.[7] A political, ideological explanation is also complicated by observing that this was a period when policy preferences on social welfare and cultural issues were unrelated in public opinion and when this alignment was still a work in progress among political elites.[8] The pro-life movement was still dominated by pro–social welfare Catholic Democrats, and conservative evangelical Christians had only recently begun joining it en masse. Yet the pairing of the social welfare liberalism Williams perceives in pregnancy centers' work with the conservatism of the movement's sexual mores was not unusual among many of those early Catholic pro-life leaders.[9]

Heartbeat International's long-tenured leader presented such an expansion of centers' scope of service as part of a learning process in which pregnancy help activists revised their thinking about the nature of the abortion problem, particularly as they gained experience with their clients, watched the incidence of abortion rise, and noticed the culture changing around them.[10] Abortion incidence did indeed climb rapidly in the years following *Roe*. The total number of abortions performed in the United States rose from at least 744,600 in 1973 to 1,553,900 in 1980 and would creep up from there to peak at an estimated 1,608,600 in 1990. Abortion rates—that is, abortions per 1,000 women aged fifteen to forty-four—climbed from 16.3 in 1973 to a high of 29.3 in 1980; in 1990 they were an estimated 27.4.[11] The idea that most pregnant women do not want abortions and can be persuaded to choose alternatives if given emotional and material support remains central to the pregnancy help movement's worldview and work, as I showed in Chapter 2. Some leaders claimed, however, that the movement came to appreciate that such humanitarian support, just like making abortion illegal, would be limited in its impact on abortion demand if changing sexual norms and what they perceive as the decline of the family were not also addressed. Heartbeat International's Margaret "Peggy" Hartshorn writes:

> The names, numbers, and variety of services reflect our response to the women, girls, and families who have been coming to us for help for over thirty years. These clients are, in a sense, "products" of a decaying culture, sometimes now called a Culture of Death. In the late '60s and '70s, we presumed that these women were in short-term crisis. . . . Now we recognize them as the walking wounded who need much more than crisis intervention. . . . Now we realize that we need to teach those [Judeo-Christian] values anew to a generation that has hardly heard of them—a generation with the scars to prove it.[12]

Similarly, a former local center director remarked that in pregnancy center work, "you realize the tide you're going against, the culture."

Pregnancy help activists frame the energy they have put into their pregnancy, parenting, and life skills education classes, and their efforts to incentivize them by linking them to material aid, with similar logic. Although it is unclear when classes on these topics started becoming a staple of pregnancy center service provision, aid-linked educational programs began to spread around the mid-1990s and into the 2000s. The growth of such incentive programs is something Heartbeat International's president identified in her interview as a "big, big change" at pregnancy centers over the course of their history. The programs represented a new way of delivering material aid and a substantial move by centers to promote lifestyle changes among their clients.

The Earn While You Learn (EWYL) Program, which I introduced in Chapter 2, was not the first of its kind but now ranks among the most popular. It traces back to an Arizona pregnancy center at which "volunteers felt as though they were giving pregnancy tests and handing out freebees but not making any long-term impact on the clients' lives." Parenting classes were offered but perceived as underused. The center reacted by moving its formerly free material aid into a "mommy store" at which clients would shop with "money" earned through participation in weekly instructional meetings with center volunteers.

The center claimed that the program was popular with clients. Eventually the program expanded into a detailed curriculum made available to other pregnancy centers.[13]

Pregnancy centers' reasoning for linking material aid to educational program participation involved some popular themes from 1990s welfare policy discourse, including bipartisan concern that aid delivered with few strings attached bred dependency and other social ills.[14] EWYL's promotional material declared, "Giving things away free only enables our clients and fosters the entitlement mentality." It boldly claimed that class lessons would "break cycles of poor parenting, neglect, and abuse."[15] Another educational incentive program used at pregnancy centers, Bridges, called itself "a hand up, not a handout."[16]

To what extent concurrent welfare policy debates actually influenced pregnancy centers' increasing interest in abstinence or other lifestyle-oriented programming cannot be discerned from my research. As tentative evidence against it, I discuss in Chapter 6 and elsewhere that many pregnancy help leaders claimed little interest in politics and showed little overt antiwelfare sentiment. By contrast, political pro-life groups after *Roe*'s first decade moved more closely into alliance with conservative "New Right" political forces.[17] Moreover, evangelical Christians' influence in the pregnancy center movement has increased over time, and political advocacy groups reflecting this tradition did lobby for welfare reforms that decreased access to cash assistance and added policy tools to promote abstinence and discourage nonmarital childbearing.[18] That the rise of conservative Christian cultural ideology in US politics might have affected pregnancy centers' expanding scope of services thus cannot be ruled out. If it has mattered, however, it has been mixed with other influences and adapted by pregnancy centers' woman-focused frames.

BABY-CENTERED RADICALISM

To the extent that pregnancy centers' practices reflected the radical character of the pro-life movement's "rescue" wing, involving aggressive protests at abortion clinics and doctors' homes, this approach appears to have been most prevalent in the second decade after *Roe*. Indeed, some of the scholarly books that group pregnancy centers with pro-life "radicalism" or "street-level" activism were produced contemporaneously.[19] Staggenborg located the problem in what she said was a wave of centers founded after 1983.[20] Even movement leaders acknowledged a phase in which some centers, in their distress over rising numbers of abortions and their desperation to stop them, adopted a "baby-centered" approach associated with some disreputable practices.[21]

Pro-choice sociologist Kimberly Kelly suggests that the most troubling practices were confined to a small share of centers, but these and other failures to demonstrate professionalism greatly damaged pregnancy centers' reputations and served as important context for a set of reforms she links to the movement's resurgence.[22] My interviewees generally agreed, though the stories they told about innovation and growth in the movement cited other factors as well. Here I share more of what is claimed, known, or believed about baby-centered radicalism at pregnancy centers as part of the story of this innovation and growth.

MEDICALIZATION AND PROFESSIONALIZATION

Perhaps the most salient change in the pregnancy center movement's history involves the inseparable phenomena of medicalization and professionalization. Because of their significance to the movement, and other features that make them theoretically interesting, I discuss them extensively in this chapter. Unlike the programming I discussed earlier in this chapter, which involved expansion of pregnancy centers' missions, medicalization and professionalization constitute new approaches the movement has taken to its original mission of crisis pregnancy intervention and support. Interestingly, national organizations began actively promoting these organizational changes in the mid-1990s, which followed the Supreme Court upholding *Roe* in two high-profile abortion cases, the election of pro-choice president Bill Clinton, and continued congressional dominance by the increasingly pro-choice Democratic Party. Medicalization and professionalization also required the pregnancy center movement to substantially increase its resources—which it did. Because of this, studying this development might shed light on the sources of the current appeal of pro-life individual outreach to activists and their supporters— and enable a tougher test of whether the opportunity structure of the pro-life movement's political stream spurred innovation and resource growth in its individual outreach stream.

Professionalization alone would be unremarkable. Scholars often treat it as part of the life course of social movement organizations (SMOs). Establishing formal, stable, institutional structures potentially enhances credibility and can enable social movements to be sustainable over the long term.[23]

However, in the pregnancy center movement, professionalization and medicalization proceeded nearly simultaneously. Although one finds in the movement's history instances of professionalization that preceded medicalization, particularly in some changes happening within the national offices of today's three major pregnancy center networks, activists commonly point to medicalization as an accelerator of this process; regulations, client expectations, and norms of the medical field, among other things, entailed professionalization. For this reason, I approach this phenomenon as a tactical innovation by pregnancy centers.

The Path to Organizational Change

The move toward medicalization and professionalization began in California, where pregnancy centers faced a lawsuit that foreshadowed the scrutiny they would attract from pro-choice activists up through the present day. A case initiated in a Los Angeles court in 1985 by a now-prominent feminist attorney charged that pregnancy centers' performance of pregnancy tests constituted illegal practice of medicine without a license. Although the judge did not rule on whether centers actually were practicing medicine, he cited perceptions that they were doing so as grounds for his order barring them from performing pregnancy tests.[24] As NIFLA president Tom Glessner and Pregnancy Clinic director Pam Palumbo both told me, in what was merely a defensive move to retain a core service, the California centers affected by the ruling responded by becoming state-licensed medical clinics.

Eventually, other events, concerns, and ideas converged to encourage interest in this strategy among other pregnancy centers. Of special concern to pregnancy center leaders in the late 1980s and early 1990s was what they perceived as an attack campaign pro-choice activists were waging against pregnancy centers. NIFLA's Glessner reported getting an early, if extreme, taste of the opposition pregnancy centers would encounter from pro-choice activists at the Seattle pregnancy center he and his wife had founded. He said pro-choice activists had picketed the center and at one point threw bricks at its windows. He said that his center was also subject to tactics pro-choice activists more regularly and openly encourage: routine visits from fake clients and the generation of negative press.[25] Pro-choice activists' media campaign even appeared as the subject of an academic journal article, in which a key Planned Parenthood of New York City employee divulged to the author her strategy and goals, and reporters admitted their extensive reliance on that Planned Parenthood staffer and the sources she provided.[26] Among other things, pro-choice activists alleged that pregnancy centers advertised as if they were abortion clinics and then subjected the women who fell for the deception to "counseling" that featured false information about abortion, photos of aborted fetuses, and psychological abuse.[27] These allegations spurred governmental investigations, including hearings by the Democrat-controlled US House of Representatives in 1991.[28] Targeted regulation of pregnancy centers' advertising was proposed. Some pregnancy centers were sued and had to close.[29] Glessner, elevated to the presidency of the Christian Action Council (CAC; now called Care Net) in the late 1980s, eventually became so concerned about the legal threat to pregnancy centers that he left his post at CAC in 1992 to start a new organization, the National Institute of Family and Life Advocates (NIFLA). Its purpose was to help pregnancy centers prevent and defend themselves against these kinds of legal attacks.

Glessner, in his interview with me, and Heartbeat International's Peggy Hartshorn, in a publication, acknowledged unprofessional or disreputable practices at some local centers, but they also charged that pro-choice organizations and their allies blew the problems that did exist out of proportion, tarring all centers with the sins of a minority.[30] A 1984 pregnancy center training manual written by Hawai'i activist Robert Pearson did recommend deceptive practices, such as advertising under "abortion" in the yellow pages and confronting abortion-minded clients with hard-hitting fetal imagery. Yet Pearson's approach, according to Kelly, represented "the extreme end of the crisis pregnancy center movement, both then and now."[31] Only about 5 percent of all pregnancy centers were affiliated with Pearson's network, although select Pearson recommendations, such as the use of graphic visual aids, were taken up by some centers outside his network.[32]

Perhaps unsurprisingly, some pregnancy help leaders began to notice their centers were struggling to attract abortion-minded women. Pregnancy centers' bruised reputations surely contributed to this, but leaders also cited other considerations. Falling prices and greater availability of the at-home pregnancy tests eroded the value of the longtime free testing at the core of centers' services, Glessner said he had perceived. He and Hartshorn also blamed the excessive caution some centers exercised in response to the pro-choice activists' exposés and lawsuits. Beyond just avoiding deception, for example, Hartshorn suggested that many centers took pains to "warn" potential clients about their opposition to abortion.[33] In response to a 1990 Canadian law regulating abortion speech by nonprofit organizations, Birthright ordered its US centers, along with its Canadian ones, to refrain from speaking with clients about abortion unless they first brought up the topic.[34] Glessner said that many pregnancy centers, in order to avoid being accused of illegally practicing medicine, altered their implementation of pregnancy testing in a way that damaged their credibility: they would hand the client a self-test kit that she could "buy at the dollar store" and then instruct her to call a doctor if her test was positive. What centers had to offer abortion-minded women, leaders suggested they gradually concluded, was out of step with what research and experience were increasingly demonstrating about the attitudes and decision making of pregnant women and the resources they wanted. Glessner voiced a perception that centers were straying from their original mission of intervention in crisis pregnancies, and as a result their staffs were becoming demoralized. He recounted as particularly striking a conversation in which the executive director of one pregnancy center told him she wanted to resign. The director allegedly complained that she had not started working at a pregnancy center to be a "diaper distribution service" and provided statistics indicating that fewer than 1 percent of her center's clients were women testing positive for pregnancy who seemed at risk for abortions.

On top of that, philosophical division and other internal problems contributed to a generally challenging period for the pregnancy center movement. As negative stories about pregnancy centers proliferated, mistrust of each other festered within the movement.[35] Transitions in and disagreement among the AAI leadership, coupled with financial trouble, left that organization facing possible extinction.[36] Birthright suffered a schism over the association's enforcement of the 1990 Canadian abortion speech law on its US centers, a dispute complicated by the death of its founder and president, Louise Summerhill.[37]

By the early 1990s, as reported to me by Glessner and a former local center director who also served at that time on Heartbeat International's board of directors, some key leaders were questioning their organizations' effectiveness and concluding that changes were needed.[38] As leaders told it, this conclusion was reinforced by indicators of the rising incidence of abortion and the political and legal environment surrounding abortion. First, the total number of abortions performed in the United States continued to climb until it peaked in 1990.[39] On top of persistently high abortion counts, the pro-life movement's lack of progress toward constitutional protection for the unborn was not lost on activists. Heartbeat International's Hartshorn, in an interview, identified the early 1990s as a period of big change for pregnancy centers and explained that she and others in the pregnancy help movement were "highly motivated by the election of Bill Clinton." Because she and others "thought we would never again have a pro-life president," they suspected that the pro-life movement's future success was going to have to come mostly from its "service arm." Hartshorn also acknowledged the 1989 *Webster v. Reproductive Health Services* and 1992 *Casey v. Planned Parenthood of Southeastern Pennsylvania* Supreme Court decisions as big disappointments that would prove influential on the movement, saying that many pro-life activists had expected that the Court would overturn *Roe* at those times.[40] As she recounted it in an interview, the disappointment associated with *Webster* and Clinton's election quickly gave way to a new sentiment. These events, she said, prompted questions in the pregnancy help movement about how they should be spending their resources and time. They inspired a "recommitment to the vision and to doing it better." She said she also suspected that those events drew more people into the pregnancy help movement, reporting that she had met many pregnancy center personnel who marked their first involvement as being in response to the *Webster* case or Clinton's election. NIFLA president Glessner, perhaps the leading advocate of pregnancy center medicalization, similarly identified recognition that abortion might never be outlawed as part of his reasoning that pregnancy centers would need to step up their game.

In the midst of this challenging period, the California pregnancy centers affected by the 1985 medical practice ruling were learning information that would eventually inspire some key leaders to propose medicalization as a solution to the multiple problems pregnancy centers faced. According to Glessner, those centers, after converting to state-licensed medical clinics, began supplementing their pregnancy testing with ultrasound imaging, a tool they could use to offer authoritative medical confirmation of pregnancy. They also began seeing more pregnant, abortion-minded clients. This confirmed Glessner's suspicion that a medicalized setting would appeal to abortion-minded women. Glessner also attributed his enthusiasm for ultrasound to a report published in a 1983 issue of the *New England Journal of Medicine* in which the authors offered preliminary, anecdotal evidence that viewing an early ultrasound image could promote bonding between mothers and their fetuses.[41] The leadership of Glessner's newly founded organization, NIFLA, began to discuss whether promotion of centers' medicalization should be one of its projects.

A realization eventually cemented Glessner's commitment to the medical conversion project. He said that while watching his children play one day, he recalled two numbers he had proposed off the top of his head at separate meetings on a possible medical conversion project: 1,000 medicalized centers as the goal NIFLA should set, and 1,500 abortion-minded clients each of those centers might expect to see each year. It occurred to him that, multiplied, those figures equaled the number of abortions then being performed annually in the United States. Glessner said the realization hit him then that "we can do this," that is, end abortion, community by community, even if the pro-life movement never achieved the changes in abortion law it was seeking.

Glessner, a lawyer in his former career, has since actively promoted the conversion of pregnancy centers to licensed medical clinics. His organization has developed resources to facilitate that change. NIFLA trains nurses in "limited obstetrical ultrasound," a term referring to use of ultrasound technology to confirm pregnancy rather than to diagnose fetal anomalies. NIFLA has developed a training manual that it says uses the standards of specific professional medical associations. The organization hosts three-day training sessions several times a year and offers opportunities for continuing education. Between 1998 and his 2012 interview, Glessner stated that NIFLA had trained 2,700 nurses. NIFLA also aids centers with the legal aspects of conversion to medical clinics.

Local centers began medicalizing in the mid-1990s, shortly after NIFLA began promoting the project in 1994.[42] Though pregnancy help movement leaders disagree about the extent to which centers should exchange what Glessner calls a "social services model" for a "medical model" of operation, local centers outside the Birthright network have generally added ultrasound machines and other medical services with enthusiasm.[43] Certainly, Glessner says, local leaders seek to protect their centers against the charge of practicing medicine without a license. Beyond that, however, leaders of local centers that I interviewed often described "going medical," a phrase within the movement that signaled the addition of an ultrasound machine, conversion to a licensed medical clinic, and adoption of any operational changes those entail, as a landmark in their center's history that ushered in much positive growth and change. The director of the center the Pregnancy Clinic, featured in this chapter's opening, told me her center was one of the earliest to go medical and professed that the percentage of clients who changed their intentions about having an abortion increased rapidly after the addition of ultrasound. Others in the pregnancy center movement told me they appreciated the opportunity the new technology provided for them to raise the overall level of professionalism at their centers and rethink other aspects of their work. Respondents to my 2012 Pregnancy Center Staff Survey overwhelmingly agreed (95 percent, 58 percent strongly), "If all women could learn the facts of fetal development and see an ultrasound image of their unborn child, the number of U.S. abortions would drop substantially."

In addition to medicalizing, pregnancy centers in the early to mid-1990s began updating their approach to counseling. Specifically, former Heartbeat International board member Mary Hamm said in her interview, they more thoroughly and consciously embraced the "woman-centered" counseling approach (see Chapter 2) that the movement still claims to use today. The "baby-centered" approach of the 1980s was left behind. Hamm also credited specific researchers' work for inspiring revision to pregnancy centers' thinking about the psychology of abortion decision making and how they might most effectively reach abortion-minded women. She said they realized "the humanity of the unborn child was not the issue for women to choose abortion or not to choose abortion. They knew it was a baby. . . . It was a lot of their own self-image and the fact that having a baby at this time in their life felt like a threat to the inner core." This perspective can be reconciled with pregnancy centers' new emphasis on ultrasound imaging by understanding what pregnancy centers said they expected to accomplish with that tool. The goal was not to change a woman's cognition about the humanity of the fetus but to encourage her to embrace what she saw on the screen as her unborn child, promoting emotional bonding. The aim was also to deliver a service leaders hoped would attract clients. If the testimony of one local center director I interviewed is representative, the sequelae of medicalization, professionalization, and renewed commitment to woman-centered service has included reforms to the way some evangelizing centers handled that work. That director said her center switched from being "really evangelical in a bad way" to "doing it in a better way" in which they strove to let clients see Christ through their love rather than thrusting Bibles into their hands.

Pregnancy centers have taken still other steps to increase their professionalism. Though the movement still greatly depends on volunteers, national leaders said their centers are increasingly adding paid employees to their staff. Although likely a minority of centers, some pregnancy centers even include licensed social workers on their counseling staff.[44] Beginning in 2001, major national pregnancy center associations released the first version of what is now called their "Commitment of Care and Competence," which lays out ethical standards these organizations and their affiliated local centers are expected to meet. As of 2011, according to Hartshorn, all national pregnancy center associations except for Birthright, which says it agrees with the standards but has a policy against collaborations with other organizations, had adopted the commitment.[45] National pregnancy center associations have also begun partnerships with outside organizations, usually Christian professional associations, to offer credentials to pregnancy center staff who had completed relevant training and demonstrated certain competencies, in fields such as peer counseling and financial management. Care Net, Heartbeat International, and NIFLA offer consulting services to their affiliates, and a number of independent organizations also offer training, consulting, materials, prepackaged programs, and other professional services to pregnancy centers. Many of these were developed by individuals with histories of working in the pregnancy help movement, including the EWYL program; Plans for You, a consulting enterprise run by one of my interviewees that specializes in teaching fund-raising and effective evangelization; and Loving and Caring, a producer of materials for pregnancy centers founded by former maternity home directors well regarded among pregnancy help leaders.

This expansionary period for pregnancy centers has included other efforts geared toward attracting more clients at risk for abortion. Among other things, although they are perceived to have lagged in embracing it, centers have more recently been harnessing modern online information technologies to reach and communicate with, as well as make themselves more accessible to, their target audience. Heartbeat International and Care Net jointly launched the Option Line crisis pregnancy contact center in 2003 and gradually enhanced its capacities; Care Net launched its own Pregnancy Decision Line in 2012. By 2012, 96 percent and 69 percent, respectively, of centers affiliated with the three biggest networks reported on my Pregnancy Center Director Survey that they used websites and Facebook pages to reach clients. One-quarter of centers said they offered clients the option to contact them by text message or web chat outside of normal business hours, and 23 percent said they advertised on Google. In

2005, Care Net and Heartbeat International announced a joint effort to start more pregnancy centers in urban areas, where women seeking abortions are believed to disproportionately reside and where abortion providers have concentrated.[46] Promotion of this project was a major theme of Care Net's 2011 conference. Consistent with Johnson's recommendations, Care Net at the time of my research had been challenging pregnancy centers to update their cosmetic appearance to make them more appealing to abortion-minded clients: its vice president, in an interview, reported sending trainers out to local centers to help their directors assess how they might be perceived through the eyes of a twenty-one-year-old, abortion-minded woman. The vice president also noted that Care Net had been commissioning research to inform its outreach to target clientele, such as a survey of women who had undergone or considered abortion.

Resource Growth

The medicalization and professionalization of pregnancy centers has required expenditures not only for the ultrasound machines but also nurses' and other employees' salaries, administration, and larger, redecorated office space. Donors appear to have responded. Kelly suggests that the professionalization trend has indeed coincided with strong financial growth in the movement, citing the expanding budgets of the Care Net and Heartbeat International national offices and the favorable comparison of their financial situations to those of other pro-life groups.[47] Well known throughout the movement is the Baby Bottle Boomerang, a popular fund-raising program invented by one of my interviewees, Elaine Ham, when she was tasked with raising money for her pregnancy center's medicalization. It involves collecting money in physical baby bottles passed through churches. Pro-life and Christian organizations from outside the pregnancy help movement, including Focus on the Family, the Southern Baptist Convention, and the Knights of Columbus (a Catholic men's fraternal group), offer grants to help pregnancy centers purchase ultrasound machines and cover related costs.[48] Meanwhile, donors continue to support pregnancy centers' provision of material aid through means such as "baby showers" organized by church groups.

Multiple leaders speculated that this resource growth in the pregnancy center movement was, perhaps ironically, in part because of pro-choice activists' attacks on pregnancy centers. The press they generated, these leaders reasoned, raised pro-life citizens' awareness that the pregnancy center movement existed in the first place.

When asked specifically about whether they thought political circumstances contributed to resource growth at their organizations, a handful of interviewees speculated that they might have. The Pregnancy Clinic's director observed that the pro-choice agendas of former presidents Clinton and Barack Obama did "wake up the churches a bit" to supporting her pregnancy center, contrasting those periods to the complacency she had perceived during the Reagan years. A second leader detected a similar phenomenon at her center. "People who donate to us want to do something because they are frustrated by the lack of respect for the sanctity of human life," she stated. Between eight years of Clinton, eight years of George W. Bush, and four years of Obama, she attested, her center received more donations when there was an "anti-life person" in the White House. She said she was puzzled by that but suspected donors were responding to what they heard in the media. She also said people came to her frequently, stirred up over what was happening in politics: "It seems we get more passionate about what we do . . . when anti-life rhetoric is spoken all the time." This perception was not universal, for one local center leader denied that donations rose and fell with political events.

Interviewees allowing a role for the political opportunity structure did not suggest that political setbacks spurred resource shifts from political to pregnancy center activism. Instead, they portrayed setbacks in abortion politics as creating a sense of threat that mobilized otherwise inactive pro-life citizens into doing something about abortion. Pregnancy centers were merely one of many beneficiaries of this renewed pro-life mobilization. Hartshorn attested in her interview to increasingly meeting people in her movement who attributed their involvement to the 2008 election of Obama. "I think people are realizing they've got to do something," Birthright's Weaver speculated. Although echoing the view that the Obama presidency had spurred public support for pregnancy centers and other pro-life organizations, the Baby Bottle Boomerang's Ham shared a hunch that political events "helped to educate people that there is such a [pregnancy center] movement."

Interviewees also credited some of the movement's resource growth to divine inspiration and intervention. Ham traces the Baby Bottle Boomerang's origins to the banquet of the pregnancy center for which she had then worked as development director, when the center's board of directors surprised her by announcing that "as God provided the funds, they would purchase ultrasound for all three locations." Ham told me that as she later pondered the immensity of the challenge of raising $100,000, "He [God] directed my eyes to a baby bottle that was sitting on my credenza." She calls her program "a gift from God to pregnancy centers." James Farmer, a Catholic priest who had helped some Maryland citizens raise money to start a new pregnancy center, reported that after starting to come in rapidly, donations dried up with the group just halfway to its goal. One day, however, on a fishing trip he took with some men from his parish, one of the men caught an unusually high number of fish and apparently discerned in that a prompting from God to make a major donation to the future pregnancy center. Right afterward, a second man Farmer had fished with years before contacted him seemingly out of the blue to donate the rest of the money the center needed. The priest contended, "You just can't explain that in human terms." That new center's director, during her interview with me, commented on a much smaller way in which she suggested she saw God providing for her center, in response to a comment I had made upon arriving about a painting that adorned the lobby. That painting, she said, had captured the attention of two separate groups shopping for decorations for the center, but its $40 price had exceeded their budget. Not long afterward, a supporter donated to the center a painting she bought for a relative, but that the relative had not needed—the very painting center staff had coveted.

Continued Medicalization

As data collection for my study proceeded, a segment of pregnancy center leaders continued to voice concerns that their movement had suffered some "mission drift." Specifically, staff at many local centers had grown too comfortable with the relatively safe and rewarding work of offering classes and material aid to women who had chosen to be mothers, and in the process the staff had lost sight of the movement's original "crisis intervention" mission—meaning outreach to pregnant women at risk for having abortions. Too heavy an emphasis on material aid and social services in centers' marketing and physical appearance, some further suggested, might even be undermining that mission. Leader interviews suggested a growing willingness in the movement to face up to a realization research and experience were increasingly making clear: many of the women not visiting pregnancy centers were having abortions because they did not want to be mothers at the time the pregnancy occurred.

Given that, the typical contemporary, abortion-minded woman would likely be bothered, if not repelled, by the stocks of baby clothing and furniture and baby-themed decor of the typical pregnancy center. Further, material aid and EWYL programs allegedly demanded much of centers' physical space and staff time but were of limited effectiveness in persuading such women to carry their pregnancies to term. Women's decision making about abortion, NIFLA's Glessner argued in his interview, involves matters "much deeper" than whether they can obtain a full closet of clothes; likewise, their ability to afford baby furniture and supplies was unlikely to be a high-priority consideration for women just learning about an unintended pregnancy. Care Net's vice president raised a similar point, citing findings from a survey her organization had recently commissioned of women who had previously chosen or considered abortion. She said that survey found that fewer than 1 percent of respondents named practical, material resources as what they most wanted while making their abortion decision; what most women wanted instead was a conversation with a trained counselor. It was only after committing to carrying the pregnancy to term that the typical woman would grow more concerned about all the things she would need to buy for the baby.

The proposed solution, along with proactive efforts to reach their target clientele, was that pregnancy centers needed to pay attention to their branding and to offer services that abortion-minded women would value. Citing such reasoning, into the 2010s, leaders within the three major networks portrayed continued medicalization of pregnancy centers as a key part of their vision for the future of the movement. For some, further medicalization would not only better position pregnancy centers to compete with abortion providers for pregnant clients but also create opportunities for the centers to communicate their messages about sexual integrity more extensively and credibly, advancing lifestyle changes they expected would reduce abortions, improve women's well-being, and strengthen families. Along these lines, Hartshorn writes of a vision in which medical pregnancy centers, in partnership with "one hundred percent pro-life medical practices," eventually could "eclipse Planned Parenthood ... and become the leading providers of true women's health care," which she defines as care that "protects and enhances a woman's gift of fertility" and that does not carry the health risks or the negative social consequences she attributed to abortion and contraceptives.[49]

Pregnancy centers' increasing involvement in offering testing and in some cases treatment for sexually transmitted infections and diseases (STI/STDs) is one step in the implementation of that vision. At Care Net's 2011 conference, representatives of one Missouri pregnancy center discussed how a location they had dedicated to STI/STDs and other reproductive health testing was enabling them to attract young clients and establish relationships with them prior to the incidence of pregnancy, not only potentially drawing more abortion-minded clients to them for pregnancy testing but also creating teachable moments intended to persuade women and men to change their sexual lifestyles.[50] According to the Charlotte Lozier Institute's pregnancy center service report, in 2017, one-quarter of pregnancy centers affiliated with any umbrella organization offered STI/STD testing, and nearly one-fifth offered STI/STD treatment.[51]

In an interview in 2012, Heartbeat International's Hartshorn shared with me a developing innovation in the delivery of her vision for women's health care: the imminent opening of Fertility Education and Medical Management (FEMM) centers. FEMM centers would teach alternative methods of family planning based on knowledge of a woman's monthly cycle and would also focus on treating reproductive and other health-care problems with approaches that did not involve a prescription for a birth control pill. Hartshorn said that FEMM centers might not be considered part of the pro-life movement but a creative outgrowth of it that would work with pregnancy centers. As of September 2018, the FEMM program's website listed twenty-seven affiliated health centers, eighteen of which were located in the United States.[52]

Johnson has been spreading a vision for pregnancy centers, and has also helped to open one in that mold, that is even bolder in its extent of medicalization. As she told the *National Catholic Register* in 2014, the ideal pregnancy center would be one capable of competing with Planned Parenthood:

> It would look like a professional medical facility. You have nursing staff there, a nurse practitioner or a mid-level clinician that would be able to see women for annual exams, breast health, pap smears, STD testing—possibly some more advanced treatment like endometrial biopsy or things like that. A center that would be able to test and treat high cholesterol, high blood pressure, diabetes; it would be able to comprehensively treat a woman.
>
> . . . It's something that Planned Parenthood can't even really do, and it is what you have to do if you want to be competitive. You have to provide services that people can't get at Planned Parenthood, and the services they can get you have to provide with better quality.

Additionally, she stated, whereas Planned Parenthood charges fees, at such pregnancy centers "you can get health care completely free."[53]

Not everyone in the pregnancy center movement endorses a strategy in which pregnancy centers aspire to compete with Planned Parenthood and transform themselves into comprehensive health clinics to do so. Birthright prohibits its centers from offering medical services, though its US director said when interviewed that her center would help women obtain and would pay for an ultrasound if the woman wanted one. The fear, according to a different center director in the Birthright/1st Way Pregnancy Centers wing, is that these services and the requisite fund-raising could shift the organizational culture away from the focus on friendship envisioned by Birthright's founder. Though some 1st Way centers have added professional staff and medical capacity, and her own center had added ultrasound technology, Denise Cocciolone of the National Life Center and 1st Way stated flatly that she did not want her center to be like Planned Parenthood, that is, to mimic some of its practices.[54] Meanwhile, in interviews, Care Net's medical consultant and Heartbeat International's president opined that it was not necessary or even desirable for all pregnancy centers to medicalize. Even for those centers offering medical services, Care Net's medical consultant said, the organization's leaders conceptualized them as additional and balanced with existing services rather than as a wholesale transition in the way a pregnancy center worked.

No one in the movement seemed willing to jettison certain key features that they suggested made pregnancy centers different from, and a threat to, Planned Parenthood. These included their alleged attention to more aspects of a woman's well-being, including her spiritual well-being, the quality of the relationships they formed with clients, and of course the idea that they saw their services as affirming rather than destroying life. Care Net's Melinda Delahoyde stated in her interview with me of pregnancy center directors, "We're the anti-Planned Parenthood."

FACTORS SHAPING TACTICAL INNOVATION IN THE PREGNANCY HELP MOVEMENT

This narrative of innovation in the pregnancy help movement's approach to fighting abortion suggests that many factors associated with the tactical choices of SMOs (see Chapter 1) contributed. Leaders suggested that the contraction of political opportunities symbolized by two near-misses at the Supreme Court and the election of a pro-choice president packed into the 1989–1992 period helped motivate a concerted effort to improve their effectiveness at reducing abortion, thus contributing indirectly to pregnancy centers' most salient innovation, the addition of ultrasound imaging. Overall, however, tactical innovation in the pregnancy help movement appears much less responsive to the opportunity structure for changing abortion policy than it is to abortion incidence itself. Leaders' accounts also highlighted their responsiveness to social conditions incorporated in their problem definitions of abortion. This sensitivity to indicators of the magnitude of a problem is arguably consistent with the humanitarian motivations several scholars have attributed to SMOs' service provision and with what Elizabeth Armstrong calls, in discussing the rise of a people- and service-intensive stream of anti-AIDS activism, the "logic of responding to an epidemic."[55] The nature of activists' responses to objective and perceived changes in the magnitude of the abortion problem—at least, the responses that had managed sufficient distribution and durability to be captured in my research—appeared constrained by ideology. This is not so much left-right political ideology, however, as activists' religious beliefs, especially about sex and sexuality but also, to some extent, about an evangelical mission. Activists portray tactical innovation as emerging from a learning process. This learning involved evolution in activists' understandings of their target group and the nature of the abortion problem as well as grassroots-level experimentation with new services and practices. As they innovated, activists appeared to take cues from reference groups in other fields, most importantly health, social services, education, and ministry.

This narrative of innovation in the pregnancy help movement also shows striking evidence of interaction between the pregnancy help movement and its pro-choice countermovement, especially that countermovement's service-providing organizations. In Chapter 2, I observed that Summerhill identified an abortion referral service as one of her inspirations for founding what appears to have been the world's first pregnancy center. Later, some women who had undergone abortions would find their way into pregnancy centers, where they would help shape centers' work and inspire a significant shift in messaging across multiple streams of the pro-life movement. Like those of Planned Parenthood, some pregnancy center staff members would enter schools and other community venues to teach about sex. As pro-choice advocates amplified some women's negative experiences at pregnancy centers, pregnancy centers fought for their own survival and relevance. As abortion providers, year after year, drew upward of 1 million pregnant women into their doors, pregnancy centers sought new ways to more effectively compete for these clients. In doing so, pregnancy centers adapted some of the features of abortion providers to their own work and are challenging themselves to continue this effort.

How well is this story of movement-countermovement competition borne out by other evidence? My Pregnancy Center Director Survey offered some indicators of centers' medicalization, professionalization, and related innovation as well as one indicator of countermovement strength: whether an abortion clinic operated in the same city, county, or metropolitan area as the pregnancy center. Table 4.1 specifies those indicators and compares them based on whether a center reported an abortion clinic in its community. Across these four indicators, results suggested that pregnancy centers with an abortion clinic in their city, county, or metropolitan area had more extensively medicalized and professionalized and were devoting more resources to attracting abortion-minded clients than were centers lacking local competition from an abortion clinic. For example, 71 percent of centers that said there was an abortion clinic in their city, county, or metropolitan area offered onsite medical services, compared with 49 percent among those responding that there was not an abortion clinic or that they did not know if one existed (chi2(1) = 24.3, p < .001).

The statistics in Table 4.1 alone are not evidence that the presence of an abortion clinic spurred pregnancy centers to medicalize, professionalize, and advertise online to reach women inclined toward abortion. Among other things, the results might signal a pregnancy center's location in a densely populated area where a larger potential donor pool might be available. However, they are consistent with such a story. They are also consistent with the policies of at least one major contributor to pregnancy centers' acquisition of ultrasound machines, Focus on the Family's Option Ultrasound Program, of which the grant-making criteria favor centers in cities with multiple abortion providers and in states with liberal abortion access policies.[56]

The Pregnancy Center Director Survey also enables preliminary tests for evidence consistent with some aspects of pregnancy centers' learning curve story—specifically, whether there is evidence of some interviewees' perceptions that medicalized settings appeal to abortion-minded women whereas a large material aid and social service operation deters them. I approximate the scale of centers' material aid and social service offerings with two variables.

Table 4.1 Pregnancy Center Innovations, by Presence of an Abortion Clinic

	Abortion Clinic in Community	No Abortion Clinic
Percent offering "onsite medical services, such as limited obstetrical ultrasound or early prenatal care"	71.2***	49.0
Percent using Google advertisements to reach clients	33.8***	14.4
Percent offering professional counseling	14.7*	7.7
Mean number of paid employees	7.3***	4.3

Source: Pregnancy Center Director Survey.

Note: *p < .05; **p < .01, ***p < .001, from chi-square (on percents) and t-tests (on means). N = 480 (medical), 454 (Google), 477 (professional counseling), 495 (employees).

One is the number of goods and services from Figure 2.1, excluding the three medical services, a center reported providing. Another is directors' estimates of the percentage of the center's clientele seeking material aid for children already born.[57]

Results are mixed. The number of material goods and social services centers report providing is uncorrelated with the share of clients estimated to be considering abortion ($r = -0.03$, $p < .59$). I find a modest negative correlation, however, between the estimated share of *total* clients who have come to obtain material aid for children already born and the estimated share of *pregnancy-test* clients who consider abortion ($r = -0.27$, $p < .001$).

Meanwhile, Figure 4.1 shows that centers that offered medical services beyond pregnancy testing reported substantially higher percentages of clients contemplating abortion than centers that did not. Of nonmedical centers, 56 percent reported that fewer than 10 percent of their pregnancy clients were considering abortion, compared with 22 percent of medical centers. Of medical centers, 16 percent reported that more than 50 percent of their clients were considering abortion, compared with just 3 percent of nonmedical centers. Repeating the cross tabulations separately for centers that did and did not report an abortion clinic in their community continued to yield large differences, in which centers offering medical services reported higher shares of clients considering abortion than centers not offering medical services. Using chi-square

Figure 4.1 Estimated Percentage of Clients Considering Abortion, by Medical Status and Presence of an Abortion Clinic

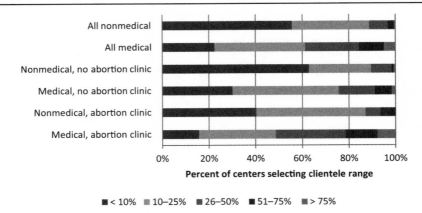

Source: Pregnancy Center Director Survey. N = 449–450.

tests, differences observed in these three comparisons were statistically significant, all at p < .001.

CONCLUSION

Over time, pregnancy centers' approach to solving the problem of abortion has evolved. Pregnancy centers have greatly increased their attention to influencing the lifestyles of clients and others in their communities, especially concerning sex, religion, and parenting. They are also working hard to attract abortion-minded clients to their offices, most importantly by highlighting medical over social service provision and professionalizing their images as well as their practices. As this has happened, especially over the past two decades, the resources of the pregnancy center movement have increased substantially.

What explains this strategy shift and the corresponding growth in resources? Activists' framing of these matters touches on a number of factors. Consistent with political process theory, receiving some mention is the contraction of political opportunity for outlawing abortion that many activists had begun to perceive by the early 1990s. Activists suggested this increased their sense of the urgency of their work. However, activists' accounts emphasized other factors more heavily. One of these is movement-countermovement interplay, involving the existential threats pro-choice activists' public relations and legal action posed to pregnancy centers as well as pregnancy centers' growing conception of themselves as competing with abortion providers for clients. Another is a learning process concerning the nature of abortion decision making, the effectiveness of various interventions, and more recent strategies for target-group outreach that activists said they were learning from research and their abortion-providing counterparts. Activists suggested that what they have learned, among other things, raises doubt about the effectiveness of a pregnancy center model that emphasizes making baby-related goods and social services available to needy women. Explaining innovation, activists also often cited the efforts of individuals who became entrepreneurs for a particular change, either at the national level or within a particular local center. To many activists, the movement's innovation and growth also reflect God's inspiration and provision.

The movement's framing of pregnancy centers' changing tactics suggests that activists' purported *goal* of serving women and *desire* to save the unborn sometimes work in tension. Activists voicing concern about "mission drift," pushing centers to practice more aggressive client outreach, and promoting increased emphasis on medical relative to social services appear to perceive that too much of a focus on serving women—or at least serving the wrong kind of women with the wrong kind of service—can compromise opportunities to save babies. Of course, widening the availability of free health-care services, should pregnancy centers continue to move in this direction, might very well be objectively good for women's well-being and a resource that poor women do value more than cribs, baby clothing, and diapers. Therefore, it is not clear that this would represent a retreat from woman-centered service, or, if the pullback from social services is largely cosmetic, a retreat from centers' commitment to meeting poor families' material needs. I revisit this idea when speculating on the future of the pregnancy help movement in Chapter 7.

The apparent tension between serving women and stopping abortion reflected in some movement leaders' efforts to refocus on a "crisis intervention" mission might also suggest something more generalizable about service-providing SMOs. People who participate in them arguably fulfill dual roles as volunteers and as activists in the social movement with which they identify. The two characters theoretically display differences in worldview, goals, methods, style, and perhaps temperament.[58] They work within venues popularly believed to be governed by different values and conventions.[59] Some conflict over the balance of volunteer and activist roles, within activists themselves and also at the movement level, where strategic decisions are made, might be inherent in the nature of service-providing SMOs. This tension might spur frequent reassessment of and adjustment to tactics, including even reevaluation of the SMOs' "logic" or "field."

I next turn to understanding the attractiveness of pregnancy help outreach to present-day pro-life activists—those whose initiative and funds make it possible for pregnancy centers to open and sustain themselves in a community (see Chapter 5)—and those who staff the centers and other service providers, on whose labor and talent the movement depends (see Chapter 6). In Chapter 5, I ask whether the same kinds of factors that activists cited in their movement's tactical innovation and resource growth also predict patterns in the distribution of pregnancy centers across the United States. Such analyses shed light on the character of the pregnancy center movement as well as the correlates of movement-linked service provision.

5. Where Service Provision Flourishes

An overflow crowd packed the chamber of the South Bend, Indiana, Common Council on a May evening in 2018 to learn whether a local pregnancy center, the Women's Care Center, would be allowed to open a new office next door to the site of a proposed abortion clinic. Whether the Women's Care Center could operate there depended on its securing a change in the property's zoning.[1] A city agency had submitted a favorable recommendation,[2] and the heavily Democratic Common Council weeks beforehand had approved the change by a five-to-four margin.[3] Democratic mayor Pete Buttigieg, however, had vetoed the zoning change, arguing that enabling a pregnancy center and an abortion clinic to exist side by side could invite conflict detrimental to the neighborhood.[4] The council was meeting to vote on whether to override that veto.

The conflict had reached the national news, perhaps because of the identities of the major players. Buttigieg was regarded as a rising star in national Democratic politics. The would-be abortion provider belonged to Whole Woman's Health Alliance, a Texas-based network of abortion clinics and the winning plaintiff in a major abortion case decided by the US Supreme Court in 2015, *Whole Woman's Health v. Cole*. The Women's Care Center also was not the typical local pregnancy center, at least in terms of scale. Founded in 1984 by a University of Notre Dame professor, by 2018 it had grown into the largest pregnancy "center" in the country, operating twenty-nine offices in ten states and claiming to serve 26,000 women per year. It was a relatively professionalized pregnancy center that offered ultrasounds and other supports, including "healthy baby education, free vitamins, parenting and life skills classes, self-sufficiency support, cribs, diapers, free children's books to promote literacy, and strong father's groups."[5] The new center would have been its fourth in South Bend. The organization's president claimed, "Two of every three babies born in South Bend now start with our centers."[6]

The case had likely also attracted attention because of its implications for abortion access in northern Indiana. South Bend, a city of just over 100,000 residents and a nearly 27 percent poverty rate, perhaps best known as the home of the University of Notre Dame, had lacked an abortion provider since

2015.[7] That former clinic had stopped offering abortions and eventually closed amid a state investigation encouraged by a local right-to-life group. That investigation eventually led to the suspension of its physician's medical license on grounds of reporting and medical practice violations.[8] Whole Woman's Health had also been facing barriers in its effort to open a South Bend clinic. It claimed that "multiple landlords refused to rent to us," and it was caught up in a legal battle over the Indiana State Department of Health's denial of its application for a license.[9]

The major arguments of each side in the high-profile case are representative of those in the national battle over pregnancy centers. Whole Woman's Health alleged that pregnancy centers generally and the Women's Care Center specifically used lies and shame to block women from accessing abortion. A Whole Woman's Health spokesperson quoted in South Bend's WNDU news alleged, "I think just having them in that close of proximity is, their purpose is to try to confuse women and trick them into coming someplace that they didn't mean to go."[10] A Women's Care Center representative argued that the center's logo, which depicts a woman kissing a baby, should clearly signal its pro-life position. She told the *South Bend Tribune*, "The choice that a woman makes is her own. Our work is not persuasion, our work is not coercion. . . . We offer women an opportunity to choose life. We don't intend or purport to do anything else."[11] She said that a donor funding the new center had mandated that it be located next to the future abortion clinic.[12] In the national media, on the *Whole Woman's Health* blog, a leader of the organization shared a story from its Peoria, Illinois, clinic in which a couple allegedly accidentally went to the adjacent Women's Care Center instead, were led to believe they were in the abortion clinic, and then were confronted with an image from the woman's ultrasound decorated with "Hi Mommy" and "Hi Daddy" stickers.[13] A writer in the conservative *National Review* offered statistics on massive abortion rate drops and the closing of abortion providers in the years after Women's Care Center offices opened in communities, arguing that these showed women gaining the resources to exercise choice.[14]

The South Bend conflict, as with debates elsewhere over policy related to pro-life pregnancy centers, turns on both sides' very different ideas about what sorts of organizations pregnancy centers are. To what extent are they service-providing versus activist organizations? Are they closer to the mainstream or the radical end of the pro-life movement? To what extent are their motives and their daily work concerned with providing tangible help to women who do not want abortions versus trying to halt those women who do?

Although the evidence I have presented so far in this book has suggested that pregnancy centers fall closer to the former option than the latter on each of these three questions, much of it has relied on words of the movement's own participants. There are also other reasons for reluctance in accepting that narrative. Among them, in Chapter 4, I attributed some important strategic changes in the pregnancy center movement to national movement leaders' responsiveness to declining abortion incidence, adversity faced by colleagues in the pro-life movement's political stream, and the activity of pro-choice activists. I also called attention to voices pushing pregnancy centers to be more aggressive in their efforts to attract women planning to have abortions. Additionally, some scholars have suggested that the pregnancy centers being opened after *Roe*'s first decade tended to be founded by different kinds of people than those early leaders I profiled in Chapter 3. Those later pregnancy center founders, unlike the humanitarian first responders, allegedly had reasons for discouragement that the legal right to abortion would be rolled back anytime soon, and their experimentation with new and increasingly aggressive tactics reflected that desperation.[15]

Motives are virtually impossible to verify empirically, but evidence more consistent with some than others might manifest itself in data not subject to possible interpretive biases: the locations of pregnancy centers. As seen in the South Bend case and elsewhere, pro-choice activists point to pregnancy centers' alleged tendencies to locate near abortion providers as evidence of their subversive character and of a mission more tightly wedded to the imperative of stopping abortions than helping women.[16] They do not lack basis for doing so, given that one of the most aggressive proponents of this strategy has been Robert Pearson, the same activist who recommended other aggressive and ethically suspect pregnancy center practices during the 1980s. During my research I encountered examples of pregnancy centers that followed it. Opening in close proximity to an abortion clinic need not mean that the pregnancy center founders are disinterested in helping women; in Chapter 2, I showed that an important part of the belief system they articulate is that most women do not really want to have abortions but merely perceive that they have no better realistic options. However, if pregnancy centers are concentrating their resources strategically near abortion providers and maintaining less of a presence in communities likely to have large numbers of low-income women who do not want abortions, this might be a clue to the prominence of stopping abortion in pregnancy centers' missions.

Analysis of geographical patterns in pregnancy centers' proliferation can also contribute to a more general understanding of where movement-linked direct service flourishes. In the analysis that follows, I look at how well indicators of problematic social conditions, activists' competition with their countermovement, and the political opportunity structure, among other factors, are associated with variation in where pregnancy centers open and where they are most numerous. I first examine variation in pregnancy centers' prevalence across states and then look at the extent to which they operate in communities with an abortion clinic and in high-poverty communities.

Research assistants and I used information from an online directory of pregnancy centers to count the number of them by state and zip code. The directory, published by a maternity home network called Several Sources Shelters, contained 2,663 entries as of spring 2013.[17] Further analysis discovered that this total included other types of service providers of pro-life pregnancy help: 155 local Catholic Charities affiliates, 51 affiliates of the Bethany Christian Services adoption agency, 166 other social service charities (e.g., Catholic Social Services, Catholic Family Services), 21 "hotlines" or "helplines," and 52 organizations known or presumed from their names to be maternity homes. The remaining 2,218 organizations, or 83.3 percent of entries, were presumed pregnancy centers. Most of the analysis I present here is limited to pregnancy centers, given that they have a shorter history and different relationship to the abortion conflict than the other types of organizations, and thus a different set of factors might influence their locations. I replicated all analysis with the full dataset, however, and share theoretically or empirically interesting differences when they appear.

EXPLAINING STATE-LEVEL DIFFERENCES
IN PREGNANCY CENTER PROLIFERATION

I look first at how and why the prevalence of pregnancy centers varies across states.[18] Excluding the District of Columbia with its three pregnancy centers, the jurisdiction with the fewest pregnancy centers is Rhode Island (four). Populous California perhaps unsurprisingly encompasses the most pregnancy

Figure 5.1 Number of Pregnancy Centers per 500,000 Population, by State, 2013

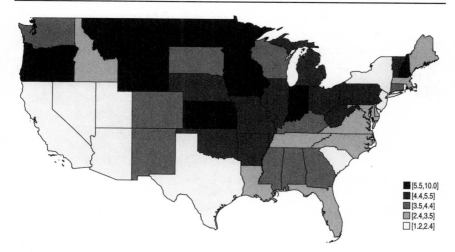

[5.5,10.0]
[4.4,5.5]
[3.5,4.4]
[2.4,3.5]
[1.2,2.4]

Source: Author's analysis of Several Sources Shelters pregnancy center directory and population data from the US Census Bureau.

centers (156). More meaningful statistics adjust for population size: the number of pregnancy centers per 500,000 state residents. This figure ranged from a low of 1.2 in Utah to a high of 10.0 in Montana and averaged 4.2 nationally.

Figure 5.1 maps population-adjusted numbers of pregnancy centers by state. This map arguably bears little relationship to the familiar red-blue Electoral College maps of US presidential elections since 2000. Pro-life pregnancy centers are generally most numerous relative to the population in the northern United States, especially the Great Plains states (which lean Republican) and the Midwestern states (which leaned Democratic in the first decade of the 2000s). They are scarcest in the Southwest. As shown in Figure 5.2, the distribution of all listed pro-life pregnancy help service providers follows a similar pattern.

I gathered data on several theoretically plausible predictors of this interstate variation in the prevalence of pregnancy centers. I will introduce these predictors and my expectations. Appendix B details data sources, indicator construction, and summary statistics.

One potential predictor is the *political opportunity structure* pro-life activists face in each state. Though states cannot ban abortion, courts have allowed them some latitude regarding how they regulate and fund abortion, potentially enabling them to reduce abortion by affecting access. Pro-life activists

Figure 5.2 Number of Pregnancy Help Service Providers per 500,000 Population, by State, 2013

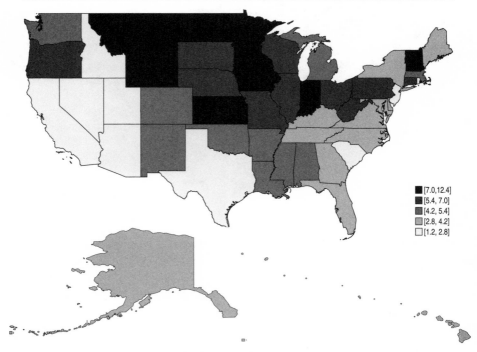

Source: Author's analysis of Several Sources Shelters pregnancy center directory and population data from the US Census Bureau.

have shown great interest in influencing state abortion policy, but some states have been much more responsive to their efforts than have others.[19] I developed a measure tapping the political opportunity structure using NARAL Pro-Choice America's ratings of governors and each state legislative chamber as "pro-choice," "mixed-choice," or "anti-choice" for each two-year election cycle in the first decade of the 2000s. I expect that as the favorability of the pro-life movement's political opportunity structure improves (represented by higher values on the measure), the number of pregnancy centers will decrease.

I measure variation in the magnitude of *problematic social conditions* (as perceived by activists) with state abortion rates (the number of abortions per 1,000 reproductive-age women). I also consider *the intensity of competition from pregnancy centers' countermovement* using the number of abortion providers per 500,000 state residents. If pregnancy centers represent a response to a perceived unmet need for "saving babies" from abortion, or if their openings are part of an effort to compete locally with abortion providers, each of these variables should be positively related to the number of pregnancy centers.

I consider tendencies in the *political ideology* of the public of each state, expecting that pregnancy centers might be most compatible with ideological moderation given their infusion of their antiabortion and proabstinence positions with talk and action promoting the well-being of women and poor people. My measure starts with a state ideological score (on a liberal-conservative spectrum) constructed by Chris Tausanovitch and Christopher Warshaw based on policy issue public opinion poll data.[20] I effectively fold that score so that the highest values of my indicator mark the most ideologically extreme (in either a liberal or conservative direction) state populations. Empirically, I expect that as ideological extremity increases, the number of pregnancy centers will decrease.

Such potential influences on the proliferation of pregnancy centers must be balanced against another important ingredient of social mobilization that might ultimately work at cross-purposes with most or all of them: *movement resources.*[21] To operate, pregnancy centers require a steady stream of donated money, goods, and volunteer labor. These are unlikely to be supplied by anyone who does not share centers' opposition to abortion. Thus, I predict that as public pro-life sentiment increases, the number of pregnancy centers will increase. Given a dearth of updated, comparable state-level opinion polls on abortion, I combine three pieces of data into a composite measure of public pro-life sentiment: Barbara Norrander's and Juliana Pacheco's estimates of state public opinion on legal abortion and the percentage of a state's population composed of white evangelical Protestants.[22]

Pregnancy centers' status as brick-and-mortar, charitable institutions makes it appropriate to control for general market-related considerations that likely affect the number of charities opening in a given area. These can include considerations such as patterns in how population is distributed across land area, perceptions of socioeconomic need, relative wealth of state populations, levels of social capital, the extent to which others are providing a similar service, and the extent to which state and local governments contract out public service provision to nonprofit organizations. Because these are too many variables to control for in a sample of fifty states, I control for the *size of the charitable sector* itself. I gathered data on the number of human service charities

Table 5.1 Correlates of Density of State Pregnancy Help Service Providers

	Pregnancy Centers	*All Pregnancy Help Service Providers*
Pro-life political opportunity index	0.003	0.016
Public pro-life sentiment	0.214	0.184
Public ideological extremity score	−0.134	−0.104
Abortion rate	−0.429**	−0.459**
Abortion providers per 500K pop.	−0.149	−0.099
Human service charities per 500K pop.	0.650**	0.775**

Source: Author's analysis of data from multiple sources, as cited in text and appendix B.

Note: Figures are Pearson correlation coefficients. Density of pregnancy centers and all pregnancy help service providers is measured as total per 500,000 of state population. N = 50. *p <. 05, **p < .01, ***p < .001.

per 500,000 state residents, and I expect that as the size of the charitable sector increases, the number of pregnancy centers will also increase.

The simple correlations in Table 5.1 demonstrate that none of these expectations are borne out, except for the strong positive relationship between the incidence of human service charities and pregnancy centers. The relationship between the abortion rate and the number of pregnancy centers—technically, the natural log of the population-adjusted number of pregnancy centers, as this log transformation is methodologically indicated by the nature of my data—is moderately strong and statistically significant but negative. All other correlation coefficients are statistically insignificant and substantively small (close to zero), indicating the lack of a relationship between variables.

The correlations in Table 5.1, however, fail to take into account the relationships potential predictors of pregnancy centers' proliferation are likely to have with each other. In states where the abortion rate is high or the political opportunity structure is very unfavorable, for example, public opposition to abortion is likely to be relatively low, limiting the resources upon which pro-life activists could draw to fund and staff pregnancy centers. Further, the negative relationship between the abortion rate and pregnancy center prevalence is unlikely to reflect any strategic targeting of states with low abortion rates by pregnancy center activists. It is also unlikely to be mostly a result of long-term impacts pregnancy centers might have had in reducing the abortion rate where they are most numerous, for states' relative rankings with regard to the abortion rate have changed little over time. Instead, the negative relationship between the abortion rate and pregnancy center rate likely signals something else about low-abortion-rate states that makes the formation of pregnancy centers attractive and feasible. I thus performed an ordinary least squares regression analysis on the data in order to estimate each variable's relationship with the number of pregnancy centers while taking into account the values of the other variables. Appendix B contains full statistical results along with additional information about the estimation and sensitivity analyses.

Overall, the six variables explain much of the state-level variation in the incidence of pregnancy centers—about 60 percent, using the model's adjusted R-squared statistic. It remains the case that the more human services charities are operating in a state, the more pregnancy centers are there and that these figures closely correspond. As the population-adjusted number of human services charities increases by 1 percent, the population-adjusted number of pregnancy centers is predicted to increase by a bit more than 1 percent. (Again, technically, I have used in the models the natural log of the number of pregnancy centers per 500,000 state residents as well as the natural logs of the population-adjusted human services charities and abortion providers, and the natural log of the abortion rate.) This suggests that the extent of pregnancy centers' distribution has much to do with that set of generic factors shaping the spread of other human service charities.

Taking this and other variables into account, I now observe some support for some of the other hypotheses. An increase in the key movement resource of public pro-life sentiment is associated with an increase in pregnancy centers. Specifically, the model predicts, an increase in public pro-life sentiment equivalent to one standard deviation corresponds to a statistically significant 17.6 percent increase in the population-adjusted number of pregnancy centers. Results also signal that, all else being equal, an increase in the favorability of the political opportunity structure might diminish the prevalence of pregnancy centers. A one-unit increase in favorability (on a thirty-one-point scale) is associated with a statistically significant decrease of 1.6 percent in the population-adjusted number of pregnancy centers. The remaining variables are not significantly related to the incidence of pregnancy centers. The only change in these basic findings when I replicate the analysis using all pregnancy help service providers in the directory is estimation of a marginally significant (p < .065), negative relationship between ideological extremity and the count of pregnancy help service providers.

Figure 5.3 Predicted Maximum Impact of Factors in State Pregnancy Center Prevalence

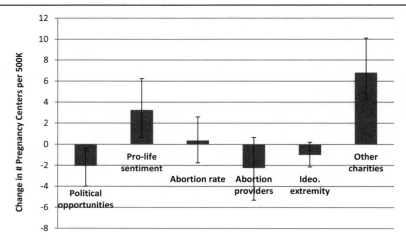

Note: Graph shows change in the state number of pregnancy centers per 500,000 people predicted for each variable's shift from its minimum to maximum value, with all other variables set at their means. Predictions are based on the ordinary least squares regression reported in Appendix B, Table B1.2. Errors bars represent 95 percent confidence intervals on the predictions. N = 50.

Figure 5.3 depicts how the variables analyzed compare in their predicted impacts on the prevalence of pregnancy centers. Specifically, the graph illustrates the change predicted in a state's number of pregnancy centers (per 500,000 people) when each independent variable increases from its minimum to maximum value. My analysis assumes that all other variables are fixed at their means.[23] Such statistical predictions carry uncertainty; thus error bars on the graph mark what quantitative researchers call "95 percent confidence intervals," or a range of likely values for each impact. When this range includes zero, it means there is a good chance the change might have no impact at all, and thus it is not considered "statistically significant."

Underscoring the importance of resources to a movement's ability to sustain service provision, the inclusion of public pro-life sentiment in the model appears especially critical to predicting the number of pregnancy centers as well as to the other findings the model appears to yield. Holding all covariates at their means, my model predicts that change in public pro-life sentiment from its minimum to maximum value will increase the number of pregnancy centers per 500,000 state residents by 3.3 centers; recall that the mean is 4.2 centers per 500,000 and that its value across states ranges from 1.2 to 10. A minimum-to-maximum shift in the favorability of the political opportunity structure, meanwhile, predicts decreases of 2.0 pregnancy centers. Though not statistically significant, the predicted impact of a minimum-to-maximum shift in the incidence of abortion providers is an even larger decrease of 2.2 pregnancy centers. Public pro-life sentiment and abortion provider supply are closely and negatively related, so that if pro-life sentiment is not controlled, the number of abortion providers picks up its effect and becomes a highly statistically significant, still negative, predictor of the prevalence of pregnancy centers.

The finding of a statistically significant relationship between the favorability of the pro-life movement's political opportunity structure and the prevalence of pregnancy centers also depends highly on accounting for public pro-life sentiment. Behind the finding is nonlinearity in the relationship between the favorability of the political opportunity structure and the prevalence of pregnancy centers. Specifically, average numbers of population-adjusted pregnancy centers peak in those states where elected officials' ratings from NARAL average just slightly to the pro-life side of a perfect "mixed choice" score. To some extent this is also the case with public pro-life sentiment, such that the prevalence of pregnancy centers generally rises with this variable but drops off in states with the highest levels of pro-life sentiment. Meanwhile, the favorability of the political opportunity structure and public pro-life sentiment are highly positively correlated ($r = 0.69$). Controlling for public pro-life sentiment effectively models this nonlinearity for political opportunities but in a way that fits the data somewhat better than if the square of the political opportunities index is substituted.[24] If public pro-life sentiment is excluded from the analysis, the estimated relationship between the political opportunity structure and the number of pregnancy centers is much smaller and not statistically significant.

What appears to be happening is that public pro-life sentiment, the favorability of pro-life activists' political opportunity structure, and the incidence of pregnancy centers initially seem to grow together. Even if pro-life movement resources are disproportionately concentrated in pregnancy centers rather than politics in states where the political environment is especially hostile to the cause—something these data cannot discern—any such concentration of resources does not appear to match the growth in pregnancy centers that comes with having more pro-life movement resources in total. Some of the states with the most favorable political opportunity structures, however, end up with fewer pregnancy help organizations than would be expected given their levels of public pro-life sentiment. However, some of the states with the highest levels of public pro-life sentiment also end up with fewer pregnancy centers than the preexisting growth pattern would have suggested. Perhaps pro-life activists in those states with the highest levels of pro-life sentiment and most promising political opportunity structures are too busy with politics—or too complacent—to invest as much into pregnancy centers as they are in states with moderate-to-high levels of these variables. Alternatively, omitted variables or error in concept measurement might explain the difference.

Overall, however, the data signal that higher concentrations of pro-life pregnancy centers in a state say much more about the *cultural strength* of the pro-life movement there than about its *political weakness,* that is, the frustration and despair activists might encounter in their efforts to change abortion policies and reduce the number of abortions. Counted relative to the population, pregnancy centers are much more numerous in those states where abortion rates are low, abortion providers are few, and larger percentages of the public oppose unrestricted access to legal abortion. Such states might offer fewer "babies" for pro-life activists to save from abortion than other states— and yet this is where the pregnancy help movement has its greatest presence.

THE LOCAL CONTEXT OF PREGNANCY CENTERS

Briefly, I zoom into pregnancy centers' local contexts. There, one might observe patterns masked at a level of aggregation as large and heterogeneous as states. I do not attempt a comprehensive model of pregnancy center variation across localities, but I do consider popular claims about where pregnancy centers are located relative to abortion providers and to another group that varies greatly in size across local communities, poor people. I also present some additional data on demographic characteristics of the communities that have pregnancy centers, considering how these compare for communities without pregnancy centers and communities with abortion clinics.

My analysis continues to use the Several Sources Shelters pregnancy center directory from 2013, but I now count centers at the zip-code level. I also use a dataset of abortion providers that I had assembled for another project, using information from 2005. Because a comprehensive directory of abortion providers was not publicly available, I attempted to build my own using multiple partial online directories and provider search functions.[25] The resulting dataset is mostly limited to clinic providers, but clinics performed nearly 95 percent of US abortions in 2005.[26] Given the small number of nonclinic providers included, the resulting dataset of 828 unique entries likely captures most of the 816 clinic-based abortion providers counted by the Alan Guttmacher Institute for 2005.[27]

To estimate pregnancy centers' tendency to locate in close proximity to abortion clinics, I matched pregnancy centers and abortion clinics on zip codes. A superior analysis would calculate proximity between abortion clinics and pregnancy centers based on street address, given that pregnancy centers' alleged strategy is to operate close enough to the abortion provider to intercept its foot traffic. However, analysis of the extent to which pregnancy centers and abortion clinics tend to share the same zip codes can provide preliminary evidence for or against this as a typical pregnancy center location strategy. It can do so by estimating a minimum share of pregnancy centers and abortion clinics *not* located in close proximity.

Geographical overlap between pregnancy centers and abortion clinics is present but not substantial. Of the 828 abortion clinics in my 2005 directory, 34 percent had a pregnancy center in their same zip code as of 2013. Meanwhile, of the 2,218 pregnancy centers, 12 percent were located in zip codes that had housed an abortion provider in 2005. It is possible that additional pregnancy centers might have once had abortion providers in their communities, but given just how many pregnancy centers lacked an abortion clinic in their zip code, accounting for clinic closures and moves is unlikely to affect the conclusion that the typical pregnancy center offers its services away from the site of an abortion clinic.[28] Overall, however, findings are consistent with the state-level results and suggest that shadowing abortion clinics is not a primary factor in most pregnancy centers' location decisions.

Further analysis of the local contexts of pregnancy centers and abortion clinics reveals substantial differences in the types of communities in which they are located. I compared these service providers' local contexts using data from the Census Bureau's American Community Survey (ACS), aggregated from 2007 to 2011 at the level of the Zip Code Tabulation Area (ZCTA). ZCTAs are geographical units used by the Census Bureau that closely correspond to zip codes. Appendix B contains details on the ACS data and on how I matched zip codes to ZCTAs.

Differences between ZCTAs with these different types of service providers say less about the distinguishing characteristics of communities with pregnancy centers, however, than they do about the distinguishing characteristics of communities with abortion clinics. Table 5.2 presents select geographic, demographic, and socioeconomic characteristics of ZCTAs with and without pregnancy centers. It also presents those characteristics for ZCTAs with and without abortion clinics. As might be expected given that providers of any service are likely to want to be located in areas easily accessible to their target clientele and their staff, ZCTAs with pregnancy centers and ZCTAs with abortion clinics are more likely than ZCTAs without them to be located within a metropolitan area and to be more densely populated than the average US ZCTA. Pregnancy centers' metropolitan bias is much less pronounced than that of abortion clinics, however. Nearly every abortion clinic is located in a metropolitan area, compared with three-quarters of pregnancy centers. Further, the data indicate that the average population size of the metropolitan areas in which abortion providers are located is considerably larger than that of the metropolitan areas in which pregnancy centers are located. This does not reflect a scenario in which pregnancy centers have avoided large metropolitan areas—they have not—but one in which the centers are more numerous and also less concentrated in the largest metropolitan areas than abortion clinics are. Not only do abortion clinics concentrate in large metropolitan areas but also they disproportionately locate in densely populated parts of those metropolitan areas. The average population density of ZCTAs with abortion clinics is more than triple that of ZCTAs with pregnancy centers, and still remains well more than double that of ZCTAs with pregnancy centers when nonmetro ZCTAs are excluded (not shown).

The socioeconomic characteristics of ZCTAs with abortion clinics differ from those of ZCTAs without them in a manner consistent with abortion clinics' highly urbanized contexts: these ZCTAs have both higher poverty rates and higher median household incomes along with larger shares of their populations that hold at least a bachelor's degree and identify racially as black. Pregnancy centers, too, just to a lesser degree than abortion clinics, are located in ZCTAs that have higher poverty rates and larger shares of the population who identify as black and who hold at least a bachelor's degree, relative to the US ZCTAs without them, although median household income is lower in ZCTAs with pregnancy centers than in ZCTAs without them. Although other scholars have hypothesized that pregnancy centers are likely to want to open

Table 5.2 Characteristics of Communities with Pregnancy Centers and Abortion Clinics

	ZCTAs w/o Pregnancy Centers	*ZCTAs w/ Pregnancy Centers*	*ZCTAs w/ Abortion Clinics*	*ZCTAs w/o Abortion Clinics*
% in metro area	56.2	74.6***	96.7***	56.5
Metro pop. size	2,796,838	2,976,460	4,730,571***	2,740,688
Pop. density	1193.1	2300.4***	7054.5***	1136.1
Median HH income	51,570.2	49,413.4***	53,220.5**	51,397.0
Poverty rate	14.3	16.5***	18.1**	14.3
% black	7.1	10.7***	16.9***	7.1
Employee % female	46.4	47.9***	47.9	46.4
% with BA degree	15.1	17.9***	24.0***	15.1
% w/ abortion clinic	1.5	11.8***	100.0	0.0
% w/ pregnancy ctr.	0.0	100.0	34.2	5.4
N	31,111	1995	691	32,415

Source: Author's analysis of data from multiple sources, as cited in text and Appendix B.

Note: Asterisks in "ZCTAs w/ Pregnancy Centers" column indicate statistical significance in comparison with "ZCTAs w/o Pregnancy Centers." Asterisks in "ZCTAs w/ Abortion Clinics" column indicate statistical significance in comparison with "ZCTAs w/ Pregnancy Centers": *p < .05, **p < .01, ***p < .001 (two-tailed). N counts total number of ZCTAs meeting column label criteria. Ns for some individual items are reduced slightly because of missing ACS data. They exclude nonmetropolitan ZCTAs in the case of metro population size means.

in areas where relatively fewer women are in the labor force, so as to secure a larger potential volunteer pool, ZCTAs with pregnancy centers and ZCTAs with abortion clinics are identical in terms of a similar measure that might tap gender roles, the percent of employed people who are female.[29]

Although the pro-life movement encounters criticism for failing to aid poor women, some pro-choice advocates have expressed concern that pregnancy centers, in their location decisions, *target* poor women. Care Net and Heartbeat International have openly promoted "Urban Initiatives" to encourage the opening of pregnancy centers in communities in which women in demographic groups with high abortion rates—and poor women's abortion rates are especially high—are likely to reside.[30] These organizations have claimed they need to locate there because their movement's presence in such communities is weak.

Here, I assess only the extent to which pregnancy centers had, as of 2013, penetrated high-poverty communities. "Communities" remain ZCTAs. I define a high-poverty ZCTA as one in which at least 30 percent of the population falls below the federal poverty line; such a figure is twice the 2012 US poverty rate of 15 percent.[31] Using my ACS data, 8.5 percent of US zip codes could be defined as high-poverty zip codes.

Table 5.3 presents the data. Although high-poverty ZCTAs were somewhat less likely to have at least one pregnancy center (5.3 percent) than all other ZCTAs (6.2 percent), the difference is not substantively striking. It also reverses itself when the analysis is limited to metropolitan areas, where high-poverty zip codes become somewhat more likely to have a pregnancy center (9.4 percent) than other ZCTAs (7.9 percent). Pregnancy centers are more likely to have a presence in high-poverty ZCTAs than abortion clinics are (3.3 percent of high-poverty ZCTAs have abortion clinics), although considering that abortion clinics are less numerous, the percentage of high-poverty ZCTAs with at least one abortion clinic exceeds that of other ZCTAs (2.0 percent). Extending the analysis beyond pregnancy centers, 6.4 percent of all high-poverty ZCTAs and 11.7 percent of high-poverty ZCTAs within metropolitan areas housed at least one pro-life pregnancy help service provider.

Another way of looking at the data is considering the percentage of pregnancy centers located in high-poverty communities: 8 percent. This sits right below the percentage of all ZCTAs high in poverty and so is close to the percentage one might expect to find if pregnancy centers were choosing ZCTAs at random. Pregnancy centers' likelihood of being in high-poverty communities increases when abortion clinics are there (15 percent versus 7 percent), although such clinics are not present in 75 percent of the high-poverty ZCTAs where pregnancy centers are located. There is stronger evidence, then, that pregnancy centers are targeting communities with abortion clinics than communities with high poverty rates, but it still leaves the vast majority of pregnancy centers in neither kind of community.

Table 5.3 Pregnancy Help Service Provision in High-Poverty Communities

	High-Poverty ZCTAs	Other ZCTAs	High-Poverty Metro ZCTAs	Other Metro ZCTAs
% w/ a pregnancy center	5.3[+]	6.2	9.4[+]	7.9
% w/ any PHSP	6.4	7.0	11.7[**]	9.0
% w/ an abortion clinic	3.3[***]	2.0	6.9[***]	3.4
N	2758	29684	1340	17180

Source: Author's analysis of data from multiple sources, as cited in text and appendix B.

Note: High-poverty ZCTAs are defined as ZCTAs with poverty rates of 30 percent or more. PHSP = pregnancy help service provider. Asterisks in "High-Poverty ZCTAs" column indicate statistical significance in comparison with other ZCTAs. Asterisks in "High-Poverty Metro ZCTAs" column indicate statistical significance in comparison with other metro ZCTAs: $+p < .10$, $*p < .05$, $**p < .01$, $***p < .001$.

CONCLUSION

Results of the analyses presented in this chapter point to the resource-intensive nature of service provision relative to many other forms of social action and suggest that this and the relative permanence of service-providing institutions inspires attention to the same market considerations that might influence the distribution of charities not linked to social movements. Findings are quite consistent with those of a county-level analysis of pregnancy center locations by McVeigh, Crubaugh, and Estep, who focus especially on Catholic and evangelical Christian adherents. The authors find a curvilinear pattern that they suggest indicates pregnancy centers' need for a "critical mass" of supporters as well as the possibility that complacency might set in when this mass becomes especially large.[32]

Results are also largely inconsistent with a view of pregnancy centers as a tactic strategically deployed by the pro-life movement in areas where opportunities to change abortion law are weakest or where the magnitude of the abortion "problem" and the strength of their countermovement appears the greatest. Other factors being equal, diminished political opportunities might increase the density of pregnancy centers in a given state. In practice, however, pregnancy centers exist in a diverse array of US communities. There is evidence of purposive effort to locate near abortion providers. Most abortion clinics, however, operate without a pregnancy center even in the same zip code, and the overwhelming majority of pregnancy centers work in communities lacking an abortion clinic. The density of these pro-life service providers is greatest in states with relatively low public support for legal abortion, low abortion rates, and few abortion providers.

This is not necessarily the geographical pattern one would expect if activists' urgency about stopping abortion is a leading motive in the establishment of pregnancy centers. It also is not necessarily the pattern one might expect if the movement were geared principally toward helping needy women who choose or want to choose an alternative to abortion, though the pregnancy help movement does not claim this as its only mission. It might not be for lack of trying. Zoning rules or other political or pragmatic barriers might keep pregnancy centers from acquiring property near abortion clinics, and there might be real resource constraints pro-life activists face in starting and maintaining pregnancy centers in the kinds of communities where abortion providers and abortion-seeking women are most likely to be. A story could also be told, consistent with pro-choice activists' narrative about pregnancy center deception, in which pregnancy center founders do not believe they need to locate near real abortion providers in order to attract abortion-seeking women; they can simply pretend to *be* the abortion provider. However, such a strategy is probably not sustainable in the age of online reviews.

The simplest answer to where the pro-life movement's service provision flourishes might be that it is in the communities where those activists who want to offer and can muster the local resources to support it live. It reflects a grassroots character that the movement still retains. Leaders, although encouraging more pregnancy centers to open near abortion providers and in "underserved" urban neighborhoods, appear to be comfortable with this. It makes sense if one accepts the claim that a central movement goal is "that no woman ever feels forced to have an abortion because of lack of support or practical alternatives."[33] The absoluteness of this goal might then render irrelevant to activists the scale of this type of social "need" for pregnancy centers when deciding where to open them. Indeed, another national leader has published a vision that every US community should have a pregnancy center, which he imagines as a cornerstone for the mass distribution of a pro-life culture.[34] Although the geographical spread of pregnancy centers bears the stamps of volunteer and activist identities and both woman-serving and baby-saving missions, it might reflect even more clearly the culture-building strategy Davis and Robinson attribute to large-scale service-providing movements "bypassing the state."[35]

Back in South Bend, pro-choice activists ran a petition drive against the zoning change but expressed the sense that they had been outmobilized. Pro Choice South Bend submitted 355 online signatures to the Common Council before its first vote and increased that somewhat in the following days.[36] The Women's Care Center, meanwhile, claimed to have collected 2,800 signatures.[37] The national "rapid response" pro-choice group Lady Parts Justice League, on the morning of the Common Council's override vote, called on activists to come to the meeting wearing purple.[38] Local news coverage, however, depicted and described the crowd witnessing the council's vote as overwhelmingly attired in the pink shirts or ribbons signaling solidarity with the Women's Care Center.[39]

Still, pro-choice activists had garnered the mayor's support. All council members repeated their original votes, and thus the veto stood.

As the debate had proceeded, however, local public officials weighed in with their perceptions of the Women's Care Center as an organization. WSBT news reported on a local police statement that "only" three reports had been filed with them over a four-year period despite the coexistence of the city's prior abortion clinic and another Women's Care Center office.[40] Other local coverage noted that a neighborhood association had begun fund-raising to buy the Women's Care Center property out of fear that if the Women's Care Center had to put it back up for sale, a "more confrontational" antiabortion group competing against the Women's Care Center to buy the site in the first place would move in instead.[41] Buttigieg's veto message recognized a written commitment the Women's Care Center had made to prohibit abortion clinic protestors from using its property but said the center's control over protest activity would be limited. It also acknowledged the Women's Care Center's addition to its website of a statement that it did not provide abortions and expressed the mayor's "great respect and appreciation for the people who serve at the Women's Care Center, and for the work that they do to support new and expecting parents."[42]

What happened after the mayor's veto was sustained arguably continues to illustrate the mix of service-provision and activist goals of pregnancy centers as well as some of the local dynamics that might be contributing to the kinds of spatial patterns observed in this chapter. Weeks after the vote, the Women's Care Center announced that it had purchased property across the street from the proposed abortion clinic that would not require a zoning change.[43] Meanwhile, Whole Woman's Health as of October 2018 continued to battle the Indiana State Department of Health to gain its license to offer abortions. Although it had persuaded a judge to take its side in the case, the Department of Health was appealing that decision.[44] Earlier, the Women's Care Center had pledged that it would open in the targeted neighborhood regardless of whether the abortion clinic did.[45]

6. The Politics of Pregnancy Help Activist Mobilization

In laying out his vision for renewal and reform of pro-lifers' efforts to end abortion and build a broader "culture of life," National Association of Family and Life Advocates (NIFLA) president Tom Glessner writes, "Perhaps one of the failings of the pro-life efforts over the last twenty-five years has been the fact that it has basically become wedded to one political party—the Republican Party. This must change if we are serious in restoring life-affirming values in our communities and life-protecting measures to the unborn." Instead of the party, he presented pregnancy centers and local church-led "restoration societies" as the best cornerstones of pro-life efforts. A political agenda should remain, but it "must be totally and completely nonpartisan" and involve members of both political parties. After all, "God is neither a Republican nor a Democrat."[1]

It is not uncommon in the pregnancy help movement to encounter statements like these. They show some consistency with a story line from literature on civic participation in which alienation from partisan politics is allegedly pushing many citizens, especially younger ones, to eschew conventional political participation in favor of volunteer work and other direct action to solve public problems.[2] Community service offers "a refuge from (and alternative to)" politics.[3] Similarly, other cheerleaders for the nonprofit sector often tout its capacity to transcend adversarial, partisan politics.[4] Whereas government gridlocks and is mired in ideological strife, the voluntary sector solves problems, employing approaches unconstrained by liberal or conservative orthodoxy.[5]

Adriane Bilous raises the possibility that volunteer work might be part of how activists resolve cross pressures related to conflicting ideologies and social allegiances. Bilous interviews young, evangelical women active in "social justice" organizations that serve and strive to empower marginalized populations, such as sex-trafficking victims and homeless people. She perceives that her subjects handled their evangelical identities gingerly, embracing the teachings of their faith on cultural issues but distancing themselves from a brand of evangelicalism tied to right-wing, Republican politics focused more on individual sin than on compassion and social engagement. She argues, "Young evangelical women struggle to work through a current reality in which the individual evangelical identities they've come to accept potentially conflict with what many would describe as leftist concerns, including social welfare, poverty, and social class disparities."[6] In the process, they grow disengaged and disenchanted with politics but find outlets for their leftist concerns in service. Sociologists Nancy Davis and Robert Robinson also invoke ideological inconsistencies to argue that a communitarian ideology—one that unites cultural conservatism and economic egalitarianism under a mandate of concern for one's neighbor—undergirds substantial investment in social service provision by religious fundamentalist movements in diverse cultures.[7] Kerry Jacoby has specifically suggested that of the various forms of pro-life activism, individual outreach should most appeal to politically left-leaning individuals.[8]

The civic participation literature also speculates that interest in service reflects perceptions that political engagement is an unproductive enterprise. Volunteers observed by Nina Eliasoph, for example, tended to associate political activism with talk and voluntarism with action.[9] This critique more closely resembles the frequent portrayal of pro-life pregnancy centers, which I introduced in Chapter 1, as arising from activists' frustration with what they could accomplish in politics toward ending abortion.

In this chapter I explore how these ideas relate to the growth and appeal of pro-life individual outreach, shifting the book's perspective to that of the individual pregnancy help activists. I examine factors associated with individual activists' mobilization into the pregnancy help movement and the extent of their participation in other streams of the pro-life movement, especially the political stream. I begin by discussing leaders' constructions of the pregnancy help movement and its activists as apolitical and describing the problems leaders perceive with political action. Next, I delve into the mobilization stories of pregnancy help leaders who joined the movement after the initial post-*Roe* burst of activity, comparing and contrasting themes in their stories with those that had emerged among activists involved with the movement's origins and early growth. I then present and analyze quantitative data on the self-reported motivations, political attitudes, and pro-life activism of staff at local Care Net, Heartbeat International, and NIFLA-affiliated pregnancy centers.

I use the term *political* narrowly, to reference activity targeting the state or unfolding in official governmental arenas. This is because such a narrow understanding appears to be especially common among volunteers for service-providing organizations (see Chapter 1). By using the term in this way, I do not intend to negate an alternative view that pregnancy help work is inherently political, in that it unfolds in and affects the "realm of the contestable."[10]

AN APOLITICAL MOVEMENT?

Leaders Construct Activist Motivations

Pregnancy help leaders often suggest that their movement is an apolitical one. Not only do pregnancy help organizations generally avoid electoral, legislative, and protest activity, as I showed in Chapter 2, but most of the national organization leaders I interviewed suggested that their movement is largely populated by people who do not care much for politics. Local center directors are generally not politically active and do not want to hear political speakers at their conferences or messages like "vote for Romney," Care Net's president said in an interview. They are generally "turned off by that politicking," said Denise Cocciolone of 1st Way Pregnancy Centers. Heartbeat International's president told me she perceived that many people in the pregnancy help movement are "intimidated" by politics or else do not believe it is appropriate for a representative of a pregnancy center to take a political position.

Leaders frequently constructed the motivation of the people in their movement as a modest humanitarian inclination toward helping a neighbor in need, borne out of tendencies toward empathy and reciprocity that one leader described to me as "written on the human heart." In doing so, they treated acts of founding, volunteering for, or otherwise supporting pregnancy help organizations not as puzzles to be explained but predictable responses to awareness of need or injustice. One leader likened the formation of her organization's pregnancy centers to the way in which people come together after a flood or hurricane to support those affected by the disasters; she said it was just something, simply, that "good people" do. "When truth hits the news and they know there are needs, I think people will react to those needs. . . . When they see the need, our country has always been a good giving country," Birthright's Terry Weaver said. Others spoke similarly. "When good people perceive injustice, there is a natural tendency to address the injustice and provide help for those who have been treated unjustly," asserted a priest who had helped multiple pregnancy centers open. In pregnancy centers, he continued, "the goodness of the community comes together to address that wrong [abortion]." Another leader described pregnancy centers as "pure Americanism": volunteers serving people in their communities. Frederica Mathewes-Green, the Maryland writer and pregnancy center promoter, argued that the movement represented an old practice "being rediscovered": women going out and looking for a neighbor in trouble. It is "one of the most ancient tasks women have [done] to help each other," she opined. Being around pregnancy centers, she said she "felt like I was watching something very primitive" in the way that women of a community came together to offer support during pregnancy.

Some leaders speculated that many activists were moved to act on this empathy for women contemplating abortion out of their own experience or a friend or family member's crisis pregnancy or abortion. Four of the twenty-two leaders I interviewed themselves cited those experiences—and a fifth had a different pregnancy story—as contributing to their involvement in the movement. Those activists, leaders said, saw involvement with the pregnancy help movement as a way to "give back" for help provided to them by others or to keep other women from suffering as they did. The head of the Nurturing Network (TNN) estimated that 90 percent of the women her organization had served later volunteered, donated, or helped the organization in another way.

Other leaders identified God with these natural human tendencies, such as NIFLA's Glessner attributing pregnancy center work to the combination of a pro-life person's hope to make a difference on the abortion issue and a "desire . . . God places on your heart" to do "something for His kingdom." "God put it on his heart," said a Care Net consultant and Connecticut center director, similarly, of the inspiration of her center's founder. What should and did motivate pregnancy center volunteers, according to Care Net's president, was a "heart commitment . . . all about Jesus Christ." "Christ calls us," a fourth interviewee said.[11]

The Problems with Politics

National and local leaders themselves, with some exceptions, also did not show much interest in, affinity for, or comfort with politics. One longtime national leader openly professed her distaste for "political baloney." Across the board, leaders neither talked about politics extensively nor appeared to do so with eagerness or ease. Ideological labels went almost entirely unused, even in re-sponse to an interview question asking whether and how the pregnancy help movement differed from other forms of pro-life activism in its "philosophy, ideology, or worldview." Leaders did not necessarily claim ignorance of the world of politics and government. Instead, they appeared to place politics, even abortion politics, outside the boundaries of their professional identities and their organizations' work. Perhaps notably, such tendencies appeared un-related to the type of pregnancy help service provider or national pregnancy center association a leader represented.

The confrontational aspects appeared to be what most repelled many preg-nancy help activists from politics. Cocciolone lumped in "politicking" with "anything that's aggressive," which she said pregnancy help activists also dis-liked. Similarly, Weaver linked political action to more aggressive forms of antiabortion activism when describing her organization as formed of people "wanting to do something" but not "shooting people," marching, or picketing. They "don't want to be caught up in the political arena," she said. Indeed, when asked to address how the philosophies, ideologies, or worldviews of people in the pregnancy help movement differed from those of other pro-life activists, several leaders quickly pointed to a difference in the tone of their work. Preg-nancy centers are "not on the strident end" of the pro-life movement, asserted one leader. Others cited their "nonconfrontational" style and their "softer ap-proach" of "be[ing] gentle, kind, and loving."

Some leaders critiqued politics in general, and abortion politics in partic-ular, for a binary, absolutist character that biased one's head over one's heart and was disconnected from real people's lives. Abortion politics, these in-terviewees suggested, could not accommodate the emotional nuances of the issue that they had come to appreciate in their direct interactions with preg-nant women. Although TNN's Mary Cunningham Agee said that she under-stood it because abortion destroyed human life, she shared that the "black-and-white" nature of abortion politics "doesn't resonate with where my heart responds." People working in politics tend to work on a "theoretical level" and take a "cerebral approach" to issues, former Heartbeat International board member and center director Mary Hamm said. In contrast, she observed of pregnancy center activists, "We're in the trenches, so I think we tend to be a lot more compassionate about women choosing abortion because we realize it's not as simple as people working on that level—the theoretical level—may think."

Several leaders differentiated their stream of pro-life activism from others for its orientation toward the practical: whereas politicians talked and activists protested, they implied, people serving women at pregnancy centers or related organizations were engaged in the much more humanitarian and constructive work of helping women. One local director pronounced her state right-to-life group ineffective and the activists holding signs outside the local abortion clinic "clueless" about women seeking abortion. The debate over the legality of abortion, Agee stated flatly in an interview, "has gone on with very little benefit" to women. Meanwhile, pregnancy centers do not just object to problems—they solve problems—Cocciolone asserted in a point also made by a local center director. Birthright's leader shared that for years she has kept in her office a personally meaningful sign that reads, "I wondered why somebody didn't do something."

For these and other reasons, several leaders, especially those active in direct client service, portrayed political action as different from or sometimes opposed to actually serving women. Local center director Susan Hoffman speculated that her pregnancy center did not interact much with the state right-to-life group because of their different philosophies and priorities. She said that at the time of her interview the political group's main priority was defunding Planned Parenthood but claimed that cause did not interest her center because the center's goal was just to be "there for the women." Sanctuaries for Life's director claimed ignorance as to whether any political events contributed to her organization's formation: "When you're a social service agency, here to serve the poor, your goal or your vision is to help serve the poor. . . . We don't even look at the politics. . . . That's too complicated."

Respecting clients meant keeping their personal politics out of the pregnancy center, some leaders suggested, as well as maintaining distance from other pro-life organizations. From Louise Summerhill's instructions to the first Birthright chapters to the views of my interviewees in 2012, movement leaders have long argued that association of pregnancy centers or their personnel with political viewpoints and activities could inhibit truly nonjudgmental service and alienate potential clients.[12] In one stark example of the seriousness with which some leaders appeared to take this idea, Hoffman told me that she had attended a pro-life prayer event—one of perhaps two pro-life movement activities in which she said she had ever taken part beyond her employment at the pregnancy center—but hid her face while she was there. She also recalled that someone at her church had once asked her if she was pro-life. She gets so used to not being overtly pro-life around clients at the center, she explained, that it carries over into other venues.

In interviews and public writing, leaders also frequently volunteered their skepticism about the effectiveness of electing antiabortion politicians and altering abortion law with respect to actually ending abortion. Part of this skepticism involved their judgments about the difficulty of the process and the sincerity of elected lawmakers. NIFLA's Glessner writes, "After 35 years of opposition to abortion, one truth rings out loud and clear to us: Abortion will not be ended by politicians in Washington, DC, as many have believed in recent years, but rather, will be ended when Christians in every community rise up and say abortion will not be tolerated."[13] Multiple leaders portrayed the quest to undo the legalization of abortion as a long-term, incremental project that they expected would be frustrating for those that engaged in it. Even if *Roe* were overturned, Cocciolone predicted, abortion would never disappear as a political issue. Jurisdiction over abortion's legality would revert to the states, and although some would ban abortion, others would not. At times leaders have included such arguments in their appeals to the pro-life public. For example, as part of a forum in *Christianity Today* magazine on how the pro-life movement should respond to "political change"—presumably, the start of the pro-choice Obama administration—Care Net president Melinda Delahoyde urged volunteering at pregnancy centers. She wrote, "While we have limited opportunities to promote a 'culture of life' on legal and political fronts, there is no limit to what you and I can do to inspire life, one person at a time."[14]

Another reason for their skepticism, leaders articulated, was their opinion that abortion was too deeply ingrained in the culture for an exogenous change in abortion law to fix the problem. Instead, the movement needed to "change the abortion mentality," Hartshorn suggested in her interview, a larger, long-term endeavor in which political action played a part but for which "any law itself is not the answer." Wrote Glessner in an op-ed for a pregnancy center magazine, "The fact that our society permits abortion on demand is a symptom of a cultural and spiritual sickness that must be addressed outside the political arena. A change in the law will not end abortion if the hearts and minds of the public, both within and without the religious communities, are not changed."[15]

Leaders cast the daily work of the pregnancy help movement as being more productive—for women and the antiabortion cause alike—and rewarding than they imagined political or protest work would be. It's "refreshing," the

Gabriel Network's director said of aiding poor women who did not want abortions but needed practical help. He opined, "People want to know that what they're doing is making a difference," and he said this sense of accomplishment would be difficult to achieve from attending pro-life marches or participating in a pro-life political group. Working at a pregnancy center, argued local center board chair Cookie Harris, people "can save a life on the spot" and give women a "hand" when they are "drowning." "Every day we have victories," Hartshorn declared, elaborating that those victories could happen even when a baby was not saved from abortion.

Though pregnancy help activists showed little love for conventional political action, and they sometimes criticized the decoupling of such action from helping women, they did not claim to oppose that method of fighting abortion. A few leaders explicitly maintained that it was important for the pro-life movement to keep trying to overturn *Roe,* citing a need for justice in the law. Some hinted at admiration for political activists who had persevered for many years with seemingly few tangible victories to show for it. Some activists shared that they understood the aggressive, black-and-white approach of pro-life activists in politics even though they personally did not feel drawn toward it: one has to "fight fire with fire," Cocciolone stated, referencing the aggression she attributed to political pro-choice activists. Even the most critical pregnancy help leaders were quick to credit other pro-life activists with good intentions. Several also maintained that the movement benefitted from diverse tactics. In a sentiment echoed by others, one local center leader opined that "all have a role to play" in the movement, as in "the Body of Christ." Rather than objecting to fighting abortion through the political process, many leaders simply did not seem to see intense political involvement as the role for which they were best suited or called to play in the pro-life movement.

Interactions with Other Pro-Life Streams

Leaders generally conceded there was fragmentation among local or national pro-life organizations, although many suggested that tension among pro-life groups was not a serious problem and that it had also been improving with time. Some said they perceived more tension among local pregnancy help organizations because they competed for donations and clients than among different types of pro-life groups. The "three pillars" of the pro-life movement "coexist amicably," Care Net's vice president, Cindy Hopkins, said. Although acknowledging some bitter episodes in pro-life movement history and some ongoing tactical disagreements, Heartbeat International's president argued that perceptions of division and acrimony in the pro-life movement were overblown.

Some leaders acknowledged occasional instances of cooperation across pro-life movement streams. Heartbeat International's Hartshorn shared in her interview that she had been part of some occasional meetings of leaders of the largest US and international pro-life groups geared toward helping leaders build fellowship, unite in prayer, and cope with their disagreements over strategy. As a result of those meetings, she said she believed she was in a place where she could call up any one of those leaders and have a good conversation. The meetings, she said, "haven't resulted in a monolithic plan, but maybe we don't need one." The pro-life movement was a grassroots movement, and such movements breed valuable creativity, she reasoned.

Consistent with Jacoby's perception that activists in the pro-life movement's political stream "use their influence to enable the other two groups [individual outreach and direct-action streams] to continue their activities without interference and to enact legislation that facilitates their success,"[16] some leaders professed benefitting in some ways from the work of political activists. One of these, named in the written history of an activist in the Birthright/1st Way wing, is keeping pregnancy center personnel informed of political issues likely to affect their work, such as pregnancy center regulations pushed by pro-choice advocates. Others included the enactment of "legislation to protect women, for example, parental notification laws" and legislation "to help pregnancy centers."[17]

In Maryland, where two of the most populous local jurisdictions had enacted targeted pregnancy center regulations and where statewide regulations had also been debated, some local leaders reported increased communications with and support from other groups in relation to that legislation. Mary Hamm called pro-choice groups' political campaign against pregnancy centers "a blessing in disguise" because she said it brought together formerly competing groups—different types of pro-life organizations as well as pregnancy centers themselves. Fighting the state legislation, she said, provided an opportunity for leaders of different pro-life groups to meet and learn from each other. Meanwhile, Carol Clews, who did not join the movement until the 2000s and whose center had been affected by a Baltimore pregnancy center ordinance, spoke glowingly of other state pro-life organizations. Among others, she described the state's right-to-life affiliate as a "wonderful group . . . pro-active and involved" that occasionally provided the center information and practical assistance, and she described the leader of another group associated with grassroots education, protest, and other activism as someone she respected, even though she called his tactics "not our M.O."

THE CHANGING PROFILE OF PREGNANCY HELP LEADERS

The professed lack of politicization among contemporary pregnancy help activists is consistent with the long-term process of professionalization in the movement, though I lack the historical data to judge whether the pregnancy help activists are less interested in, fond of, or optimistic about politics than they were in the past. Participants in the pregnancy help movement, as I shared in previous chapters, even generally eschew identification as "activists." Instead, they and the Care Net and Heartbeat International training manuals tend to refer to themselves as "staff," "volunteers," and "helpers" and in terms of their specific jobs, such as "nurse," "peer counselor," and "consultant." They tend to categorize their organizations as "service providers" or "ministries."

Although leaders associated pregnancy help service providers with the pro-life movement (see Chapter 2), I observed that several of them invoked additional reference groups when describing the work of their organizations or the movement. In several cases, this variation seemed to correspond with leaders' own professional backgrounds. The pregnancy help movement is not based on "politics, but need," stated a leader with a background in public administration and Christian social ministry. Local center director Mariana Vera, a former college instructor, characterized her staff's primary role as teachers. The Pregnancy Clinic's director, who had worked as a health-care provider before beginning her career at the pregnancy center, ran one of the first medicalized centers and emphasized her clinics' efforts to design and operate in accord with "industry standards" in health care and counseling. A fourth, whose background was in business but whose many roles in the pregnancy center movement included a position at the headquarters of the Southern Baptist Convention, where she had encouraged and supported the founding of pregnancy centers, highlighted centers' connection to the religious congregations who so often helped fund them: "Without the churches, this ministry would never function. I look at this as an arm of the local church."

Evidence of the increasing relevance of such reference groups—and the diminishing relevance of pro-life political experience—to pregnancy help activists' identities and work came from variation over time in the mobilization stories of movement leaders. The early activists, whose stories I told in Chapter 3, were largely self-starters. Distressed over the legalization of abortion, they fought back through the political process and in other ways before they settled into their roles in the pregnancy help movement. Many of these individuals built pregnancy help enterprises from scratch, and most eventually came to hold leadership positions in national pregnancy center organizations. In contrast, low salience of pro-life conviction, little to no prior involvement in pro-life activism, and a theme of compatibility between organizational needs and the professional credentials and skills of future activists marked the mobilization stories of leaders who became involved after *Roe*'s first decade.[18] To some extent, what might look like generational differences in pregnancy help leadership can reflect differences in the attributes of the kinds of people who come to lead local versus national organizations. These generalizations, however, also distinguish my one early leader interviewee whose role stayed exclusively local from those later leader interviewees who came to hold national positions.

Weakness of Pro-Life Conviction and Prior Activism

Of the thirteen pregnancy help activists I interviewed whose involvement began more than a decade after *Roe*, just one described her entry into the pregnancy help movement as the product of efforts to act on a passionate opposition to abortion. This was Harris, a Maryland mother and future pregnancy center board chair who said that she had been "hit by lightning" and "couldn't rest" after watching a film of an abortion, *The Silent Scream*, in the 1990s. Two other interviewees, both executives at a national pregnancy center association, incorporated some individual initiative in the stories of their first involvement, but neither suggested that they found their way to pregnancy centers in searching for a way to take action about abortion. One of them said she had sought advice from a pregnancy center about how to talk about abortion with compassion; she had felt tremendous guilt after failing to talk a friend out of an abortion. In particular she had been distressed by the contrast between the compassion a second friend who counseled in favor of the abortion had shown the pregnant woman and her own loss for words other than that abortion was murder. The second had entered the pregnancy help movement only a few years earlier when he was hired straight into his executive position rather than rising through the volunteer ranks at local centers, as most other interviewees did. His previous job had been at a different Christian social ministry, and he explained the attractiveness of the pregnancy center association job in terms of the opportunity it would give him to act on his standing concern about the devaluation of the lives of the unborn, seniors, and people with disabilities.

For most leaders who began their involvement more than a decade after *Roe,* pro-life beliefs appeared to function as conditions for but not direct motivators of involvement. All interviewees professed having been pro-life and/ or "Christian" at the time they got involved, though two volunteered that they had previously supported abortion rights (as did two interviewees from the wave of early leaders). That background of being pro-life and Christian put individuals in a position to be exposed to the pregnancy help movement, or to be asked or "called" into the movement, and after that to respond affirmatively, then take on increasing levels of involvement. Activists suggest that the draw of involvement in the pro-life movement, however, came more from the specific appeal of the work they would do for pregnancy help organizations than from a general urge to do something about abortion.

Perhaps unsurprisingly, then, most leaders whose involvement began after *Roe* was well-established law reported little or no involvement with the pro-life movement before becoming involved with a pregnancy help organization. Except for the Baltimore activist inspired by *The Silent Scream,* who quickly enmeshed herself in multiple streams of the pro-life movement, none of the thirteen reported any prior involvement with a political right-to-life group. The only other leader reporting any routine involvement with the pro-life movement before becoming involved with pregnancy help work said that she gave presentations about right-to-life issues to students as part of her job at an educational institute associated with a Catholic hospital.

With the exception of one activist, who began volunteering at a pregnancy center soon after emigrating from a country where abortion was not legal, activists tended to attribute their lack of involvement to a focus on their daily lives—most typically, children and careers—rather than any conscious rejection of opportunities to be active in the pro-life movement. The encounters later leaders reported with the pro-life movement were typically passing ones—most commonly, attending a March for Life—that merited no further elaboration and at which apparently nothing had happened to draw the attendee further into pro-life activism. "I was pro-life, but I was busy," explained Mary Hamm, who eventually directed a local pregnancy center and served in the national leadership of Heartbeat International. She reported that she had attended the first March for Life while she was in college but otherwise did not have "any other real involvement" in the pro-life movement until nearly twenty years and eleven children later, when her involvement with a group of "family-friendly feminists" piqued her interest in abortion and primed her to agree when a priest asked her to serve on the board of a new pregnancy center. The Gabriel Network's director, Anthony DiIulio, said that he had attended a couple of Marches for Life as a youth but had never been passionate about the abortion issue or the pro-life movement until six months into a job he held jointly with his more enthusiastically pro-life wife as a live-in maternity home director. He told me that his commitment to the movement was cemented when he witnessed a spontaneous act of kindness that a volunteer performed for the women in the home—showing up with bags of each one's favorite grocery items, right down to the specific brand—and the baffled reaction of one of the women to that demonstration of love. "This is the pro-life movement I want to be a part of," he had thought at that time and subsequently invested himself much more vigorously in the work of his organization.

The stories of these later leaders have much in common with conclusions Ziad Munson reached about the mobilization of contemporary pro-life activists. Based on interviews with activists in all four streams of the movement, and in contrast to at least one important study of earlier participants in the movement's direct-action stream, Munson argues that antiabortion conviction and strategic choice play surprisingly unimportant roles in the mobilization of today's pro-life activists and their commitment to a particular stream of activism.[19] He observed a common and seemingly more accidental path by which activists became engaged with a particular stream of pro-life activism. In the course of daily living, sometimes even before a future activist identified as pro-life, he or she was brought into a type of contact with the pro-life movement that resulted in a personal invitation to participate in some isolated pro-life movement activity. Invitations typically came from a member of the future activist's social network. Rather than concern about abortion, the perceived social benefits of participation tended to motivate acceptance of the invitation; participation also tended to be rationalized in general terms as an activity that would help others. From that initial involvement and through repeated exposure to the views of the pro-life activists in his or her social network, the activist's beliefs about abortion would develop, thicken, and intensify. Eventually, pro-life activism—usually in that stream of the movement with which the initial contact was made—became a regular part of the activist's life. The unfolding of these events, however, depended on whether activists' initial contact with the movement coincided with a transitional period in their lives in which changes to daily routines made them more logistically and psychologically "available" for a new activity.[20]

Although my later-leader interviewees made little reference to the social aspects of helping at pregnancy centers, they rather commonly shared that they first became involved in response to an invitation or request. Some of these invitations were personal, and others were appeals made to a broader audience, such as in presentations at the future activist's church. Most of these invitations were delivered through religious networks. Some activists whose involvement began with employment identified a family member, friend, or colleague as having alerted them to the opportunity.

Times of transition in activists' lives also surfaced in many stories. These were most often job changes for the activist or the activist's spouse, some of which were accompanied by a move. Changes in family status, including the birth of a child, a miscarriage, and a child's transition to college also received mention.

Professional Skills and Experience

Another notable change in the profiles of pregnancy help movement leaders, especially among those linked to Care Net, Heartbeat International, and NIFLA-affiliated pregnancy centers, appears to be the growing importance of professional experience to leaders' first involvement with pregnancy help organizations. The history I outline in Chapters 3 and 4 recognizes that professionals with prior high-status careers, such as doctors, lawyers, and college professors, have long played important roles in the pregnancy help movement. The change was not necessarily a result of newer leaders more frequently bringing outside professional experience into the movement but of newer leaders being more likely to enter the movement as employees whose skills and credentials matched their organizations' needs—and who shared their organizations' values—rather than as volunteers who had discovered pregnancy centers while seeking opportunities to do something about abortion.

This phenomenon developed gradually. Of the five interviewees whose involvement began more than a decade after *Roe* but still during the 1980s, all had prior professional training or experience relevant to their future roles in the pregnancy help movement, and all but one began at their organizations as volunteers or founders. Two of those five women, an obstetrician-gynecologist and a psychiatric nurse, specifically professed that their professional background was relevant to their entry into the movement, even though they were recruited through their churches. Eventually, the former became a local center's medical director and a national spokesperson on medical issues, and the latter came to direct a local pregnancy center and design a healing program for postabortive women. The other three included an aspiring social worker who would staff a program providing free medical care and other help to indigent women, a business manager and owner asked to manage a pregnancy center office who eventually became a prolific pregnancy center fund-raiser, and a corporate executive who tapped her networks to grow an organization she had founded to help pregnant women maintain their college education or career. Links to prior professional experiences were not relevant to every late leader interviewed because none of the three interviewees who began their involvement in the 1990s discussed such experience, but they were again highly relevant for another wave of late leaders who had each spent less than a decade in the pregnancy help movement by the time of their 2012 interviews.

Four of the latest five interviewees, signaling a further change in the profile of pregnancy help leaders, acquired their leadership positions by successfully applying for jobs for which they had relevant prior experience. These included an obstetric nurse and nursing instructor who became a pregnancy center's nurse manager and later its director, a woman who had worked in development for a disease management foundation and became a pregnancy center's development and then executive director, a public administrator who had spent most of his career in local government consumer protection agencies before becoming an executive at a national pregnancy center association, and a college-instructor-turned-pregnancy-center-executive-director who described teaching as her passion and part of the counseling work she also performed at the center. The fifth had come to the pregnancy help movement from jobs at churches and soon after earning a graduate degree in music. Not everyone in this group short-circuited the volunteer work that had preceded the employment of nearly every other interviewee holding a paid position, but even the two that did not spent little time in that stage. One of them, the obstetric nurse, was invited to apply for a poorly paid nurse manager position ($11 per hour) at about the same time she had decided to volunteer her assistance to a pregnancy center director who had given a presentation at her church about the center's plans to add medical services.

Continuity: Resonance and Religion

Some themes in leaders' mobilization stories appeared important regardless of generation. Many leaders who joined the movement after *Roe's* first decade suggested something resonated with them about an approach to abortion that involved helping women. Most of them also shared perceptions that God had been drawing them into the movement.

For some, discernment of such a call preceded involvement in the movement, and others suggested that God's call was so subtly expressed that they only recognized it retrospectively. One who had entered the movement by founding her own pregnancy assistance network said she discerned a call to do that as she shared with God her suffering over a late-term miscarriage and developed a profound sense of solidarity with women dealing with another form of pregnancy loss, abortion. Another, who had begun at the urban, multicultural pregnancy center she now directs as a volunteer pregnancy counselor, told how the center had one day stood out to her on a drive, at a time when she was a new immigrant and had not been planning to work. She said she found herself fulfilling in her work there a personal call from God to serve poor and marginalized people. Two interviewees, a female obstetrician-gynecologist and an obstetric nurse with some Spanish proficiency, shared how pregnancy center colleagues had described their arrivals as timely answers to prayers for a person with their exact characteristics and credentials. "God was drawing me in," said the doctor, Sandy Christiansen, of the "invitations" from others that had preceded each new phase of her involvement with the movement. The nurse described months of carrying her pregnancy center job application in her purse while she weighed the large pay cut she would have to accept against her growing sense that God had earmarked the position for her. "God just orchestrated everything for me," explained Michelle Williams of the twists and turns in her life that took her from prior career plans and support for abortion rights toward directing Sanctuaries for Life. A Baltimore center's executive director, Carol Clews, called it "a God thing" that she had the position she did. She told a story that involved an unexpected change in her employment status, a seeming coincidence that led her sister to discover and alert her to a pregnancy center job opening, and her later surprise promotion to executive director. Another leader, Elaine Ham, credited her transition from a successful career in business to her multiple roles in the pregnancy center movement to a series of divine signs. These began with a prophetic Bible verse that a visiting pastor said God had instructed him to give her and included a startling vision she said had interrupted one morning commute and fulfilled itself years later, in a new location, after she had begun volunteering at a pregnancy center and was eventually asked to direct a new center in a building that she recognized from her vision.

MOBILIZATION, POLITICS, AND PRO-LIFE ACTIVISM HISTORY OF PREGNANCY CENTER STAFF

Christiansen, a Care Net consultant and local center medical director, read local staff a little differently than some of her colleagues. Pregnancy centers are apolitical, she clarified, but the people within them generally are not. She reconciled the two with a story in which a former client who had changed her mind about having an abortion spoke positively to the media about her experience at the center. The client allegedly surprised center personnel by telling the media admiringly that staff "didn't care" whether she had an abortion or not. There is "a fine line to walk," Christiansen explained, between staff's pro-life views and their commitment to being nonjudgmental. She speculated that habits the staff developed while working with clients produced the appearance of disinterest in abortion and politics generally, but in her view, appearance was not always reality.

Data from the Pregnancy Center Staff Survey enable tests of leaders' perceptions.

Self-Reported Reasons for Involvement

Staff members at pregnancy centers affiliated with Care Net, Heartbeat International, or NIFLA typically rated multiple reasons (from a battery of nine) as "very important" to their "decision to start helping at a pro-life pregnancy center." This pattern provokes suspicion that responses might be a better

Table 6.1 Ratings of Reasons for First Involvement at a Pregnancy Center

	Very Important (%)	Somewhat Important (%)
God's call	92.1	6.8
A request or encouragement from someone I knew	18.8	39.5
Passion for saving babies from abortion	83.5	14.9
The opportunity to teach others about abstinence and/or wholesome sexuality	63.5	30.3
My conviction that any solution to abortion must meet women's needs	53.6	27.8
The opportunity to share the gospel with others	75.8	20.8
My desire to help the poor, vulnerable, or emotionally distressed	74.8	21.5
My concern about how gender roles have changed since the 1950s	16.5	31.2
My own or a close acquaintance's crisis pregnancy or abortion	31.2	18.2

Source: Pregnancy Center Staff Survey.

Note: Nonmissing Ns = 252–271, and 188 for "Passion from saving babies . . ." because of exclusion from one version of the questionnaire. Figures are percentages.

indicator of staff affinity for the multiple aspects of centers' missions than of the attitudes or circumstances associated with individual mobilization stories. Still, relative ratings might be informative regarding the relative salience of different values and concerns among pregnancy center staff members, especially before they developed a long-term commitment to the movement. Responses are summarized in Table 6.1.

Despite leaders' condemnation of a baby-saving mentality, the vast majority (84 percent) of respondents reported that "passion for saving babies from abortion" was very important to why they first got involved with a pregnancy center. This percentage far exceeded the share of respondents who rated "My conviction that any solution to abortion must meet women's needs" as very important, although this woman-focused motivation was nonetheless identified as a very important reason for involvement by a majority (54 percent). The prevalence of the baby-saving motivation also exceeded, but came closer to being matched by, the survey's humanitarian reason, "My desire to help the poor, vulnerable, or emotionally distressed"; this motivation drew a "very important" rating from three-quarters of respondents. The data are unable to reveal the extent to which pregnancy center training and experience over time successfully inculcated the centers' purported woman-focused orientation. The importance of the baby-saving motivation appeared slightly weaker among employees relative to volunteers, along with the most recently mobilized (fewer than two years since first involvement) center staff, but in all cases commanded large majorities.

Responses indicated that religion was highly salient to pregnancy center staff's explanations of their motivations. Three-quarters of respondents cited "the opportunity to share the Gospel with others" as very important. Consistent with the themes that arose in leaders' mobilization stories, a whopping 92 percent rated "God's call" as very important to their involvement.[21]

A notable minority of respondents identified experiences with abortion or "crisis" pregnancy as very important to their involvement at the center. "My own or a close acquaintance's crisis pregnancy or abortion" was identified as "very important" by 31 percent of respondents. Another 18 percent rated it as "somewhat important." Overall, 32 percent of respondents reported that they (or in the case of the few men, a woman with whom they had conceived a child) had experienced a "crisis pregnancy"; 13 percent disclosed an abortion.[22] In research published elsewhere, I found that reporting a crisis pregnancy or abortion of one's own was associated with a substantial and statistically significant increase in the weekly hours volunteers donated to pregnancy centers.[23]

Do Pregnancy Centers Attract Humanitarians?

My Pregnancy Center Staff Survey data offer some signs consistent with the inclinations toward nurturing, humanitarian voluntarism, and reciprocity leaders attributed to their staff. Of the respondents, 79 percent reported that in the past year they had "contributed time, money, or other resources to the poor or a charity that serves the poor"; another 16 percent reported having done so in their lifetime but not in the past year.[24] Although an imprecise comparison, a 2006 survey of the general population found that 80 percent had reported making some financial contribution to *any* charitable or religious cause in the past year.[25] Of the full sample, 7 percent had adopted children, as had 9.5 percent of those of reproductive age (eighteen to forty-four). These figures substantially exceeded the prevalence of adoption in the US adult population: the

National Center for Health Statistics estimated that as of 2002 among those aged eighteen to forty-four, 1.1 percent of women and 2.3 percent of men had adopted children.[26] Six Pregnancy Center Staff Survey respondents (2.25 percent) said they had parented foster children.

Perceptions of Pregnancy Center Effectiveness and Political Opportunity

Figure 6.1 presents the views of pregnancy center staff on the efficacy and sufficiency of political campaigns to ban abortion. Staff overwhelmingly agreed (97 percent, with 72 percent of the total agreeing strongly), "If abortion were outlawed tomorrow, pregnancy centers' work would still be needed." Although these statistics can be interpreted in multiple ways, including as an endorsement of the value of the work pregnancy centers do outside of trying to stop abortion, they suggest skepticism of the efficacy of legal change alone in actually ending abortion. Center staff perhaps unsurprisingly also expressed their faith in the efficacy of pregnancy centers' approach to abortion relative to other forms of pro-life activism—at least as a conduit for their own gifts if not also for pro-life movement strategy in general. Of the respondents, 43.9 percent agreed and 36.4 percent strongly agreed (totaling more than 80 percent in agreement) that "helping at a pregnancy center is the most effective thing I can do to end abortion." Fewer than 4 percent disagreed.

Pregnancy center staff members show less consensus in their perceptions of the pro-life movement's political opportunity structure, as represented by their predictions of the likelihood that they would live to see the movement achieve its chief policy goal. Pessimism nonetheless beats optimism. Nearly half of the sample agreed (39.9 percent) or strongly agreed (8.8 percent) that "the United States is unlikely to outlaw abortion in my lifetime." Just over one-quarter disagreed (21.8) or strongly disagreed (5 percent). Perhaps surprisingly, responses to that question were distributed independently of age (chi-square = 25.9, df = 20, p = .168).

Political and Social Issue Attitudes

Most activists in the Care Net/Heartbeat International/NIFLA pregnancy center staff sample did not appear to be alienated from the present two-party

Figure 6.1 Center Staff's Views on the Efficacy and Sufficiency of Pro-Life Political Advocacy

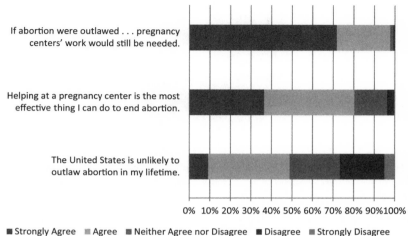

0% 10% 20% 30% 40% 50% 60% 70% 80% 90%100%

■ Strongly Agree   ■ Agree   ■ Neither Agree nor Disagree   ■ Disagree   ■ Strongly Disagree

Source: Pregnancy Center Staff Survey. N = 262–269.

system. The survey prompted, "Think about your views on a variety of political issues. Would you say that any of the major parties in the United States represents your views reasonably well?" Figure 6.2 shows a solid majority favored the Republican Party, with most of the rest claiming that neither party represented their views.

The respondents also tilted to the political right, though with considerable ambivalence, on questions about the scope of government responsibility and the social safety net. These are summarized in Figure 6.3.[27] The data show broad agreement that government has involved itself in too many areas that are properly the responsibility of the people. This restraint regarding the government's role moderates in the case of the support of poor women and children but still leaves a plurality of respondents neither agreeing nor disagreeing that, for them, "government should provide a strong safety net." Staff members divided closely over the merits of an approach to fighting abortion long associated with political liberals that periodically appears in political discourse urging pro-lifers to vote for Democrats: "If all women had access to economic supports such as affordable health care and child care, cash assistance, or several months or more of paid maternity leave, the number of U.S. abortions would drop substantially."[28] Most respondents bunched in the middle three

Figure 6.2 Center Staff's Perceived Representation by a Political Party

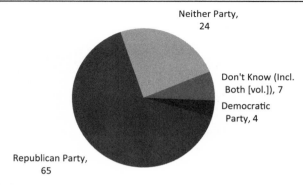

Note: Graph shows responses to the question: "Think about your views on a variety of political issues. Would you say that any of the major parties in the United States represents your views reasonably well?"

Source: Pregnancy Center Staff Survey. N = 266.

categories—agree, disagree, and neither agree nor disagree—such that each of these options garnered about 27 percent of responses. Among the rest, strong disagreement with the prediction that economic supports could greatly reduce abortion slightly exceeded strong agreement.

Some respondents showed a strong feminist consciousness, though they were only a minority of pregnancy center staff. About one-quarter of respondents agreed or strongly agreed that antiabortion politicians neglected women's needs. Though most of them did not strongly agree, 11 percent agreed that they consider themselves feminists.

At the same time, there is little evidence that pregnancy center staff members are self-consciously antifeminist. Survey respondents voiced little enthusiasm for pushing the typical clients into marriage. Fewer than 10 percent agreed (7.6 percent) or strongly agreed (1.5 percent) with the statement, "Most of our (unwed) pregnant clients should marry the father of their baby." Derived from some older scholarship on pro-life activists, the statement, "What the abortion issue is really all about is what the role of women should be" also generated substantial pushback, with 59 percent disagreeing (about half of them strongly) and 16 percent agreeing (more than two-thirds of them, not strongly).[29] Not shown in Figure 6.3, 34 percent affirmed that there had "ever been a time in your life when you believed that abortion should be legal in at least some circumstances other than danger to the life of the mother."

Figure 6.3 Select Sociopolitical Attitudes of Pregnancy Center Staff

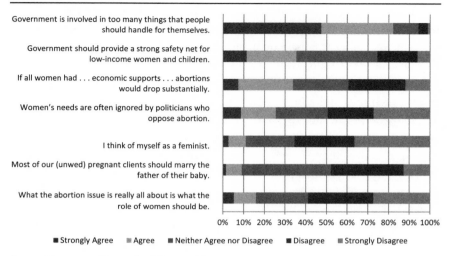

Source: Pregnancy Center Staff Survey. N = 263–268.

The responses presented in Figures 6.2 and 6.3 might overstate the conservatism of pregnancy center staff. For one, opinion researchers often describe the US public as philosophically conservative but pragmatically liberal, meaning people tend to oppose interventionist government in the abstract but support its concrete programs.[30] The Pregnancy Center Staff Survey asked only about abstract principles. Second, some previously noted biases in the sample are plausibly associated with political conservatism. Centers agreeing to serve as study sites were smaller than the average for all centers from which the sample was drawn (those completing the Pregnancy Center Director Survey). They operated in communities with lower population densities and were more likely to be located in the former Confederacy, in states casting Republican electoral votes in 2008, and in communities without abortion clinics. Another relevant bias was the disproportionately evangelical Protestant (versus Catholic) character of the sample, which resulted from the exclusion of Birthright centers from the survey and the superior response rates of Care Net relative to Heartbeat International centers to the Pregnancy Center Director Survey, the first step in the sampling process. The Pregnancy Center Staff Survey did not include any geographical variables or identifiers that could be used to assess this kind of variation.

Although results should be taken cautiously given the low number (forty-six) of nonevangelical respondents, the survey did reveal substantial and statistically significant differences of opinion between evangelical Protestants and others, nearly all of whom were Catholic, on some of the opinion questions. Nonevangelicals most notably showed greater support for the social safety net: 58 percent agreed or strongly agreed in principle that it should be strong, and fewer than 10 percent chose any level of disagreement (chi2(4) = 19.0, p < .001). Nonevangelicals were also more willing to identify themselves as feminists (chi2(4) = 14.1, p < .007), at 21 percent overall, to call out antiabortion politicians for ignoring women's needs (chi2(4) = 11.5, p < .022, 28 percent agreeing, the vast majority of them strongly), and to express faith that increased economic support could greatly reduce abortions (chi2(4) = 12.2, p < .016, 52 percent agreeing). Such differences are unsurprising. Though studies of economic and social welfare attitudes in the United States do not consistently find, especially after taking into account racial, class, or other differences, that evangelicals are significantly more conservative than others, research suggests the gap is growing.[31] Prominent evangelical political activists, from whom evangelicals active in the pregnancy center movement might be likely to take cues, have long expressed suspicion of the "welfare state." Scholars attribute this attitude to a host of deeply rooted ideas, including a "Calvinist ethic" reifying free markets, hard work, and individual responsibility for economic outcomes, anticommunist sentiment and related fears that a secular state could undermine evangelical Christian values and institutions, growing loyalty to the Republican Party, and the availability of a counternarrative in which faith-based service providers can care more effectively for the poor than the government can.[32] Still, even if Figure 6.3 might overstate the conservatism of the broader population of pregnancy center activists on gender and the role of government, feminism and social welfare liberalism would hardly appear to be defining characteristics of these activists' worldviews and identities.

Political Interest and Pro-Life Activism

Statistics from the Pregnancy Center Staff Survey showed varying levels of political interest but offered no evidence that local center personnel are less interested in politics than members of the general public. In response to a survey question about their interest in "politics and public affairs," 38 percent described themselves as "very interested," and 40 percent described themselves as "somewhat interested." Of the rest, 17 percent were "slightly interested," and 5 percent were "not at all interested." Larger shares of volunteers (41 percent) than employees (30 percent) described themselves as "very interested," but overall, the differences in the distributions of these groups' responses were not statistically significant (p = .302). In response to an identical question asked in 2009 of a national adult sample that participated in the Evaluations of Government and Society Study (EGSS), 26 percent described themselves as "very interested," 35 percent described themselves as "somewhat interested," 24 percent called themselves "slightly interested," and 15 percent professed to be "not at all interested." The percentage describing themselves as "very interested" fell further, to 20 percent, in an EGSS subsample more demographically similar to that of pregnancy center staff: women attending religious services at least once per week. However, the fact that the Pregnancy Center Staff Survey was fielded during the spring and summer of a presidential election year might have boosted the level of political interest in that sample relative to what might have been observed in 2009.

Though political apathy is not the norm for pregnancy center staff, neither is broad involvement with other forms of pro-life activism in particular or "political activity" in general. Figures 6.4 and 6.5 present the evidence, broken down separately for employees and volunteers. The data come from questions about whether a respondent had been involved with each of the following activities in the past year, in her or his lifetime but not in the past year, or never:

- Contacted a public official about abortion-related legislation or regulation
- Testified at a legislative, administrative, or court hearing about abortion-related policy
- Donated time, money, or other resources to elect an anti-abortion candidate, defeat a pro-abortion candidate, or influence votes on an abortion-related ballot question
- Taken part in some public pro-life demonstration such as a march, rally, life chain, or prayer vigil
- Attempted to educate or persuade the public on abortion, by means such as giving talks, writing letters to newspapers, or producing a newsletter or blog
- Engaged in any kind of political activity on matters unrelated to abortion

Figure 6.4 Employees' Pro-Life Activism and Political Participation as of 2012

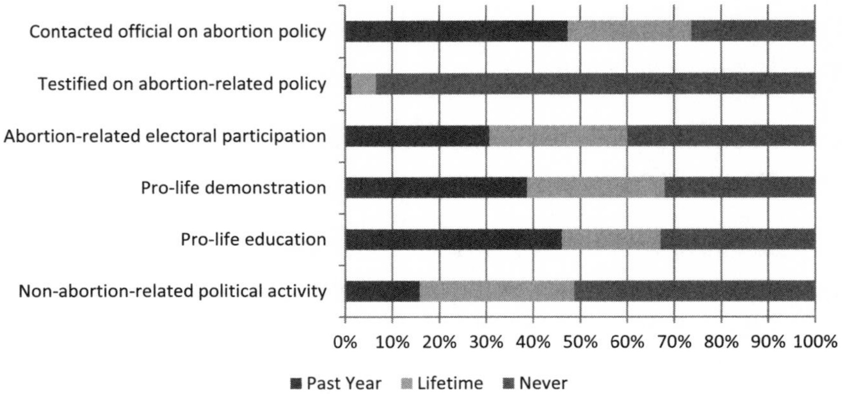

Source: Pregnancy Center Staff Survey. N = 76 employees.

Among volunteers, majorities for every item except pro-life demonstrations (where the relevant figure is still a 48 percent plurality) said that they had never done the activity in question. Most (78 percent), however, appear to have at least dabbled in some other form of antiabortion activism at some point in their lives; 43 percent of volunteers reported having performed one of the queried antiabortion activities within the past year. Looking only at institutional political pro-life activity, measured with the first three items, 61 percent of volunteers said they performed at least one in their lifetimes, and 29 percent reported doing at least one of those activities within the past year.

Employees were somewhat more politically active, perhaps as a result of their longer tenures in the movement, invitations they might have received given their positions, or the need they might have felt to respond to legislation targeting pregnancy centers. Of the respondents, 89 percent reported having performed at least one of the five acts of pro-life activism at some point in their lives, and 71 percent said they had performed at least one such activity in the past year. More than three-quarters, 78 percent, had performed at least one institutional political activity in their lives, and 54 percent had done so in the past year. Political activity outside the abortion issue was much less common, however, as a slim (51 percent) majority reported having never engaged in it, and few (16 percent) reported having done it in the past year.

Figure 6.5 Volunteers' Pro-Life Activism and Political Participation as of 2012

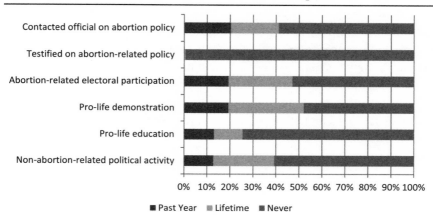

Source: Pregnancy Center Staff Survey. N = 188–192 volunteers.

These data suggest a few conclusions about how experiences with other forms of pro-life activism, especially institutional political activism targeting the state, contributed to the mobilization of pregnancy center activists. First, the data show that a nontrivial minority of pregnancy center staff, if not more, began their involvement at pregnancy centers without having ever performed even a simple, single act of antiabortion activism, such as attending a March for Life or writing to a legislator. A more precise percentage cannot be estimated from my sample because the data cannot say whether, for those reporting instances of other pro-life activism, performance of the activity preceded involvement at the pregnancy center. Second, the data suggest that most pregnancy center staff, in practice, were not engaged in *any* institutional political activism, even in their private lives. Third, however, the minority of personnel lacking any activism history was offset by another minority that reported recent contributions to multiple other streams of the pro-life movement. Taken together, these data do not strongly support the idea that many contemporary pregnancy center staff shifted into the individual outreach stream of the pro-life movement after experiencing frustration, discouragement, or burnout in other, earlier efforts to stop abortion.

Data also offer some clues about how pregnancy center staff members participate in other forms of pro-life activism in particular, and politics in general, after they have settled into the movement's service-providing stream. Involvement with service provision at pregnancy centers does not uniformly inhibit involvement in activities that might be called political "activism." Leaders' perceptions that the typical pregnancy center staff member avoided such activity, however, generally appeared accurate.

EXPLAINING PARTICIPATION IN OTHER PRO-LIFE ACTIVISM

In this chapter I began by entertaining ideas that pro-lifers might opt for volunteer service over conventional political action out of ideological cross-pressures or alienation from partisan politics or because of pessimism about prospects that political action would achieve its desired goals. Lacking variation in whether activists are involved in pregnancy help service and the ability to measure these concepts prior to involvement in the pro-life movement, my conclusions about these matters must be limited. I can gain some leverage over them, however, by exploiting variation in pregnancy center staff's involvement with other forms of pro-life activism.

Hypotheses, Variables, and Statistical Model

I performed multivariate statistical analysis on the Pregnancy Center Staff Survey data aimed at explaining variation in two outcome, or dependent, variables:

- Whether a respondent reported no involvement at all in any of the five forms of pro-life activism measured on the survey (19 percent)
- Whether a respondent reported no involvement within the past year in any of the five forms of pro-life activism measured on the survey (49 percent)

I tested three hypotheses.

The political opportunity hypothesis predicted that *as strength of agreement that abortion will not be outlawed increases, the likelihood of reporting other forms of pro-life activism will decrease.* Representing perceptions of the long-term political opportunity structure the pro-life movement faces, the independent variable was measured on the five-point Likert-style scale portrayed in Figure 6.1. I expected that this variable was more likely to predict variation in recent pro-life activism than lifetime pro-life activism because respondents' judgments about the prospects of banning abortion might have changed over time. They might also have changed *because* of respondents' participation in other forms of pro-life activism. Inability to detect this potential reversal of the causal arrow is an important limitation to keep in mind when interpreting the results.

A second hypothesis concerned the possibility that activists might have been deterred from participation in pro-life political activism, confining themselves to pregnancy centers instead, because antiabortion political elites did not represent activists' views or identities on issues other than abortion. Because pregnancy help activists claim that their stream of the pro-life movement shows a special sensitivity to women and the poor, I focused on activists' attitudes and identities in relation to gender and social welfare issues. I anticipated that pregnancy help activists who identify as advocates for women and who support an active role for the government in solving problems, providing for the poor, and coping with hardships in women's lives that might be part of abortion decisions could have been hesitant to engage with political activists who mainly work with conservative Republicans and who often face criticism for insensitivity to women. I built a measure of what I called "social welfare and gender liberalism" using six items from Figures 6.2 and 6.3. One of these items was whether a respondent provided an answer other than the Republican Party to the party representation question I introduced earlier in this chapter. The rest were extent of agreement (measured on a five-point scale ranging from strongly disagree to strongly agree) with the following five statements:

- "Women's needs are often ignored by politicians who oppose abortion."
- "If all women had access to economic supports such as affordable health care and child care, cash assistance, or several months or more of paid maternity leave, the number of U.S. abortions would drop substantially."
- "Government should provide a strong safety net for low-income women and children."
- "Government is involved in too many things that people should handle for themselves."
- "I think of myself as a feminist."

The measure was a principal components factor score. It resulted from a statistical analysis of patterns in these items' variation, indicating that they were related and thus might be tapping the same underlying concept. Statistically speaking, all six items had loaded onto a single factor with an eigenvalue greater than two. The cross-pressures hypothesis predicted that *as social welfare and gender liberalism increases, the likelihood of reporting other forms of pro-life activism will decrease.*

The data also enabled a test of the pattern emerging in leaders' mobilization stories, in which the pregnancy center movement appeared to be increasingly attracting an unpoliticized staff. The Pregnancy Center Staff Survey asked how many years it had been since respondents first started helping at any pregnancy center, and I reported descriptive statistics in Chapter 2. The activist change hypothesis predicted that *as years since first involvement with a pregnancy center increase, the likelihood of reporting other forms of pro-life activism will increase.* Statistical support for such a hypothesis, however, would not necessarily confirm that activist cohorts differed in experience prior to pregnancy center mobilization. This is because observation of a positive relationship between the variables could also have resulted if working at a pregnancy center, over time, drew individuals more extensively into the wider pro-life movement. I return to that point later in this chapter.

Models of pregnancy center activists' experience with pro-life activism controlled for age (five dummy variables marking age categories), status as a volunteer or employee, and three socioeconomic characteristics that might affect whether one had the financial, time, or informational resources often thought to promote political participation: household income (eight categories), employment (whether one had a full-time job), and education (whether one held a bachelor's degree or higher). I estimated these multivariate models using logistic regression.

Results

Figure 6.6 summarizes key results. It presents the percentage-point increase in the probability of each activism outcome that the model predicted would result if an independent variable increased from its minimum to its maximum value. These predictions were made with all other variables fixed at their mean values, thus approximating an "average" respondent.[33] Appendix C, Table C1.1

Figure 6.6 Predicted Impact of Political Opportunity Prospects, Ideological Cross Pressures, and Activist Change on Participation in Other Pro-Life Activism

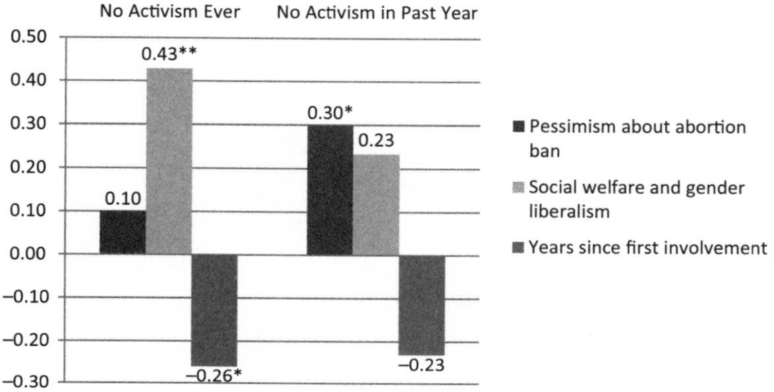

Note: Graph shows predicted probabilities when all covariates are set at their means from the logistic regression model in Appendix C, Table C1.1. *p < .05, **p < .01 for statistical significance of underlying regression coefficient.

Source: Pregnancy Center Staff Survey. N = 219.

presents full results, including logit coefficients and standard errors for all variables.

Results support the political opportunity hypothesis with respect to whether pregnancy center staff members participated in other pro-life activism within the past year. The model predicted that, all else being equal, a shift from strongly disagreeing to strongly agreeing that abortion would not be banned in one's lifetime was associated with a 30 percentage-point increase in the likelihood that a pregnancy center staff member reported no other forms of recent pro-life activism. As anticipated, the small increase in the likelihood of reporting no pro-life activism ever is not statistically significant, suggesting that the variables are unrelated.

Ideological cross-pressures appear strongly related to whether a pregnancy center staff member ever participated in other forms of pro-life activism. All else being equal, an increase in social welfare and gender liberalism from its minimum to maximum value was associated with a predicted 43 percentage-point increase in the likelihood of reporting no past or present engagement in other streams of the pro-life movement. The increase in the likelihood of reporting no recent involvement in other forms of pro-life activism that the model predicted for such a shift is also substantial (23 percentage points), but the underlying statistical estimates are so imprecise that the increase is not statistically significant—that is, observing an increase this large in such a sample could very well be a result of chance.

The activist change hypothesis likewise performs well as a predictor of whether a pregnancy center staff member reported having ever participated in other pro-life activism, but its impact on whether one reported any other recent pro-life activism is less clear. As the number of years since first involvement at a pregnancy center increased, from a minimum value of zero to a maximum value of thirty-one, the predicted likelihood of reporting no involvement in any other stream of the pro-life movement fell by 26 percentage points. The predicted decrease this shift made in the likelihood of reporting no recent pro-life activism is similar in magnitude (23 percentage points) but is estimated with so much uncertainty that the result is not statistically significant.

Before concluding the statistical analysis, I repeated it using outcome variables that measured only whether a respondent had engaged in conventional political pro-life activism—that is, I disregarded whether pregnancy center staff members had reported participating in pro-life demonstrations or educational efforts. Results of hypothesis tests remain the same.

DOES SERVICE MOBILIZE OR DEMOBILIZE?

An important limitation of the Pregnancy Center Staff Survey data is that they do not enable me to distinguish attitudes present at the time an activist first became involved with pregnancy centers from those that developed as a function of experience in the pregnancy help movement. Similarly, I cannot tell whether the greater likelihood of engaging in other forms of pro-life activism found among those with longer tenures in the pregnancy help movement reflected changes in the types of people who worked at pregnancy centers or a process in which experience at the pregnancy center gradually drew participants into wider engagement with the rest of the pro-life movement. The latter scenario is consistent with studies finding that volunteer work tends to heighten political engagement.[34] Theoretically, it does so by increasing individuals' exposure to public problems, which eventually prompts them to ask questions about justice and structural change.[35] On the contrary, given that pregnancy help leaders said they tried to cultivate apolitical organizational cultures and that their centers were moving toward greater professionalization and medicalization, one might wonder whether contemporary pregnancy centers provide the conditions that politically mobilize volunteers. Some researchers have argued that whether service cultivates political engagement depends upon how much space civic organizations create for political discussion.[36] In a field study of nonpolitical civic organizations in a US community, Eliasoph observed the active suppression of political discussion and concluded that volunteer work can instead demobilize participants and retard demands for social change.[37]

With that in mind, the Pregnancy Center Staff Survey solicited respondents' perceptions about whether and how they had changed as a result of their involvement at the pregnancy center. Items included:

- Your involvement in other forms of pro-life activism?
- Your interest in politics?
- How much you care about economic issues such as poverty and unemployment?

The third item was designed to tap the possibility that pregnancy center work, even if its main appeal to activists is the chance to prevent abortions, eventually promotes greater interest in those women's welfare issues "owned" by the political left. It would also enable examination of whether activists who perceived themselves growing in concern about poverty also perceived themselves drifting away from politics and other forms of pro-life activism. Respondents were asked to specify whether helping at a pregnancy center had increased, decreased, or had no impact upon each of these.

Shown in Figure 6.7, pregnancy center staff typically did credit their work with increasing their engagement of these topics. Even if pregnancy center staff might have been avoiding politics in their official capacities at the centers, majorities did perceive that their work there had interested them more in politics (63 percent) and drawn them more deeply into involvement in the pro-life movement (53 percent). A solid majority (65 percent) also professed an increase in the salience to them of economic issues. On each item, just 2 percent or fewer associated their pregnancy center work with decreases.

Figure 6.8 indicates that when pregnancy center staff reported increases in caring about economic issues such as poverty, they also tended to report increases in their political interest and involvement with pro-life activism. Thus, coming to care about the economic aspects of women's well-being in the

Figure 6.7 Perceived Impact of "Helping at a Pregnancy Center" on Select Political Outcomes

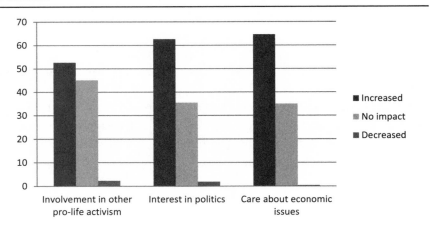

Source: Pregnancy Center Staff Survey. N = 265–266.

Figure 6.8 Reported Increases in Political Interest and Pro-Life Mobilization, by Changes in Level of Caring about Economic Issues

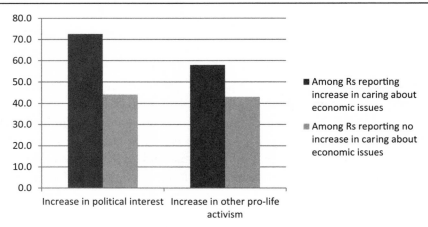

Note: The question asked, "For each item below, would you say that it has increased as a result of helping at a pregnancy center, decreased as a result of helping at a pregnancy center, or has helping at a pregnancy center had no impact?"

Source: Pregnancy Center Staff Survey. N = 264.

course of working for a pregnancy help organization did not appear to depress their interest in politics or participation in other streams of pro-life activism. In further analysis, the positive relationships among these variables persisted even after accounting for whether respondents supported or opposed a strong public safety net.

These observations are consistent with comments from one of my interviewees, Care Net consultant and local center director Linda Cochrane, who during our conversation had associated pregnancy center work with participants' development of nonjudgmental compassion for the pregnant women and increased interest in social action. Citing Gary Haugen's book *Good News about Injustice,* she claimed that people involved in ministries that care for suffering people would eventually also involve themselves in seeking justice for those they served. Compassion made one want to speak out about justice and put justice into the law, she said, not only about abortion: "You become a voice for all the issues."

CONCLUSION

Pregnancy help movement leaders claimed their movement is a nonpolitical one. For people who regard any efforts to influence individual choices or cultural norms, especially on matters contested in the realm of politics, as exercises of power and therefore "political," such claims might be unpersuasive. On the contrary, it does appear true that the typical pregnancy center staff member was not highly active in institutional or street politics, and that pregnancy help leaders tried to cultivate organizational cultures that avoided talk or practice of such activities.

Though pregnancy help leaders sometimes market their movement to potential volunteers by discussing the limits of antiabortion political action, the movement is not in large part composed of activists who have given up on pro-life political activism. Many activists, especially those who have joined the movement most recently, simply do not appear politicized at all. Consistent with Ziad Munson's research, I see little evidence that contemporary activists are coming to pregnancy help organizations after abandoning other streams of the pro-life movement.[38] In the case of late leader mobilization, where my data are richer, neither does the typical activist seem to find the movement out of a conscious intention to take action about abortion. Instead, seemingly chance exposure to the pregnancy help movement collided with latent pro-life and "Christian" values. Something made these stick, so that leading, volunteering, or working in the pro-life individual outreach stream became a routinized commitment, whereas any previous exposure to the pro-life movement had not. Munson's idea of "availability" surely played a part, and my subjects also suggest that pregnancy centers' helping work felt comfortable and right in terms of its problem-solving logic, their personalities, their emotional dispositions toward abortion, their occupational interests and skills, and their sense about what God wanted them to do with their time and talent. Less than an alternative to political action on abortion, pregnancy help activism looks more like an alternative to an unconscious pattern of *no* action—or else a complement to political or other action.

The Gabriel Network's DiIulio described his organization to me as existing "in a no man's land between conservative and liberal . . . conservative by makeup doing work that's traditionally liberal." He said that early in his tenure he had anticipated that his organization would grow by attracting support from "left-leaning" people. Instead, he professed to have observed that growth had been concentrated mainly among "pro-lifers" who were "broadening their efforts" against abortion while still staying engaged in abortion politics, despite the dismal political prospects presented by the Obama presidency and disappointment in what had not been accomplished under George W. Bush.

Data on the political attitudes and engagement of pregnancy center staff are somewhat consistent with this picture, with the caveat that the apparently more left-leaning Catholics in the movement are underrepresented by these data. Activists in my sample leaned politically to the right, although their ranks included some displaying signs of a liberal orientation on social welfare and gender politics. Left-leaning pregnancy center staff members did seem reluctant to aid the pro-life movement in other ways, consistent with some scholars' fears that partisan polarization prompts moderates to substitute service for politics. However, many others combined their service with at least isolated acts of participation in other pro-life movement streams. Rather than service channeling their interests and activities away from political issues and the rest of the pro-life movement, most pregnancy center staff members indicated the opposite. This might also have been true of the organizational leaders, who though busy with and partial to their pro-life individual outreach work nonetheless maintained awareness of and some degree of communication and collaboration with leaders in other movement streams.

7. The Impact and Future of the Pregnancy Help Movement

For several years now, in an event held at least annually called Babies Go to Congress, Heartbeat International has brought former clients, their children, and the pregnancy center staff who assisted them to Capitol Hill, where the clients share their stories in personal meetings with elected officials. In July 2012, lawmakers heard from four mothers whose testimonials are also published online. Emily Behny discussed how a day-care program and teen mother support groups provided through a pregnancy center helped her graduate from high school on time.[1] Shelly Louis relayed how she canceled an abortion appointment after pregnancy center staff gave her the clarity and encouragement she needed to resist pressures from finances and her boyfriend and how practical support continued throughout her pregnancy.[2] Jessica Gore lauded the transformative experience of viewing an ultrasound image of her daughter, the preparation for parenthood she received from center classes, and the opportunity to "earn" through those classes supplies that had seemed "impossible" for an eighteen-year-old to provide for her baby.[3] Teen mother Sarah Seely contrasted the kindness, personal attention, and constructive information she reported receiving at a pregnancy center with the uncaring treatment and lack of support for options other than abortion she said she had encountered at Planned Parenthood.[4] The women also spoke of gratitude for their children and pride in their own life accomplishments. Their testimonies were intended to deliver a message: "Pregnancy Help Centers Are Good for America!"[5] Heartbeat International's president described the event as a "pro-active effort to make friends with influencers in our nation's capitol" that the organization encourages affiliates to replicate in their state legislatures.[6]

With efforts like these, pregnancy centers are countering pro-choice activists' framing of their work with their own. They inspire the questions that drive this chapter: First, what has been the impact of the pro-life pregnancy help movement on pregnant women, and to what extent is it accomplishing its goals? Second, as national leaders push local centers to compete more aggressively with Planned Parenthood for clients, how likely will the movement be to change the defining features of its forms of social action? In this chapter I address these matters in turn and then offer a focused discussion of another topic some critics have linked to the impact and future of pregnancy centers and the larger pro-life movement: the potential that preference for a privatized response to poverty might undermine activists' efforts to reduce abortion and expand their movements' mass appeal, especially among racial minorities.

IMPACT OF THE PREGNANCY HELP MOVEMENT

Despite the powerful analytical tools at the disposal of social scientists, impact assessment is often challenging and contested. This is especially the case when one wishes to attribute causation and when working on topics for which the very definition of success, not to mention the data and methods used to measure it, is politically controversial. In the case of the pregnancy help movement's work, not only the subjectivity of available evidence but also often sheer lack of data hinders clear-cut assessments of the results of the work. Much of my discussion in this chapter, then, is speculative and geared toward setting an agenda for future research and debate. That said, this section addresses the impacts of the pregnancy help movement in three areas: the larger pro-life movement, the incidence of abortion, and women's well-being.

Impacts on the Pro-Life Movement

Although the pregnancy help movement does not articulate this goal for itself, social movement organizations (SMOs) often aim to build activists' engagement in their movement. That the typical pregnancy center volunteer has been involved with the movement for several years suggests that it is succeeding in this way. Chapter 6 also presented evidence of activists' perceptions that pregnancy center work had deepened their engagement in the wider pro-life movement. A related way in which the pregnancy help movement has *not* affected the pro-life movement, however—in contrast to the experiences of some other service-providing SMOs (see Chapter 1)—is by mobilizing beneficiaries of their services into state-directed antiabortion activism. I encountered no evidence in my research of any attempt or plan to do this. This makes sense given the perhaps unusual relationship pregnancy help activists have with their target group: they are not necessarily on the same side of the abortion issue.

Pregnancy help leaders have long challenged other Christians and pro-life activists to change. They have challenged them to stop stigmatizing unwed mothers, show greater sensitivity to postabortive women, and back up their claims to be pro-life with concrete support for alternatives to abortion. Available evidence suggests that their targets have responded in some ways but not others.

Some scholars have identified pregnancy centers as contributors to the increasing participation of women who have had abortions in the pro-life movement and to the movement's increasing use of "woman-protective" or "pro-woman" arguments.[7] Two leading pro-life activists confirm these observations.[8] Some of my interviewees expressed cautious agreement that activists elsewhere in the pro-life movement had progressed in showing sensitivity to women. Meanwhile, though one cannot know how pregnancy centers' messages to the more visible wings of the pro-life movement might have contributed to this phenomenon, members of the public who oppose abortion have become more liberalized over the past few decades in their support for gender equality, closing an earlier gap with pro-choice advocates.[9]

Activists still see work to be done. For example, as I began my 2012 interview with Margaret "Peggy" Hartshorn just days after US Representative Todd Akin, a Republican from Missouri, made infamous comments that seemed to minimize rape, she brought up the controversy.[10] She expressed frustration and disappointment that Akin had not spoken in a more "woman-centered" fashion, lamenting the example of dedicated antiabortion "champions" like him who "don't know how to frame the issue." In 2018, Care Net emailed its blog subscribers a link to an earlier post reminding readers that although sex outside of marriage was a sin, unwed pregnancy was not.[11] A survey commissioned by Care Net of women who had abortions found that more than one-third of them were attending a Christian church at least monthly at the time of their first abortion. Care Net found that the most commonly received or anticipated reactions from churches toward all of the women surveyed were judgment and condemnation. However, it also observed that reports of positive reactions from churches increased greatly among women who attended church regularly, relative to those who did not, and that a slim majority of the full sample agreed at least somewhat that "churches are prepared to provide material, emotional, and spiritual support to women who chose to keep a child resulting from an unplanned pregnancy."[12]

Whether pregnancy help activists have contributed to the increased acceptance of unwed childbearing in the United States cannot be known.[13] Mary
Cunningham Agee, president of the Nurturing Network (TNN) told me she
believed its messages had helped inspire families to embrace those young family members who experienced unplanned pregnancy. While she shared in her
interview the important periods of growth and change at her organization,
Agee implied that the number of women calling her organization for help had
decreased from a period decades beforehand when she said they received about
1,000 calls per year. She also claimed to hear less desperation in the women's
voices recently. When it was founded in the 1980s, TNN was prepared to completely relocate women cast out by their families, colleges, or workplaces (or
who feared they would be) because of pregnancy. As the stigma surrounding
unplanned pregnancy diminished, Agee said, there was less need in the United
States for an "underground railroad" like her organization had provided.

The flow of resources into the pregnancy help movement offers mixed evidence that churches and pro-lifers are responding to pregnancy centers' calls
for more concrete aid to women living in poverty. Donations are supporting
such social welfare activities as pregnancy centers' material aid operations and
their opening of maternity homes.[14] Much of the cash flow into the pregnancy
help movement, however, appears to be tied to the ultrasound machine, which
has nothing to do with easing the pragmatic hardships women carrying unintended pregnancies face. Data are not available to assess whether pro-life
activists have expanded over time their propensity to perform individual acts
of kindness to parents likely to be at risk for abortion or to donate to poverty-related charities. Interviewee Frederica Mathewes-Green, however, who
over a long tenure of involvement had contributed to multiple streams of the
pro-life movement, argued that pro-life activists outside the individual outreach stream had long shown great generosity in their private lives to pregnant
women and pregnancy centers despite the insensitive-sounding, baby-focused
comments they sometimes made in public.

Activists in the pro-life movement's political stream might point to legislation they backed directing funds to pregnancy help organizations as evidence of
increased support of alternatives to abortion. In Chapter 2, I summarized relevant state policies. Meanwhile, analysis I performed of federal lobbying disclo-
sure forms filed between 1998 and 2011 by the National Right to Life Committee
(NRLC), the nation's leading pro-life advocacy group, showed that at various
points it had promoted bills to help pregnancy centers purchase ultrasound

machines and to reallocate some public welfare funding toward state programs for alternatives to abortion, of which pregnancy centers would have likely been beneficiaries. Though none of these bills were enacted, the federal government under President George W. Bush made administrative changes that permitted states to spend portions of their federal Temporary Assistance to Needy Families (TANF) grants on programs for alternatives to abortion.[15]

The area in which pro-life activists—with some notable exceptions, such as the U.S. Conference of Catholic Bishops—clearly have *not* responded to the pregnancy help movement's calls for practical support for women "choosing life" is with advocacy for public social welfare programs. There is no indication that pregnancy help activists *are* challenging their peers to support such programs. Nonetheless, the movement's political stream appears to have backed away from this area since the 1960s and 1970s, when legislation to expand publicly funded medical care and other economic assistance was very much a part of right-to-life groups' political agendas.[16] To be clear, single-issue, pro-life groups generally confine any lobbying against social welfare spending or program expansions to specific provisions relating to abortion, euthanasia, or other narrowly defined right-to-life issues. My analysis of NRLC lobbying disclosures as well as those filed by the three other groups categorized by the Center for Responsive Politics as antiabortion lobbies, reveals just one exception.[17] This occurred when NRLC shifted its position on the Affordable Care Act (ACA) from calls to strike specific provisions to lobbying for full repeal. However, neither have these groups done much over the same period to advance legislation that would maintain or expand the social safety net.

In the present political climate, this is unsurprising. Maintenance of a narrow issue agenda is rational in the face of resource constraints and at a time when taking on new positions could create a wedge in an ideologically diverse membership.[18] Several scholars have explicitly credited the pro-life movement's single-issue focus with uniting in collective action citizens who would not agree on many other political issues.[19] Over time, a process of elite partisan realignment, in which opposition to abortion rights has increasingly become bundled with Republican Party affiliation and conservative policy preferences on social welfare issues, has arguably raised the political costs to pro-life organizations of lobbying for public antipoverty initiatives, whereas it lowers those costs for pro-choice organizations.[20]

One might speculate, as Jacoby suggests, that pregnancy help organizations' work frees pro-life political advocacy groups from social welfare lobbying so that they can focus on changing abortion law.[21] Whether the kind of aid extended by pro-life pregnancy help organizations sufficiently substitutes for what the government could do, however, to help women bear the costs of unintended pregnancy, is a different matter.

Impacts on Abortion

Pregnancy help discourse often denies that stopping abortions, or "saving babies," is a movement goal (see Chapter 2). They describe it instead as a desirable consequence of meeting the more immediate goals of serving God while serving women with compassion and truth.[22] Nonetheless, the movement's promotional materials celebrate those instances in which clients considering abortion opt to give birth instead, and its leaders talk boldly about ending abortion (see Chapter 2). For this reason, it seems fair to ask how effective the pregnancy help movement has been at reducing abortions.

The incidence of abortion in the United States has trended downward for decades and by some measures now sits at its lowest levels since 1973, or earlier.[23] The potential causes of this decline—whether improved contraceptive technology, access, and use; declines in teenagers' sexual activity; increased moral discomfort with abortion; tighter abortion regulations; or otherwise—are multiple and highly debated in public discourse. Future empirical research is needed to rigorously examine whether and how pregnancy help service providers have contributed to these trends.

It does appear that pregnancy centers have contributed to some women's decisions to continue their pregnancies. To begin, 67 percent of all respondents to the Pregnancy Center Staff Survey reported having been "personally involved in a situation in which a client at this or another pro-life pregnancy center had been seriously considering abortion and then later chose to give birth." This figure rises to 81 percent of respondents among those whose roles at the center had included being a "peer counselor." Of everyone saying they had been personally involved in such a situation, 86 percent said they had been involved in more than one such situation. Client testimonies cited in news features and the movement's promotional materials help to affirm these claims.

How such instances scale up to aggregate numbers of averted abortions is less clear. Pregnancy centers with the three major networks have been ramping up their collection and analysis of client data but often cannot track what

Figure 7.1 Changed Views on Having an Abortion among Pregnancy Center Clients, 2017

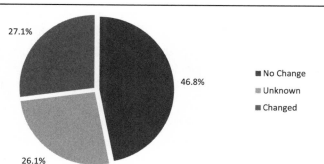

27.1%

46.8%

26.1%

■ No Change
■ Unknown
■ Changed

Source: Author's analysis of eKYROS.com data. N = 51,733 pregnancy test clients initially stating they were undecided about or planning to abort their pregnancies.

happens in clients' lives after those women leave the center. However, they do now often record how clients' pregnancy intentions change over the center visit. Data on these attitude changes are available online from more than 1,300 pregnancy centers using the popular eKYROS client management software system, according to the company's website as of 2018. The reports are automatically generated and continuously updated based on the data the centers' staff enter into the system.

Using that data for 2017, Figure 7.1 summarizes those pregnancy centers' record at changing clients' minds about having abortions. The system showed that of those clients who had received positive pregnancy tests and indicated they were planning or undecided about abortion, 27 percent decided instead to carry their pregnancies to term. Meanwhile, 47 percent did not, and the views of the rest upon exit were unknown.[24] Data from 2010 to 2016 yield similar figures (28–30 percent annually choosing to carry to term) and represent a substantial increase over the earlier available years (2004–2009). Because the number of clients covered by the system has increased greatly over time, however, variation in this figure might reflect changes in the number of or characteristics of centers using the system rather than the centers' performance.

If one is willing to assume experiences at the eKYROS centers are representative (though they might not be), extrapolation of their data can produce a crude estimate of the number of abortions prevented at all US pregnancy centers. For 2017, eKYROS centers reported that 14,022 women changed their minds about having an abortion – that is, they had told the pregnancy center counselor they were planning or considering abortions but later committed to carrying their pregnancies to term. We next need some estimate of the percentage of US pregnancy center service volume for which eKYROS centers account. One can be derived from the limited available national statistics by comparing the number of pregnancy tests and ultrasounds CLI attributes to all US pregnancy centers to those reported by eKYROS centers. The sum of CLI's numbers exceeded the sum of the eKYROs numbers by a factor of nearly 2.8.[25] Simple math then yields an estimate of just under 39,000 women that US pregnancy centers persuaded to give birth. By comparison, Guttmacher Institute researchers report 926,200 abortions performed in the United States in the most recent year for which data are available, 2014.[26]

Whether this loose estimate signals success is subjective. Kimberly Kelly, also working with the eKYROS.com data, transforms the number of women recorded as having changed their minds about abortion into a percentage of all pregnant clients and argues on that basis that pregnancy centers are largely ineffective at meeting their most important goal.[27] Performing the same calculations on the 2017 eKYROS.com data, I find that women recorded as changing their minds about abortion constituted 5.6 percent of "pregnancy cases" established through a pregnancy test and/or ultrasound. This is an increase from the 4 percent Kelly reports from 2010 data, but still an underwhelming figure.

As Kelly recognizes, driving these figures are the low shares of women considering abortion in the first place. She reports statistics from the eKYROS.com data on stated pregnancy intentions similar to the estimates my Pregnancy Center Director Survey yielded for the typical center in Chapter 2. EKYROS .com no longer directly reports initial client pregnancy intention data.[28] It now prominently reports "abortion vulnerability," a measure of clients' risk for having abortions determined by pregnancy center counselors during intake meetings. It might not necessarily be the same as intentions stated by the clients. For example, a client who states an intention to continue the pregnancy might be coded as "abortion vulnerable" rather than "likely to carry" because she indicates that she has not ruled out abortion or that she is being pressured by others to have an abortion, among other reasons.[29] Depicted in Figure 7.2, after subtracting approximately 35,000 cases coded as "not applicable" for pregnancy intention, pregnancy center staff members during the intake process assessed nearly 11 percent of clients as "abortion minded" and another 29 percent as "abortion vulnerable."[30] In the perception of the counselors,

Figure 7.2 Counselors' Initial Assessments of Client Abortion Risk, 2017

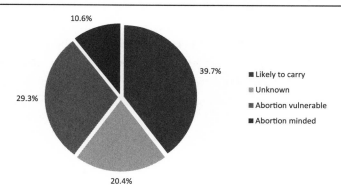

Source: Author's analysis of eKYROS.com data. N = 297,554 pregnancy test clients.

"abortion-minded" clients plan to have abortions, whereas "abortion-vulnerable" clients are deemed by them to be at risk for having an abortion.

A low percentage of pregnant clients considering or at risk for abortion need not indicate that pregnancy centers are unsuccessful at preventing abortions. An article by a Heartbeat International official argues that a woman a counselor assesses as being likely to carry her pregnancy to term might not be revealing everything on her mind, might not be making her choice from a truly "pro-life" motivation, and might later waver in her stated plans as her pregnancy, with all its pressures, proceeds. A pregnancy center that fails to direct resources at such a woman, he suggests, might expose her current pregnancy and any future ones to a risk of abortion and might miss the chance to change her heart and build up a "culture of life."[31] Thus, it is unclear what this group's percentage of clientele would need to be to pronounce pregnancy centers "effective."

With these and other matters in mind, the actual number of abortions pregnancy centers avert might well be substantially higher or lower than the rough estimate presented here. In addition to the concerns about data quality and the possibility that clients might not follow through on their stated intentions—whether abortion or birth—there is the impossibility of determining what the outcome would have been in the absence of the pregnancy centers' intervention. Some women "choosing life" might have opted for that eventually, and others seemingly committed to carrying might not have persisted with that intention absent the preemptive effect of any support they received at the pregnancy centers. Pregnancy centers might also plausibly exercise influence over clients before they enter the centers' doors. This could happen if centers are enjoying any success in spreading their "pro-life" values in the culture or if advance knowledge that help is available from the pregnancy center contributes to the number of clients arriving in search of practical assistance with a pregnancy that they did or are planning to continue. Such possibilities would be extraordinarily difficult to test empirically.

Impacts on Women's Well-Being

Future research on the impact of pregnancy help service providers might strive to assess how well they have contributed to various aspects of women's well-being they say they aim to foster. These include women's economic security, their physical health, the health of their pregnancies, their senses of self-efficacy and self-worth, and the stability and satisfaction level of their relationships with crucial others, such as romantic partners, children, and parents. The movement offers ample testimonies in promotional materials, events such as Babies Go to Congress, and the client stories some leaders fondly volunteered to me during interviews about individual women who are thriving. Yet there is no basis for judging how representative an experience this is or how pregnancy center clients fare relative to their counterparts who do not reach out to the centers.

A more ambitious outcome for women's well-being sought by many pregnancy centers, life transformation, would be still more difficult to measure and attribute credit for even if pregnancy centers gained the resources to study their clients longitudinally. Counseling at a pregnancy center, a former local center director who had done this remarked in an interview, leaves one "sowing seeds and not necessarily seeing the harvest." A pregnancy counselor might not help a woman save her child from abortion, she continued, but many years later, that counseling session and the compassion shown at the center might bear fruit in the woman's life. Based on the scale and reach of the movement and the nature of the assistance it offers, pregnancy centers might more easily claim credit for something else they suggest promotes women's well-being: simply being present in their communities as a resource to ensure that women have help acting on alternatives to abortion.

Do Pregnancy Centers Harm Women?

Many pro-choice advocates and allies portray pregnancy centers as harmful to women's well-being. Of particular concern to these advocates is that counseling delivered at pregnancy centers allegedly inflates the health risks associated with abortion, especially regarding whether abortion heightens the risk of breast cancer and various mental health problems. Critics also take issue with the fact that pregnancy centers neither provide nor refer for abortions and also often do not help women learn medically accurate information about and access contraception. Because of this, two doctors recently charged in the *AMA Journal of Ethics,* pregnancy centers' counseling on these topics "falls outside accepted medical standards and guidelines for providing evidence-based information and treatment options."[32] They say that when dealing with pregnancy centers, women seeking abortions face potentially costly and harmful delays in obtaining them, given that the health risks, cost, and ease of accessing abortion increase with the age of the fetus. "Why Are Crisis Pregnancy Centers Not Illegal?" asked the headline of an article in the left-leaning *Slate* magazine.[33]

Citing such arguments, several state and local governments over the past decade have enacted laws regulating what pregnancy centers must tell clients in their advertisements and/or in notices posted or distributed at their centers. Two of these came from jurisdictions in the state where my local center interviews focused. Baltimore City's 2009 ordinance mandated signs disclosing that a center neither provided nor referred for abortion or birth control.[34] Montgomery County, Maryland's 2010 ordinance, which applied to pregnancy centers with no licensed medical professional on their staffs, required centers to post signs in their waiting rooms in English and Spanish including statements that "the Center does not have a licensed medical professional on staff" and that "the Montgomery County Health Officer encourages women who are or may be pregnant to consult with a licensed health care provider."[35] Elsewhere, California's 2015 Reproductive "FACT" Act required one of two types of notices depending on whether a pregnancy center was licensed as a state medical facility. The law required pregnancy centers not licensed by the state to post a specific statement declaring so in signage at the center and in "clear and conspicuous" fashion on their websites and in all advertisements. The message was to be conveyed in at least forty-eight-point type and in multiple languages.

Pregnancy centers holding state medical licenses were required to post signs in their lobbies, using at least twenty-two-point font, informing their clients about how to access services that include publicly funded abortion and contraception or to individually distribute a print or digital notice to clients at the center. The mandated language read: "California has public programs that provide immediate free or low-cost access to comprehensive family planning services (including all FDA-approved methods of contraception), prenatal care, and abortion for eligible women. To determine whether you qualify, contact the county social services office at [insert the telephone number]."[36] Hawai'i enacted a similar law. Meanwhile, Illinois's 2016 Health Care Right of Conscience bill (SB 1954) went further. It amended the state's right-of-conscience code in a way that would have required medical pregnancy centers to discuss with pregnant patients all "legal treatment options," including the "benefits" of those options. It also mandated that if the facility or its medical staff raised conscience objections to providing any legal treatment option requested by the patient, they must direct the patient through referral, transfer, or written document to another health care provider that offered that option.

Challenges to these laws by pregnancy centers and their allies have fared well in the courts. Leading up to a five-to-four Supreme Court ruling striking down California's Reproductive FACT Act in *NIFLA v. Becerra* (2018), pregnancy centers' track record included victories in cases challenging the Baltimore City and Montgomery County laws as well as an Austin, Texas, law and two out of three provisions of a New York City law. Hawai'i's law was struck down in the wake of *NIFLA v. Becerra,* but litigation of the Illinois law had not yet been resolved at the time of this writing. Except for in Austin, where the judge deemed the law to be impermissibly vague, courts ruling in favor of pregnancy centers all upheld arguments that the signage was a form of compelled speech.[37]

What can available information tell us about the extent of pregnancy centers' engagement in what pro-choice advocates label ethically problematic and potential harmful practices? My data offer little more than observations that the major networks' volunteer training manuals and leader statements condemn dishonesty and coercion and call on staff members to respect each client (Chapter 2). As Kelly also finds, most of pregnancy centers' work is with clients who might not be pregnant at all or even considering abortion.[38] I did not observe pregnancy counseling, a limitation shared by all existing scholarly research on pregnancy centers. Other sources, however, bear on this question.

Pregnancy Center Portrayals of Abortion Risks

Amy Bryant and colleagues argue that pregnancy centers commonly provide information contested by medical authorities. Their review of the websites of 254 pregnancy centers listed in twelve states' resources directories for women with unplanned pregnancies concluded that 80 percent "provided at least one false or misleading statement," typically about the health risks of abortion.[39] A different analysis by Bryant and Erika Levi of narratives collected from the undercover visits or phone calls a pro-choice activist group made to North Carolina pregnancy centers, concluded that 53 percent of the thirty-two centers the group reached uttered at least one piece of misleading or incorrect information about the medical risks of abortion or the effectiveness of birth control.[40]

Adjudicating debates about the ethics of the abortion-related information pregnancy centers present to women might be complicated by the observation that pregnancy centers' volunteer training manuals and a Care Net client brochure, "Before You Decide," that I reviewed cite peer-reviewed scientific studies in defense of their claims, such as those that associate abortion with increased risks of depression, anxiety, drug and alcohol abuse, suicide, and breast cancer. The conclusions and methods of such studies, however, have been contested by other studies and represent a minority view among scientific authorities.[41] The American Psychological Association (APA) states, "The best scientific evidence published indicates that among adult women who have an *unplanned* pregnancy the relative risk of mental health problems is no greater if they have a single elective first-trimester abortion than if they deliver that pregnancy."[42] The APA concedes that there might be negative mental health consequences in cases of wanted pregnancies or multiple abortions but says it is uncertain whether these are caused by the abortions or by other, related factors. Meanwhile, the National Cancer Institute (NCI) in 2003 issued an oft-cited report rejecting a link between abortion and breast cancer.[43] Some of the authors of research associating abortion with negative health consequences allege that organizations such as the APA and NCI, along with the mainstream press, have unfairly ignored or discredited their studies and looked past weaknesses in those with different conclusions to protect a political agenda.[44] I am not in a position to evaluate these claims.

In the meantime, pregnancy centers cling apparently quite sincerely to their beliefs that abortion harms women and privilege some types of evidence over others.[45] Care Net's national medical consultant, an obstetrician, cited in her interview the stories aggregated on the website of the Silent No More

Awareness Campaign (a platform for the perspectives of women who regret a previous abortion, sponsored by Priests for Life and Anglicans for Life) as an important motivator of the importance pregnancy centers attached to warning women about abortion's risks. She said that although scientific evidence is important to consider when assessing the aftereffects of abortion, "you can't argue with someone's story."

Pregnancy Centers Posing as Abortion Clinics?
Available evidence suggests that women visiting pregnancy centers under the impression that they are actually abortion providers has not recently been a widespread problem. Bryant and colleagues acknowledge that "a few imply that they offer abortion services."[46] Their analysis of pregnancy center websites reports that 90 percent declared their centers did not refer for abortions. Bryant et al. also found that 56 percent declared a religious affiliation.[47] Katrina Kimport and colleagues, in a short survey of 114 clients at a Louisiana abortion clinic in 2015, found that 7 women (6 percent) said they had visited a pregnancy center in relation to that pregnancy; the study did not indicate how many of these visits were under a misconception. They also found that 5 percent of 269 surveyed Louisiana prenatal clinic patients said they had visited a pregnancy center. Among them, one woman said she contacted the pregnancy center as a result of searching online for an abortion clinic but also said that the center disclosed when she called for an abortion appointment that it did not offer abortions.[48]

Opinions of the courts in the Baltimore City and Montgomery County cases raised doubts regarding the quality of the evidence that pregnancy centers dupe women and cause them harmful delays in obtaining medical care. The opinion of a federal district judge in *Centro Tepeyac v. Montgomery County et al.* cited the county's lack of evidence that any women had ever been harmed by misinformation delivered at a pregnancy center. Among other observations, it noted that statements in the county council's legislative record favoring the resolution came from those "who were universally volunteers from a pro-choice organization sent to investigate LSPRCs' [limited services pregnancy resource centers] practices" and cited acknowledgment before the court by the county's chief health officer that she had never received a complaint from a woman who had been harmed by visiting one of the relevant pregnancy centers.[49] In the Baltimore City case, the majority opinion of the Court of Appeals for the Fourth Circuit concluded: "Here, the record establishes, at most, only isolated instances of misconduct by pregnancy centers generally, and, as the City concedes, none by the Pregnancy Center itself. Indeed, the record contains no evidence that any woman has been misled into believing that any pregnancy center subject to Ordinance 09-252 was a medical clinic or that a woman in Baltimore delayed seeking medical services because of such a misconception."[50]

On the contrary, a pro-choice writer claims that women's fear of going public, rather than lack of harm by pregnancy centers, explains the dearth of firsthand evidence from real clients—so clearly, more research is needed, particularly by outside scholars, on women's experiences at pregnancy centers.[51] Such research might compare experiences with counseling there to experiences with counseling received at Planned Parenthood and other clinics that perform or refer for abortions, including how they address all of women's pregnancy options.

In the meantime, pregnancy centers offer as evidence that they are legitimate and respected service providers the fact that government health and social service agencies refer clients to them. CLI, a conservative pro-life think tank, provided website links from twenty states in an amicus curiae brief it filed with the Supreme Court in a pregnancy-center-related case.[52] Most, but not all of these, belonged to Republican-leaning states. My research in highly Democratic and pro-choice Maryland (which did not appear on CLI's list) suggests that this practice might be even more common. There, interviewees from the Gabriel Network, Sanctuaries for Life, and pregnancy centers in the Baltimore City and Washington, DC, metropolitan regions proudly reported serving clients referred by public agencies. Referrals mentioned by these leaders were for material assistance; housing; personalized, bilingual assistance in navigating the public health and welfare system; and other core services. Additionally, one center's director noted that her center's free classes for fathers fulfilled parenting education requirements attached to some child support orders. Court opinions in the Baltimore City and Montgomery County pregnancy center cases verified that public health and welfare agencies referred women to the affected centers.[53]

Client Satisfaction

Pregnancy centers claim high rates of client satisfaction with their services. Care Net reported that on client exit surveys done in 2013, 2014, and 2015, at least 97 percent of clients in each of those years described their experiences at the center as positive.[54] A national telephone survey CLI commissioned for pregnancy centers in 2014 of 1,000 women and 300 men aged eighteen to forty-four also yielded high favorability ratings. In a follow-up question addressed to the minority of respondents who said that they or someone they knew had visited or used the services of a pregnancy center, 89 percent of women and 78 percent of men said that the person's experience had been "very positive" or "somewhat positive."[55] Confidence in these conclusions could be increased if the research were replicated by parties without a stake in the results.

The study of Louisiana prenatal care clinic patients by Kimport and colleagues is an important step in that direction, though its conclusions are highly limited because of the small sample size. The researchers conducted in-depth interviews with twelve of the fourteen women in their study who said they had visited a pregnancy center, including three who said they did so while planning or considering abortion. Kimport and her coauthors say that their research subjects "uniformly described their CPC experience as positive," citing especially the free goods and services they received. They noted the women's praise for finding at a pregnancy center the opportunity to talk in-depth with someone who seemed to care about them, along with the ease and speed of obtaining an appointment the center offered. Kimport and colleagues also observed that those women who encountered religious messages at pregnancy centers said they appreciated them.[56] For the three women contemplating abortion who later decided against it, Kimport and colleagues suggest that "the visit operated like a final push toward continuing the pregnancy," given other factors involved in their decisions, and that all three reported being happy with the decision to continue their pregnancies.[57]

THE FUTURE OF THE PREGNANCY HELP MOVEMENT

In Chapter 4, I outlined some ways in which pregnancy centers are adapting, or talking about adapting, tactics from Planned Parenthood in order to compete more effectively with it and other abortion providers for clients. This strategy, however, arguably risks eroding some key features of the pregnancy help movement I highlighted in Chapter 1, including "trespass" on territory associated with the pro-choice movement, operation in relatively privatized venues, and general avoidance of targeting the state. Data collected in this research provide some basis for reasoning about how likely this is to happen in the near future.

Future Attention to Poverty

Pregnancy centers' provision of material aid and social services to poor women arguably challenges the pro-choice movement's reputational advantage on poverty, yet medicalization and the talk of "mission drift" might signal a retreat from this work. In an interview, Heartbeat International's Hartshorn acknowledged an effort over the previous twenty years to encourage pregnancy centers to think over the extent of aid they are "called" to offer. However, most local pregnancy centers, she said, regarded material aid as an important resource that should be provided to their clients, and even those centers that did not offer a lot of material aid would make arrangements with other organizations to meet those needs. Thomas Glessner of the National Institute of Family and Life Advocates (NIFLA) reported in his interview that his advice to pregnancy centers regarding social services is, "Don't reinvent the wheel." If other organizations in the community can provide economic assistance to pregnancy center clients in a "workable" way, centers should refer clients to those organizations. They should only directly offer those goods and services not provided adequately elsewhere. Hartshorn in her interview implied that the decision about how much aid to provide was best left for God to reveal to center personnel. The key question, she said, was "what was the call to their founders." It might have been to emphasize engagement of abortion-minded women in a medical setting, but it might also have been to include among their services long-term care and material support to families.

Comments from other leaders I interviewed underscored their firm and widespread commitment, even as the pregnancy center movement medicalized, to continue helping their clients meet their material needs. Citing Biblical passages about the importance of meeting the needs of poor people, Care Net's national consultant for medical issues argued that pregnancy centers must not eliminate social services as they medicalized; they were important features of the "cohesive, well-run Christian organization" that Care Net had invested itself in teaching people how to run. Said the director of the Pregnancy Clinic, although her center had reduced and outsourced some of its material aid provision in order to project an "upscale" image, some in-house material aid was still valuable "for us to be able to assure someone. . . . It's another piece of the support puzzle" (see Chapter 4).

Leaders also credited material aid with facilitating clients' use of other resources the leaders deemed important. Provision of material aid "allows for intangible things to happen," the Gabriel Network's director said; clients might contact his organization to obtain housing, but the housing is coupled with other supportive services that he said boosted clients' sense of self-worth and hope for the future. Another pregnancy center director, in explaining her center's practice of offering material assistance broadly to poor families in its community, raised the possibility that the mothers might face crisis pregnancies later and then come to the center for counseling, remembering the care it provided earlier.

Some leaders envisioned the diminished salience of economic aid as mostly a cosmetic change. So that pregnancy centers could update their decor to make the setting more welcoming to women uneager to be mothers without sacrificing the centers' ability to aid poor women who did, Care Net personnel expressed interest in separating the types of resources they offered at the pregnancy decision phase from the types of resources they offered to women already committed to carrying their pregnancies to term. In a 2011 Care Net conference presentation, representatives of a Missouri pregnancy center discussed how they maintained two locations with different names. One was a medical office that conducted pregnancy and STI/STD testing and counseling. That office referred financially at-risk pregnant clients to the center's second location, which offered material aid and social services, only after their decisions to carry their pregnancies to term had been made.[58] It is largely at this stage that economic assistance becomes important to pregnant women, Care Net's vice president explained, and then "it will be there for them."

Consistent with these sentiments, my Pregnancy Center Director Survey offers just limited evidence that medical pregnancy centers offer a thinner range of material aid than do nonmedical centers. Out of the sixteen types of nonmedical material goods and social services listed in Figure 2.1, nonmedical pregnancy centers reported offering just a slightly higher mean number: 5.7 versus 5.5. The difference in a t-test was not statistically significant ($p = .144$ for a null hypothesis of zero difference). Centers offering medical services reported a lower percentage of clients that appeared to be poor or near-poor (chi-square = 17.7, df = 4, $p = .001$), but they did not necessarily serve fewer poor clients in absolute terms. This is because medical centers' mean 2011 client total exceeded that of nonmedical centers by a factor of about three (477 versus 1,462, $t = -7.96$, $p < .001$). At medical and nonmedical centers alike, the majority of directors reported that poor or near-poor individuals formed the majority of their clients.

Future Institutionalization and Dependence on the State

I suggested in Chapter 4 that some pregnancy help activists aspire to the scale, name recognition, and aura of credibility among women at risk for abortion enjoyed by Planned Parenthood. Planned Parenthood's "more than 600 health centers" number fewer than pregnancy centers and appear to see somewhat similar client loads, though differences in the type of statistics reported by Planned Parenthood and CLI's pregnancy center service report preclude a precise comparison. Clearly, however, the two institutions diverge in the range of services they offer and the pregnancy intentions of the clients they attract. In its 2017 fiscal year, Planned Parenthood reported providing medical services to 2.4 million patients in the United States, including nearly 1.1 million pregnancy tests and more than 330,000 abortions.[59] That only 4 percent of those surveyed in a June 2018 Gallup Poll reported having "no opinion" of Planned Parenthood suggests widespread recognition of the organization.[60] Planned Parenthood's longevity advantage over pregnancy centers—the organization is more than 100 years old—surely contributes to this. However, its relatively uniform branding and its degree of professionalization contribute as well. Further, government grants and reimbursements, which totaled $563.8 million, or 34 percent of Planned Parenthood's revenue, in fiscal 2018, likely enable its volume of medical services.[61]

Pregnancy centers will likely inch toward this model, continuing their trend toward professionalization and expanding their efforts to obtain public funds. Some in the movement have long acknowledged the advantages of public funds.[62] One of the local leaders I interviewed, whose pregnancy center's Pennsylvania office locations received money from a state alternatives to abortion program, argued that the funds had benefitted the center and its clients most importantly by helping the center hire more paid staff and fostering greater accountability.

By contrast, some leaders' statements expose some important brakes on this process that will likely limit the share of centers that eventually do seek government funding and the extent to which centers adopt increasingly professionalized, medicalized, and uniform identities and practices. Regarding government funds, Care Net's vice president reported to me that constraints on evangelization deter many Care Net centers from applying. Other interviewees expressed resistance to seeking government funds out of what appeared to be a more generalized distrust of government. If an organization receives government funding, the New Jersey–based National Life Center's president explained, "that means they can control you." The director of Maryland's Gabriel Network volunteered that his organization's board of directors maintained a firm, "visceral" opposition to applying for those government grants for which the organization would qualify. He traced these to the organization's origins in the wake of Bill Clinton's election and the triumph of pro-abortion policy in a state referendum that same year. The failure of government at its basic responsibility to protect innocent human life, he asserted, drove pro-lifers "deeper into the mindset that you can't trust government."

Many activists also express suspicion, if not disdain, toward a model of service provision characterized by size, formality, and standardization. Louise Summerhill, the founder whose model Birthright and 1st Way centers still try to follow, strongly resisted the idea of growing Birthright into "a highly structured, bureaucratic international agency. If that should ever happen," she predicted, "the sensitive, person-to-person nature of our work will disappear, volunteers will leave, and the true spirit of Birthright will vanish from the earth. Our mission will have ended."[63] Even in the bigger, more professionalized networks, pregnancy help activists highlight as the most fundamental of their resources their staff's availability to give individualized attention and compassion to pregnant women and to enter into long-term relationships with them.[64] National leaders, in my observation, showed sensitivity toward balancing the advantages of setting standards for local centers with deference to the judgments of local leaders and the "calls" some believed God had given those leaders. Disagreement over the degree of uniformity to demand from local centers is an important reason multiple pregnancy center umbrella groups exist (see Chapters 2 and 3). Although local centers might increasingly try to implement some of Planned Parenthood's branding strategies within their own networks and communities, it is hard to imagine much enthusiasm for it nationally.

Future Political Engagement

The institution some pregnancy help leaders aspire to compete with reported spending $76.9 million on "advocacy" and $45 million on "public policy" in the year ending on June 30, 2018. Planned Parenthood encompasses not only its 501(c)(3) service providers but also a 501(c)(4) advocacy group (Planned Parenthood Action Fund) and two entities that spend money on federal election campaigns.[65] The *Atlantic*, a left-leaning magazine, credits Planned Parenthood's recently retired president, Cecile Richards, with "knitting together" the organization's service-providing and advocacy wings "into a brand unlike any other in American politics," creating "a political powerhouse."[66] Given that model, one might wonder if the pregnancy help movement's growth in resources, visibility, and perception of threat might lead it to more actively target the state in its efforts to serve women, deter abortions, and defend its institutional interests.

Although some of my interviewees expressed commitments to avoiding politics, national leaders at Care Net and Heartbeat International suggested their movement could no longer afford this luxury under current political circumstances. Legislation regulating pregnancy centers' advertisements and signage, in their view, threatened centers' freedoms, inaccurately tarnished their reputations, and warranted a call to action regarding the need to educate elected officials about pregnancy centers' work and impact. That is the rationale behind Heartbeat International's Babies Go to Congress event and similar efforts, such as visits to legislatures and the development of pithy statistical reports on pregnancy centers' services to their communities, recommended at a workshop at Care Net's 2011 conference.

A second circumstance some of my interviewees raised as calling for greater political involvement by pregnancy help activists involved perceptions of increasing threats to religious freedom and freedom of conscience. Care Net's national office leaders professed to being worried about an Obama administration mandate that health insurance plans cover all federally approved contraceptives, though they said that the organization had not taken any direct action on the issue other than providing public comments. Care Net consultant and local center medical director Sandy Christiansen said in an interview that she occasionally spoke on political issues, especially what she called "conscience" issues, though not always as an official representative of Care Net. She traced her interest in that matter to discrimination she said she had experienced early in her medical career because of her refusal to perform abortions. Care Net "is not political at all," Christiansen said, but there existed "times when you have to speak out." My interviews took place before the enactment of the state laws requiring pregnancy centers to provide information on accessing abortion, a situation Heartbeat International said "compels" its California centers "to speak a message not only with which they profoundly disagree, but which directly contravenes their very reason for existence."[67]

Because pregnancy help service providers often connect their clients with public antipoverty programs such as Medicaid, some readers might wonder whether the movement would ever advocate on behalf of those programs. Although a local center might occasionally take such a step, it is unlikely that pregnancy centers would do this en masse or that their national associations would take up this cause. Chapter 6 noted the apolitical images pregnancy help organizations strive to cultivate as well as the diversity and ambivalence of local center staff attitudes on social welfare issues. My interviews of local and national leaders also yielded relevant insights, though these should be read cautiously because they arose in various contexts rather than in response to any solicitation of interviewees' social welfare policy positions. They suggest that the pregnancy help movement's relationship to the welfare state is complicated.

National and local leaders typically did not frame social welfare programs as normatively good or bad but rather as one of many appreciated community resources available to help their clients. "Whatever it takes to help that woman carry the baby to term and get started" on her own as a parent, "I think we were all in on," a former Care Net executive said in response to a question about the importance of material aid and social welfare programs to pregnancy centers' missions. In a point also shared by a current executive, this included "helping to connect people to services they're entitled to under the law." Sanctuaries for Life's director stated, "I don't think it matters who's available to help the woman who is uninsured and pregnant, as long as she's served." Even a local center leader who volunteered that she disagreed with "some" welfare programs defended her center's welfare referrals because of the programs' availability.

Ambivalence about the programs also surfaced. One form it took, generally appearing in writing from or references to a period predating national cash welfare time limits, was a view that long-term welfare receipt would be detrimental to clients. A second form of ambivalence combined general support for safety net programs with laments over some programs' perceived entanglements with abortion. One local center director I interviewed expressed gratitude for local public assistance programs that provided medical care to the uninsured but called it ironic that they also financed abortions. Another local interviewee complained that the social safety net did not do more to prevent abortion and that in some cases seemed to be set up to encourage it. He cited eligibility rules for public housing programs that he said made it difficult for pregnant women to receive assistance before their babies were born and also said that a state agency's suspension of new group-home permits made it hard for private agencies to open homes for those women. He also alleged that women participating in safety net programs frequently encountered the message that abortion was the most prudent response to their pregnancies: "So the implicit attitude is [in the safety net], why are they having a baby in the first place?"[68]

Years after the conclusion of my data collection, national pregnancy help umbrella groups continued to express reluctance to advocate institutionally for public policy on abortion. For example, a Heartbeat International representative marking the 2015 anniversary of *Roe v. Wade* promoted for distribution on Twitter: "Laws can only go so far; it is up to us to change the hearts."[69] After New York's 2019 Reproductive Health Act expanded abortion rights in that state, including late in pregnancy, a Care Net blog told readers that "changing the law is only part of the battle" against abortion. It suggested that readers could respond with prayer and contacting elected leaders but especially called them to speak up about their pro-life views and to redouble their support of pregnancy centers.[70] Heartbeat International and NIFLA condemned the law but expressed similar sentiments about potential responses.[71]

In sum, although pregnancy help service providers have increasingly engaged the state in defense of their narrow institutional interests, there is little sign they will substantively extend that effort to other public policy issues.

Competing with Planned Parenthood

This discussion of pregnancy centers' future services, institutionalization, and engagement of the state has suggested there are serious limits to how much of Planned Parenthood's model pregnancy centers would be willing to adopt in order to compete for clients. Here and in Chapter 4, however, I have observed several changes that have gained traction within the pregnancy center movement. These include updating their offices' appearances, expanding their online outreach and geographical proximity to women likely to consider abortion, enlarging their medical service offerings (though excluding abortion and artificial contraception), and hiring more paid staff with relevant professional backgrounds in fields such as health care, social services, and administration.

An interesting question is how far the types of changes pregnancy centers have embraced can go in persuading women who do not want to be pregnant to walk through their doors. Evidence reported earlier in this chapter and in

Chapter 4 suggests that medical pregnancy centers are making progress toward this goal. However, there might be a ceiling. How high that ceiling is, absent further cultural changes that pregnancy centers are also working to achieve, might depend on the accuracy of the pregnancy help movement's theories about abortions and the women who have them. If pro-life activists are correct that large proportions of unintentionally pregnant women, deep down, prefer not to have abortions, are unhappy with their lifestyles, and crave the kinds of personal relationships and mentorship that pregnancy centers want to keep at the heart of their work, then pregnancy centers could greatly increase their target clientele with greater visibility and the resources to implement their plans. If they are wrong, their strategy alone might not erode Planned Parenthood's "market share."

THE POLITICS OF RACE, POVERTY, AND PREGNANCY CENTERS

Striving for Racial Diversity

Another challenge the pregnancy help movement has assigned itself for the future is the racial diversification of its pregnancy centers' leadership and staff. National leaders have adopted initiatives and appealed to their supporters and affiliates to open more pregnancy centers in minority—especially urban, black—communities and recruit more people of color into pregnancy center work. Indeed, 90 percent of my Pregnancy Center Staff Survey sample identified as white, with just under 4 percent identifying as black. The data I presented in Chapter 5 showed that communities with pregnancy centers have substantially lower percentages of black residents than communities with abortion clinics. Meanwhile, Kelly speculates that the current situation in which pregnancy center clients are considerably more likely to be racial minorities (as well as lower in income) than the staff members who serve them compromises pregnancy centers' effectiveness at building relationships with and influencing the decisions of their clients.[72] Because black women make up a disproportionately large share of clients opting for abortion, reaching them appears critical to pregnancy centers' efforts to connect with more abortion-minded women.[73]

Pregnancy centers do not appear unusual in their underwhelming mobilization of racial minorities by pro-life movement streams. Others have observed the high proportion of whites across the movement, including the 93 percent among Munson's four-city activist sample.[74] Black people do play some visible roles as leaders of pro-life organizations in various movement streams, including the individual outreach stream, and one salient movement frame portrays abortion as black genocide, but some scholars question these efforts' persuasiveness to the majority of the black population, much less mainstream civil rights leaders.[75]

Meanwhile, though there are signs that this is changing, the mainstream pro-choice movement has also long underrepresented women of color.[76] Scholars attribute this to the increasingly narrow focus on abortion rights that developed as the movement institutionalized. This contributed to the erosion of an early, racially diverse network of grassroots activists whose multi-issue reproductive rights agenda included social and economic reforms they said facilitated a right to give birth. Moreover, black activists tended to view with suspicion the population control groups and antiwelfare frames the pro-choice movement once more visibly embraced.[77]

The mass mobilization of blacks into pro-life or pro-choice activism, some scholars have suggested, depends on the movements' abilities to acknowledge and address the socioeconomic structural problems they say affect many aspects of black women's lives, including their childbearing decisions and political behavior. Since the 2000s, mainstream pro-choice groups have increasingly adopted "reproductive justice" language to signal a broader orientation and have been working more closely with a resurgent network of activist groups representing women of color and backing a broad reproductive rights agenda.[78] Meanwhile, as Kia Heise has observed, black pro-life leaders tend to support Republican politicians and adhere to conservative social and economic worldviews that place much responsibility for issues such as poverty with individuals. She says this limits their credibility with "reproductive justice" advocates and perhaps with blacks more broadly.[79] Similarly, Kelly and Gochanour characterize pregnancy centers' increasing use of black spokespeople as a largely "surface-level" phenomenon that alone is bound to be ineffective.[80] The problem, they say, is that pregnancy centers tend to offer "individualistic solutions to deeply entrenched societal problems, demanding that poor Black women adapt their lifestyles to those of white evangelicals in order to lift themselves out of poverty."[81]

Pregnancy help activists might still be better positioned than others in the pro-life movement to mobilize blacks. As Kelly and Gochanour agree, some of their frames do, at least, acknowledge contextual social and economic factors in women's reproductive decisions. Also consistent with Kelly and Gochanour's perceptions that some pregnancy center activists are taking seriously the perspectives of generally liberal-leaning blacks, my book recognizes a range of political opinions among pregnancy help activists and resources offered to pregnancy center clients that go far beyond calls for lifestyle change.[82] Because pregnancy help activists operate outside of official political venues and do not target the state, they are arguably freer than pro-life activists in other streams to grapple with issues that might divide political coalitions or alienate key elite allies. Moreover, the faith-based identities embraced by many pregnancy help organizations offer a more promising alternative than forms of political identity as a basis for a racially diverse coalition.

Although not the focus of my study, I saw activists engaging these kinds of arguments at Care Net's 2011 Pregnancy Center Conference, where outreach to blacks was a salient theme. The conference prominently featured several black speakers, some of whom delivered messages that might not have been expected at a gathering of largely white, evangelical pro-life activists. Lamenting that political expediency and the power of moneyed interests had limited pro-life activists' gains when they thought they had allies in the White House, a married couple active in multiple pro-life movement streams and with abstinence education called for the pro-life movement to reinvigorate itself with outreach to "the African American church." Although the couple portrayed that church as transcending ideological categories, the effort envisioned would apparently be implemented through personal friendships, prayer, and pregnancy center service. "Politics is messy," they declared.[83] A conference workshop challenged attendees to better appreciate "the impact of racism in the life of the African-American client" and to use what they learned to "help end racism *and* abortion."[84] Prayer led by Alveda King, a pro-life activist and niece of civil rights leader Martin Luther King, called for unity in the pro-life movement, including "those caring for the poor," along with those serving at pregnancy centers, working in politics, and praying outside of abortion clinics. Headlining speaker Tony Evans, a pastor whose megachurch runs a pregnancy center offered by Kelly and Gochanour as an example of one that took structural problems seriously, praised attendees for "offer[ing] hope in the midst of hopelessness."[85] Evans, like other speakers, conveyed a vision in which Christians worked together across racial and political divides to support the pro-life cause, stating, "This cause is bigger than partisan politics and racial differences."[86]

Considering pregnancy help activists' lack of interest in conventional political advocacy, the success of their racial diversification project might turn on how extensively their cultural transformation work recognizes and attempts to combat the social and economic hardship and disparity faced by many of their clients. Through my research, I perceived a great deal of awareness and concern about these issues. This included recognition of the inadequacy of the material aid pregnancy centers provide relative to what would be needed to ensure economic security for a poor woman choosing to raise a child as a single parent. The aid is a "drop in the bucket," Care Net's former executive director, Curtis Young, conceded. The Gabriel Network's director bemoaned that the "industry of alternatives to abortion" he said was needed to cope with the consequences of "choosing life" for poor women and for society was "not all there."

Whether the pregnancy help movement is able to marshal the resources and will for greater cultural activism on these issues is another matter. Scholars' recognition of an evangelical movement toward racial healing and a "new evangelical social engagement" characterized by service and advocacy in a wide range of policy areas increases its plausibility.[87] However, the pregnancy help movement has already substantially broadened its mission and work beyond intervention in the pregnancy decisions of women contemplating abortion, and some leaders now call for a recovery of some of that focus.

Pregnancy Help versus the Welfare State

Related to this matter is some critics' charge that the pro-life movement is limiting not only its mass appeal but also its impact on abortions by failing to adequately address the leading cause of abortion in their estimation: poverty.[88] In some critics' eyes, an expansion of the welfare state as well as reforms of economic and social structures are needed more than expansion of pregnancy center work. Pro-choice advocates have expressed concern that in some states, money directed to pregnancy centers has come from block grants dedicated to TANF, a program providing cash assistance and other social services to low-income families with the stated goal of moving them toward economic self-sufficiency.[89] Texas has also diverted funds from other women's health and public health projects to support pregnancy centers.[90]

Although my research showed some support among pregnancy help activists for these critics' argument, activists tended toward skepticism about how far economic aid could go at dissuading abortions, at least in isolation from other supports. Many national and local leaders I interviewed credited their organizations' offers of material support with incremental or indirect contributions to clients' decisions to carry their pregnancies to term but—with some exceptions—tended to characterize the situations in which such economic support made the difference alone in a decision between abortion and childbearing as relatively rare. My national sample of pregnancy center staff seems to agree. Just over half of Pregnancy Center Staff Survey respondents who affirmed they had been "personally involved in a situation in which a client at this or another pro-life pregnancy center had been seriously considering abortion and then later chose to give birth" rated "receiving help with affording a child" as very important to women's changes of mind about abortion. It was rated as unimportant or inapplicable by only 4.5 percent (see Table 7.1). A plurality, 44 percent, rated "resolving conflicts with education or employment" as very important. Of the nine potential factors assessed on the survey regarding women's changes of mind about abortion, however, staff rated an average of six as very important.

A small (n = 45) survey of postpartum pregnancy center clients that I fielded in Baltimore in 2005 as part of a different research project produced a similar set of views. A battery of questions regarding the importance of various factors in a woman's decisions to "have and raise your baby" included two potential solutions to financial need: "I got help affording a baby from a government program like welfare (TANF), food stamps, Medicaid, child care assistance, or housing assistance" and "I got help affording a baby from family, friends, my employer, school, or church or another organization." Of the respondents, 49 percent rated government assistance as "very important" to their decision, whereas 59 percent rated nongovernmental assistance as "very important." However, respondents also identified an average of 4.5 reasons (out of a possible 9) as "very important" to their decision, and the economic reasons were never cited on their own. Psychological and social factors were cited far more commonly than economic ones, including a belief that motherhood is very fulfilling (89 percent), the experience of seeing an ultrasound image of the fetus (75 percent), the support of special people in the woman's life (68 percent), and moral objection to abortion (66 percent). Of the respondents, 45 percent rated "counseling or help from this (or another) pregnancy center" as "very important" to their decision, a figure that rose to 67 percent after removing the nearly one-third of respondents who indicated that they had not visited a

Table 7.1 Pregnancy Center Staff's Ratings of Factors in Changes of Mind about Abortion

	% Very Important	% Not Important/ NA	Mean Total V.I. Reasons When V.I.
Receiving help with affording a child	52.5	4.5	7.2
Resolving conflicts with education or employment	44.4	12.8	7.6
Seeing an ultrasound image of their unborn child	95.5	0.0	6.2
Learning facts about fetal development	83.3	0.6	6.5
Learning about abortion's risks to their physical or mental health	56.7	1.7	7.1
A religious experience	55.0	8.3	7.0
Support from the father of the child	56.5	2.3	7.1
Encouragement from a parent or friend	84.5	0.6	6.5
Time to reflect on their situation and values	80.1	0.6	6.5

Source: Pregnancy Center Staff Survey

Note: Respondents saying they were personally involved in a woman's change of mind only (N = 176).

pregnancy center during their pregnancy. Still excluding those respondents, 13 percent of the rest rated counseling or help provided by a pregnancy center as "not important."

The survey also included the question: "Think about the help you got from government programs, family, friends, or others, with your expenses like baby supplies, child care, health care, housing, and time off from work or school. Do you think you would have had an abortion if you had not received this help?" There, a solid majority (59 percent) of respondents professed that they would not have made a different decision. Eight women (18 percent) said that they would have had an abortion in the absence of that support, and 23 percent said they were unsure.

These findings should be taken extremely cautiously. Survey results might not be generalizable given the small and localized sample and other facts about the research design described in Appendix D. It might also be relevant that, as with many other pregnancy center clients, the large majority of respondents (71 percent) reported deciding "almost immediately" to continue the pregnancy and raise the baby. Nonetheless, they offered tentative and preliminary corroboration of pregnancy center leaders' views that helping low-income women cope with the costs of a child plays a valuable but complex and not often singularly decisive role in encouraging the choice of alternatives to abortion.

Pregnancy centers' in-house antipoverty aid, of course, pales in comparison with the resources the state does or could marshal for this cause. As I showed in Chapter 6, a nontrivial minority of my Pregnancy Center Staff Survey sample endorsed the view that a greatly expanded welfare state could greatly reduce abortions. Available empirical research is insufficient to assess this conclusively but does offer some basis for speculation.

First, studies on the relationships of US welfare program generosity and receipt to abortion suggest that welfare might have a discernible "pro-life" effect but a modest one conditional on characteristics of the woman or her context.[91] Public assistance in the United States, however, is modest relative to what European countries typically offer. A more interesting exploration of the opportunity cost of pregnancy centers might therefore consider the relationship between welfare generosity and abortion rates cross nationally. Surprisingly, no such study appears to have been published.

A vast social science literature on the economics of fertility, encompassing cross-national evidence, meanwhile expresses caution about governments' capacity to influence childbearing using tools such as social welfare and tax policies. A review by Anne Gauthier observes that studies' findings are "mixed" in multiple policy areas, with some reporting small, positive impacts of policy on fertility and others reporting no impact. Gauthier concludes that family policies might have some impact on fertility, but that any impact is substantively small and driven more by changes in the timing of births than in total family size.[92] An analysis of Russia's pronatalist family policies suggests a similar conclusion.[93] Another review of the literature expresses somewhat more optimism about government's capacity to boost fertility but points to government's role in shaping the cultural context of those policies as the key mechanism.[94] Because many European countries expanded their welfare states long ago, however, and in the context of concern about falling birth rates, it is unclear how well conclusions about the impact of those policies would generalize to the contemporary United States.[95]

Perhaps tellingly, many pro-choice activists as well as researchers writing in pro-choice and other academic journals share the doubt or uncertainty of many pregnancy help activists that economic aid alone could substantially reduce US abortions. In describing women's reasons for having abortions, pro-choice writers emphasize the unique attributes of each woman's situation and that women typically articulate multiple, often interlocking, reasons for their abortions.[96] Early studies projected that this would make it difficult to design interventions to significantly reduce abortions after pregnancy has occurred.[97] In a prominent book arguing in favor of abortion rights, feminist writer Katha Pollitt similarly questions whether many women will choose to give birth even if given more money, adding to the multiple reasons the assertion that financial aid would not sway the minds of the many women having abortions who simply do not want to be mothers at a particular time.[98]

With limits, a companion survey to my 2005 Baltimore pregnancy center client survey—this one of patients at three Baltimore-area abortion clinics—potentially offers insights on this matter. This effort, described in Appendix D, also might not be generalizable because of the small sample size (n = 63), geographical restriction, and other concerns. The survey did, however, directly pose to clients opting for abortion a question other scholars have not asked. The data also provided an opportunity for original analysis of women's self-reports about the importance of different factors in their reproductive decisions.

Consistent with previously cited research, my respondents commonly cited financial need as a reason for choosing abortion. The two financial need reasons my survey included for women to rate as "very important," "somewhat important," "not important" or "not applicable" were the least likely of all the thirteen items in the battery to be rated as unimportant or inapplicable. These were: "I cannot afford to have a baby because I struggle to afford my own and my family's basic needs," and "I can afford my own and my family's basic needs, but I cannot afford to have a baby." However, also consistent with previous research, women who identified one or both of the financial need responses as very important to their abortion decision cited an average of 4.6 very important reasons for their abortion, a figure statistically (p < .001) and substantially higher than the 1.1 very important reasons identified by women who did not rate financial need as very important.

Uniquely, the survey presented clients who chose abortion a safety net scenario similar to that available in the most generous European welfare states, asking:

Other countries provide a lot of assistance to women and their families that the government, employers, and schools in the U.S. do not provide. These countries give women things like free child care, free health care, money they can use to pay their family's expenses, and the chance to take months or even years off of work with pay after giving birth. Would you have made a different decision about your pregnancy if you could get that kind of help?

A plurality of respondents, 44 percent, professed that they would not have made a different decision. Half that number (22 percent) said that they would have. The rest said they were unsure.

These figures, albeit from a small and localized sample, join other research reviewed and reported in this section to suggest that a more expansive welfare state might well reduce the incidence of abortions but would come with a ceiling and considerable uncertainty regarding the magnitude of any reduction. It is therefore not obvious that pro-life activists or their allies in government are passing up a tremendous opportunity to reduce abortion when channeling aid to poor women through pregnancy centers rather than existing or expanded welfare programs, although there clearly seems to be more that could be done through either route to ease the substantial economic costs of childbearing.

CONCLUSION

Because the pregnancy help movement perceives itself as under attack from pro-choice forces, it has shown increasing consciousness about the need to demonstrate its pregnancy centers' impact and to engage, to a limited extent, with government. As it does this, it has not backed down from its conviction that abortion harms, or can harm, women. Others' research indicates that the majority of pregnancy centers make claims about abortion's risks to women, including openly on their websites, deemed by scientific authorities as misleading or false. In contrast, despite episodic reports of its occurrence, available evidence does not suggest that large numbers of women are coming to pregnancy centers under the mistaken impression that they can obtain an abortion there. Available evidence also indicates pregnancy centers provide services that women who do not want or who are ambivalent about abortion appreciate and that most women have positive experiences there. Because much of that evidence comes from individual testimonies or from research performed or sponsored by pregnancy centers and their allies, however, confidence in these conclusions would be strengthened by further scholarly research.

Differing perspectives on whether pregnancy centers should be evaluated as volunteer organizations serving women or activist organizations trying to stop abortions color evaluations of their performance. Though pregnancy centers struggle to attract and change the minds of women considering abortion in the proportions that many believe successful enterprises ought to, in absolute terms the numbers are not trivial. The general approach to social change reified by pregnancy centers and many other volunteer groups, which Nina Eliasoph calls "changing the world one x at a time," frequently receives criticism for limited results and distracting attention from pursuit of more sweeping state-led reforms.[99] It might well apply to the pro-life pregnancy help movement. Considerable uncertainty surrounds the magnitude of its impacts on abortion incidence and women's well-being, necessitating more research. However, there is not compelling evidence that state-led efforts to improve women's economic security—although potentially incrementally impactful— would dramatically reduce demand for abortion, either. Yet this, too, is an open question, given the limits of existing research and the data presented here.

The pregnancy help movement might continue to talk of competing with Planned Parenthood. It might continue to expand its scope, tinker with its image, and step up its political engagement to defend its institutions' reputations and their freedom to operate as they wish. Despite this, it is unlikely to abandon its fundamental strategy of fighting abortion through privatized outreach and charitable aid.

8. Conclusions: Targets, Trespass, Service, and Foundations in Faith

This book began with the proposition that the work being performed at pro-life pregnancy centers, maternity homes, and other charitable agencies represents a form of pro-life activism distinguished by several strategic features. The pro-life pregnancy help movement directs its work for change at nonstate targets, operates in largely privatized venues, employs service provision as its primary tactic, and aims to address causes popularly associated with its countermovement such as women's (including poor women's) well-being and empowerment. When it comes to the movement's pregnancy centers, however, its motives and the nature of the most salient "services" it delivers have become the subjects of competing political narratives—but little empirical research. In this book, I thus set out to explore the identity, work, history, and impact of pro-life pregnancy centers and related service providers as well as their relations with the larger US antiabortion movement.

In this concluding chapter, I synthesize evidence presented throughout the book to develop a coherent account of why and how a form of antiabortion activism with these strategic features emerged, grew in its scale and tactical scope, and appeals to activists today. I begin by assessing how well potential factors in social movement organizations' (SMOs') strategic choices and service provision perform in accounting for the pro-life pregnancy help movement. I next elaborate on an important aspect of activists' identities I suggest is key to understanding the forms the movement's actions have taken: their religious faith. I then turn to the nature of pregnancy help work itself: To what extent is it primarily geared at serving women versus "saving babies?" The book closes by considering the implications of this answer and my broader study for scholarship on social action and the pro-life movement, and for the future of the abortion conflict.

ASSESSING EXPLANATIONS

Political Opportunity and Frustration

Little evidence exists that there was ever a moment in the pro-life movement's history when some conscious decision was made to change tactics and begin devoting attention to supporting women facing problem pregnancies. Pro-life pregnancy centers began sprouting in the United States as repeal of criminal abortion prohibitions arose on state legislative agendas in the late 1960s and early 1970s. By the time of the *Roe v. Wade* decision in 1973, pro-life activists had already founded two associations to facilitate the work and the spread of pregnancy centers. Individuals who would found pregnancy centers played active roles in the networks of the newly emerging pro-life movement. From the start, the plans for collective action against the legalization of abortion developed within the early pro-life movement's key institution, the Catholic Church, included outreach to pregnant women and support of alternatives to abortion.

Other features of the developmental path of pregnancy help activism are also largely inconsistent with the idea that actual or perceived contractions of political opportunity (in this case, to outlaw abortion) prompted activists to seek new targets, promoting growth in the numbers and resources of the pregnancy help movement. Expansions in pro-life individual outreach only rarely appear to be tied to the ebbs and flows of the pro-life movement's political prospects, whether in activists' own narratives or in a more objective attempt to map major events in the individual outreach stream onto the timing of apparent changes in political opportunity. Many of the startups of pregnancy centers and the diversification of the types of organizations that would support alternatives to abortion had already been accomplished by the time the pro-life movement's political prospects appeared to dim considerably in the early 1990s. Pregnancy centers' history shows an apparently consistent march of programmatic growth as centers added such functions as postabortion support, abstinence education, parenting and life skills classes, and medical services beyond the pregnancy test. An important exception is that national pregnancy center leaders promoted a burst of innovations in the early to mid-1990s, and some grounded this in perceptions that ending abortion through the political process was increasingly unrealistic. However, they also identified many other factors as contributing to these innovations and the resource growth that would make them possible.

Data from contemporary pregnancy center activists and on the distribution of pregnancy help organizations across states largely corroborate the conclusion that neither perceptions of limited political opportunity nor the political feelings of frustration or despair contribute substantially to the appeal of pregnancy help activism to its practitioners and donors. There is evidence that such feelings might contribute to some pregnancy center activists' avoidance of political activities. Overall, however, pregnancy center activists report varying levels of interest in and experience with pro-life political activism as well as a wide range of opinions about the prospects for banning abortion through the political process. Data suggest that the most recently mobilized activists are less likely to come to pregnancy help work with experience with other forms of pro-life activism than earlier cohorts of activists, and leaders in general express little fondness for politics. At the state level, the number of pregnancy centers established relative to the population is related to variation in political opportunity only after taking into account public support for the pro-life position on abortion. As a general rule, increasing numbers of pregnancy centers are much more clearly a sign of the pro-life movement's cultural strength than of its political weakness.

Responding to Unmet Need

The distribution of pregnancy centers across states appears to have much more in common with that of other human service charities. Beyond that, however, my analyses find either no relationship or a counterintuitive relationship with indicators of the relative magnitude of the "need" for pregnancy centers. Pregnancy centers exist in both high-poverty and low-poverty communities. Pregnancy center proliferation is inversely related to abortion rates at the state level, without taking any other variables into account. Resource availability in high-abortion-rate states, coupled with the movement's decentralized, grassroots nature, is likely an important constraint on the deployment of pregnancy centers to places where the "need" for their services would appear to be greatest.

Exploring how "need" varies cross sectionally, however, might insufficiently test whether the pregnancy help movement has arisen and grown in response to some objective indicator of "need" for its services. For a movement logically organized around helping individuals and also aimed at making abortion "unwanted and unthinkable" rather than merely reducing it, "need" theoretically exists anywhere, and its magnitude is irrelevant. Further, exploration of the types of activities in which pregnancy help outreach workers are engaged and the goals they have set for themselves suggests that activists envision themselves meeting types of "need" that go well beyond that for information and support during a problem pregnancy.

Stronger evidence surfaces for unmet need's appearance as a framing strategy than as an objective measure. Pregnancy help activists regularly and saliently sell their movement to potential volunteers, donors, and clients for its collective effort to counter the lack of support in women's lives they say leaves those women feeling they have no choice but abortion. They have rationalized their movement on these grounds since its inception, and among pregnancy help activists there is near-unanimous agreement that most women having abortions are pressured into them by others or by their circumstances. Pregnancy help leaders and staff have tried to pass on this sympathetic view of the abortion-seeking woman to other pro-life activists and have critiqued those who have not yet internalized it. They define themselves in relation to other pro-life activists in terms of their attention to this human need, and they draw heavily on secular and Christian versions of humanitarianism for the moral basis for their work. Statements volunteered by some activists suggested a belief that their centers are filling voids other institutions—from the welfare state to Planned Parenthood to local charities, not to mention significant people in the woman's life—do not. Need for practical resources to cope with the financial burdens of parenthood is included among these voids, but pregnancy center activists, who stress relationships in their theory of and approach to reducing the incidence of abortion, seem to see a response to social and spiritual, rather than material, poverty as closer to the heart of their work. Thus the *perception* of need among abortion-seeking women and others appears to be an original and enduring motivation of pro-life pregnancy help work, even if supply-side concerns might limit where, when, and the scale on which pregnancy help activists respond.

Ideology and Attitudes toward the State

Pregnancy help activists' rhetorical trespassing on pro-choice territory and the tangible assistance they provide to poor women do not appear inspired by political ideologies—feminism and social welfare liberalism—not traditionally associated with the pro-life movement. Neither is the movement an oppositional one within the larger pro-life movement. Activists sympathetic with feminism and social welfare liberalism surely do work in the pro-life pregnancy help movement, and those views are negatively associated with the likelihood activists involve themselves in political and other pro-life activism in addition to pregnancy center work. Overall, however, left-leaning activists appear to be in the minority among pregnancy center staff.

At the same time, there is little evidence that activists have refrained from targeting the state in their efforts to support alternatives to abortion because of ideological objections to the welfare state. During the late 1960s, when pregnancy centers were introduced, and into the 1970s as they spread, liberal Democrats led much of the pro-life movement.[1] Differences in party platforms and party activist opinions on abortion were not especially stark. Neither were activist attitudes on abortion and social welfare as tightly bundled as they are today.[2] Today, many rank-and-file pregnancy center activists express the view that government is doing too much, but both leaders' statements about public programs and the ways in which the typical pregnancy center works in partnership with government and community agencies to serve women suggest that much of this support for limited government is nuanced and conditional. I find evidence in the movement of ambivalence toward the welfare state, in which appreciation for its direct aid to women mixes with doubt about its long-term efficacy, suspicion of its promotion of abortion, and fear that its resources could be used to suppress Christian expression.

In the end, though, political ideology simply is not salient to the way pregnancy help activists frame their work. Although most pregnancy help leaders identify with the pro-life movement, the typical pregnancy center identifies itself as a ministry or a service provider rather than an activist organization. Consistent with this identity, its personnel tend to distance themselves from overtly political activity when representing the center.

Activists often describe themselves as attracted to pregnancy centers' problem-solving work, which many see as more productive in ending abortion and helping women than addressing those issues through the political process. This and the apolitical image pregnancy centers try to project might have aided activist recruitment by making their work resonate with unpoliticized, pro-life citizens, as it did for some of my interviewees and as might also be seen in new activists' relatively lower levels of pro-life movement participation. However, evidence suggests that over time, pregnancy centers do not lull their personnel into avoiding politics in their private lives but rather spark interest in politics, social issues, and other forms of pro-life activism.

Movement-Countermovement Dynamics

I find evidence of movement-countermovement dynamics at work in the development of the pro-life pregnancy help movement, especially in pregnancy centers' efforts to attract more pregnant women at risk of choosing abortion.[3] Many pregnancy centers have adapted frames, tactics, and various other attributes of abortion providers and abortion rights advocates as they compete to offer their services to overlapping core client groups. Birthright founder Louise Summerhill, for example, claimed to have borrowed the very idea of a pregnancy center from a British telephone service that aimed to help women procure abortions while they were still heavily restricted.[4] Over time, pregnancy centers' adoption of "woman-centered counseling," medicalization, professionalization, online advertising and outreach, and initiatives to establish more urban locations have to some extent reflected learning from their opposition and responses to their opposition's attempts to discredit them. Consistent with this story, I find an association between individual pregnancy centers' uptake of some of these innovations and the presence of an abortion clinic in the pregnancy center's city, county, or metropolitan area.

These changes are not merely superficial ones in which pregnancy centers try to look like abortion clinics. My interviewees suggested that medicalization in particular has meant significant change in the way pregnancy centers operate, even as their implementation of this practice has been infused with their own values. It has also been backed by substantial resource growth.

As important as this drive to compete with abortion clinics is to understanding some of pregnancy centers' actions (see Chapter 4), it is incomplete. My research suggests that pregnancy centers' strategies to compete are sometimes exaggerated in the popular press. This includes alleged deceptive and coercive practices. Additionally, although various voices within the pro-life movement have encouraged pregnancy centers to obtain property in close proximity to abortion clinics, in part in the hopes that women will accidentally enter the pregnancy center instead, the typical pregnancy center does not appear to be shadowing an abortion clinic. There is, in fact, an inverse relationship between numbers of pregnancy centers and numbers of abortion providers at the state level. The majority of abortion clinics have no pregnancy center within even the same zip code, and the vast majority of pregnancy centers operate in communities without abortion clinics. Some within the pregnancy help movement actively resist the idea of mimicking some of abortion providers' strategies, especially the formality of their operations. Further, pregnancy center personnel indicated that their movement's job will not be finished even if abortion is outlawed.

WHAT MAKES THE MOVEMENT "TICK"

The discussion above suggests that many ideas appearing in the scholarly literature on SMOs' strategies and engagement in service provision help us understand the pregnancy help movement's development, appeal, and tactical choices. However, taking all these things together still misses what makes the contemporary pro-life pregnancy help movement "tick," in the sense that it is a source of the movement's energy, goals, ideas, and enduring appeal to activists and supporters. This source is important to identify, given how clashes over policy related to pregnancy centers now unfolding in legislatures and courts turn on dramatically different characterizations of pregnancy center activists' motives and the nature of their organizations' work.

Nina Eliasoph argues that we can understand what makes a movement "tick" by asking, "*How* do people in a civic association connect or disconnect 'caring about people' and 'caring about politics'?"[5] As I have shown especially in Chapter 6, pro-life pregnancy help activists often treat whatever "caring" they show toward politics as a matter of compulsion: it is something they must do from time to time if they want to save women and the unborn from abortion, slow cultural slides down a slippery slope, and retain the freedom for themselves to "care about people" in their institutions in the way that they see fit. The scope of their political activism is tightly limited to cultural issues linked clearly to pregnancy, abortion, and the operation of pregnancy help institutions. Meanwhile, defining their centers as ministries, many express a reluctance to care (or at least, to appear to care) too much about politics for fear that it could interfere with their demonstration of caring about people.

What makes pro-life individual outreach tick does not appear to be an issue as understood in the realms of policy and politics. Activists often describe their movement as being most fundamentally about something different than this—a way of caring for people that arguably cannot be accomplished by an impersonal and secular state. As pregnancy help activists construct it, the heart of their work is supposed to be about loving God and neighbor, especially one's most vulnerable and suffering neighbors. "We are not primarily workers for God or for His causes; we are first and foremost lovers of God," Heartbeat International's training manual tells its staff.[6] Care Net tells its staff, "The goal of pregnancy center ministry is to reach out and offer hurting people the love of Christ. This love is demonstrated by sharing life-affirming alternatives to abortion, ministering healing and reconciliation for those who have experienced abortion, and offering eternal hope for the future in Jesus Christ."[7] "The essence of the Birthright service is love," wrote the organization's founder.[8]

Pregnancy Help and the Practice of Love

References to love are ubiquitous in pregnancy help organizations' official frames of their work. Adding to the evidence, Heartbeat International's training manual, *The LOVE Approach,* argues that "love or charity, whose ultimate source is God, should be our deepest *motive* for helping."[9] It adds that love is "the ultimate source of our wisdom and strength" and also "our behavior" and "practical approach."[10] Care Net's training manual states, "Pregnancy center ministry is rooted in the compassion and love of Jesus Christ."[11] Pregnancy centers' mission with respect to the client, the organization instructs its staff, is "loving her with action and in truth."[12]

These ideas are just as present when local centers' leaders speak freely of what they do. Local center director Mariana Vera professed that her center's "code" was to treat women with "love." Another director framed the material goods provided through her centers as communicating the "love" of donors for the women who would receive them. Local center board president Cookie Harris said she was most proud of her center for the way it cared for women, specifically: "They get love here."

Key movement documents define love as involving an other-regarding perspective, nonjudgmental attitudes, and action. Birthright founder Summerhill wrote, "Love means to care and serve and be responsible for other people, so that, as soon as we see another in distress, we immediately respond."[13] To Care Net, citing Jesus as its model, love "values and esteems others and is unselfish—ready to serve others and put their needs first."[14] Heartbeat International defines love with a famous Biblical passage listing its characteristics, including patience, kindness, humility, selflessness, and constancy.[15] It and Care Net both teach that love should be shown unconditionally.[16]

Love, representatives of some major pregnancy center associations have suggested, is ultimately the solution to abortion. "Love is the most needed ingredient in solving the problems of abortion," Birthright's Summerhill argued in 1973.[17] Heartbeat International's Margaret "Peggy" Hartshorn argued in a 2013 speech to national pro-life leaders that "the root problem in the Culture of Death is selfishness. The answer is selflessness. That's love. In the pro-life movement of the future, we must make selflessness, personal investment, healing, restoration, new vision, and sharing the Good News . . . part of everything we do, because of the sin and woundedness around us."[18] Care Net suggests that the gospel and the rest of God's word in the Bible, which its pregnancy center Bible calls God's "love letter to you," helps people to make the hard choices that it sees as key to ending abortion.[19] "The Gospel is the long-term solution to a client's problems in lifestyle, relationships, or pregnancy choices. The Gospel is what allows women who come to your center to make life-affirming decisions that have eternal consequences."[20]

Leaders, of course, also endorse pragmatic, concrete responses to abortion, but they cast the effectiveness of *any* message or resource as dependent on the context of its delivery. The most effective context, interviews and training documents suggested, was an authentic, loving, supportive relationship. Messages about abortion or Christianity would be rejected, they presumed, if not delivered in a loving manner, respectful of the woman's dignity, priorities, and degree of openness to such a message. Messages about the "sanctity of human life," Care Net's volunteer training manual warns, lose power as they are unmoored from messages about God's love for humankind.[21] Sharing the gospel itself, it says, "is not about religion—it is about relationships."[22] Heartbeat International's Hartshorn argues that the movement's "tools . . . do not work very well unless incorporated with the personal touch, the personal involvement and love of one person shared with another."[23] Her organization's volunteer training manual claims that even exposing a pregnant woman to an ultrasound image will be unlikely to dissuade her from abortion if not "done within a pregnancy help medical clinic . . . in the context of relationship building with the mother of the child."[24] It continues, "Our influence is not as much through our knowledge, professionalism, authority, equipment, or some other factor that comes from outside of us, or is conferred on us. . . . Our influence is effective because of who we are and because of the relationship that we form with the client or patient."[25]

The Example of Jesus Christ

Individual outreach activists often described the love they aspired to show as modeled on the example and teaching of Jesus Christ. Heartbeat International's president, when interviewed, said she frequently presented the Bible's Good Samaritan, from a parable Jesus told, as a model for pregnancy center staff and the Biblical basis for her organization. She explained that the story of the Good Samaritan nicely reflected her organization's dual religious and secular motives, defining the secular one as helping a person in need.[26] In her interview, the Nurturing Network's (TNN) founder rooted her emphasis on practical action over other antiabortion strategies in the way that Jesus allegedly addressed social ills and "broken" people: "He would roll up his sleeves . . . bind up their wounds. . . . To me, it's rooted in my faith." Explaining her agency's aid to the poor, Michelle Williams of Sanctuaries for Life also invoked Jesus' attention to material human needs as well as his listening skills. Care Net observes, "Jesus never exerted political influence to usher in the Kingdom of God . . . never lobbied for political reform, nor did He endorse rival candidates to the corrupt Roman occupiers." Instead, Jesus showed love to individuals.[27] It further notes that the "love and concern" Christ showed was "for the powerless, the poor, the widows, and the orphans."[28] Heartbeat International tells its volunteers, "It is by sacrificial service, modeled on Christ as the Servant of His Father and Our Savior who died for us, that we save lives and change lives."[29]

Pregnancy help activists also follow cues they say Jesus' ministry sent in privileging direct, person-to-person service as a strategy for coping with human need. Writes TNN's Mary Cunningham Agee, Jesus ministered

almost always to one, uniquely blessed, soul at a time. For every miraculous incident where Jesus fed the masses with a few loaves and fish, there are far more instances where He healed a certain leper, cured a chosen blind man, and forgave the sins of a specific sinner. . . . He refused to keep a safe distance . . . He reached out and touched one broken hurting person at a time.[30]

Faith-Based Character

The degree to which interviewees and movement communications provided faith-based reasoning for what they do contrasts with the much less overtly religious face pregnancy help organizations seem to present to clients and the public at local centers. Although a large image of the Virgin Mary adorned a waiting room wall of one of the pregnancy centers I visited, one that had not styled itself after a medical office, in no other location did religious decor catch my attention. With some exceptions, casual glances at local center websites I visited during this research typically did not make it immediately evident that those centers were faith-based organizations. The movement's faith-based character is not necessarily concealed. One interviewee, for example, asserted that Care Net and the staff at the local center where she worked do not believe in hiding their Bibles. The pregnancy center featured at the start of this book, on the same glass storefront advertising its services, identifies itself as "A Ministry for Life." Upon close scrutiny of the walls inside, tucked amid pictures of babies and teddy bears and flyers and brochures advertising various public health and social service resources, I did find signs of the center's faith-based identity, such as a framed sketch of what appeared to be Jesus embracing a woman and quotes conveying what appear to be intended as inspirational messages from religious sources. The pregnancy center should not overflow with messages about Jesus's love, Care Net's president cautioned, because the client is in a "different place."

Regardless of the varied ways in which pregnancy help service providers addressed religion in their client- and public-facing communications, it was clear that behind the scenes, their staff members drew tremendous strength and energy from their faith.[31] Despite her organization's nonevangelizing nature, Birthright's then-director professed that it "runs on prayer power." Another local center director said that she and the rest of her center's staff regularly prayed together. Programs of both Care Net and Heartbeat International conferences are generously sprinkled with "praise and worship" and other religious devotions and activities, in addition to the more standard secular conference material such as informational and training sessions, networking and fellowship opportunities, motivational speeches, and recognition of notable individual and organizational accomplishments. At Care Net's conference, I observed participants praying at length over each other, a ritual Heartbeat International also claims to include.[32]

Heartbeat International and Care Net training manuals impress upon staff members the importance of tending to their own relationships with God and using those as the basis of their work at pregnancy centers. Heartbeat International instructs its volunteers, "The heart of ministry must be the Lord God Himself. Only through an intimate love relationship with Him will we be ready to enter into the work He has prepared for us. Know God. Love God. Then, love His people."[33] Staff members appeared to have responded: 75 percent of Pregnancy Center Staff Survey respondents professed that their "religious commitment" had increased as a result of their service at the pregnancy center, and just a single person out of 268 professed that it had decreased.

Heartbeat International in particular has been moving in recent years to adopt a more explicitly faith-based identity. Until 1993, it labeled itself "nondenominational and nonsectarian." It then began calling itself "an interdenominational Christian association" to reflect the presence of Protestants in its ranks, and it now calls itself a "Christ-centered association."[34] The association's then-president reported in her interview that her organization made other changes over her tenure to reflect its Christian identity. It updated its filings with the Internal Revenue Service (IRS) to add "religious purposes" to its reasons for requesting its 501(c)(3) tax status and encouraged its affiliates to follow. It introduced religious services and practices into its conferences with increasing volume and variety. It also crafted Biblically based training materials. These changes, the president writes in a book on her organization's history and work, were welcomed by local personnel. She also professes in that book to have gradually arrived at the insight that encouraging a greater awareness of and adherence to "God's plan for our sexuality" among individuals and in the culture properly belonged at the "core" of her organization's varied activities—and would relieve tremendous human suffering.[35]

Trusting in God's Guidance and Provision for the Movement

In my book, I have already shown how commonly participants in the pro-life pregnancy help movement attributed their involvement as well as the rise of new organizations and innovations within it to divine inspiration or calls. In doing so, activists expressed a particular spirituality and religious worldview of a God constantly active in human affairs, who watches his creatures, who desires good for them, and who has plans for every individual. This God persistently tries to catch humans' attention. He speaks back, though not necessarily in words, to those who take time to engage him and listen. He personally calls people to particular levels of involvement or action within the movement, and he supplies every resource necessary for fulfillment of his plans. Although no activist stated this explicitly, enlisting the power of the state, plausibly, is not necessary for solving problems (though sometimes helpful) with such a God on the movement's side. Pregnancy help activists rhetorically committed themselves and in practice did appear to make efforts to address a variety of needs associated with alternatives to abortion. However, the idea that God is ultimately in control relieves pressure on activists to have a preplanned answer to every problem that might arise as a result of their work for individuals, society, or the organization itself.

Financial matters were volunteered often by interviewees as requiring trust in God's provision. One local center director said that employees at her center have to be prepared for the possibility that they will not be paid sometimes but claimed that she left finances to God: "He's in charge of the boat," she stated. Another leader, Linda Cochrane, marveled, "God totally blesses us and fulfills all our needs, really. We might not have everything we want, but we have everything we need."

Leaders frequently credited God as the source of new ideas and the supplier of labor and of people with specific talents needed in the movement. Some referred to other leaders as people God "brought forth"[36] or "raised up."[37] A local center director who claimed to have felt unqualified for her job when it fell into her lap in the 1980s marveled at how "God brought people" with gifts she did not have to sustain and grow the center. Heartbeat International's Hartshorn described the pregnancy help movement as "another entire army of pro-life warriors that was being raised up by the Lord."[38] In an interview, she called the pregnancy help movement "one of the greatest achievements" of the pro-life movement and stated further, "I attribute it to the Lord."

Leaders also presented God's guidance as something people in their movement should look for and could trust when carrying out their work. Heartbeat International's Hartshorn said how much material assistance a pregnancy center should offer must be determined by the nature of "the call to their founders." Local center director Susan Hoffman suggested that God had intervened twice when her center had attempted to cut back its material assistance, first when donations of a particular children's clothing size poured in after the center had decided to stop carrying it and then again to thwart the center's plans to move material assistance offsite when the center leaders ran into trouble obtaining the space they had selected. Coping with the emotional stresses of pregnancy counseling and finding the right words and help for a woman were also constructed as areas in which staff should seek and expect to receive God's guidance, although the major pregnancy center associations insist activists do their part with appropriate training.[39] "The Lord is willing to work with us; are we willing to work with Him? As we rely on Him to work through us, we will find our ministry to be more effective and less burdensome," Care Net teaches.[40] Activists also expressed faith that God was capable of helping their clients through all of their trials, even if that help came through human instruments, including professionals outside the pregnancy center. "My God, if he created a baby . . . He's going to help us find help for her," Birthright's Weaver proclaimed. "It looks impossible, but for God it's not impossible," said Vera of women's recovery, even from tragic circumstances such as rape.

The idea that God, working directly in the world and through human instruments, was himself a resource that could ultimately end abortion and other ills surfaced across interviews and in other communications. Though most interviewees showed little enthusiasm for other forms of pro-life activism (see Chapter 6), several praised an initiative called 40 Days for Life. The initiative brings citizens together virtually and in front of abortion clinics in specific local communities for forty-day periods of intense prayer to end abortion.[41] Heartbeat International titled its 2013 conference, which coincided with the fortieth anniversary of *Roe* and took place in the same city, Dallas, where *Roe*'s path through the courts began, "He Reigns." "Nothing, including political climates, cultural shifts, or even the unspeakable worldwide tragedy of abortion, can dethrone the God whose glory is set above the heavens," stated the organization's website, in explaining the conference theme.[42] Despite the immensity of the threats to human life and dignity in the culture, the group's president argued in a speech that year to pro-life leaders, the movement must keep working in a spirit of hope, for "the power behind us is the Lord."[43]

From the origins of the pregnancy center movement until the present day, key leaders have portrayed their movement as having a special role in God's plan. "When we give our love to a lonely, downcast girl, a victim of the cruelty of people and circumstances, we, whether we believe it or not, are the instruments of the restorative power of God," wrote Birthright founder Summerhill decades ago.[44] "We believe that the Lord is using Heartbeat International in a mighty way to help create a Culture of Life around the world," wrote

Hartshorn.[45] "I think the pregnancy center movement is God's answer to the injustice of abortion," asserted Cochrane, implying that God would one day "deliver" the United States from abortion just as God had eventually largely delivered it from past injustices such as child labor and slavery. According to leaders, activists cooperated in that plan with their loving service and sharing of the gospel in word or deed.

Membership in the "Body of Christ"

Just as the idea that God has the resources to ultimately solve abortion and other problems is available to comfort pregnancy help activists when their capacity to address those problems seems relatively modest, so is another theological idea with which activists contextualize their work. This is that pregnancy help activists are members of a much larger and diverse body that seeks the same goals. Consistent with the increasing salience of a faith-based identity to the movement, Hartshorn's 2013 speech to national pro-life leaders stated that pregnancy centers thought of themselves as "church-in-action" and as belonging to the "Body of Christ."[46]

Some interviewees referenced the "Body of Christ" in how they linked their approach to the abortion issue with those of other pro-life activists. Even when touting the virtues of individual outreach, they claimed to recognize the value of the division of labor that had evolved in the pro-life movement. One local center leader opined that "all have a role to play" in the movement, as in "the Body of Christ." "All those organizations play a part," conceded TNN's Agee, similarly, despite articulating some of the sharpest criticisms of activists involved in antiabortion politics and protest. "We're all in the same ministry of saving lives . . . like people are called to different roles in the church," declared fund-raiser Elaine Ham.

In the statements I quoted in this section and elsewhere, activists held a worldview in which God creates human beings with different gifts and personality dispositions that suit them to the unique purposes God has in mind for them. As they fulfill their unique callings, they accomplish something bigger than any one person or organization could. A possible implication of this worldview is that it helps activists to rationalize the boundaries they draw around their own work, even as they forge increasingly complex connections between the immediate problem they are trying to solve and other issues. It does not rest on any one group of activists or any one tactical approach to take on the full web. Also, it is not inevitable that the only institution with the capacity to solve it is the highest level of government.

THE POLITICS OF PREGNANCY HELP'S RELIGIOUS IDEOLOGY

The US pro-life movement might be, as Munson argues, jointly a religious and political phenomenon, but the energy, the character, and the behavior of the movement stream most directly concerned with women's welfare appears to be much more substantially motivated, animated, and shaped by religious faith than by the strategic or ideological concerns linked with the world of politics.[47] Notably, the kind of religious faith activists professed is neither the "personal morality" or "sin avoidance" variety of Christianity typically associated with pro-life activists. Neither is it the kind of "social justice" or "social gospel" variety of Christianity often associated with antipoverty work.[48] Instead, activists in the pro-life pregnancy help movement fuse these two faces of Christianity by reifying the Biblical command to love both God and neighbor. A Bible verse and prayer quoted by Heartbeat International's president that she said had personally touched her during her participation in National Day of Prayer events and that she deemed a "fitting close" to her book on her organization's first forty years exemplifies this linkage. The Bible verse as she quoted it, drawn from James 1:27 in the New International Version, reads: "Religion that God our Father accepts as pure and faultless is this: to look after orphans and widows in their distress and to keep oneself from being polluted by the world." The prayer she quoted as paired with that verse, credited to the 30-Day Prayer Guide associated with the National Day of Prayer, exalts self-giving love, the crossing of cultural boundaries, and reliance on God's grace, directed to the end of eliminating need:

> Lord, the first chapters of the Book of Acts provide a reflection of the loving, healing community that the Church is meant to be, so much so that "there were no needy persons among them." I want to reach out and touch others with Your love. It might take a miracle, but help me to extend myself to my neighbors, across cultural, racial, and Church barriers. I confess that I can't do this on my own, but that You can change me through the power of Your Holy Spirit. Father,

breathe life into Your Church so that it can be written that there are no needy persons among us. The need is overwhelming, but Your grace and ability to provide is greater. Revive our hearts to rise up and give and give and give. May we reflect You to a dying world, Lord Jesus, and love as You love. Amen.[49]

In this study, I did not set out to collect data on the religious views of activists; my lens instead had been the political. Although this will limit what this book can say to scholars of religion about how different aspects of religious affiliation, belief, or practice channel themselves into different approaches to social problems, conclusions from political scientist Nancy Wadsworth's study of evangelicals' engagement of race relations resonated powerfully with my own observations.[50] Wadsworth documents a substantial investment made by otherwise conservative, white evangelicals in the project of ending racism within the Christian Church, a project that has included repentance for past treatment of minorities, forging social ties across racial and ethnic lines, and steps toward creating multiethnic and multiracial houses of worship and other religious bodies. Yet many of those participating in such work, Wadsworth observes, stop short of taking this project into overtly political venues, where a natural next step might be the advocacy of public policies long sought by leaders of black Christian churches and the civil rights movement. Wadsworth concludes that conservative ideology is relatively unimportant, although not necessarily irrelevant, to this "ambivalence" about political activism. Instead, she highlights aspects of evangelical faith and culture. These have enabled racial change efforts to flourish within the socially safe spaces of religious venues, accepted as settings in which God can work to transform human beings. They also starkly contrast with how Wadsworth's subjects understood the characteristics, norms, and practices of the secular, political realm. They constructed that realm as separated from religious faith and characterized by artificiality and ineffectiveness in both its relationships and programmatic initiatives. In it, one risked becoming corrupted by worldly matters. Perhaps most importantly, the political realm was portrayed as a place that accentuated differences and invited conflict, traits religious venues tended to suppress. This suspicion of the secular political world, Wadsworth further suggests, is neither specific to whites nor to the issue of race. It was also shared by nonwhites participating in evangelical racial healing efforts and consistent with long-standing evangelical Christian thought about political engagement, which viewed it as a worldly activity best limited to states of "dire emergency," which abortion, for example, was understood to be.[51]

Wadsworth criticizes an alleged evangelical tendency to anchor social problems in personal sin, in this case referring to racism. This sets up evangelicals' argument that the path to social change is through the conversion of hearts, which will prompt God to change problematic conditions in the world, rather than pressing for systemic reforms.[52] Some exceptions to a lack of interest in systemic reform within the pregnancy help movement have appeared in various places throughout this book. The tendency Wadsworth recognizes, however, clearly manifests itself in the pro-life pregnancy help movement despite the fact that it is not correct to call it purely an "evangelical" movement. That this tendency applies not only to reforms that might be favored by the political left but also to *abortion* laws, however, enhances the case that conservative political ideologies and limited interest in issues cannot take one far in explaining the political ambivalence of Christians whose activism has been concentrated in nongovernmental venues.

Understanding how important "church" has become as a reference group for much of the contemporary pro-life pregnancy help movement is arguably critical for understanding how pregnancy help activists have come to engage social priorities of both the left and right, why they have largely confined their work for change to nongovernmental venues, and why this stream of pro-life activism is now believed to be thriving. The concept of "church," the content of its teaching, and perhaps also the relationships formed there offer an intellectual framework, moral imperative, and sense of social solidarity upon which activists can draw to justify their humanitarian and cultural reform work, its place in the larger pro-life movement, and their prioritization of person-to-person service. Activists did not appear to be unaware of the large scale of the cultural, social, and perhaps even economic forces that affect their work. Instead, there is evidence that they rationalized their approach with the belief that they are part of some greater whole both human and mystical and potentially powerful enough to take on great social problems.

SERVING WOMEN OR SAVING BABIES?

Are pro-life pregnancy centers primarily in the business of serving women or saving babies? In activists' ideal world, they accomplish both: saving babies as a result of serving women. Volunteers are also taught that in serving women, they are really serving God.

We do not know to what extent pregnancy centers offer lies, shame, and emotional coercion to abortion-inclined women in their counseling rooms instead of the approach they claim (see Chapter 2), but the offer of pregnancy-related help with which they lure clients is real and substantial. Nearly every pregnancy center provides baby-related consumer goods plus other aid and referrals geared toward meeting basic needs for food, shelter, clothing, and medical care. Sometimes these referrals are to other pro-life pregnancy service providers who will meet that need, free of charge. Pregnancy help organizations aim to improve the long-term well-being of women and their families by offering in-house educational programming, mentorship, and/or case management dealing with pregnancy health and parenting basics. That might include practical help with economic matters such as obtaining employment and child care. They extend this assistance broadly, even in parts of the country where abortion rates are low and abortion providers are scarce and to women who do not plan to have abortions or are no longer pregnant.

Some pregnancy help organizations' efforts to advance women's long-term well-being also often aim to change the woman herself. They seek to inspire her to change her values and lifestyle, though they say that to do so, they try to build her sense of capacity and self-worth and embed in her a desire for what they understand to be healthy, supportive relationships. If she has had an abortion and that seems to be troubling her, they encourage her to seek God's forgiveness as well as to forgive herself and the others involved, projecting that this will lead to peace. They aim to save her—not only from abortion, but from the suffering they attribute to her background, her choices, and the way she has been treated by others. This strategy might not serve all women the way they want to be served—but it is arguably only loosely connected to a hypothetical fixation with stopping abortions.

Indeed, if pregnancy centers have a hidden agenda behind their claims to provide practical and emotional support through unplanned childbearing, it is more likely an agenda to transform the lives of clients through sharing faith-based messages than one to stop all the abortions that they can. Such an agenda might even compromise success at baby-saving, as the longtime director of a nonevangelizing center in the Birthright/1st Way wing of the movement has speculated in her memoir about the movement. This is because abortion-minded women might avoid centers that gain reputations for evangelizing.[53] Some women, of course, might later appreciate the effort, especially if local center staff members follow training manuals' cautions (see Chapter 2) about listening carefully to see who might be open to the message and respecting clients' desires not to hear a message. It is also true that not all pregnancy centers overtly evangelize, and not all address lifestyle issues, even in the wing of the movement anchored by Care Net, Heartbeat International, and NIFLA centers. Regardless of religious stance, pro-life pregnancy help activists depart in an important way from the judgment popularly associated with people of their religious and political profiles. Conditional on pregnancy having occurred, they not only support but also celebrate the motherhood of women who have long faced social marginalization: the unwed, low-income, and racial and ethnic minority mothers who make up their core clientele.[54]

This hardly means that pregnancy center activists are not strongly motivated to save the unborn from abortion. This is, in fact, a common reason local staff members disclosed in an anonymous survey for their first involvement with a pregnancy center, and it is an outcome of their work that they track. The strong wording to "baby-focused" activists I quoted in Chapter 2 notwithstanding, I often encountered spoken or written words from leaders that treated saving "babies" from abortion as part of their movement's work. They almost exclusively did so, however, while including in the same breath a commitment to saving *women* from abortion as well. My book suggests some tension exists within the pregnancy center movement regarding how it will balance the more active work some envision for the movement in competing with abortion providers for clients with the more passive work of providing goods, services, and what they hope will be transformative encounters to women who do not want or did not have abortions.

Adding to the case that serving women is central to pro-life individual outreach, even if it is part of how activists facilitate other missions, the pregnancy help movement is operationally distinct from pro-life direct action and political advocacy—streams of the movement that might be more closely associated with baby-saving missions. It works with a largely different set of activists and claims a different philosophy, even though embracing a shared pro-life identity. Pregnancy help staff members sometimes dabble in these streams' activities in their private lives, but they often keep their distance out of preference and in many cases, organizational policy.

COMMON GROUND ON ABORTION?

Several scholars and journalists have opined that pro-life and pro-choice activists should be able to forge common ground in providing for poor and other women who do not want to have abortions.[55] It is tempting to ask, in light of the research presented in this book, whether pregnancy help activists could be persuaded to participate in such a project.

Two leaders raised this potential for common ground with pro-choice workers in their interviews. "There's a very soft side to pro-choice," opined Agee. Another interviewee, Frederica Mathewes-Green, had personally helped to organize a formal Common Ground movement in the mid-1990s. Through that experience, she said, she observed that people who worked at pregnancy centers and people who worked at abortion clinics had much more in common with each other than political pro-life and pro-choice advocates. At least among those who self-selected into Common Ground, she claimed, pregnancy center workers held realistic ideas of the challenges pregnant women face, whereas the abortion clinic workers expressed surprising ambivalence about abortion and recognized that many women seemed coerced into their decisions.

The Common Ground Network for Life and Choice and similar such movements have not fared well. Political parties, the media, and political activists on both sides of the abortion issue have expressed disinterest in, and in some cases suspicion of, compromise.[56] Despite my two interviewees' personal enthusiasm for common ground projects, they too implied pessimism about the likelihood that they would work in light of reactions they said their pro-life work had received from pro-choice advocates. Agee suggested it was difficult to convince pro-choice advocates that in her organization's work of assisting childbearing women, "we're not trying to remove an alternative," that is, that her service was not disguising a hidden legal agenda to overturn abortion rights. Mathewes-Green said that she had felt stung by the way political pro-choice advocates had treated her and her pro-life colleagues during what she called her last attempt at political pro-life activism, in 1992. She had served then as communications director for a group lobbying Maryland voters to overturn a pro-choice law that had enshrined a state right to abortion and considerably loosened regulation of abortion providers. She recounted that during the political campaign, opponents had branded her and other pro-life advocates as "anti-choice" and had charged that the pro-lifers' arguments about wanting to protect women were lies. Otherwise possessing feminist credentials, she had converted from pro-choice to pro-life in adulthood when she learned what happened in an abortion procedure and came to connect it to her feminist philosophy. During that campaign, she said, she "saw the willingness of the other side to put women at risk" as they rejected what pro-lifers saw as the modest regulations previously in place. Meanwhile, pro-choice activists' continued work to regulate and influence public opinion about pregnancy centers adds to the case that formation of a pro-life/pro-choice coalition to aid women remains highly unlikely.

LESSONS FOR THE STUDY OF SOCIAL ACTION AND SERVICE POLITICS

My research on pro-life pregnancy help activism affirms and extends some developments in the study of social movements and civic participation, though offering less support to others.

First, this account of pro-life people's mobilization into the stream of the movement that engages in direct service is arguably consistent with literature on activist mobilization and the tactical choices of SMOs that have downplayed political instrumental rationality relative to more pedestrian aspects of the human experience. In this view, uptake of a particular form of activism reflects in large part its consistency with such factors as individual or collective emotion, identity and the values and ideas that create meaning in life, and availability for integrating activism into one's lifestyle and routines.[57] Whether and how people participate in political and civic life, Orum and Dale suspect, might simply grow from an orientation toward daily living in which "participation must feel so natural to the lives of people, so much a part of their everyday circumstances, that it feels both important and necessary to the workings of their lives."[58] These individual decisions can aggregate in a way that produces a useful result for the movement, making it look like a strategic, top-down decision, when in fact it is not.

Ruth Braunstein's account of the forms of social action as governed by "perceptions of appropriateness" regarding what kind of action people with identities like theirs ought to take fits especially well with how participants in the pregnancy help movement frame their work.[59] In the pregnancy help movement, "people like us" appear to be most commonly understood as

Christian, pro-life (not just antiabortion), and women. Some also bring to the movement identities as mothers, neighbors, and women who have also experienced a crisis pregnancy as well as particular occupational identities. Taking such a perspective on social action, it would not be surprising to observe that the kind of lock-in to a particular style or "stream" of activism that Munson observed in the pro-life movement, and that I see some evidence for as well, is common to other social movements.[60] It might also be why sitting on the fence of service and activism, as pregnancy center staff do, is not necessarily a comfortable place. Perhaps in such cases one might expect that such SMOs can perform better at some activities than others, depending on which dimension of identity is most salient.

Strategic calculations regarding political opportunities and methods for fighting problematic conditions—here, reducing demand for abortion—show up more visibly when one considers innovations in the forms service provision takes. Even then, as they are implemented, they appear to be filtered through activists' identities and affect for their targets. These delimit what service-providing staff will and will not do to realize their movement's activist goals.

Second, my book adds to recent research that has rediscovered a role for religious faith in motivating social action beyond the cultural issues linked to sex, marriage, childbearing, and parenting often assumed to animate the Christian Right.[61] In this case, although pregnancy centers concern themselves very much with all these traditional Christian Right issues, the key example is their substantial investment in material aid and social services, even in cases in which an abortion is not at stake. Religious activists' involvement in this work is consistent with a growing body of evidence linking religiosity to expressions of "humanitarian" and "prosocial" values, to the increased likelihood of charitable giving, voluntarism, and various altruistic acts, and even to stereotypically liberal policy preferences on select issues, such as opposition to the death penalty or, in some contexts, support for social welfare programs.[62]

Although my study of the pregnancy help movement did not set out to collect this information, it offers some light on the mechanisms through which religiosity promotes helping values and behavior. Certainly activists draw from the substantive teachings of their faith. Their examples of the role of religious events and social networks in exposing them to pregnancy help work or facilitating the founding of a pregnancy help organization are consistent with other research that highlights churches' capacity to mobilize and to foster such precursors of altruism as friendship and social trust.[63] Still more clearly, it points to subjects' understandings of God, God's relationship to the world, and God's relationship with them personally as factors justifying their work. Schafer's literature review summarizes a number of specific understandings believed to link religiosity and prosocial behavior.[64] Meanwhile, a study in which the conclusions dovetail with the accounts of pregnancy help activists, en route to explaining an association between religiosity and opposition to the death penalty, proposes as a key aspect of religiosity perception of a close personal relationship with a God whose character is painted as more loving and merciful than judgmental and punitive. The authors also find that this close personal relationship with a loving God increases empathetic dispositions and motivation to help the needy.[65] Another study has linked this kind of understanding of and relationship with God to volunteering, at least among college women.[66]

It is not clear from this or other research, however, that religion exogenously moves pro-life activists to compassionate action. Munson suggests that among pro-life activists generally, the causal arrow runs more strongly from pro-life commitment to religiosity than the other way around.[67] Recent research by Samuel Perry points explicitly to pro-life attitudes as a correlate of support for transracial adoption among Catholics and evangelicals.[68] This research suggests that both matter and that religious and pro-life commitments reinforce each other as drivers of pregnancy help outreach. Religious commitment commonly put activists in this study in a position to be mobilized. Work within the movement then exposed them to leaders' efforts to nurture activists' religious faith and deepen the intellectual connections they drew between that faith, their pro-life beliefs, and the service they performed at pregnancy centers and other movement organizations.

Third, my research confirms some suspicions about who participates in "service politics," although it might also allay fears that volunteer work can diminish citizens' engagement with democratic processes. In this research, subjects' substitution of service for political action was assessed using variation in pregnancy center activists' participation in protest or activities to influence legislation, elections, or public opinion. Roughly consistent with suspicions that citizens who concentrate their activism in community service tend to be younger and turned off by partisan polarization, if not ideologically cross pressured themselves, I find that those who began their service most recently and those who express the most liberal opinions on economic and gender issues are the most likely among pregnancy help activists to report no involvement in other pro-life activism.[69] Even though pregnancy help activists distanced their work from political action and often expressed negative attitudes about politics, however, it is not clear that they had been disengaged in their private lives. Pregnancy center staff members appeared to self-report more political interest than the general public, and solid majorities perceived that their interest in politics, involvement with other forms of pro-life activism, and caring about economic issues increased because of their pregnancy center service. There is also evidence that many participated in politics in order to defend their interests as Christian service providers. This is consistent with theory that service ultimately facilitates, rather than detracts from, political engagement and that participation in volunteer work and conventional political action are correlated.[70]

PREGNANCY HELP AND THE PRO-LIFE MOVEMENT IN A POST-ROE UNITED STATES

Pro-choice advocates have sounded the alarm that abortion accessibility, if not the right itself, is in grave danger. According to the pro-abortion rights Guttmacher Institute, between the *Roe* decision in 1973 and July 2016, states had enacted more than 1,100 abortion restrictions, with 30 percent of them occurring since 2010. Although the organization portrayed abortion rights as having dodged a bullet in 2016 when a five-to-four majority of the US Supreme Court struck down a package of Texas regulations on abortion providers in *Whole Woman's Health v. Cole,* it voiced concern about a wave of new laws and policy proposals that would divert public money from Planned Parenthood and ban certain late-term abortions.[71] To make matters grimmer for the pro-choice side, in 2018, Brett Kavanaugh was sworn in as a Supreme Court justice. It is widely believed that he would supply, if given a suitable case, the fifth vote to overturn *Roe.*

At an earlier seemingly watershed moment for the pro-life movement, after the Supreme Court's *Webster* and *Casey* rulings had begun to open the door to greater state regulation of abortion, political scientists Dran and Bowers speculated on what political will might exist in the United States to cope with the pragmatic problems they expected women to face should abortion be made illegal. "Policy alternatives to abortion will not be easy," they warned, presenting data from a poll assessing US citizens' endorsement of and support for increasing federal spending on one alternative to abortion, adoption.[72] Their analyses located barriers to compromise in a segment of pro-life citizens who endorsed but were unwilling to fund an adoption alternative and in a segment of otherwise pro-choice citizens reluctant to endorse an alternative to abortion.

Today, a similar prediction is easy to make. However, the pro-life movement has shown itself to be quite willing to spend its resources on alternatives to abortion through institutions of its own making. Although not created strategically to achieve such goals, the development of pregnancy centers and other service providers addresses some practical problems for the pro-life movement. Working in civil society enables the movement to address a broader issue agenda than it could when targeting the state, for when use of the state's coercive power is not at stake, ideologies are less rigid and political alliances are less relevant.[73] There is evidence that the pregnancy help movement, as Jacoby predicted, provides a comfortable place in the pro-life movement for citizens who dislike partisan politics and whose empathy for women is salient. Further, it might eventually draw those citizens into more extensive activism.[74] The pregnancy help movement also serves as the pro-life movement's response to challenges on what it is doing for women who might suffer hardship as a result of forgoing abortion.[75]

Pregnancy help activists, however, signaled that they intended for their institutions to endure beyond *Roe*—when the need to "save babies," for some, might not seem so pressing. Even now, some pregnancy centers are moving into former abortion clinics.[76] Heartbeat International's leader foresees pregnancy centers' continued expansion into the field of women's health care (minus abortion and artificial contraception), pledging that if Planned Parenthood one day loses its government funding, pregnancy centers will "fill the void that will be left when this Goliath falls."[77] That pregnancy centers remain quite numerous in areas of the country where abortion access is limited lends credibility to activists' statements about the longevity they foresee for their movement. So does the evidence suggesting that the movement's motives and energy are more strongly grounded in activists' attachments to a loving vision of Christianity than in the intensity of their stakes in the political conflict over abortion. Already the pregnancy help movement is fighting battles other than abortion. They might also find new ones: one leader predicted that pregnancy centers would eventually become involved in the fight against sex slavery because their administration of pregnancy tests and counseling could put them in a position to learn such details of women's backgrounds.

Although pregnancy centers have long maintained a presence in foreign countries, the increasingly transnational character their movement is acquiring enhances the case for its longevity. For example, as of 2012, Agee's TNN reported a presence in thirty-three countries and identified expansion of its outreach overseas as an important future focus for the organization. As of October 2018, Heartbeat International's "Worldwide Directory of Pregnancy Help" listed 6,852 pregnancy centers and other pregnancy help service providers globally, including those outside its own network.[78] It claimed affiliates operating in fifty countries on all inhabited continents.[79] Emails I received during this research communicating highlights of the group's annual conferences showcased the different nationalities and cultures of the pregnancy center directors underneath the organization's umbrella, and the organization's history also celebrates this development in the movement.[80]

Information about the substance and scale of the pro-life movement's individual outreach arguably challenges scholars and the general public to think differently about the character of the pro-life movement and its attention to women's well-being. This is especially the case if accepting propositions of social movement scholars that tactical choices communicate activists' feelings, identities, values, and worldviews.[81] Perhaps it should not surprise anyone, however, that a movement increasingly identified with ideological conservatism would concern itself with caring for those who would be affected by its policy goals. The pro-choice movement and the political left enjoy superior reputations for compassion and action on behalf of women and poor people, yet empirical research demonstrates that a concern with caring and the prevention of harm is a nearly universal component of human morality, espoused by liberals and conservatives alike.[82] Instead, the chief ideological differences in moral systems concern the greater number of criteria that make up conservative morality, including the values of authority, loyalty, and purity, which relate to their positions on abortion, sex, and related cultural issues.[83]

It might or might not be fair to use activists' policy positions as a barometer of that caring, but there was a time when support for antipoverty programs and other aid to families was quite common and vocal among pro-life activists and the pro-life public, and that support has not necessarily disappeared.[84] Andrew Lewis, based on empirical analysis, has suggested that the primacy of the abortion issue has shaped how many US Christians and their leaders frame and take positions on other issues.[85] Meanwhile, Rose Ernst has explained leading feminist groups' lackluster support for social welfare programs in the

1960s and 1970s in terms of constraints posed by political alliances.[86] It is interesting to speculate, therefore, how extensively pro-life activists might target the state to increase support for alternatives to abortion if partisan and interest alignments were different.

Social entrepreneur Adam Kahane argues that movements solve social problems most effectively when they balance natural human drives toward wielding power and giving love. Some activists' characters dispose them toward thinking and acting more strongly on one of these drives than the other, and therefore striking that balance requires cooperation and compromise among activists with these diverse propensities as well as conscious individual efforts to develop their weaker drive in order to facilitate that compromise.[87] Individual outreach activists present themselves as the force of love in the pro-life movement, a force that deals with the human hardships activists striving for power in political arenas or the streets—whether rightly or wrongly—appear to neglect. Pregnancy help activists' changing tactics over time also suggest their ongoing search for that balance within their stream of the movement and within themselves; perhaps that is inherent to the work of providing service in the context of a social movement. At present, they appear to be challenging themselves to exercise power more boldly—albeit, also ethically—to reach those abortion-minded women who might not be initially attracted to the form of love activists think they are expressing in their offers of material help and social services for women who choose to have babies. In doing this throughout their history, they have shown an interest in learning from their countermovement.

There is still much to be learned from careful social science about how much pro-life pregnancy help organizations have contributed to making abortion "unwanted and unthinkable," and how women's well-being has been affected, positively or negatively, by their efforts. Subjectivity concerning exactly what advances women's well-being will likely ensure contested conclusions. The movement's refusal to help women obtain abortions (and, often, contraceptives) will undermine in the eyes of some its claim to be woman-centered, as will some of its activists' efforts to change the culture around sex. However, neither have the pro-choice and feminist movements and the service providers they encompass escaped blame for what they allegedly do not provide: support and advocacy for low-income, often minority women who say they want motherhood to be a feasible choice.[88]

The fight over pro-life pregnancy centers represents an extension of the US abortion conflict into yet another set of venues. As it gains visibility, the likelihood that pro-life pregnancy help outreach will be viewed through any other prism arguably dims. To some, their work is a threat. Participants in the movement see themselves differently—as offering "sanctuaries" from the battles in politics and women's lives and as pursuing by other means the US abortion conflict's Holy Grail: a social arrangement that reconciles the lives of the unborn with the welfare of women.[89]

Appendix A
Methodological Appendix for Chapter 1

This appendix provides additional methodological detail on my three major data sources.

PREGNANCY CENTER DIRECTOR SURVEY

This was an online survey about pregnancy center characteristics, consisting mostly of close-ended, multiple-choice questions. I fielded it between February and May 2012.

The sample consisted of pregnancy centers affiliated with Care Net, Heartbeat International, or the National Institute of Family and Life Advocates (NIFLA), the three largest associations of pregnancy help organizations in the United States. At the time this research began, those organizations were estimated to encompass as many as 90 percent of US pregnancy centers (Family Research Council 2009), though the difficulty of counting independent centers makes it hard to know for certain. Respondents were recruited through emails containing the survey link sent on my behalf by Care Net, Heartbeat International, and NIFLA to their affiliate contact lists. Care Net centers also received an invitation to complete the online survey as part of their affiliate renewal paperwork packets, which the organization's national office mailed at the time the survey was entering the field, a feature that likely contributed to superior response rates of Care Net centers, relative to the others. Responding on behalf of 734 pregnancy centers, 510 directors completed the survey. The larger number of centers relative to directors results from the fact that some pregnancy center office locations belong to local chains, sharing the same director. These 734 centers constituted 37.3 percent of 1,969 pregnancy centers affiliated with Care Net, Heartbeat International, or NIFLA as of 2010. Participating centers came from every state but Delaware (and the District of Columbia).

PREGNANCY CENTER STAFF SURVEY

The Pregnancy Center Staff Survey was a self-administered, anonymous paper survey offered at thirty-one pregnancy center office locations in twenty states and returned via mail. All questions were close ended. To preserve anonymity, my Institutional Review Board waived documentation of informed consent. Information sheets were attached to all questionnaires instead. Survey forms did not identify study sites but only with which of the three national networks the study site affiliated.

Study sites were recruited from the 85 percent of centers responding affirmatively to a Pregnancy Center Director Survey question soliciting willingness to consider participation in the staff study. Stratified random sampling was used to select a pool of those centers to approach with a formal request to be part of the study.

The stratified sampling worked as follows: After the originally planned closing date of the Pregnancy Center Director Survey, a random sample was drawn for study site recruitment. I soon decided to extend the Pregnancy Center Director Survey and send reminder emails, however, eliciting more responses. From this pool, I drew a second, smaller random sample for study site recruitment. I contacted directors via the email addresses they provided to request that their centers be Pregnancy Center Staff Survey study sites. After I had recruited my target number of study sites, I observed an over-representation of sites affiliated with Care Net relative to sites affiliated with Heartbeat International. To lessen this imbalance in the Pregnancy Center Staff Survey, I sent recruitment emails to additional centers randomly selected from my second pool of Pregnancy Center Director Survey respondents, confining these only to centers affiliated with Heartbeat International and not Care Net.

Of fifty-eight center directors to whom a request was emailed, twenty-six ultimately participated. Because local chain centers offered them at their multiple office locations, there were thirty-one total study sites. The large majority of nonparticipating centers reflected nonresponse to requests rather than explicit declines.

Directors of participating pregnancy centers were asked to inform their staff about the survey in the way they normally communicated center business and to place the surveys in a central location accessible to staff but not clients. Willing respondents returned completed, anonymous surveys to me by mail. Surveys were made available at each study site for a period of approximately one month. Representing 48.5 percent of the number of employees and volunteers directors reported having at their centers during the survey month, 272 completed surveys were received.

Table A1.1 displays descriptive statistics for the Pregnancy Center Staff Survey sample.

PREGNANCY HELP MOVEMENT LEADER INTERVIEWS

I conducted interviews during summer and fall 2012. The typical interview lasted about one hour. I took detailed notes but did not record the sessions. One interviewee was recontacted in 2014 to clarify a historical detail.

Though consent forms included anonymity as an option, all interviewees granted permission to be identified by name. Table A1.2 lists interviewees and their roles at the time of the interview.

Table A1.1 Characteristics of Pregnancy Center Staff Sample

	Volunteers	Employees	All
Volunteer	100.0	0.0	71.6
Female	96.8	97.4	97.0
Catholic	13.6	13.0	13.4
Evangelical Christian	82.2	84.4	82.9
Attends church once a week or more	93.7	92.2	93.3
Employment status			
Employed full time	13.2	36.4	19.8
Employed part time	17.9	63.6	30.6
Not employed, looking for work	4.7	0.0	3.4
Not employed, not looking for work	64.2	0.0	46.3
Bachelor's degree or higher	51.8	52.0	51.9
Student	6.8	10.5	7.8
Household income			
Less than $40,000	14.7	22.3	17.0
$40,001–$70,000	19.4	30.3	23.6
$70,001–$100,000	24.1	21.1	23.1
More than $100,000	41.8	23.7	36.4
Age			
18–24	5.3	3.9	4.9
25–34	5.8	15.6	8.6
35–44	9.5	13.9	10.5
45–54	23.3	32.5	25.8
55–64	29.1	29.9	29.2
65+	27.0	5.2	21.0
White	91.1	88.2	90.3
Married and living with spouse	83.3	85.7	84.0
Reports bio., step, adopted, or foster children	89.4	89.6	89.5
Children currently in home	20.2	37.5	25.2

Source: Pregnancy Center Staff Survey. Modified versions of this table appeared in Laura S. Hussey, "Political Action versus Personal Action: Understanding Social Movements' Pursuit of Change through Nongovernmental Channels," *American Politics Research* 42 (2014): 409–440; Laura S. Hussey, "Crisis Pregnancy Centers, Poverty, and the Expanding Frontiers of American Abortion Politics," *Politics and Policy* 41, no. 6 (2013): 985–1011.

Note: N = 272. All figures are percentages.

Table A1.2 Leaders Interviewed

Name	Role (at time of interview)	Date
Agee, Mary Cunningham	Founder and president, the Nurturing Network	October 18, 2012
Breeden, Lawrence	Chief operations officer, anonymous national pregnancy center association	August 15, 2012
Christiansen, Sandra	National consultant, Care Net; medical director of Care Net Pregnancy Center of Frederick, Maryland	July 9, 2012
Clews, Carol	Executive director, Greater Baltimore Center for Pregnancy Concerns	August 14, 2012
Cocciolone, Denise	Founder and president, National Life Center (parent of 1st Way Pregnancy Centers); local pregnancy center director; former head of Birthright's USA branch	October 23, 2012
Cochrane, Linda	National consultant, Care Net; other relevant experience includes current and prior director positions at local pregnancy centers	October 16, 2012
Delahoyde, Melinda	President, Care Net; other relevant experience includes other roles in Care Net leadership	August 15, 2012
DiIulio, Anthony	Executive director, the Gabriel Network, Maryland	September 11, 2012
Farmer, James	Former director of Respect Life Office for Catholic Archdiocese of Baltimore; helped to found multiple pregnancy centers in Maryland	October 9, 2012
Glessner, Thomas	President, National Institute of Family and Life Advocates; other relevant experience includes a former leadership position at Christian Action Council (CAC)/Care Net and founding a pregnancy center	June 29, 2012
Ham, Elaine	Founder and national consultant, Plans for You (enterprise assisting pregnancy centers with fund-raising and other matters); other relevant experience includes former leadership roles at a local center and the Southern Baptist Convention's pregnancy center ministry	October 3, 2012

Name	Role (at time of interview)	Date
Hamm, Maria Suarez	Former executive director, Tepeyac Silver Spring (Maryland) Women's Center; other relevant experience includes service on Heartbeat International's board of directors	October 12, 2012
Harris, Cookie	Chair of the board, Pregnancy Center North, Maryland	August 3, 2012
Hartshorn, Margaret	President, Heartbeat International; other relevant experience includes founding and directing a pregnancy center	August 23, 2012, and September 8, 2014
Hoffman, Susan	Executive director, Tender Care Pregnancy Center, Maryland and Pennsylvania	September 20, 2012
Hopkins, Cynthia	Vice president for center services, Care Net; other relevant experience includes directing a pregnancy center	August 15, 2012
Mathewes-Green, Frederica	Author and speaker promoting pregnancy centers and alternatives to abortion	September 18, 2012
Palumbo, Pamela	Executive director, the Pregnancy Clinic, Maryland	July 17, 2012
Vera, Mariana	Executive director, Tepeyac Silver Spring (Maryland) Women's Center	October 25, 2012
Weaver, Terry	US Birthright director; local pregnancy center director	October 23, 2012
Williams, D. Michelle	Director, Sanctuaries for Life (Maryland), Catholic Charities of Washington, DC	October 2, 2012
Young, Curtis	Former executive director, Christian Action Council (CAC)/Care Net	August 8, 2012

Source: A modified version of this table appeared in Laura S. Hussey, "Political Action versus Personal Action: Understanding Social Movements' Pursuit of Change through Nongovernmental Channels," *American Politics Research* 42 (2014): 409–440.

Appendix B
Methodological Appendix for Chapter 5

This appendix includes additional information about the indicators used and data analysis performed in chapter 5.

INDICATORS IN THE STATE-LEVEL ANALYSIS

Summary statistics for all indicators are in Table B1.1, while additional information about indicator sources and construction is below.

Pro-life political opportunities index: Data were drawn from the 2001, 2003, 2005, 2007, and 2009 editions of NARAL Pro-Choice America's *Who Decides?* series. I assigned codes to governors and each state legislative chamber corresponding to NARAL's ratings of these institutions as "pro-choice" (–1), "mixed-choice" (0), or "anti-choice" (1) and then summed these three codes for each two-year election cycle in the first decade of the 2000s. I treated Nebraska's unicameral legislature as bicameral, entering the unicameral score twice.

Abortion rates: Data came from the Guttmacher Institute.[1] I used the version of this statistic that assigns abortion rates based on the woman's state of residence and averaged all available data by state from the first decade of the 2000s (2000, 2004, 2005, 2007, and 2008).

Abortion providers per 500,000 state population: Provider counts came from the Guttmacher Institute.[2] I averaged all available data by state from the first decade of the 2000s (2000, 2005, and 2008).

Ideological extremity: Tausanovitch and Warshaw constructed the ideology measure on which I based this indicator, using a host of policy issue opinion questions asked in several large national surveys between 2000 and 2011. I analyzed the version of the data estimated using multilevel regression with poststratification (MRP).[3] Ideological scores originally assigned to the individuals on whom state-level results are based were centered on zero. I converted ideological scores (on a liberal-conservative spectrum) to ideological extremity scores by taking the absolute value of states' mean ideology scores.

Public pro-life sentiment: The indicator was a principal components factor score comprising the three items in the text. The Norrander state abortion opinion measure I used was the percentage of the public saying abortion should always be illegal, based on responses to the 1988–1990–1992 Senate Election Study. I used the most recent available year, 1998, from Pacheco's state abortion opinion estimates. Her measure estimated the percent of the public saying abortion should be legal in all cases. I considered the percentage of white, evangelical Protestants in a state because this group is believed to supply many contemporary pro-life activists. These data were collected in the 2010 U.S. Religion Census: Religious Congregations and Membership Study.[4] The three indicators are highly correlated and load onto a single factor.

Human services charities: Data were extracted from the National Center for Charitable Statistics database at the Urban Institute and had their original source in the Internal Revenue Service's April 2010 Exempt Organizations Business Master File.[5]

Population adjustments for pregnancy help organizations, abortion providers, and human services charities: These employed the state populations as of July 1, 2011 (in 500,000s). Population data were published online by the US Census Bureau, Table 1: Estimates of the Resident Population by Selected Age Groups for the United States, States, and Puerto Rico: July 1, 2011 (SC-EST2011-01) (Release date May 2012).

ESTIMATION OF STATE-LEVEL MODELS

The full regression results behind Figure 5.3 are in Table B1.2.

Sensitivity Analysis

Sensitivity analysis included estimation of negative binomial regression models of each state's pregnancy center and total pregnancy help service provider counts. These controlled for population and its square and did not make population adjustments to any provider-count variables or use natural log transformations. All other variables were the same. Results were similar to those reported in Table B1.2 except that the negative abortion rate coefficient became statistically significant and negative in modeling counts of pregnancy centers and of all pregnancy help service providers. Additionally, the ideological extremity coefficient lost the marginal statistical significance it had in the pregnancy help service provider OLS model.

ANALYSIS OF ZCTA-LEVEL LOCATIONS OF
PREGNANCY CENTERS AND ABORTION CLINICS

Assembly of a dataset of US zip code tabulation areas (ZCTAs) linked to information about the locations of pregnancy centers and abortion clinics began with the retrieval of missing zip codes from the Several Sources Shelters pregnancy center directory. Out of all 2,663 pregnancy help organization entries, 302 lacked zip codes. I located all but 29 (4 of which were hotlines) of these manually, finding the vast majority by using the US Postal Service's online zip code lookup tool. For the rest, when directory address information was insufficient for identifying a single zip code, I found zip codes through

Table B1.1 Summary Statistics for State-Level Analysis

Variable	Mean	S.D.	Min.	Max.
PHSPs/500k	5.16	2.53	1.24	12.43
Ln (PHSPs/500K)	1.52	0.50	0.22	2.52
PCs/500k	4.16	1.94	1.24	10.02
Ln (PCs/500k)	1.32	0.46	0.22	2.30
Pro-life pol. opp. index	2.74	9.65	−15.00	15.00
Public pro-life sentiment	0.00	1.00	−1.65	2.49
Public ideo. extremity score	0.16	0.10	0.01	0.39
Abortion rate	16.04	7.01	6.40	37.60
Ln (abortion rate)	2.69	0.42	1.86	3.63
Abortion providers/500k	2.81	2.64	0.34	15.27
Ln (Abortion providers/500k)	0.70	0.82	−1.07	2.73
HS charities/500k	512.72	175.42	264.09	1,036.87
Ln (HS charities/500k)	6.19	0.31	5.58	6.94

Source: Author's analysis of data from multiple sources, as cited in Chapter 5 and Appendix B.

Note: N = 50 states; PHSP = pregnancy help service providers; PCs = pregnancy centers; HS = human services.

internet searches for the organization. I did the same for a small number of abortion clinics missing zip codes.

I merged the pregnancy help and abortion clinic directories on zip code. I then transformed the datasets so that postal zip codes became unique cases, totaling up along the way the number of each service provider per zip code. The number of zip codes containing at least one pregnancy help organization totaled 2,293 (2,020 zip codes housed at least one pregnancy center), whereas the number of zip codes containing at least one abortion clinic totaled 694.

To enable a merge with contextual data, postal zip codes then required conversion to Census ZCTAs. These five-digit numbers are identical in most but not all cases. I therefore converted the postal zip codes to ZCTAs using the 2010 zip code to ZCTA "crosswalk" file produced by and available for download from the UDS Mapper Project, a federally funded effort of the American Academy of Family Physicians' policy research unit, the Robert Graham Center.[6] At the end of this process, fourteen zip codes assigned to the service providers in my 2005 and 2013 directories could not be matched to a 2010 ZCTA and were dropped. I then identified those cases in which

Table B1.2 Correlates of Pregnancy Center Diffusion

	Ln (PCs per 500K pop.)	Ln (PHSPs per 500K pop.)
Pro-life political opportunity index	−0.016*	−0.017**
	(0.007)	(0.006)
Public pro-life sentiment	0.176*	0.189**
	(0.070)	(0.063)
Public ideological extremity score	−0.693	−0.726[+]
	(0.425)	(0.383)
Ln (Abortion rate)	0.056	0.046
	(0.165)	(0.149)
Ln (Abortion providers per 500K pop.)	−0.154	−0.138
	(0.105)	(0.094)
Ln (Human service charities per 500K pop.)	1.072**	1.290**
	(0.175)	(0.158)
Constant	−5.202**	−6.329**
	(1.385)	(1.248)
Adjusted R-squared	0.595	0.720
N	50	50

Source: Author's analysis of data from multiple sources, as cited in Chapter 5 and Appendix B.

Note: Table presents coefficients (standard errors in parentheses) from ordinary least squares regression models. $^+p < .10$, $^*p < .05$, $^{**}p < .01$, $^{***}p < .001$ (two-tailed). PCs = pregnancy centers. PHSPs = pregnancy help service providers.

multiple postal zip codes corresponded to a single ZCTA. In those cases, I retallied the total numbers of service providers per ZCTA and then removed duplicate ZCTAs.

I next merged this file of ZCTAs containing a pregnancy help organization or abortion clinic to a ZCTA-level dataset of select demographic and economic variables extracted from the US Census Bureau's American Community Survey (ACS) data. The Census Bureau aggregates the annual survey data across years (in this case 2007–2011) to improve data quality at low levels of aggregation such as the ZCTA. Only ZCTAs located within the fifty US states and the District of Columbia were used. The final dataset consisted of 33,106 ZCTAs, 2,682 of which contained any pregnancy help organization and/or an abortion clinic and 2,450 of which contained a pregnancy center and/or an abortion clinic. ACS data for select variables were unavailable for some ZCTAs, often those with small populations. For example, poverty rates were available for 32,442 out of 33,106 ZCTAs.

I placed ZCTAs within particular metropolitan areas using the "2010 Zip Code Tabulation Area (ZCTA) to Metropolitan and Micropolitan Areas Relationship File," available for download from the US Census Bureau. This file also contained data on the population size of metropolitan areas.

NOTES

1. Guttmacher Institute, www.guttmacher.org, accessed October 8, 2014.

2. Guttmacher Institute, www.guttmacher.org, accessed October 8, 2014.

3. American Ideology Project, http://www.americanideologyproject.com, accessed February 9, 2015.

4. Clifford Grammich et al., "2010 U.S. Religion Census: Religious Congregations and Membership Study," ed. American Association of Statisticians of American Religious Bodies (2012), http://www.rcms2010.org/. www.thearda.com.

5. Urban Institute, National Center for Charitable Statistics, http://nccsdataweb .urban.org, accessed February 9, 2015.

6. American Academy of Family Physicians, Robert Graham Center, http://uds mapper.org/docs/Zip_to_ZCTA_crosswalk_2010_JSI.xls, accessed May 23, 2012.

Appendix C
Methodological Appendix for Chapter 6

Table C1.1 reports full results for the regression model summarized in Figure 6.6.

Table C1.1 Predictors of Lack of Participation in Pro-Life Activism

	No Activism Ever	No Activism in Past Year
Pessimism about abortion ban	0.223	0.308*
	(0.191)	(0.143)
Social welfare and gender liberalism	0.685**	0.202
	(0.212)	(0.162)
Years since first involvement	−0.163*	−0.031
	(0.067)	(0.028)
Age 18–24	0.372	0.855
	(0.820)	(0.736)
Age 25–34	0.000	0.515
	(0.765)	(0.617)
Age 35–44	1.130	1.045+
	(0.708)	(0.618)
Age 45–54	0.257	1.017*
	(0.615)	(0.504)
Age 55–64	0.167	0.690
	(0.608)	(0.478)
Volunteer	0.835	1.274**
	(0.554)	(0.367)
Household income (8 categories)	0.026	0.002
	(0.094)	(0.078)
Has full-time job	−0.647	−0.411
	(0.594)	(0.403)
Has BA degree or higher	−0.192	−0.387
	(0.398)	(0.312)
Constant	−2.535*	−2.083**
	(1.023)	(0.756)
Pseudo R-squared	0.179	0.118
N	219	219

Source: Pregnancy Center Staff Survey.

Note: Table displays logit coefficients, with standard errors in parentheses. +p < .10, *p < .05, **p < .01, ***p <. 001.

Appendix D
Methodological Appendix for Chapter 7

This appendix includes information beyond that provided in Chapter 7 about the 2005 surveys of clients at Baltimore abortion clinics and pregnancy centers.

In late 2005, as part of a different research project, I fielded two specialized surveys designed to solicit recently pregnant women's own perspectives about the roles of financial need and economic assistance in their decision making about their pregnancies. These considered the welfare state as it is and as it could be. One survey was offered at the offices of three abortion providers to clients returning for an optional but recommended one-week postabortion follow-up visit. The other was offered at four pregnancy centers to new mothers (women who had given birth within the past year) visiting the center to receive the gift layettes the centers provided to clients upon the birth of a child or for reasons other than a pregnancy test, such as to receive material aid or to participate in a parenting class or support group. I chose pregnancy centers as the sites through which to reach new mothers under the assumption that a large share of those mothers' pregnancies would have been unintended. All service providers were located in Baltimore City (Maryland) proper or nearby suburbs.

Data were gathered by means of a self-administered questionnaire offered to clients by staff at the study sites. The survey was anonymous, facilitated by a waiver from my Institutional Review Board allowing subjects to provide informed consent with a checkbox in lieu of a signature. Participation was restricted to subjects over eighteen years of age. Subjects completed the survey at the study site. Abortion clients received $5 cash upon returning a survey. Because pregnancy center staff objected to handling cash, their clients received a $5 gift certificate. Among other items, the questionnaire asked women about the importance of various concerns at the time they were pregnant, about the resources they could have accessed if they chose to have and raise a baby, and about whether they might have made a different decision about their pregnancy if they had (or had not) received help in overcoming some important economic barriers to motherhood. In all, 108 useable surveys were collected, 45 from women who chose childbirth and 63 from women who chose abortion.

Table D1.1 reports the demographic characteristics of both samples of women. With regard to age (excepting the exclusion of minors), marital status, and religious affiliation, the abortion client sample tracked reasonably well with the characteristics of a large sample of abortion clients conducted at 100 geographically diverse abortion providers in 2000 and 2001.[1] Likely reflecting Maryland's high ranks among US states for income and educational attainment, the abortion client sample reports higher levels of both and less participation in Medicaid relative to national surveys of abortion clients.[2] Consistent with the larger percentage of blacks living in the Baltimore metropolitan area (28.7 percent in 2006) and Baltimore City itself (65.2 percent in 2005) relative to the country as a whole, the percentage of black women in the abortion patient sample exceeds that found in the national survey.[3]

Table D1.1. Characteristics of Baltimore-Area Abortion and Pregnancy Center Client Samples

	Abortion Clinic Clients	*Pregnancy Center Clients (post-birth)*
Pregnancy intention		
Unplanned	84.1	55.6
Unplanned, but open to idea	12.7	22.2
Planned	3.2	22.2
Age		
18–19	11.1	17.8
20–24	30.2	28.9
25–29	23.8	22.2
20–24	19.1	15.6
35 and above	15.9	15.6
Marital Status		
Currently married	20.6	13.3
Divorced/separated/widowed	14.3	11.1
Never married	65.1	75.6
Race/Ethnicity		
Black	47.6	71.1
White	44.4	17.8
Latina, Asian, Native American, or Other	7.9	11.1
Household Income		
Less than $10,000	17.5	48.8
$10,001–$25,000	14.3	41.5
$25,001–$40,000	20.6	4.9
$40,001–$55,000	14.3	4.9
$55,001–$70,000	12.7	0.0
$75,001–$85,000	4.8	0.0
$85,001–$100,000	6.4	0.0
More than $100,000	9.5	0.0
Education		
Less than high school	3.2	35.6
High school diploma or GED	30.2	42.2
Some college or two-year degree	34.9	17.8
Bachelor's degree or higher	31.8	4.4
Student status at survey		
Full-time student	15.9	11.1
Part-time student	15.9	4.4
Not a student	68.3	84.4

Employment status at survey		
Employed full time	60.3	22.7
Employed part time	20.6	11.4
Not employed; looking for work	11.1	52.3
Not employed; not looking for work	7.9	13.6
Children at time of pregnancy		
0	49.2	33.3
1	30.2	26.7
2	17.5	26.7
3 or more	3.2	13.3
Public assistance receipt		
Yes, at pregnancy	14.3	66.7
Yes, at survey	20.6	93.3
Abortion opinion at pregnancy		
"Pro-life"	14.3	44.2
"Pro-choice"	74.6	9.3
"Don't know"	11.1	46.5
Church attendance		
Once a week or more	20.9	35.6
At least once a month	12.9	15.6
A few times a year	38.7	37.8
Never	27.4	11.1

Source: Author's survey of Baltimore-area abortion and pregnancy center clients, 2005.

Note: All figures are percentages. Maximum nonmissing Ns = 63 for abortion clinic clients and 45 for pregnancy center clients.

The childbirth sample does not align as well with national data gathered on women who gave birth following unintended pregnancies from 2006 to 2010, but this is unsurprising given that study sites were expected to attract disproportionate shares of financially needy women.[4] The sample of women at pregnancy centers reflects slightly but not strikingly higher ages, in part because of the exclusion of minors. It includes larger percentages of never-married women and much larger percentages of black women. Based on rough comparisons between household income data I collected in my survey and measures of household income relative to the poverty line reported for the national survey, the pregnancy center sample appears to contain larger shares of women with low incomes. The women in the pregnancy center sample also appear to have been more likely to be receiving help from a social welfare program at the time of their children's birth. Not all pregnancies in the sample had been unintended; ten women (22 percent) reported that they had been planning to conceive (so, too, did two women among the abortion clients).

Aside from the pregnancy center sample's lower socioeconomic status and greater likelihood of identifying as black, other characteristics separate the two samples of women. Pregnancy center clients are more likely than abortion clients to have children, to have larger family sizes, to claim a religious affiliation, and to attend church, and they are much less likely to identify their position on abortion as pro-choice. They are less likely to report employment, although many say they are looking for work, but about as likely to be attending school.

NOTES

1. Rachel K. Jones, Jacqueline E. Darroch, and Stanley K. Henshaw, "Patterns in the Socioeconomic Characteristics of Women Obtaining Abortion in 2000–2001," *Perspectives on Sexual and Reproductive Health* 34, no. 5 (2002): 226–235.

2. See, for example, data and maps produced by "Measure of America," Social Science Research Council, accessed September 9, 2016, http://www.measureofamerica.org /maps.

3. US Census Bureau, "Table B-3: Metropolitan Areas—Population by Age, Sex, Race, and Hispanic Origin: April 1, 2000 to July 1, 2006," August 9, 2007, http://www .census.gov/popest/datasets.html; Table D-2, "Places—Population by Race and Hispanic Origin," in *County and City Data Book: 2007* (Washington, DC: Government Printing Office, 2007).

4. William D. Mosher, Jo Jones, and Joyce C. Abma, *Intended and Unintended Births in the United States, 1982–2010* (Hyattsville, MD: National Center for Health Statistics, 2012).

Notes

CHAPTER 1. THE PUZZLE OF PREGNANCY HELP ACTIVISM

1. Carol Clews, in discussion with the author, August 14, 2012.

2. "Center for Pregnancy Concerns," Center for Pregnancy Concerns, accessed August 16, 2018, http://pregnantandneedhelp.org/.

3. Nancy Gibbs, "The Grass-Roots Abortion War," *Time,* February 15, 2007, http://www.time.com/time/magazine/article/0,9171,1590444,00.html.

4. Pam Belluck, "Pregnancy Centers Gain Influence in Anti-Abortion Arena," *New York Times,* January 4, 2013, http://www.nytimes.com/2013/01/05/health/pregnancy-centers-gain-influence-in-anti-abortion-fight.html?_r=0.

5. Margaret H. Hartshorn, *Foot Soldiers Armed with Love: Heartbeat International's First Forty Years* (Virginia Beach, VA: Donning, 2011), 15.

6. Hartshorn, *Foot Soldiers,* 16.

7. Ziad Munson, *The Making of Pro-Life Activists: How Social Movement Mobilization Works* (Chicago: University of Chicago Press, 2008).

8. James Davison Hunter, *Before the Shooting Begins: Searching for Democracy in America's Culture War* (New York: Free Press, 1994).

9. Melody Rose, *Safe, Legal, and Unavailable? Abortion Politics in the United States* (Washington, DC: Congressional Quarterly Press, 2007); Laurence Tribe, *Abortion: The Clash of Absolutes* (New York: Norton, 1990).

10. Melody Rose, "Pro-Life, Pro-Woman? Frame Extension in the American Anti-abortion Movement," *Journal of Women, Politics, and Policy* 32, no. 1 (2011): 1–27; Glen A. Halva-Neubauer and Sara L. Zeigler, "Promoting Fetal Personhood: The Rhetorical and Legal Strategies of the Pro-Life Movement," *Feminist Formations* 22, no. 2 (2010): 101–123.

11. Dallas A. Blanchard, *The Anti-Abortion Movement and the Rise of the Religious Right: From Polite to Fiery Protest* (New York: Twayne, 1994).

12. For example, see Rose, *Safe, Legal, and Unavailable?;* Glen Harold Stassen, "Pro-Life? Look at the Fruits," *SojoMail,* October 13, 2004, http://www.sojo.net/index.cfm?action=sojomail.display&issue=041013).

13. Kurt Eichenwald, "America's Abortion Wars (and How to End Them)," *Newsweek,* December 17, 2015, https://www.newsweek.com/2015/12/25/abortion-war-overif-you-want-it-be-406137.html

14. Munson, *Making of Pro-Life Activists,* 113

15. "Worldwide Directory of Pregnancy Help," Heartbeat International, accessed July 24, 2018, https://www.heartbeatinternational.org/worldwide-directory.

16. Moira S. Gaul and Mai W. Bean, *A Legacy of Life and Love: Pregnancy Center Service Report,* 3rd ed. (Arlington, VA: Charlotte Lozier Institute, 2018), 8, https://www.heartbeatinternational.org/images/assets/pressroom/PRC-report-2018.pdf

17. Rachel K. Jones and Jenna Jerman, "Abortion Incidence and Service Availability in the United States, 2014," *Perspectives on Sexual and Reproductive Health* 49, no. 1 (2017): 3–14.

18. Munson, *Making of Pro-Life Activists*, 113.

19. Faye D. Ginsburg, *Contested Lives: The Abortion Debate in an American Community,* updated ed. (Berkeley: University of California Press, 1998); Munson, *Making of Pro-Life Activists.*

20. Kimberly Kelly, "Evangelical Underdogs: Intrinsic Success, Organizational Solidarity, and Marginalized Identities as Religious Movement Resources," *Journal of Contemporary Ethnography* 43, no. 4 (2014): 419–455; Kimberly Kelly, "In the Name of the Mother: Renegotiating Conservative Women's Authority in the Crisis Pregnancy Center Movement," *Signs* 38, no. 1 (2012): 203–230; Kimberly Kelly, "In the Name of the Mother: Gender and Religion in the Crisis Pregnancy Center Movement," PhD diss., University of Georgia, 2009.

21. Dr. and Mrs. John C. Willke, *Abortion and the Pro-Life Movement: An Inside View* (West Conshohocken, PA: Infinity, 2014).

22. Olivia Gans and Mary Spaulding Balch, *When They Say . . . You Say: Defending the Pro-Life Position and Framing the Issue by the Language We Use* (Washington, DC: National Right to Life Committee, 2009).

23. Dave Andrusko, "The 'Little Things' That Help Turn a Woman from Abortion to a Choice for Life," *NRL News Today,* August 10, 2018, https://www.nationalrightto lifenews.org/news/2018/08/the-little-things-that-help-turn-a-woman-from-abortion -to-a-choice-for-life/.

24. NARAL Pro-Choice America Foundation, *The Truth about Crisis Pregnancy Centers* (Washington, DC: NARAL Pro-Choice America Foundation, 2010).

25. NARAL Pro-Choice America, *Crisis Pregnancy Centers Lie: The Insidious Threat to Reproductive Freedom* (Washington, DC: NARAL Pro-Choice America, 2015), http:// www.prochoiceamerica.org/assets/download-files/cpc-report-2015.pdf.

26. Dawn Laguens, "Remarks from Dawn Laguens, Executive Vice President of Planned Parenthood Federation of America, as Prepared," Planned Parenthood, March 20, 2018, https://www.plannedparenthood.org/uploads/filer_public/ec/85/ec85816d-34 f1–4877–80de-bf37ce0fc363/remarks_from_dawn_laguens.pdf.

27. Kelly, "In the Name of the Mother"; Marvin N. Olasky, "Abortion Rights: Anatomy of a Negative Campaign," *Public Relations Review* 13, no. 3 (1987): 12–23; Suzanne Staggenborg, *The Pro-Choice Movement: Organization and Activism in the Abortion Conflict* (New York: Oxford University Press, 1991).

28. Melia Robinson, "Pro-Choice Activists Followed Google Employees on Their Way to Work This Week to Call Attention to a Little-Known Problem with Search Results," *Business Insider,* April 4, 2018, https://www.businessinsider.com/google-protest-over -anti-abortion-clinic-ads-2018–4; Hayley Tsukayama, "Google Removes 'Deceptive' Pregnancy Center Ads," *Washington Post,* April 28, 2014, https://www.washingtonpost .com/news/the-switch/wp/2014/04/28/naral-successfully-lobbies-google-to-take-down -deceptive-pregnancy-center-ads/?noredirect=on&utm_term=.08d57e7eb57c.

29. Nikolas T. Nikas, Dorinda C. Bordlee, and Thomas M. Messner, "Brief for Amici Curiae, Charlotte Lozier Institute, March for Life Education Fund, and National Pro-Life Women's Caucus in Support of Petitioners, NIFLA v. Becerra, 138 S. Ct. 2361 (2018)," January 12, 2018, https://s27589.pcdn.co/wp-content/uploads/2018/01/16–1140 -Amicus-Brief-on-the-Merits-003-Jan-12–2018.pdf.

30. Guttmacher Institute, "'Choose Life' License Plates," September 1, 2018, https:// www.guttmacher.org/state-policy/explore/choose-life-license-plates; Bryce Covert and Josh Israel, "The States That Siphon Welfare Money to Stop Abortion," Think-Progress, October 3, 2016, https://thinkprogress.org/tanf-cpcs-ec002305dd18/.

31. Blanchard, *Anti-Abortion Movement,* 68.

32. Blanchard, *Anti-Abortion Movement,* 53.

33. James Risen and Judy L. Thomas, *Wrath of Angels: The American Abortion War* (New York: Basic Books, 1998).

34. Joshua Wilson, *The Street Politics of Abortion: Speech, Violence, and America's Culture Wars* (Palo Alto, CA: Stanford University Press, 2013).

35. Alesha Doan, *Opposition and Intimidation: The Abortion Wars and Strategies of Political Harassment* (Ann Arbor: University of Michigan Press, 2007), 106.

36. Kelly, "In the Name of the Mother"; Kelly, "Gender and Religion."

37. Gibbs, "Grass-Roots Abortion War."

38. Sara Diamond, *Not by Politics Alone: The Enduring Influence of the Christian Right* (New York: Guilford, 1998), 154.

39. Ginsburg, *Contested Lives*; Munson, *Making of Pro-Life Activists.*

40. James R. Kelly, "Pro-Life Politics: From Counter-Movement to Transforming Movement," in *Consistently Opposing Killing: From Abortion to Assisted Suicide, the Death Penalty, and War,* ed. Rachel M. MacNair and Stephen Zunes (Westport, CT: Praeger, 2008), 163.

41. Kelly, "Gender and Religion."

42. Kelly, "Gender and Religion," 246.

43. Kelly, "Gender and Religion," 252–253.

44. John R. Petrocik, "Issue Ownership in Presidential Elections, with a 1980 Case Study," *American Journal of Political Science* 40, no. 3 (1996): 825–850; Helmut Norpoth and Bruce Buchanan, "Wanted: The Education President: Issue Trespassing by Political Candidates," *Public Opinion Quarterly* 56, no. 1 (1992): 87–99.

45. Elizabeth A. Armstrong and Mary Bernstein, "Culture, Power, and Institutions: A Multi-Institutional Politics Approach to Social Movements," *Sociological Theory* 26, no. 1 (2008): 74–99; Katherine MacFarland Bruce, "LGBT Pride as a Cultural Protest Tactic in a Southern City," *Journal of Contemporary Ethnography* 42, no. 5 (2013): 608–635; Verta Taylor et al., "Culture and Mobilization: Tactical Repertoires, Same-Sex Weddings, and the Impact on Gay Activism," *American Sociological Review* 74, no. 6 (2009): 865–890; Nella Van Dyke, Sarah A. Soule, and Verta A. Taylor, "The Targets of Social Movements: Beyond a Focus on the State," *Research in Social Movements, Conflicts, and Change* 25 (2004): 27–51; Edward T. Walker, Andrew W. Martin, and John D. McCarthy, "Confronting the State, the Corporation, and the Academy: The Influence

of Institutional Targets on Social Movement Repertoires," *American Journal of Sociology* 114, no. 1 (2008): 35–76.

46. Russell J. Dalton, *The Good Citizen: How a Younger Generation Is Reshaping American Politics*, rev. ed. (Washington, DC: Congressional Quarterly Press, 2009); Jennifer Oser, Marc Hooghe, and Sofie Marien, "Is Online Participation Distinct from Offline Participation? A Latent Class Analysis of Participation Types and Their Stratification," *Political Research Quarterly* 66, no. 1 (2013): 91–101; Patricia Strach, "Political Participation in a Consumer Era: Why Americans Choose Politics," paper presented at the Annual Meeting of the Midwest Political Science Association, Chicago, IL, April 12–14, 2012; Cliff Zukin et al., *A New Engagement: Political Participation, Civic Life, and the Changing American Citizen* (Oxford, UK: Oxford University Press, 2006).

47. William A. Galston and Peter Levine, "America's Civic Condition: A Glance at the Evidence," in *Community Works: The Revival of Civil Society in America*, ed. E. J. Dionne (Washington, DC: Brookings Institution, 1998), 30–36; Stephen Macedo et al., *Democracy at Risk: How Political Choices Undermine Citizen Participation and What We Can Do about It* (Washington, DC: Brookings Institution, 2005); Sheilah Mann, "What the Survey of American College Freshmen Tells Us about Their Interest in Politics and Political Science," *P.S.: Political Science and Politics* 32 (1999): 263–268; Craig A. Rimmerman, *The New Citizenship: Unconventional Politics, Activism, and Service*, 3rd ed. (Boulder, CO: Westview, 2005).

48. Nina Eliasoph, *Avoiding Politics: How Americans Produce Apathy in Everyday Life* (New York: Cambridge University Press, 1998).

49. Amy Blackstone, "'It's Just about Being Fair': Activism and the Politics of Volunteering in the Breast Cancer Movement," *Gender and Society* 18, no. 3 (2004): 350–368; Adriane Bilous, "'We Need a Revival': Young Evangelical Women Redefine Activism in New York City," in *The New Evangelical Social Engagement*, ed. Brian Steensland and Philip Goff (Oxford, UK: Oxford University Press, 2014), 109–128; Samantha Majic, "Serving Sex Workers and Promoting Democratic Engagement: Rethinking Nonprofits' Role in American Civic and Political Life," *Perspectives on Politics* 9, no. 4 (2011): 821–839.

50. Nancy J. Davis and Robert V. Robinson, *Claiming Society for God: Religious Movements and Social Welfare in Egypt, Israel, Italy, and the United States* (Bloomington: Indiana University Press, 2012).

51. Daniel M. Shea, "Young Voters, Declining Trust and the Limits of 'Service Politics,'" *Forum* 13, no. 3 (2015): 459–479, https://doi.org/10.1515/for-2015-0036; Strach, "Political Participation in a Consumer Era"; Zukin et al., *New Engagement*.

52. Blanchard, *Anti-Abortion Movement*; Kimberly H. Conger, *The Christian Right in Republican State Politics* (New York: Palgrave-Macmillan, 2009), 140–141; Ginsburg, *Contested Lives*; Staggenborg, *Pro-Choice Movement*, 129; Wilson, *Street Politics*, 14.

53. Ginsburg, *Contested Lives*, 122. Ginsburg notes variations in the origins of pregnancy centers, however, and also suggests that in practice different types of activists than those active in politics and street protest ended up arriving to support pregnancy help organizations.

54. Ginsburg, *Contested Lives*, 100.

55. Blanchard, *Anti-Abortion Movement*; Doan, *Opposition and Intimidation*; Kerry N. Jacoby, *Souls, Bodies, Spirits: The Drive to Abolish Abortion since 1973* (Westport, CT: Praeger, 1999); Carol J. C. Maxwell, *Pro-Life Activists in America: Meaning, Motivation, and Direct Action* (Cambridge, UK: Cambridge University Press, 2002), 241; Wilson, *Street Politics*, 158.

56. Melody Rose, *Safe, Legal, and Unavailable?*, 2.

57. Wilson, *Street Politics*, 4.

58. Wilson, *Street Politics*, 5.

59. Doug McAdam, *Political Process and the Development of Black Insurgency* (Chicago: University of Chicago Press, 1982); David S. Meyer, "Tending the Vineyard: Cultivating Political Process Research," in *Rethinking Social Movements: Structure, Meaning, and Emotions*, ed. J. Goodwin and J. M. Jasper (Lanham, MD: Rowman and Littlefield, 2004): 47–59.

60. Doug McAdam, "Conceptual Origins, Current Problems, Future Directions," in *Comparative Perspectives on Social Movements: Political Opportunities, Mobilizing Structures, and Cultural Framings*, ed. Doug McAdam, John D. McCarthy, and Mayer N. Zald (Cambridge, UK: Cambridge University Press, 1996), 27.

61. David S. Meyer and Suzanne Staggenborg, "Movements, Countermovements, and the Structure of Political Opportunity," *American Journal of Sociology* 101 (1996): 1628–1660.

62. Walker, Martin, and McCarthy, "Confronting the State," 71.

63. Meyer, "Tending the Vineyard"; Meyer and Staggenborg, "Movements, Countermovements, and the Structure of Political Opportunity"; Walker, Martin, and McCarthy, "Confronting the State."

64. Jo Freeman, "A Model for Analyzing the Strategic Options of Social Movement Organizations," in *Waves of Protest: Social Movements since the Sixties*, ed. Jo Freeman and Victoria Johnson (Lanham, MD: Rowman and Littlefield, 1999): 221–240.

65. Walker, Martin, and McCarthy, "Confronting the State."

66. Doan, *Opposition and Intimidation*.

67. Daniel K. Williams, *Defenders of the Unborn: The Pro-Life Movement before* Roe v. Wade (New York: Oxford University Press, 2016).

68. Williams, *Defenders of the Unborn*.

69. Deborah R. McFarlane and Kenneth J. Meier, *The Politics of Fertility Control* (New York: Chatham House, 2001).

70. Williams, *Defenders of the Unborn*.

71. McFarlane and Meier, *Politics of Fertility Control*; Williams, *Defenders of the Unborn*.

72. Alan I. Abramowitz, "It's Abortion, Stupid: Policy Voting in the 1992 Presidential Election," *Journal of Politics* 57, no. 1 (1995): 176–186.

73. Doan, *Opposition and Intimidation*.

74. Jacoby, *Souls, Bodies, Spirits*; Williams, *Defenders of the Unborn*.

75. Elizabeth Nash et al., *Laws Affecting Reproductive Health and Rights: State Trends at Midyear, 2016* (New York: Guttmacher Institute, 2016), https://www.guttmacher

.org/article/2016/07/laws-affecting-reproductive-health-and-rights-state-trends-mid
year-2016.; Rose, *Safe, Legal, and Unavailable.*

76. Williams, *Defenders of the Unborn.*

77. Munson, *Making of Pro-Life Activists.*

78. Munson, *Making of Pro-Life Activists*, 128. ·

79. Munson, *Making of Pro-Life Activists*, 125.

80. Jacoby, *Souls, Bodies, Spirits.*

81. Kathleen M. Blee, *Inside Organized Racism: Women in the Hate Movement* (Berkeley: University of California Press, 2002); Ruth Braunstein, *Prophets and Patriots: Faith in Democracy across the Political Divide* (Berkeley: University of California Press, 2017); Hahrie Han, *How Organizations Develop Activists: Civic Associations and Leadership in the 21st Century* (New York: Oxford University Press, 2014); Jon A. Shields, *The Democratic Virtues of the Christian Right* (Princeton, NJ: Princeton University Press, 2009).

82. Maxwell, *Pro-Life Activists in America*; Risen and Thomas, *Wrath of Angels.*

83. Debra C. Minkoff, *Organizing for Equality: The Evolution of Women's and Racial-Ethnic Organizations in America, 1955–1985* (New Brunswick, NJ: Rutgers University Press, 1995); Barbara G. Collins and Mary B. Whalen, "The Rape Crisis Movement: Radical or Reformist?," *Social Work* 34, no. 1 (1989): 61–63; Carol S. Wharton, "Establishing Shelters for Battered Women: Local Manifestations of a Social Movement," *Qualitative Sociology* 10, no. 2 (1987): 146–163; John J. Chin, "The Limits and Potential of Nonprofit Organizations in Participatory Planning: A Case Study of the New York HIV Planning Council," *Journal of Urban Affairs* 31, no. 4 (2009): 431–460; Deborah B. Gould, *Moving Politics: Emotion and ACT UP's Fight against AIDS* (Chicago: University of Chicago Press, 2009); Benjamin Shepard, "From Community Organization to Direct Services: The Street Trans Action Revolutionaries to Sylvia Rivera Law Project," *Journal of Social Service Research* 39, no. 1 (2013): 95–114; Majic, "Serving Sex Workers"; Daniel M. Cress, "Nonprofit Incorporation among Movements of the Poor," *Sociological Quarterly* 38, no. 2 (1997): 343–360; Helen Deines, "The Catholic Worker Movement: Communities of Personal Hospitality and Justice," *Social Work and Christianity* 35, no. 4 (2008): 429–448.

84. Collins and Whalen, "Rape Crisis Movement."

85. Meyer and Staggenborg, "Movements, Countermovements, and the Structure of Political Opportunity."

86. Verta Taylor and Nellie Van Dyke, "'Get Up, Stand Up': Tactical Repertoires of Social Movements," in *The Blackwell Companion to Social Movements*, ed. David A. Snow, Sarah A. Soule, and Hanspeter Kriesi (Malden, MA: Blackwell, 2004): 262–293; Walker, Martin, and McCarthy, "Confronting the State."

87. Elizabeth A. Armstrong, *Forging Gay Identities: Organizing Sexuality in San Francisco, 1950–1994* (Chicago: University of Chicago Press, 2002), 13–14.

88. Freeman, "Strategic Options"; McAdam, *Political Process.*

89. Taylor and Van Dyke, "'Get Up, Stand Up.'"

90. Braunstein, *Prophets and Patriots.*

91. Gould, *Moving Politics.*

92. Freeman, "Strategic Options."

93. Armstrong, *Forging Gay Identities.*

94. Braunstein, *Prophets and Patriots,* 153.

95. Taylor and Van Dyke, "'Get Up, Stand Up,'" 277.

96. Taylor and Van Dyke, "'Get Up, Stand Up,'" 276.

97. Debra C. Minkoff, "The Emergence of Hybrid Organizational Forms: Combining Identity-Based Service Provision and Political Action," *Nonprofit and Voluntary Sector Quarterly* 31 (2002): 377–400; Elizabeth S. Clemens, "Organizational Repertoires and Institutional Change: Women's Group and the Transformation of U.S. Politics, 1890–1920," *American Journal of Sociology* 98, no. 4 (1993): 755–798.

98. Minkoff, "Emergence of Hybrid Organizational Forms," 378.

99. Minkoff, "Emergence of Hybrid Organizational Forms."

100. Majic, "Serving Sex Workers."

101. Collins and Whalen, "Rape Crisis Movement"; Deines, "Catholic Worker Movement"; Gould, *Moving Politics.*

102. Shepard, "Community Organization to Direct Services"; Deines, "Catholic Worker Movement"; Davis and Robinson, *Claiming Society for God.*

103. Gould, *Moving Politics.*

104. Armstrong, *Forging Gay Identities,* 173.

105. Deines, "Catholic Worker Movement"; Nancy D. Wadsworth, *Ambivalent Miracles: Evangelicals and the Politics of Racial Healing* (Charlottesville: University of Virginia Press, 2014).

106. Davis and Robinson, *Claiming Society for God.*

107. Bilous, "'We Need a Revival'"; Blackstone, "'Being Fair.'"

108. Nina Eliasoph, *The Politics of Volunteering* (Cambridge, UK: Polity, 2013); Hahrie Han, *Moved to Action: Motivation, Participation, and Inequality in American Politics* (Palo Alto, CA: Stanford University Press, 2009).

109. James Douglas, "Political Theories of Nonprofit Organizations," in *The Nonprofit Sector: A Research Handbook,* ed. W. W. Powell (New Haven, CT: Yale University Press, 1987): 43–54; Dennis R. Young, "Alternative Models of Government-Nonprofit Sector Relations: Theoretical and International Perspectives," *Nonprofit and Voluntary Sector Quarterly* 29, no. 1 (2000): 149–172.

110. Collins and Whalen, "Rape Crisis Movement"; Cress, "Nonprofit Incorporation"; Majic, "Serving Sex Workers"; Shepard, "Community Organization to Direct Services."

111. Gould, *Moving Politics*; Majic, "Serving Sex Workers."

112. Collins and Whalen, "Rape Crisis Movement"; Shepard, "Community Organization to Direct Services."

113. Davis and Robinson, *Claiming Society for God*; see also Deines, "Catholic Worker Movement."

114. Williams, *Defenders of the Unborn.*

115. Kelly, "In the Name of the Mother."

116. Minkoff, "Emergence of Hybrid Organizational Forms."

117. Luther P. Gerlach and Virginia H. Hine, *People, Power, Change: Movements of Social Transformation* (Indianapolis, IN: Bobbs-Merrill, 1970), xxi.

CHAPTER 2. OVERVIEW OF THE PREGNANCY HELP MOVEMENT

1. Margaret H. Hartshorn, *Foot Soldiers Armed with Love: Heartbeat International's First Forty Years* (Virginia Beach, VA: Donning, 2011), 15.

2. National Institute of Family and Life Advocates, "Mission and Vision," accessed August 3, 2011, http://www.nifla.org/about-us-mission-and-vision.asp.

3. Thomas Glessner, *The Emerging Brave New World* (Crane, MO: HighWay, 2008), 139.

4. Hartshorn, *Foot Soldiers*, 16.

5. Heartbeat International, "Worldwide Directory of Pregnancy Help," accessed July 24, 2018, https://www.heartbeatinternational.org/worldwide-directory.

6. Respondents in multilocation networks were given the option of responding on behalf of an individual center or all centers in the network. In the small number of instances in which I received responses from an individual center in a network in addition to a response for the entire network, the entire network response was used and the individual center response was removed from the data. National pregnancy center totals typically count each separate office location as a distinct "pregnancy center."

7. Curtis Young, in discussion with the author, August 8, 2012.

8. Women's Care Center Foundation, "About," accessed August 27, 2018, http://womenscarecenterfoundation.org/about/.

9. Heartbeat International, "Worldwide Directory of Pregnancy Help."

10. All will be called "national associations," even though some have affiliated centers in countries other than the United States.

11. Family Research Council, *A Passion to Serve,* 2nd ed. (Washington, DC: Family Research Council, 2012).

12. Both figures come from my interviews with these associations' national directors.

13. Family Research Council, *A Passion to Serve, a Vision for Life: Pregnancy Resource Center Service Report 2009* (Washington, DC: Family Research Council, 2009).

14. Hartshorn, *Foot Soldiers*; Susan Hoffman, in discussion with the author, September 20, 2012.

15. Hartshorn, *Foot Soldiers*; Terry Ianora, *Crisis Pregnancy Centers: The Birth of a Grassroots Movement* (Bloomington, IN: AuthorHouse, 2009); Terry Weaver, in discussion with the author, October 23, 2012.

16. Ianora, *Crisis Pregnancy Centers*; Andrew Nelson, "Birthright Leader Stepping Down after 45 Years Helping Women in Crisis Pregnancies," *Georgia Bulletin*, December 23, 2014, https://georgiabulletin.org/news/2014/12/birthright-leader-stepping-45-years-helping-women-crisis-pregnancies/.

17. Heartbeat International, "Worldwide Directory of Pregnancy Help."

18. Mary Cunningham Agee, in discussion with the author, October 18, 2012; Karen Walker, "From the Boardroom to the Battle for Life," *National Catholic Register* 74, no. 8 (1998).

19. Gabriel Project, "National Portal to the Gabriel Project," accessed September 22, 2014, http://www.gabrielproject.us/index.html.

20. Anthony DiIulio, in discussion with the author, September 11, 2012.

21. Gabriel Network, "About," accessed August 1, 2012, http://gabrielnetwork.org /about.

22. D. Michelle Williams, in discussion with the author, October 2, 2012.

23. Nelson, "Birthright Leader Stepping Down."

24. Mary Cunningham Agee, *The Nurturing Network: Serving the Urgent and Practical Needs of Mothers in Crisis for 25 Years* (St. Helena, CA: Nurturing Network, 2007/2010).

25. The data do not differentiate between those who have been involved continuously over the time span identified and those who have not.

26. See also Kimberly Kelly, "In the Name of the Mother: Renegotiating Conservative Women's Authority in the Crisis Pregnancy Center Movement," *Signs* 38, no. 1 (2012): 203–230.

27. Kelly, "In the Name of the Mother."

28. Care Net, *Serving with Care and Integrity: A Training Resource for Pregnancy Center Volunteers* (Lansdowne, VA: Care Net, 2003), 33, 38.

29. Heartbeat International, *The LOVE Approach Training Manual*, 3rd ed. (Columbus, OH: Heartbeat International, 2011), 71.

30. Heartbeat International, *LOVE Approach*, 196.

31. Heartbeat International, *LOVE Approach*, 196.

32. Frederica Mathewes-Green, *Real Choices: Listening to Women; Looking for Alternatives to Abortion* (Ben Lomond, CA: Conciliar, 1997), 11.

33. See also Ziad Munson, *The Making of Pro-Life Activists: How Social Movement Mobilization Works* (Chicago: University of Chicago Press, 2008).

34. Mathewes-Green, *Real Choices*, 22–23.

35. Heartbeat International, *LOVE Approach*, 196.

36. Care Net, *Serving with Care and Integrity*, 28.

37. Care Net, *Serving with Care and Integrity,* 27; Heartbeat International, *LOVE Approach*, 12.

38. Pamela Palumbo, in discussion with the author, July 17, 2012.

39. Cookie Harris, in discussion with the author, August 3, 2012.

40. See also Kimberly Kelly, "In the Name of the Mother: Gender and Religion in the Crisis Pregnancy Center Movement," PhD diss., University of Georgia, 2009).

41. Care Net, *Serving with Care and Integrity*, 38.

42. Care Net, *Serving with Care and Integrity,* 38.

43. Gabriel Network, "About."

44. Maria Suarez Hamm, in discussion with the author, October 12, 2012.

45. Louise Summerhill, *The Story of Birthright: The Alternative to Abortion* (Libertyville, IL: Prow/Franciscan Marytown, 1973/1984), 74–75.

46. Care Net, *Serving with Care and Integrity*, 33.

47. Care Net, *Serving with Care and Integrity*, 156.

48. Care Net, *Serving with Care and Integrity*, 37.

49. Heartbeat International, *LOVE Approach*, 187.

50. Mariana Vera, in discussion with the author, October 25, 2012.

51. Margaret H. Hartshorn, "Pregnancy Help Centers, Abstinence, STDs, and Healing: Putting It All Together," in *Back to the Drawing Board: The Future of the Pro-Life Movement*, ed. Teresa R. Wagner (South Bend, IN: St. Augustine's, 2003), 106–120; Hartshorn, *Foot Soldiers*.

52. Heartbeat International, *LOVE Approach*, 12.

53. Heartbeat International, *LOVE Approach*, 73.

54. Birthright International, https://birthright.org/, accessed October 2, 2018.

55. Mary Cunningham Agee, *A Call to Effective Action: When Being Right Is Not Enough* (Washington, DC: Respect Life Program, 2004).

56. Care Net, *Serving with Care and Integrity*, 55.

57. Care Net, *Serving with Care and Integrity*, 53.

58. Care Net, *Serving with Care and Integrity*, 55.

59. Care Net, *Serving with Care and Integrity*; Heartbeat International, *The LOVE Approach*.

60. Care Net, *Serving with Care and Integrity*, 6.

61. Care Net, *Serving with Care and Integrity*, 53–55; Heartbeat International, *LOVE Approach*, 13–14.

62. Cindy Hopkins, in discussion with the author, August 15, 2012.

63. Margaret Hartshorn, in discussion with the author, August 23, 2012.

64. Frederica Mathewes-Green, in discussion with the author, September 18, 2012.

65. Summerhill, *Story of Birthright*, 36–37.

66. Melinda Delahoyde, *Fighting for Life: Defending the Newborn's Right to Live* (Ann Arbor, MI: Servant, 1984), 76.

67. Agee, *Call to Effective Action*.

68. Denise Cocciolone, in discussion with the author, October 23, 2012.

69. Tony Evans, "September 29 Dinner General Session" speech, Care Net National Pregnancy Center Conference, Orlando, FL, September 29, 2011.

70. Heartbeat International, *LOVE Approach*, 83.

71. Heartbeat International, *LOVE Approach*, 88.

72. Glessner, *Emerging Brave New World*, 139.

73. This leader fleshes out that argument in some of her public writing, including: Frederica Mathewes-Green, "The Bitter Price of Choice," in *Prolife Feminism: Yesterday and Today*, ed. Rachel MacNair, Mare Krane Derr, and Linda Naranjo-Huebl (New York: Solzburger and Graham, 1995), 181–184.

74. Agee, *Call to Effective Action*.

75. Reva B. Siegel, "The Right's Reasons: Constitutional Conflict and the Spread of Woman-Protective Antiabortion Argument," *Duke Law Journal* 57 (2008): 1641–1692.

76. Summerhill, *Story of Birthright*, 27.

77. Care Net, *Before You Decide* (Lansdowne, VA: Care Net, 2011).

78. Heartbeat International, *LOVE Approach.*

79. She pointed, in particular, to the personal testimonies posted on the website of Silent No More, a group of women who regret past abortions and seek by sharing their stories to discourage other women from having abortions.

80. Sandra Christiansen, in discussion with the author, July 9, 2012.

81. Agee, *Call to Effective Action.*

82. For example, NARAL Pro-Choice America, *Crisis Pregnancy Centers Lie: The Insidious Threat to Reproductive Freedom* (Washington, DC: NARAL Pro-Choice America, 2015), http://www.prochoiceamerica.org/assets/download-files/cpc-report-2015.pdf.

83. Care Net, *Serving with Care and Integrity*, 6.

84. Summerhill, *Story of Birthright*, viii.

85. Summerhill, *Story of Birthright*, 69.

86. Cited in Ianora, *Crisis Pregnancy Centers*, 41.

87. Glessner, *Emerging Brave New World*, 191.

88. Linda Cochrane, in discussion with the author, October 16, 2012.

89. Timothy Dolan, "Al Smith Foundation Dinner," *The Gospel in the Digital Age* (blog), October 19, 2012, http://blog.archny.org/index.php/al-smith-foundation-dinner/.

90. Quoted in *Birthright v. Birthright, Inc.*, 827 F. Supp. 1114 (1993).

91. Melinda Delahoyde, "Volunteer at a Center," *Christianity Today*, October 14, 2009, http://www.christianitytoday.com/ct/2009/october/26.56.html; Mary Cunningham Agee, *Compassion in Action: Maternal Profiles in Courage and Those Who Gave Them Hope* (St. Helena, CA: Nurturing Network, 2006).

92. Hartshorn, *Foot Soldiers*, 65; Glessner, *Emerging Brave New World*, 1.

93. Susan Hoffman, in discussion with the author, September 20, 2012.

94. For example, the author's observations in person (2012) or over live television (2013).

95. Jo Freeman, "A Model for Analyzing the Strategic Options of Social Movement Organizations," in *Waves of Protest: Social Movements since the Sixties*, ed. Jo Freeman and Victoria Johnson (Lanham, MD: Rowman and Littlefield, 1999), 221–240.

96. Elizabeth A. Armstrong, *Forging Gay Identities: Organizing Sexuality in San Francisco, 1950–1994* (Chicago: University of Chicago Press, 2002).

97. Heartbeat International, "Option Line," accessed September 10, 2018, https://www.heartbeatinternational.org/our-work/option-line.

98. Moira S. Gaul and Mai W. Bean, *A Legacy of Life and Love: Pregnancy Center Service Report*, 3rd ed. (Arlington, VA: Charlotte Lozier Institute, 2018), 8, https://www.heartbeatinternational.org/images/assets/pressroom/PRC-report-2018.pdf. CLI's data come from online surveys of pregnancy centers that it distributed through Care Net, Heartbeat International, NIFLA, and smaller pregnancy center "parent organizations."

99. Heartbeat International, *LOVE Approach.*

100. Heartbeat International, *LOVE Approach*, 22.

101. Care Net, *Serving with Care and Integrity*, 47–51.

102. Care Net, *Serving with Care and Integrity*, 50.

103. Heartbeat International, *LOVE Approach*, 15.

104. Ianora, *Crisis Pregnancy Center*, 81–82.

105. Birthright International.

106. Kelly, "In the Name of the Mother."

107. Care Net, *Serving with Care and Integrity*, 109.

108. Heartbeat International, *LOVE Approach*, 73.

109. Care Net, *Serving with Care and Integrity*, 65.

110. Gaul and Bean, *Legacy of Life and Love*, 8.

111. I have redrawn the figure using the same data from: Laura S. Hussey, "Crisis Pregnancy Centers, Poverty, and the Expanding Frontiers of American Abortion Politics," *Politics & Policy*, 41, no. 6 (2013), 999.

112. Andrea K. McDaniels, "Covering a Common Need: A New Diaper Bank Offers Parents a Necessary Supply, Peace of Mind," *Baltimore Sun*, September 29, 2015, A1.

113. Heartbeat International, "Worldwide Directory of Pregnancy Help."

114. Lindsay E. Beyerstein. "Sent Away: A New Look at Maternity Homes," RH Reality Check, June 21, 2007, http://rhrealitycheck.org/article/2007/06/21/sent-away-a-new-look-at-maternity-group-homes/; Jane Gross, "Anti-Abortion Revival: Homes for the Unwed," *New York Times*, July 23, 1989.

115. Marnie Eisenstadt, "Grandmothers Turn Their Fight against Abortion into a Syracuse Home for Babies," *Central NY Real-Time News Blog, Syracuse Post-Standard*, March 20, 2014, http://blog.syracuse.com/news/print.html?entry=/2014/03/grandmothers_turn_their_fight_against_abortion_into_a_syracuse_home_for_babies.html; Lara Hulsey, *Maternity Group Homes Classification and Literature Review: Final Report* (Princeton, NJ: Mathematica Policy Research, 2004); Loving and Caring, "Today's Maternity Homes," accessed December 22, 2014, http://lovingandcaring.org/housing/todays-maternity-homes/.

116. I asked pregnancy center directors, "As a general rule, if asked, does your center provide material assistance to the following groups?"

117. Heartbeat International, "Our Story," accessed October 15, 2018, https://www.heartbeatinternational.org/about/our-story.

118. Gaul and Bean, *Legacy of Life and Love*, 30.

119. Gaul and Bean, *Legacy of Life and Love*, 8.

120. Earn While You Learn, "The EWYL Impact," accessed June 24, 2013, http://www.ewylonline.org.

121. Earn While You Learn, "Main Curriculum," accessed June 24, 2013, http://www.ewylonline.org/Main_Curriculum.asp.

122. Earn While You Learn, "Life Skills Pack," accessed June 24, 2013, http://www.ewylonline.org/Life_Skills.asp.

123. Assure Pregnancy Clinic, "Bridges," accessed June 25, 2013, http://www.assurelife.org/what-we-do/our-programs/bridges/.

124. Gaul and Bean, *Legacy of Life and Love*, 8.

125. Respondents were instructed to count only people who came to the center for goods, information, or services—not attendees at public or classroom presentations—as clients.

126. Kimberly Kelly, "Evangelical Underdogs: Intrinsic Success, Organizational Solidarity, and Marginalized Identities as Religious Movement Resources," *Journal of Contemporary Ethnography* 43, no. 4 (2014): 419–455.

127. Rachel K. Jones and Jenna Jerman, "Abortion Incidence and Service Availability in the United States, 2011," *Perspectives on Sexual and Reproductive Health* 46, no. 1 (2014): 17–27.

128. Care Net, "Mission and Vision," accessed October 15, 2018, https://www.care-net .org/mission-and-vision.

129. Heartbeat International, *LOVE Approach*, 11.

130. Gaul and Bean, *Legacy of Life and Love*, 35.

131. "Care Net Presents Linda Cochrane the Dr. Harold O.J. Brown Sanctity of Human Life Award," Christian Newswire, accessed April 1, 2015, http://www.christian newswire.com/news/675574347.html.

132. Linda Cochrane, *Forgiven and Set Free* (Grand Rapids, MI: Baker Books, 1996).

133. Elaine Ham, in discussion with the author, October 3, 2012.

134. Heartbeat International, *LOVE Approach*, 254.

135. Gaul and Bean, *Legacy of Life and Love*, 33.

136. Care Net, *Serving with Care and Integrity*, 164.

137. Heartbeat International, *LOVE Approach*, 252.

138. Hartshorn, *Foot Soldiers*, 104.

139. Hartshorn, *Foot Soldiers*; Heartbeat International, *LOVE Approach*.

140. Karolyn Schrage, "Effectively Reaching the Abortion-Minded Woman," workshop presented at the Care Net National Pregnancy Center Conference, Orlando, FL, September 28, 2011.

141. Care Net, *Serving with Care and Integrity*, 171.

142. Care Net, *Serving with Care and Integrity*, 171.

143. Care Net, *Serving with Care and Integrity*, 101.

144. *Beautiful Everyday Holy Bible,* New Living Translation, 2nd ed. (Carol Stream, IL: Tyndale House, 2007).

145. Heartbeat International, *LOVE Approach*, 85–86.

146. Ianora, *Crisis Pregnancy Centers.*

147. Gaul and Bean, *Legacy of Life and Love*, 65.

148. US House of Representatives, Committee on Government Reform Minority Staff, *False and Misleading Health Information Provided by Federally Funded Pregnancy Resource Centers* (Washington, DC: Government Printing Office, 2006).

149. Teddy Wilson, "Trump Gives Away Millions to Anti-Choice Fake Clinics," Rewire.News, September 7, 2017, https://rewire.news/article/2017/09/07/trump-gives -away-millions-anti-choice-fake-clinics/.

150. Teddy Wilson, "State-Level Republicans Pour Taxpayer Money into Fake Clinics at an Unprecedented Pace (Updated)," Rewire.News, February 16, 2018 (Updated March 20, 2018), https://rewire.news/article/2018/02/16/state-level-republicans -pour-taxpayer-money-fake-clinics-unprecedented-pace/.

151. Guttmacher Institute, "'Choose Life' License Plates," September 1, 2018, https:// www.guttmacher.org/state-policy/explore/choose-life-license-plates.

152. Bryce Covert and Josh Israel, "The States That Siphon Welfare Money to Stop Abortion," ThinkProgress, October 3, 2016, https://thinkprogress.org/tanf-cpcs-ec00 2305dd18/.

153. Kelly, "Gender and Religion," 163.

CHAPTER 3. ORIGINS AND EARLY GROWTH

1. Family Research Council, *A Passion to Serve, a Vision for Life: Pregnancy Resource Center Service Report 2009* (Washington, DC: Family Research Council, 2009); Family Research Council, *A Passion to Serve,* 2nd ed. (Washington, DC: Family Research Council, 2012); Marvin N. Olasky, *The Tragedy of American Compassion* (Wheaton, IL: Crossway, 1992); Terry Ianora, *Crisis Pregnancy Centers: The Birth of a Grassroots Movement* (Bloomington, IN: AuthorHouse, 2009).

2. Kathy Rudy, *Beyond Pro-Life and Pro-Choice: Moral Diversity in the Abortion Debate* (Boston: Beacon Press, 1996).

3. For example, Lindsay E. Beyerstein, "Sent Away: A New look at Maternity Homes," RH Reality Check, June 21, 2007, http://rhrealitycheck.org/article/2007/06/21 /sent-away-a-new-look-at-maternity-group-homes/; Ann Fessler, *The Girls Who Went Away: The Hidden History of Women Who Surrendered Children for Adoption in the Decades before* Roe v. Wade (New York: Penguin, 2006).

4. Samuel O. Miller, "Maternity Homes: The Case of a Dying Institution," *Journal of Sociology and Social Welfare* 1, no. 1 (October 1973).

5. Regina G. Kunzel, "The Professionalization of Benevolence: Evangelicals and Social Workers in the Florence Crittenton Homes, 1915 to 1945," *Journal of Social History* 22, no. 1 (1988); Marian J. Morton, "Fallen Women, Federated Charities, and Maternity Homes, 1913–1973," *Social Service Review* 62, no. 1 (1988).

6. Maureen Fitzgerald, *Habits of Compassion: Irish Catholic Nuns and the Origins of New York's Welfare System, 1830–1920* (Urbana: University of Illinois Press, 2006); Kunzel, "Professionalization of Benevolence"; Morton, "Fallen Women."

7. Fitzgerald, *Habits of Compassion.*

8. Kunzel, "Professionalization of Benevolence"; Morton, "Fallen Women, Federated Charities, and Maternity Homes."

9. Kunzel, "Professionalization of Benevolence."

10. Rudy, *Beyond Pro-Life and Pro-Choice.*

11. Rickie Solinger, *Beggars and Choosers: How the Politics of Choice Shapes Adoption, Abortion, and Welfare in the United States* (New York: Hill and Wang, 2001).

12. Miller, "Maternity Homes."

13. Margaret H. Hartshorn, *Foot Soldiers Armed with Love: Heartbeat International's First Forty Years* (Virginia Beach, VA: Donning, 2011); Margaret Hartshorn, in discussion with the author, September 8, 2014; Ianora, *Crisis Pregnancy Centers.*

14. Hartshorn, in discussion with the author, September 8, 2014; Terry Weaver, in discussion with the author, October 23, 2012. See also Ianora, *Crisis Pregnancy Centers.*

15. Family Research Council, *A Passion to Serve,* 2nd ed.; Hartshorn, in discussion

with the author, September 8, 2014; Daniel K. Williams, *Defenders of the Unborn: The Pro-Life Movement before* Roe v. Wade (New York: Oxford University Press, 2016).

16. Hartshorn, *Foot Soldiers.*

17. Dawn Stacey, *The Pregnancy Center Movement: History of Crisis Pregnancy Centers* (Crisis Pregnancy Center Watch, n.d.), http://www.motherjones.com/files/cpc history2.pdf.

18. Hartshorn, *Foot Soldiers*; Ianora, *Crisis Pregnancy Centers.*

19. Williams, *Defenders of the Unborn*, 123.

20. Moira S. Gaul and Mai W. Bean, *A Legacy of Life and Love: Pregnancy Center Service Report*, 3rd ed. (Arlington, VA: Charlotte Lozier Institute, 2018), 4, https://www .heartbeatinternational.org/images/assets/pressroom/PRC-report-2018.pdf; Andrew Nelson, "Birthright Leader Stepping Down after 45 Years Helping Women in Crisis Pregnancies," *Georgia Bulletin,* December 23, 2014, https://georgiabulletin.org/news /2014/12/birthright-leader-stepping-45-years-helping-women-crisis-pregnancies/; Weaver, in discussion with the author; Williams, *Defenders of the Unborn.*

21. Williams, *Defenders of the Unborn.*

22. Christopher Z. Mooney and Mei-Hsien Lee, "Legislative Morality in the American States: The Case of Pre-*Roe* Abortion Regulation Reform," *American Journal of Political Science* 39, no. 3 (1995): 599–627.

23. Right to Life League of Southern California, "About Us," accessed January 20, 2015, http://rtllsc.org/life/About%20Us/index.php; see also Hartshorn, *Foot Soldiers.*

24. Hartshorn, *Foot Soldiers*; Hartshorn, in discussion with the author, September 8, 2014; Ianora, *Crisis Pregnancy Centers.*

25. Williams, *Defenders of the Unborn.*

26. Carol Buchanan, in discussion with the author, October 12, 2012. This individual was not part of my elite interview sample.

27. Louise Summerhill, *The Story of Birthright: The Alternative to Abortion* (Libertyville, IL: Prow/Franciscan Marytown, 1973/1984): viii.

28. United Nations, Population Division, *Abortion Policies: A Global Review,* vol. 1 (New York: United Nations, 2001).

29. Summerhill, *Story of Birthright*, 5.

30. Summerhill, *Story of Birthright*, 6.

31. Hartshorn, *Foot Soldiers.*

32. Hartshorn, *Foot Soldiers*; Ianora, *Crisis Pregnancy Centers.*

33. Hartshorn, *Foot Soldiers*; Ianora, *Crisis Pregnancy Centers.*

34. Hartshorn, *Foot Soldiers*, 9.

35. Ianora, *Crisis Pregnancy Centers.*

36. Hartshorn, *Foot Soldiers*; Ianora, *Crisis Pregnancy Centers.*

37. Hartshorn, *Foot Soldiers*, 29.

38. Ianora, *Crisis Pregnancy Centers.*

39. Ianora, *Crisis Pregnancy Centers*, xv–xvi.

40. Margaret H. Hartshorn, "Pregnancy Help Centers, Abstinence, STDs, and Healing: Putting It All Together," in *Back to the Drawing Board: The Future of the Pro-Life Movement,* ed. Teresa R. Wagner (South Bend, IN: St. Augustine's, 2003), 107.

41. Summerhill, *Story of Birthright*, 9.

42. Hartshorn, *Foot Soldiers*.

43. Summerhill, *Story of Birthright*, 27.

44. Summerhill, *Story of Birthright*, 4.

45. Hartshorn, "Pregnancy Help Centers, Abstinence, STDs, and Healing," 107.

46. Hartshorn, *Foot Soldiers*, 14.

47. Hartshorn, *Foot Soldiers*; Margaret Hartshorn, in discussion with the author, August 23, 2012.

48. Summerhill, *Story of Birthright*, 21.

49. Ianora, *Crisis Pregnancy Centers*.

50. Summerhill, *Story of Birthright*, 24.

51. Summerhill, *Story of Birthright*, 6–7.

52. Summerhill, *Story of Birthright*, 7–8.

53. Andrew R. Lewis, "Abortion Politics and the Decline of the Separation of Church and State: The Southern Baptist Case," *Politics and Religion* 7, no. 3 (2014): 521–549.

54. Jill Quadagno and Deana Rohlinger, "The Religious Factor in U.S. Welfare State Politics," in *Religion, Class Coalitions, and Welfare States,* ed. Kees van Kersbergen and Philip Manow (New York: Cambridge University Press, 2009), 236–266; Daniel K. Williams, "The Partisan Trajectory of the American Pro-Life Movement: How a Liberal Catholic Campaign Became a Conservative Evangelical Cause," *Religions* 6, no. 2 (2015): 451–475.

55. Mayer N. Zald and John D. McCarthy, "Religious Groups as Crucibles of Social Movements," in *Social Movements in an Organizational Society,* ed. Mayer N. Zald and John D. McCarthy (New Brunswick, NJ: Transaction, 1987), 67–96.

56. Ianora, *Crisis Pregnancy Centers*, 52.

57. National Conference of Catholic Bishops, "Pastoral Plan for Pro-Life Activities: A Statement Issued by the National Conference of Catholic Bishops," November 20, 1975,   http://www.priestsforlife.org/magisterium/bishops/75-11-20pastoralplanforpro lifeactivitiesnccb.htm.

58. For example, Denise Cocciolone, in discussion with the author, October 23, 2012; Ianora, *Crisis Pregnancy Centers*; Summerhill, *Story of Birthright*.

59. Hartshorn, "Pregnancy Help Centers, Abstinence, STDs, and Healing."

60. Myra Marx Ferree et al., *Shaping Abortion Discourse: Democracy and the Public Sphere in Germany and the United States* (Cambridge, UK: Cambridge University Press, 2002).

61. Hartshorn, *Foot Soldiers*, 41.

62. Lewis, "Abortion Politics"; Daniel Schlozman, *When Movements Anchor Parties: Electoral Alignments in American History* (Princeton, NJ: Princeton University Press, 2015); Daniel K. Williams, *God's Own Party: The Making of the Christian Right* (Oxford, UK: Oxford University, 2010).

63. Melinda Delahoyde, in discussion with the author, August 15, 2012.

64. Thomas Glessner, in discussion with the author, June 29, 2012.

65. Geoffrey Layman, *The Great Divide: Religious and Cultural Conflict in American Party Politics* (New York: Columbia University Press, 2001); Williams, *God's Own Party*.

66. For example, Layman, *The Great Divide*; Duane Murray Oldfield, *The Right and the Righteous: The Christian Right Confronts the Republican Party* (Lanham, MD: Rowman and Littlefield, 1996); Carol J. C. Maxwell, *Pro-Life Activists in America: Meaning, Motivation, and Direct Action* (Cambridge, UK: Cambridge University Press, 2002); Williams, *God's Own Party*; Williams, "Partisan Trajectory."

67. See also Williams, *God's Own Party*.

68. Robert A. Case II, "Joe Brown, CAC, and Me," *Case in Point* (blog), May 10, 2011, https://robertcaseinpoint.com/tag/christian-action-council/.

69. Case, "Joe Brown, CAC, and Me"; Susan Wunderink, "Theologian Harold O. J. Brown Dies at 74," *Christianity Today*, July 9, 2007, http://www.christianitytoday.com /ct/2007/julyweb-only/128-13.0.html; Curtis Young, discussion with the author, August 8, 2012.

70. Case, "Joe Brown, CAC, and Me."

71. A text-only version of this brochure is available on the *Case in Point* blog of its author, Robert A. Case II, https://robertcaseinpoint.com/tag/christian-action-council /page/2/, accessed February 20, 2014.

72. James Risen and Judy L. Thomas, *Wrath of Angels: The American Abortion War* (New York: Basic Books, 1998); Williams, *God's Own Party*.

73. Oldfield, *Right and the Righteous*; Clyde Wilcox and Carin Larson, *Onward Christian Soldiers? The Religious Right in American Politics*, 3rd ed. (Boulder, CO: Westview, 2006); Williams, *God's Own Party*.

74. Melinda Delahoyde, *Fighting for Life: Defending the Newborn's Right to Live* (Ann Arbor, MI: Servant, 1984), 72–73.

75. Delahoyde, *Fighting for Life*, 76.

76. Delahoyde, *Fighting for Life*, 73.

77. Carol A. Clews, "A History of the Center for Pregnancy Concerns" speech, n.d.

78. My interviewee's account of the center's founding is largely consistent with that told by Risen and Thomas in *Wrath of Angels*. Risen and Thomas, however, also credit a local right-to-life affiliate with pushing to create the center and place greater weight than my interviewee did on the role of one of the church's pastors, Michael Bray, who had been inspired by the testimony of the woman who had undergone four abortions. They note that Bray would later assist with the nonfatal bombings of several abortion clinics.

79. Summerhill, *Story of Birthright*.

80. Kimberly Kelly, "In the Name of the Mother: Gender and Religion in the Crisis Pregnancy Center Movement," PhD diss., University of Georgia, 2009, 91.

81. Hartshorn, *Foot Soldiers*.

82. Other than its year, data on the founding story of one interviewee's center were not collected. That interviewee suggested that at the time she became involved, however, members of her church had been heavily involved with running and supporting the center.

83. James Farmer, in discussion with the author, October 9, 2012.

84. Ronald Reagan, "Abortion and the Conscience of the Nation," *Human Life Review*, February 3, 1983, http://www.humanlifereview.com/abortion-and-the-conscience -of-the-nation-ronald-reagan-the-10th-anniversary-of-the-supreme-court-decision

-in-roe-v-wade-is-a-good-time-for-us-to-pause-and-reflect-our-nationwide-policy -of-abortion-o/.

85. House of His Creation, "History," accessed December 22, 2014, http://hohc.org /about-us/history/.

86. Kerry N. Jacoby, *Souls, Bodies, Spirits: The Drive to Abolish Abortion since 1973* (Westport, CT: Praeger, 1999); Liberty Godparent Foundation, "About Us," accessed March 31, 2015, http://www.godparentfoundation.org/maternity/about-us/.

87. Jane Gross, "Anti-Abortion Revival: Homes for the Unwed," *New York Times*, July 23 1989.

88. See also Karen Walker, "From the Boardroom to the Battle for Life," *National Catholic Register* 74, no. 8 (1998).

89. Diocese of Austin, "History of the Gabriel Project," accessed April 1, 2015, http://www.austindiocese.org/offices-ministries/offices/pro-life-activities-and-chaste -living-office/ministries/gabriel-project-0; Anthony DiIulio, in discussion with the author, September 11, 2012.

90. Gabriel Network, "History," accessed August 2, 2016, http://gabrielnetwork.org /who-we-are/vision-mission-history.

91. Gabriel Network, "History."

92. Summerhill, *Story of Birthright.*

93. Miller, "Maternity Homes."

94. Hartshorn, *Foot Soldiers*; Kristin Luker, *Abortion and the Politics of Motherhood* (Berkeley: University of California Press, 1984).

95. Suzanne Staggenborg, *The Pro-Choice Movement: Organization and Activism in the Abortion Conflict* (New York: Oxford University Press, 1991).

96. Williams, *Defenders of the Unborn.*

97. Layman, *Great Divide.*

98. Greg D. Adams, "Abortion: Evidence of an Issue Evolution," *American Journal of Political Science* 41 (1997); David Karol, *Party Position Change in American Politics: Coalition Management* (Cambridge, Uk: Cambridge University Press, 2009); Williams, *Defenders of the Unborn.*

99. Kelly, "Gender and Religion"; Kimberly Kelly, "In the Name of the Mother: Renegotiating Conservative Women's Authority in the Crisis Pregnancy Center Movement," *Signs* 38, no. 1 (2012); Ziad Munson, *The Making of Pro-Life Activists: How Social Movement Mobilization Works* (Chicago: University of Chicago Press, 2008).

CHAPTER 4. STRATEGY CHANGE AND RESOURCE GROWTH

1. Abby Johnson, "Morning General Session" speech, Care Net National Pregnancy Center Conference, Orlando, FL, September 30, 2011. This account is based on personal observations and the official publicly available audio recording of the session.

2. Lori Freedman and Tracy A. Weitz, "The Politics of Motherhood Meets the Politics of Poverty," *Contemporary Sociology* 41, no. 1 (2012): 36–42.

3. Reva B. Siegel, "The Right's Reasons: Constitutional Conflict and the Spread of Woman-Protective Antiabortion Argument," *Duke Law Journal* 57 (2008): 1641–1692.

4. Margaret H. Hartshorn, "Pregnancy Help Centers, Abstinence, STDs, and Healing: Putting It All Together," in *Back to the Drawing Board: The Future of the Pro-Life Movement,* ed. Teresa R. Wagner (South Bend, IN: St. Augustine's, 2003): 106–120; Siegel, "Right's Reasons."

5. Margaret H. Hartshorn, *Foot Soldiers Armed with Love: Heartbeat International's First Forty Years* (Virginia Beach, VA: Donning, 2011), 100.

6. Moira S. Gaul and Mai W. Bean, *A Legacy of Life and Love: Pregnancy Center Service Report,* 3rd ed. (Arlington, VA: Charlotte Lozier Institute, 2018), 33, https://www.heartbeatinternational.org/images/assets/pressroom/PRC-report-2018.pdf.

7. Daniel K. Williams, *Defenders of the Unborn: The Pro-Life Movement before* Roe v. Wade (New York: Oxford University Press, 2016); Kerry N. Jacoby, *Souls, Bodies, Spirits: The Drive to Abolish Abortion since 1973* (Westport, CT: Praeger, 1999).

8. Edward G. Carmines and James Woods, "The Role of Party Activists in the Evolution of the Abortion Issue," *Political Behavior* 24, no. 4, *Special Issue: Parties and Partisanship,* Part 3 (2002): 361–377.

9. Williams, *Defenders of the Unborn.*

10. Hartshorn, "Pregnancy Help Centers, Abstinence, STDs, and Healing"; Hartshorn, *Foot Soldiers.*

11. Rachel K. Jones et al., "Abortion in the United States: Incidence and Access to Services, 2005," *Perspectives on Sexual and Reproductive Health* 40, no. 1 (2008): 6–16.

12. Hartshorn, "Pregnancy Help Centers, Abstinence, STDs, and Healing," 106–107.

13. Earn While You Learn, "The Origin of EWYL," accessed June 24, 2013, http://www.ewylonline.org/origin.asp.

14. Harrell R. Rodgers, Jr., *American Poverty in a New Era of Reform,* 2nd ed. (Armonk, NY: M. E. Sharpe, 2006).

15. Earn While You Learn, "The EWYL Impact," accessed June 24, 2013, http://www.ewylonline.org.

16. Assure Pregnancy Clinic, "Bridges," accessed June 25, 2013, http://www.assurelife.org/what-we-do/our-programs/bridges/.

17. Mary Ziegler, *After Roe: The Lost History of the Abortion Debate* (Cambridge, MA: Harvard University Press, 2015).

18. Jill Quadagno and Deana Rohlinger, "The Religious Factor in U.S. Welfare State Politics," in *Religion, Class Coalitions, and Welfare States,* ed. Kees van Kersbergen and Philip Manow (New York: Cambridge University Press, 2009), 236–266.

19. Dallas A. Blanchard, *The Anti-Abortion Movement and the Rise of the Religious Right: From Polite to Fiery Protest* (New York: Twayne, 1994); Suzanne Staggenborg, *The Pro-Choice Movement: Organization and Activism in the Abortion Conflict* (New York: Oxford University Press, 1991).

20. Staggenborg, *Pro-Choice Movement;* see also Faye D. Ginsburg, *Contested Lives: The Abortion Debate in an American Community,* updated ed. (Berkeley: University of California Press, 1998).

21. Hartshorn, "Pregnancy Help Centers, Abstinence, STDs, and Healing."

22. Kimberly Kelly, "In the Name of the Mother: Gender and Religion in the Crisis Pregnancy Center Movement," PhD diss., University of Georgia, 2009; Kimberly Kelly, "In the Name of the Mother: Renegotiating Conservative Women's Authority in the Crisis Pregnancy Center Movement," *Signs* 38, no. 1 (2012).

23. Staggenborg, *Pro-Choice Movement.*

24. Dorothy Townsend, "Judge Rules Out Pregnancy Tests at 25 Right-to-Life League Centers," *Los Angeles Times,* September 27, 1985, http://articles.latimes.com/1985-09-27/local/me-18237_1_pregnancy-test.

25. See Kelly, "Gender and Religion"; Kelly, "In the Name of the Mother."

26. Marvin N. Olasky, "Abortion Rights: Anatomy of a Negative Campaign," *Public Relations Review* 13, no. 3 (1987): 12–23.

27. Kelly, "In the Name of the Mother."

28. See, for example, Associated Press, "Congressional Inquiry Examines Reports of Bogus Abortion Clinics," *New York Times,* September 21, 1991, http://www.nytimes.com/1991/09/21/us/congressional-inquiry-examines-reports-of-bogus-abortion-clinics.html; Mimi Hall, "Pregnancy Centers Target of Maryland Probe," *USA Today,* July 25, 1991, 3A.

29. Hartshorn, "Pregnancy Help Centers, Abstinence, STDs, and Healing"; Kelly, "In the Name of the Mother."

30. Hartshorn, "Pregnancy Help Centers, Abstinence, STDs, and Healing."

31. Kelly, "Gender and Religion," 94.

32. Kelly, "Gender and Religion"; Olasky, "Abortion Rights"; Hartshorn, "Pregnancy Help Centers, Abstinence, STDs, and Healing".

33. Hartshorn, "Pregnancy Help Centers, Abstinence, STDs, and Healing," 110.

34. Terry Ianora, *Crisis Pregnancy Centers: The Birth of a Grassroots Movement* (Bloomington, IN: AuthorHouse, 2009).

35. Hartshorn, "Pregnancy Help Centers, Abstinence, STDs, and Healing."

36. Hartshorn, *Foot Soldiers;* see also Thomas Glessner, in discussion with the author, June 29, 2012.

37. Denise Cocciolone, in discussion with the author, October 23, 2012; Ianora, *Crisis Pregnancy Centers.*

38. See also Hartshorn, "Pregnancy Help Centers, Abstinence, STDs, and Healing."

39. Jones et al., "Abortion in the United States."

40. See also Hartshorn, *Foot Soldiers;* Margaret Hartshorn, in discussion with the author, August 23, 2012.

41. John C. Fletcher and Mark I. Evans, "Maternal Bonding in Early Fetal Ultrasound Examinations," *New England Journal of Medicine* 308 (1983): 392–393.

42. Hartshorn, *Foot Soldiers.*

43. Birthright maintains a policy against offering medical services at its centers.

44. Ziad Munson, *The Making of Pro-Life Activists: How Social Movement Mobilization Works* (Chicago: University of Chicago Press, 2008).

45. Hartshorn, *Foot Soldiers.*

46. Melinda Delahoyde, in discussion with the author, August 15, 2012; Family Re-

search Council, *A Passion to Serve, a Vision for Life: Pregnancy Resource Center Service Report 2009* (Washington, DC: Family Research Council, 2009); Hartshorn, *Foot Soldiers*; Jones et al., "Abortion in the United States."

47. Kelly, "Gender and Religion."

48. Family Research Council, *Passion to Serve*; Neela Banerjee, "Church Groups Turn to Sonogram to Turn Women from Abortions," *New York Times,* February 2, 2005, https://www.nytimes.com/2005/02/02/us/church-groups-turn-to-sonogram-to -turn-women-from-abortions.html; Knights of Columbus, "Ultrasound Initiative," accessed August 2, 2016, http://www.kofc.org/en/members/programs/culture-of-life /ultrasound-initiative.html#/.

49. Hartshorn, *Foot Soldiers,* 106.

50. Karolyn Schrage, "Effectively Reaching the Abortion-Minded Woman," workshop presented at the Care Net National Pregnancy Center Conference, Orlando, FL, September 28, 2011.

51. Gaul and Bean, *Legacy of Life and Love,* 19.

52. FEMM, "Locations," accessed September 19, 2018, https://femmhealth.org /health-centers/locations/.

53. Peter Jesserer Smith, "Abby Johnson: Only Modern Pro-Life Women's Centers Can Beat Planned Parenthood," *National Catholic Register,* February 19, 2014, http://www .ncregister.com/daily-news/abby-johnson-only-modern-pro-life-womens-centers -can-beat-planned-parenthoo.

54. Ianora, *Crisis Pregnancy Centers,* 104.

55. Elizabeth A. Armstrong, *Forging Gay Identities: Organizing Sexuality in San Francisco, 1950–1994* (Chicago: University of Chicago Press, 2002), 173.

56. Sanctity of Human Life, "What's the First Step in the Option Ultrasound Process?," Focus on the Family, accessed March 15, 2016, http://www.heartlink.org/directors /A000000738.cfm.

57. See Figure 2.3 for descriptive statistics for this measure and the dependent variable, directors' estimates of the share of pregnancy-test clients who consider abortion.

58. Nina Eliasoph, *Avoiding Politics: How Americans Produce Apathy in Everyday Life* (New York: Cambridge University Press, 1998); Nina Eliasoph, *The Politics of Volunteering* (Cambridge: Polity Press, 2013).

59. R. Allen Hays, "Community Activists' Perceptions of Citizenship Roles in an Urban Community: A Case Study of Attitudes That Affect Civic Engagement," *Journal of Urban Affairs* 29, no. 4 (2007): 401–424; Tobi Walker, "The Service/Politics Split: Rethinking Service to Teach Political Engagement," *P.S.: Political Science and Politics* 33, no. 3 (2000): 647–649.

CHAPTER 5. WHERE SERVICE PROVISION FLOURISHES

1. Jeff Parrott, "Buttigieg Veto Survives South Bend Council," *South Bend Tribune,* May 15, 2018, https://www.southbendtribune.com/news/local/buttigieg-veto-survives -south-bend-council/article_dfd77812-528f-531b-9790-a82c7f734746.html.

2. Pete Buttigieg, "Letter to Clerk Fowler and Council President Scott," cited in Melissa Hudson, "Mayor Buttigieg Vetoes Zoning Decision for Women's Care Center," *ABC 57 News*, April 27, 2018, https://www.abc57.com/news/mayor-buttigieg-vetoes -womens-care-center-zoning.

3. Jeff Parrott, "Will Council Override South Bend Mayor's Veto of Women's Care Center Rezoning?," *South Bend Tribune*, May 11, 2018, https://www.southbendtribune .com/news/local/will-council-override-south-bend-mayor-s-veto-of-women/article _3cee80f9-b399-53f6-85ea-7b317e6ebe0a.html.

4. Buttigieg, "Letter to Clerk Fowler and Council President Scott."

5. Ann Manion, "Women's Care Center President: South Bend Mayor's Veto Is a Setback," *South Bend Tribune*, May 10, 2018, https://www.southbendtribune.com /news/opinion/viewpoint/women-s-care-center-president-south-bend-mayor-s-veto /article_8e327506–6567–526a-a718-75efa5a622ed.html; Women's Care Center Foundation, "About," accessed August 27, 2018, http://womenscarecenterfoundation.org /about/.

6. Manion, "Women's Care Center President."

7. US Census Bureau, "Quick Facts: South Bend City, Indiana—Population Estimates, July 1, 2017," accessed October 11, 2018, https://www.census.gov/quickfacts /southbendcityindiana.

8. Niki Kelly, "State Suspends Medical License of Former South Bend Abortion Doctor," *South Bend Tribune*, August 26, 2016, https://www.southbendtribune.com /news/local/state-suspends-medical-license-of-former-south-bend-abortion-doctor /article_13cf1480-6b85-11e6-b0f7-6b2daa9decdd.html; Amanda Gray, "Women's Pavilion to Close March 18, Ending 38 Years of Controversy," *South Bend Tribune*, March 12, 2016, https://www.southbendtribune.com/news/local/women-s-pavilion-to-close -march-ending-years-of-controversy/article_06d287c2-b2c3-59b9-b6be-2c00bc295dbf .html.

9. Sharon Lau, "From Indiana: Words on Fake Clinics," *Whole Woman's Health Blog*, June 11, 2018, https://wholewomanshealthblog.com/2018/06/11/from-indiana-words -on-fake-clinics/; Parrott, "Will Council Override South Bend Mayor?"

10. Mark Peterson, "Officials React to Women's Care Center Changing Plans for Pregnancy Help Facility," WNDU, June 5, 2018, https://www.wndu.com/content/news /Officials-react-to-Womens-Care-Center-changing-plans-for-pregnancy-help -facility--484623971.html.

11. Jeff Parrott, "South Bend Council Allows Anti-Abortion Group to Open Site Next to Proposed Abortion Clinic," *South Bend Tribune*, April 24, 2018, https://www .southbendtribune.com/news/local/south-bend-council-allows-anti-abortion-group -to-open-site/article_f516f3b8-3e60-5bd9-9889-3b6ee69e606e.html.

12. Parrott, "Will Council Override South Bend Mayor?"

13. Lau, "From Indiana."

14. Alexandra DeSanctis, "Pro-Choice Movement Opposes Abortion Alternatives in South Bend," *National Review*, May 1, 2018, https://www.nationalreview.com/2018/05 /crisis-pregnancy-center-south-bend-indiana-pro-choice-oppposition/.

15. Faye D. Ginsburg, *Contested Lives: The Abortion Debate in an American Community,* updated ed. (Berkeley: University of California Press, 1998); Suzanne Staggenborg, *The Pro-Choice Movement: Organization and Activism in the Abortion Conflict* (New York: Oxford University Press, 1991).

16. Jennifer Ludden, "States Fund Pregnancy Centers That Discourage Abortion," *All Things Considered,* March 9, 2015, https://www.npr.org/sections/health-shots/2015/03/09/391877614/states-fund-pregnancy-centers-that-discourage-abortion; NARAL Pro-Choice America, *Crisis Pregnancy Centers Lie: The Insidious Threat to Reproductive Freedom* (Washington, DC: NARAL Pro-Choice America, 2015), http://www.prochoiceamerica.org/assets/download-files/cpc-report-2015.pdf.

17. Several Sources Shelters, accessed May 2013, http://www.lifecall.org/cpc.html.

18. This analysis builds upon and represents a major revision of an analysis I published earlier. See Laura S. Hussey, "Political Action versus Personal Action: Understanding Social Movements' Pursuit of Change through Nongovernmental Channels," *American Politics Research* 42, no. 3 (2014): 409–440.

19. Laura S. Hussey, "Moral Issues," in *Guide to State Politics and Policy,* ed. Richard C. Niemi and Joshua J. Dyck (Washington, DC: Congressional Quarterly Press, 2013): 343–354; Deborah R. McFarlane and Kenneth J. Meier, *The Politics of Fertility Control* (New York: Chatham House, 2001); Melody Rose, *Safe, Legal, and Unavailable? Abortion Politics in the United States* (Washington, DC: Congressional Quarterly Press, 2007).

20. Chris Tausanovitch and Christopher Warshaw, "Measuring Constituent Policy Preferences in Congress, State Legislatures, and Cities," *Journal of Politics* 75, no. 2 (2013): 330–342.

21. John D. McCarthy and Mayer N. Zald, "Resource Mobilization and Social Movements: A Partial Theory," *American Journal of Sociology* 82, no. 6 (1977): 1212–1241.

22. Barbara Norrander, "Measuring State Public Opinion with the Senate National Election Study," *State Politics and Policy Quarterly* 1 (2001): 113–127; Julianna Pacheco, "Measuring and Evaluating Changes in State Opinion across Eight Issues," *American Politics Research* 42, no. 6 (2014): 986–1009; Clifford Grammich et al., "2010 U.S. Religion Census: Religious Congregations and Membership Study," ed. American Association of Statisticians of American Religious Bodies (2012), http://www.rcms2010.org/; www.thearda.com.

23. Predictions were estimated using *Clarify:* Michael Tomz, Jason Wittenberg, and Gary King, "CLARIFY: Software for Interpreting and Presenting Statistical Results," *Journal of Statistical Software* 8, no. 1 (2003), https://www.jstatsoft.org/article/view/v008i01.

24. Adjusted R-squared values differ by 7 percentage points. The square of the political opportunities score does not approach statistical significance when substituting for pro-life sentiment or when added to the model.

25. These were: a membership directory offered online by the National Coalition of Abortion Providers, a trade group; listings on a website designed to help women locate abortion clinics and to facilitate clinic advertising (www.abortionclinicspages

.com); clinic locator functions on the websites of the Planned Parenthood Federation of America and its individual regional affiliates; and entries in the online yellow pages under the heading "Abortion Clinics."

26. Rachel K. Jones et al., "Abortion in the United States: Incidence and Access to Services, 2005," *Perspectives on Sexual and Reproductive Health* 40, no. 1 (2008): 12.

27. Jones et al., "Abortion in the United States," 8.

28. In fact, clinic-based abortion providers did not decrease greatly in number between 2005 and 2011: Rachel K. Jones and Kathryn Kooistra, "Abortion Incidence and Access to Services in the United States, 2008," *Perspectives on Sexual and Reproductive Health* 43, no. 1 (2011): 41–50; Rachel K. Jones and Jenna Jerman, "Abortion Incidence and Service Availability in the United States, 2011," *Perspectives on Sexual and Reproductive Health* 46, no. 1 (2014): 3–14.

29. Andrew Yuengert and Joel Fetzer, "Location Decisions of Abortion Clinics and Crisis Pregnancy Centers in California," *Catholic Social Science Review* 15 (2010): 211–235.

30. Rachel K. Jones, Lawrence B. Finer, and Susheela Singh, *Characteristics of U.S. Abortion Patients, 2008* (New York: Guttmacher Institute, 2010).

31. Carmen DeNavas-Walt and Bernadette D. Proctor, *Income and Poverty in the United States: 2013* (Washington, DC: Government Printing Office, 2014).

32. Rory McVeigh, Bryant Crubaugh, and Kevin Estep, "Plausibility Structures, Status Threats, and the Establishment of Anti-Abortion Pregnancy Centers," *American Journal of Sociology* 122, no. 5 (2017): 1533–1571.

33. Margaret H. Hartshorn, *Foot Soldiers Armed with Love: Heartbeat International's First Forty Years* (Virginia Beach, VA: Donning, 2011), 16.

34. Thomas Glessner, *The Emerging Brave New World* (Crane, MO: HighWay, 2008), 139.

35. Nancy J. Davis and Robert V. Robinson, *Claiming Society for God: Religious Movements and Social Welfare in Egypt, Israel, Italy, and the United States* (Bloomington: Indiana University Press, 2012).

36. Jeff Parrott, "Pro–Abortion Rights Group Urging South Bend Mayor to Veto Anti-Abortion Group's Rezoning," *South Bend Tribune*, April 25, 2018, https://www.southbendtribune.com/news/local/pro-abortion-rights-group-urging-south-bend-mayor-to-veto/article_ec97b871-0625-5d76-b4b8-268fe5af64a1.html.

37. Manion, "Women's Care Center President."

38. "LPJL Daily Takedown—South Bend Needs Your Help!," *Daily Takedown,* May 14, 2018. https://ladypartsjusticeleague.com/lpjl-daily-takedown-south-bend-needs-your-help/.

39. Parrott, "Buttigieg Veto Survives South Bend Council."

40. Heather Black, "Pro-Choice Petitions Rezoning Approval to Keep Women's Care Center from Moving Next Door," WSBT, April 25, 2018, https://wsbt.com/news/local/pro-choice-petitioning-rezoning-approval-to-keep-womens-care-center-from-moving-next-door.

41. Parrott, "Buttigieg Veto Survives South Bend Council."

42. Buttigieg, "Letter to Clerk Fowler and Council President Scott"; Hudson, "Mayor Buttigieg Vetoes Zoning."

43. Peterson, "Officials React to Women's Care Center."

44. Associated Press, "Indiana Health Department Appealing South Bend Abortion Clinic Recommendation," WNDU, October 2, 2018, https://www.wndu.com/content /news/Indiana-health-department-appealing-South-Bend-abortion-clinic-recom mendation-494957201.html.

45. Parrott, "South Bend Council Allows Anti-Abortion Group."

CHAPTER 6. THE POLITICS OF
PREGNANCY HELP ACTIVIST MOBILIZATION

1. Thomas Glessner, *The Emerging Brave New World* (Crane, MO: HighWay, 2008), 194.

2. Daniel M. Shea, "Young Voters, Declining Trust and the Limits of 'Service Politics,'" *Forum* 13, no. 3 (2015): 459–479, https://doi.org/10.1515/for-2015–0036; Russell J. Dalton, *The Good Citizen: How a Younger Generation Is Reshaping American Politics,* rev. ed. (Washington, DC: Congressional Quarterly Press, 2009); Brian D. Loader, Ariadne Vromen, and Michael A. Xenos, "The Networked Young Citizen: Social Media, Political Participation, and Civic Engagement," *Information, Communication, and Society* 17, no. 2 (2014): 143–150.

3. William A. Galston and Peter Levine, "America's Civic Condition: A Glance at the Evidence," in *Community Works: The Revival of Civil Society in America,* ed. E. J. Dionne (Washington, DC: Brookings Institution, 1998), 36.

4. R. Allen Hays, "Community Activists' Perceptions of Citizenship Roles in an Urban Community: A Case Study of Attitudes That Affect Civic Engagement," *Journal of Urban Affairs* 29, no. 4 (2007): 401–424.

5. Pam Solo and Gail Pressberg, "Beyond Theory: Civil Society in Action," in *Community Works: The Revival of Civil Society in America,* ed. E. J. Dionne (Washington, DC: Brookings Institution, 1998), 81–87; E. J. Dionne, *The Vitality of Society Rests on the Independent Sector,* Conversations with Leaders Series (Washington, DC: Independent Sector, 2000); cited in Stephen Macedo et al., *Democracy at Risk: How Political Choices Undermine Citizen Participation and What We Can Do about It* (Washington, DC: Brookings Institution, 2005).

6. Adriane Bilous, "'We Need a Revival': Young Evangelical Women Redefine Activism in New York City," in *The New Evangelical Social Engagement,* ed. Brian Steensland and Philip Goff (Oxford, UK: Oxford University Press, 2014), 119.

7. Nancy J. Davis and Robert V. Robinson, *Claiming Society for God: Religious Movements and Social Welfare in Egypt, Israel, Italy, and the United States* (Bloomington: Indiana University Press, 2012).

8. Kerry N. Jacoby, *Souls, Bodies, Spirits: The Drive to Abolish Abortion since 1973* (Westport, CT: Praeger, 1999).

9. Nina Eliasoph, *Avoiding Politics: How Americans Produce Apathy in Everyday Life* (New York: Cambridge University Press, 1998).

10. Stanley Fish, "Is Everything Political?," *Chronicle of Higher Education*, March 29, 2002, https://www.chronicle.com/article/Is-Everything-Political-/45993.

11. Lawrence Breeden, in discussion with the author, August 15, 2012.

12. Louise Summerhill, *The Story of Birthright: The Alternative to Abortion* (Libertyville, IL: Prow/Franciscan Marytown, 1973/1984).

13. Glessner, *Emerging Brave New World*, 182–183.

14. Melinda Delahoyde, "Volunteer at a Center," *Christianity Today*, October 14, 2009, http://www.christianitytoday.com/ct/2009/october/26.56.html.

15. Tom Glessner, "Achieving an Abortion-Free America," *At the Center* 1, no. 3 (2000), http://www.atcmag.com/v1n3/article1.asp?pf=1.

16. Jacoby, *Souls, Bodies, Spirits*, 189.

17. Terry Ianora, *Crisis Pregnancy Centers: The Birth of a Grassroots Movement* (Bloomington, IN: AuthorHouse, 2009), 6.

18. I use *Roe*'s ten-year anniversary as the cutoff to distinguish early from later leaders, for it is just long enough to include those who played founding roles in evangelicals' large-scale movement into pregnancy center ministry in the early 1980s. It also marks the end of what Mary Ziegler describes as an unsettled period in the abortion conflict, when important transformations in argument, ideology, and alliances were taking place within the pro-life and pro-choice movements that would give the abortion debate the polarized, single-issue character still seen today. See Ziegler, *After Roe: The Lost History of the Abortion Debate* (Cambridge, MA: Harvard University Press, 2015).

19. Carol J. C. Maxwell, *Pro-Life Activists in America: Meaning, Motivation, and Direct Action* (Cambridge, UK: Cambridge University Press, 2002).

20. Ziad Munson, *The Making of Pro-Life Activists: How Social Movement Mobilization Works* (Chicago: University of Chicago Press, 2008).

21. Though there are statistically significant differences between evangelicals and nonevangelicals in the distribution of these religion-related responses (Chi2 = 17.7, p < .001 for sharing the gospel and Chi2 = 7.5, p < .05 for God's call), large majorities of both groups believed them important.

22. This prevalence of abortion histories is lower than the 32 percent Kimberly Kelly finds in her interviews of thirty-eight pregnancy center activists, but it is unclear whether the samples are comparable. See Kelly, "In the Name of the Mother: Renegotiating Conservative Women's Authority in the Crisis Pregnancy Center Movement," *Signs* 38 no. 1 (2012): 203–230.

23. Laura S. Hussey, "Political Action versus Personal Action: Understanding Social Movements' Pursuit of Change through Nongovernmental Channels," *American Politics Research* 42 (2014): 409–440.

24. The question instructed respondents to exclude pregnancy centers.

25. Robert D. Putnam and David E. Campbell, *American Grace: How Religion Divides and Unites Us* (New York: Simon and Schuster, 2010), 447.

26. Jo Jones, *Who Adopts? Characteristics of Women and Men Who Have Adopted Children* (Hyattsville, MD: National Center for Health Statistics, 2009). Pregnancy center staff might be even more likely to adopt children than the general population than this comparison suggests, because the NCHS adoption statistics include adoption of stepchildren. My Pregnancy Center Staff Survey gave no instruction regarding how to count adopted stepchildren but did separate respondents' reporting of their number of stepchildren from reporting of their number of adopted children. Of the sample, 16 percent reported having stepchildren. I thank a reviewer for this insight.

27. With modification to items included, the figure is based on Laura S. Hussey, "Crisis Pregnancy Centers, Poverty, and the Expanding Frontiers of American Abortion Politics," *Politics & Policy* 41, no. 6 (2013): 1002.

28. Daniel K. Williams, *Defenders of the Unborn: The Pro-Life Movement before* Roe v. Wade (New York: Oxford University Press, 2016); Ziegler, *After* Roe; Mark W. Roche, "Voting Our Conscience, Not Our Religion," *New York Times,* October 11, 2004, A23; James R. Kelly, "A Catholic Votes for John Kerry," *America,* September 27, 2004, http ://www.americamagazine.org/content/article.cfm?article_id=3769; Stephen Schneck, "Remarks to the Democratic National Convention," Democrats for Life of America panel, September 6, 2012, http://www.democratsforlife.org/index.php?option=com _content&view=article&id=770:remarks-by-steve-schneck-democratic-national -convention&catid=24&Itemid=205; Charles J. Reid Jr., "Catholic, Pro-Life, and Voting for Barack Obama," *Huffington Post,* October 26, 2012, http://www.huffingtonpost .com/charles-j-reid-jr/catholic-pro-life-and-voting-for-barack-obama_b_2024427 .html.

29. For example, see Dallas A. Blanchard, *The Anti-Abortion Movement and the Rise of the Religious Right: From Polite to Fiery Protest* (New York: Twayne, 1994); Kristin Luker, *Abortion and the Politics of Motherhood* (Berkeley: University of California Press, 1984).

30. Matt Grossman and David A. Hopkins, "Ideological Republicans and Group Interest Democrats: The Asymmetry of American Party Politics," *Perspectives on Politics* 13, no. 1 (2015): 119–139; Benjamin I. Page and Lawrence R. Jacobs, *Class War? What Americans Really Think about Economic Inequality* (Chicago: University of Chicago Press, 2009).

31. Melissa Deckman, Dan Cox, Robert Jones, and Betsy Cooper, "Faith and the Free Market: Evangelicals, the Tea Party, and Economic Attitudes," *Politics and Religion* 10, no. 1 (2017): 82–110.

32. Jason Hackworth, *Faith-Based: Religious Neoliberalism and the Politics of Welfare in the United States* (Athens: University of Georgia Press, 2012); Jill Quadagno and Deana Rohlinger, "The Religious Factor in U.S. Welfare State Politics," in *Religion, Class Coalitions, and Welfare States,* ed. Kees van Kersbergen and Philip Manow (New York: Cambridge University Press, 2009), 236–266.

33. All predicted probabilities were estimated using *SPost*: J. Scott Long and Jeremy Freese, *Regression Models for Categorical Dependent Variables Using Stata,* 2nd ed. (College Station, TX: Stata, 2006).

34. Macedo et al., *Democracy at Risk;* Patricia Strach, "Political Participation in a Consumer Era: Why Americans Choose Politics," paper presented at the Annual Meeting of the Midwest Political Science Association, Chicago, IL, April 12–14, 2012; Cliff Zukin et al., *A New Engagement: Political Participation, Civic Life, and the Changing American Citizen* (Oxford, UK: Oxford University Press, 2006).

35. Nina Eliasoph, *The Politics of Volunteering* (Cambridge, UK: Polity Press, 2013); Craig A. Rimmerman, *The New Citizenship: Unconventional Politics, Activism, and Service,* 3rd ed. (Boulder, CO: Westview, 2005).

36. Bonnie H. Erickson and T .A. Nosanchuk, "How an Apolitical Association Politicizes," *Canadian Review of Sociology* 27, no. 2 (1990).

37. Eliasoph, *Avoiding Politics;* see also Eliasoph, *Politics of Volunteering.*

38. See Munson, *Making of Pro-Life Activists.*

CHAPTER 7. THE IMPACT AND FUTURE OF
THE PREGNANCY HELP MOVEMENT

1. Heartbeat International, "Emily's Story," accessed July 31, 2012, http://www.heart beatinternational.org/emily-behny.

2. Heartbeat International, "From Fear to Family," accessed July 31, 2012, https:// www.heartbeatinternational.org/shelly-louis-kiree.

3. Heartbeat International, "Pregnant and Scared," accessed July 31, 2012, https:// www.heartbeatinternational.org/jessica-gore.

4. Heartbeat International, "Sarah's Story," accessed July 31, 2012, https://www .heartbeatinternational.org/sarah-seely.

5. Heartbeat International, email to supporters, July 26, 2012.

6. Margaret H. Hartshorn, *Foot Soldiers Armed with Love: Heartbeat International's First Forty Years* (Virginia Beach, VA: Donning, 2011), 90.

7. Reva B. Siegel, "The Right's Reasons: Constitutional Conflict and the Spread of Woman-Protective Antiabortion Argument," *Duke Law Journal* 57 (2008): 1641–1692; Melody Rose, "Pro-Life, Pro-Woman? Frame Extension in the American Antiabortion Movement," *Journal of Women, Politics, and Policy* 32, no. 1 (2011): 1–27.

8. Dr. and Mrs. John C. Willke, *Abortion and the Pro-Life Movement: An Inside View* (West Conshohocken, PA: Infinity, 2014).

9. Jon A. Shields, "The Politics of Motherhood Revisited," *Contemporary Sociology* 41, no. 1 (2012): 43–48.

10. John Eligon and Michael Schwirtz, "Senate Candidate Provokes Ire with 'Legitimate Rape' Comment," *New York Times,* August 19, 2012, https://www.nytimes .com/2012/08/20/us/politics/todd-akin-provokes-ire-with-legitimate-rape-comment .html.

11. Chad Ashby, "Brothers and Sisters, Unwed Pregnancy Is Not a Sin," *Care Net Churches Blog,* August 24, 2015, https://www.care-net.org/churches-blog/brothers-and -sisters-unwed-pregnancy-is-not-a-sin.

12. Care Net, *Study of Women Who Have Had an Abortion and Their Views on Church* (Lansdowne, VA: 2016).

13. Arland Thornton and Linda Young-DeMarco, "Four Decades of Trends in Attitudes Toward Family Issues in the United States: The 1960s through the 1990s," *Journal of Marriage and Family* 63, no. 4 (2001): 1009–1037.

14. Marnie Eisenstadt, "Grandmothers Turn Their Fight against Abortion into a Syracuse Home for Babies," *Central NY Real-Time News Blog, Syracuse Post-Standard,* March 20, 2014, http://blog.syracuse.com/news/print.html?entry=/2014/03/grand mothers_turn_their_fight_against_abortion_into_a_syracuse_home_for_babies .html; Maryann Gogniat Eidemiller, "Baby-Bottle Drives, Showers Help Support Pro-Life Efforts," *Our Sunday Visitor (OSV) Newsweekly,* January 22, 2017, https://www.osv .com/MyFaith/Stewardship/Article/TabId/689/ArtMID/13732/ArticleID/21465/Baby -bottle-drives-showers-help-support-pro-life-efforts.aspx.

15. Bryce Covert and Josh Israel, "The States That Siphon Welfare Money to Stop Abortion," October 3, 2016, https://thinkprogress.org/tanf-cpcs-ec002305dd18/.

16. Daniel K. Williams, *Defenders of the Unborn: The Pro-Life Movement before Roe v. Wade* (New York: Oxford University Press, 2016).

17. These are Feminists for Life, the American Life League, and the Susan B. Anthony List.

18. Suzanne Staggenborg, *The Pro-Choice Movement: Organization and Activism in the Abortion Conflict* (New York: Oxford University Press, 1991); William P. Browne, "Organized Interests and Their Issue Niches: A Search for Pluralism in a Policy Domain," *Journal of Politics* 52, no. 2 (1990): 477–509.

19. Gene Burns, *The Moral Veto: Framing Contraception, Abortion, and Cultural Pluralism in the United States* (New York: Cambridge University Press, 2005); Faye D. Ginsburg, *Contested Lives: The Abortion Debate in an American Community,* updated ed. (Berkeley: University of California Press, 1998); Kerry N. Jacoby, *Souls, Bodies, Spirits: The Drive to Abolish Abortion since 1973* (Westport, CT: Praeger, 1999); Clyde Wilcox and Carin Larson, *Onward Christian Soldiers? The Religious Right in American Politics,* 3rd ed. (Boulder, CO: Westview, 2006).

20. Greg D. Adams, "Abortion: Evidence of an Issue Evolution," *American Journal of Political Science* 41 (1997): 718–737; David Karol, *Party Position Change in American Politics: Coalition Management* (Cambridge, UK: Cambridge University Press, 2009); Geoffrey C. Layman et al., "Activists and Conflict Extension in American Party Politics," *American Political Science Review* 104, no. 2 (2010): 324–346.

21. Jacoby, *Souls, Bodies, Spirits,* 188–189.

22. Heartbeat International, *The LOVE Approach Training Manual,* 3rd ed. (Columbus, OH: Heartbeat International, 2011); Care Net, *Serving with Care and Integrity: A Training Resource for Pregnancy Center Volunteers* (Lansdowne, VA: Care Net, 2003). See also Kimberly Kelly, "In the Name of the Mother: Gender and Religion in the Crisis Pregnancy Center Movement," PhD diss., University of Georgia, 2009.

23. Rachel K. Jones et al., "Abortion in the United States: Incidence and Access to Services, 2005," *Perspectives on Sexual and Reproductive Health* 40, no. 1 (2008): 6–16; Rachel

K. Jones and Jenna Jerman, "Abortion Incidence and Service Availability in the United States, 2014," *Perspectives on Sexual and Reproductive Health* 49, no. 1 (2017): 17–27.

24. "PRC Statistics—Changed Abortion View," eKYROS.com, accessed September 24, 2018, http://www.ekyros.com/Pub/DesktopModules/ekyros/ViewStats.aspx ?ItemId=8&mid=89&tabid=16.

25. Moira S. Gaul and Mai W. Bean, *A Legacy of Life and Love: Pregnancy Center Service Report,* 3rd ed. (Arlington, VA: Charlotte Lozier Institute, 2018), https:// www.heartbeatinternational.org/images/assets/pressroom/PRC-report-2018.pdf. The percentage of testing services that are ultrasounds are similar between the eKYROs and CLI figures, suggesting that the eKYROs data may not necessarily be unrepresentative in terms of the clientele share served by medical pregnancy centers. eKYROs centers reported performing 249,891 pregnancy tests and 138,958 ultrasounds (388,849 services, with 35.7 percent ultrasounds). CLI reports for the United States 679,600 pregnancy tests and 400,100 ultrasounds (1,079,700 testing services, with 37.1 percent ultrasounds). Using only pregnancy tests to compare eKYROs to CLI service volume reduces my estimate of the total number of women changing their minds about abortion only slightly, to just over 38,000.

26. Jones and Jerman, "Abortion Incidence and Service Availability in the United States."

27. Kimberly Kelly, "Evangelical Underdogs: Intrinsic Success, Organizational Solidarity, and Marginalized Identities as Religious Movement Resources," *Journal of Contemporary Ethnography* 43, no. 4 (2014), 423.

28. Another section of its reports from which it might be discerned appears to be based on fewer pregnancies than are otherwise recorded in the data.

29. Focus on the Family, *Excellence of Care: Standards of Care for Providing Sonograms and Other Medical Services in a Pregnancy Medical Clinic* (Colorado Springs, CO: Focus on the Family, 2009), 8.

30. "PRC Statistics—Abortion Vulnerability," eKYROS.com, accessed September 24, 2018, http://www.ekyros.com/Pub/DesktopModules/ekyros/ViewStats.aspx ?ItemId=16&mid=89&tabid=16.

31. Heartbeat International, "4 'Abortion-Minded' Myths," accessed October 9, 2018, https://www.heartbeatservices.org/4-abortion-minded-myths.

32. Amy G. Bryant and Jonas J. Swartz, "Why Crisis Pregnancy Centers Are Legal but Unethical," *AMA Journal of Ethics* 20, no. 3 (2018): 271.

33. Meaghan Winter, "Why Are Crisis Pregnancy Centers Not Illegal?," Slate. com, June 17, 2015, http://www.slate.com/articles/double_x/doublex/2015/06/crisis _pregnancy_centers_three_legal_strategies_for_bringing_them_down.html.

34. Greater Baltimore Center v. Mayor and City Council, no. 11-1111 (4th Cir. 2012).

35. Centro Tepeyac v. Montgomery County et al., no. 8:10-cv-01259-DKC—Document 73 (D. Md. 2014).

36. Assem. Bill 775, 2015–2016 Reg. Sess., ch. 700, Cal. Stat. 2015.

37. Greater Baltimore Center v. Mayor and City Council of Baltimore, no. 16-2325 (4th Cir. 2018); Centro Tepeyac v. Montgomery County et al., no. 8:10-cv-01259-

DKC—Document 73 (D. Md. 2014); Austin LifeCare, Inc. v. City of Austin, no. 1:11-cv-00875-LY—Document 146 (W.D. Tex.2014); Evergreen Association, Inc. v. City of New York, nos. 11-2735-cv, 11-2929-cv. (2nd Cir. 2014); NIFLA v. Becerra, 138 S. Ct. 2361 (2018); *Calvary Chapel Pearl Harbor v. Suzuki,* no. 1:17-cv-00326-DKW-KSC—Document 53 (D. Haw. 2018)

38. Kelly, "Evangelical Underdogs."

39. Amy G. Bryant et al., "Crisis Pregnancy Center Websites: Information, Misinformation, and Disinformation," *Contraception* 90, no. 6 (2014): 603.

40. Amy G. Bryant and Erika E. Levi, "Abortion Misinformation from Crisis Pregnancy Centers in North Carolina," *Contraception* 86, no. 6 (2012), 754.

41. Bryant and Swartz, "Why Crisis Pregnancy Centers Are Legal but Unethical."

42. Brenda Major et al., *Report of the APA Task Force on Mental Health and Abortion* (Washington, DC: American Psychological Association, 2008), http://www.apa.org/pi/wpo/mental-health-abortion-report.pdf.

43. National Cancer Institute, "Abortion, Miscarriage, and Breast Cancer Risk," January 12, 2010, http://www.cancer.gov/types/breast/abortion-miscarriage-risk.

44. For example, Joel Brind, "The Abortion-Breast Cancer Connection," *National Catholic Bioethics Quarterly* (Summer 2005); Priscilla K. Coleman, "Misinformation and Naivety on Abortion and Mental Health," *Corner* (blog), November 15, 2010, http://www.nationalreview.com/corner/253296/misinformation-and-naivety-abortion-and-mental-health-priscilla-k-coleman.

45. See also Alexei Koseff, "Battle over Abortion Rights in California Shifts to Crisis Pregnancy Centers," *Sacramento Bee,* December 6, 2015, www.sacbee.com/news/politics-government/capitol-alert/article48338410.html.

46. Bryant et al., "Crisis Pregnancy Center Websites," 602.

47. Bryant et al., "Crisis Pregnancy Center Websites," 603.

48. Katrina Kimport, Rebecca Kriz, and Sarah C. M. Roberts, "The Prevalence and Impacts of Crisis Pregnancy Center Visits among a Population of Pregnant Women," *Contraception* 98, no. 1 (2018): 70–72.

49. Centro Tepeyac v. Montgomery County et al., 51.

50. Greater Baltimore Center v. Mayor and City Council, no. 11-1111, 36.

51. Winter, "Why Are Crisis Pregnancy Centers Not Illegal?"

52. Brief for Amici Curiae Charlotte Lozier Institute, March for Life Education Fund, and National Pro-Life Women's Caucus, NIFLA v. Becerra, 585 U.S. ___ (2018), https://s27589.pcdn.co/wp-content/uploads/2018/01/16–1140-Amicus-Brief-on-the-Merits-003-Jan-12-2018.pdf.

53. Centro Tepeyac v. Montgomery County et al., 7; Greater Baltimore Center v. Mayor and City Council, no. 11-1111, 37.

54. Care Net, *The Truth about "Crisis Pregnancy Centers"* (Lansdowne, VA: Care Net, 2016), 10.

55. Charles A. Donovan Sr. and Moira Gaul, *Turning Hearts toward Life II: New Market Research for Pregnancy Help Centers* (Washington, DC: Charlotte Lozier Institute, 2015), 17–18.

56. Kimport, Kriz, and Roberts, "The Prevalence and Impacts of Crisis Pregnancy Center Visits," 71.

57. Kimport, Kriz, and Roberts, "The Prevalence and Impacts of Crisis Pregnancy Center Visits," 72.

58. Karolyn Schrage, "Effectively Reaching the Abortion-Minded Woman," workshop presented at the Care Net National Pregnancy Center Conference, Orlando, FL, September 28, 2011.

59. Planned Parenthood Federation of America, *2017–2018 Annual Report* (New York: Planned Parenthood Federation of America, n.d.), https://www.plannedparenthood .org/uploads/filer_public/4a/0f/4a0f3969-cf71–4ec3–8a90–733c01ee8148/190124-annual report18-p03.pdf.

60. Gallup News Service, "Gallup Poll News Service: June Wave 1," 2018, accessed February 21, 2019, https://news.gallup.com/poll/236174/americans-views-planned -parenthood-trends.aspx?g_source=link_newsv9&g_campaign=item_236126&g _medium=copy.

61. Planned Parenthood, *2017–2018 Annual Report.*

62. Margaret H. Hartshorn, "Pregnancy Help Centers, Abstinence, STDs, and Healing: Putting It All Together," in *Back to the Drawing Board: The Future of the Pro-Life Movement,* ed. Teresa R. Wagner (South Bend, IN: St. Augustine's, 2003): 106–120.

63. Louise Summerhill, *The Story of Birthright: The Alternative to Abortion* (Libertyville, IL: Prow/Franciscan Marytown, 1973/1984), 118.

64. See also Ziad Munson, *The Making of Pro-Life Activists: How Social Movement Mobilization Works* (Chicago: University of Chicago Press, 2008).

65. Planned Parenthood, *2017–2018 Annual Report.*

66. Michelle Cottle, "Planned Parenthood Was Always Meant to Be Controversial," *Atlantic,* May 7, 2018, https://www.theatlantic.com/politics/archive/2018/05/cecile -richards-legacy/559781/.

67. Brief for Heartbeat International as Amicus Curiae, NIFLA v. Becerra, 585 U.S. ___ (2018), https://www.supremecourt.gov/DocketPDF/16/16–1140/27865/201801 16133050516_1%20-%20Main%20Document.pdf.

68. Though he acknowledged that his fear was based on hearsay, social scientists' observations of welfare offices lend merit to the concern. Research finds that pregnancy is not an uncommon discussion topic in interactions between welfare caseworkers and clients and that clients in welfare offices are often subject to veiled if not open criticism of their pregnancy-related behavior. See Irene Lurie, *At the Front Lines of the Welfare System: A Perspective on the Decline in Welfare Caseloads* (Albany, NY: Rockefeller Institute, 2006); Norma M. Riccucci, *How Management Matters: Street-Level Bureaucrats and Welfare Reform* (Washington, DC: Georgetown University Press, 2005), 95; Celeste Watkins-Hayes, *The New Welfare Bureaucrats: Entanglements of Race, Class, and Policy Reform* (Chicago: University of Chicago Press, 2009), 5. For another example of a pregnancy center leader's ambivalence toward and concern about abortion promotion in welfare programs, see Terry Ianora, *Crisis Pregnancy Centers: The Birth of a Grassroots Movement* (Bloomington, IN: AuthorHouse, 2009).

69. Kirk Walden, "We Are about to End Abortion," January 21, 2015, http://pregnancy helpnews.com/quick-commentary/item/333-we-are-about-to-end-abortion.

70. Creekmore, Heather, "Did New York Legalize Late Term Abortion? What New York's Bill Really Means for the Pro-Life Movement," *Abundant Life Blog,* January 24, 2019, https://www.care-net.org/abundant-life-blog/did-new-york-legalize-late-term -abortion-what-new-yorks-bill-really-means-for-the-pro-life-movement.

71. Andrew Wood, "New York's Abortion Law Empowers Abusers, Not Women," February 22, 2019, https://pregnancyhelpnews.com/new-york-s-abortion-law-empowers -abusers-not-women; National Institute of Family and Life Advocates, "Newly Passed Law Allows Abortion up until Birth: A Horrific Human Rights Violation," January 24, 2019, https://nifla.org/newly-passed-law-allows-abortion-up-until-birth-a-horrific -human-rights-violation/.

72. Kimberly Kelly and Amanda Gochanour, "Racial Reconciliation or Spiritual Smokescreens? Blackwashing the Crisis Pregnancy Center Movement," *Qualitative Sociology* 41 (2018): 424.

73. Jenna Jerman, Rachel K. Jones, and Tsuyoshi Onda, *Characteristics of U.S. Abortion Patients in 2014 and Changes since 2008* (New York: Guttmacher Institute, 2016), 5–6.

74. Munson, *Making of Pro-Life Activists,* 26.

75. Luigi Esposito and Victor Romano, "Benevolent Racism and the Co-optation of the Black Lives Matter Movement," *Western Journal of Black Studies* 40, no. 3 (2016): 161–173; Kia Heise, *Interactive Framing Dynamics and Ideological Boundaries in the American Abortion Debate,* PhD diss., University of Minnesota, 2015, https://conservancy .umn.edu/bitstream/handle/11299/175461/Heise_umn_0130E_16389.pdf.; Kelly and Gochanour, "Racial Reconciliation?"

76. Zakiya T. Luna, "Marching toward Reproductive Justice: Conditional (Re)framing of the March for Women's Lives," *Sociological Inquiry* 80, no. 4 (2010): 554–578.

77. Jennifer Nelson, *Women of Color and the Reproductive Rights Movement* (New York: New York University Press, 2003); Staggenborg, *Pro-Choice Movement.*

78. Luna, "Marching toward Reproductive Justice."

79. Heise, *Interactive Framing Dynamics and Ideological Boundaries in the American Abortion Debate.*

80. Kelly and Gochanour, "Racial Reconciliation?," 436.

81. Kelly and Gochanour, "Racial Reconciliation?," 433.

82. Kelly and Gochanour, "Racial Reconciliation?," 440.

83. Jeffrey Wright and Lakita Wright, "September 29 Lunch General Session," speech at the Care Net National Pregnancy Center Conference, Orlando, FL, September 29, 2011.

84. Carole Alexander and Phyllis Esposito, "Cultural Sensitivity and the African American Client: The Missing Piece of the Puzzle," workshop presented at the Care Net National Pregnancy Center Conference, Orlando, FL, September 30, 2011.

85. Kelly and Gochanour, "Racial Reconciliation?," 438–439.

86. Tony Evans, "September 29 Dinner General Session," speech at the Care Net National Pregnancy Center Conference, Orlando, FL, September 29, 2011.

87. Brian Steensland and Philip Goff, eds., *The New Evangelical Social Engagement* (New York: Oxford University Press, 2014); see also David P. Gushee, *The Future of Faith in American Politics: The Public Witness of the Evangelical Center* (Waco, TX: Baylor University Press, 2008); Marcia Pally, *The New Evangelicals: Expanding the Vision of the Common Good* (Grand Rapids, MI: Eerdmans, 2011); Nancy D. Wadsworth, *Ambivalent Miracles: Evangelicals and the Politics of Racial Healing* (Charlottesville: University of Virginia Press, 2014).

88. E. J. Dionne Jr., *Souled Out: Reclaiming Faith and Politics after the Religious Right* (Princeton, NJ: Princeton University Press, 2008), 197; Kurt Eichenwald, "America's Abortion Wars (and How to End Them)," *Newsweek,* December 17, 2015, https://www.newsweek.com/2015/12/25/abortion-war-overif-you-want-it-be-406137.html; Stephen Schneck, "Remarks to the Democratic National Convention," Democrats for Life of America panel, September 6, 2012, http://www.democratsforlife.org/index.php?option=com_content&view=article&id=770:remarks-by-steve-schneck-democratic-national-convention&catid=24&Itemid=205.

89. Covert and Israel, "States That Siphon Welfare Money to Stop Abortion."

90. Mary Tuma, "Crisis Pregnancy Centers: Money for Nothing," *Austin Chronicle,* July 20 2018, https://www.austinchronicle.com/news/2018-07-20/crisis-pregnancy-centers-money-for-nothing/.

91. For reviews and additional findings, see Laura S. Hussey, "Welfare Generosity, Abortion Access, and Abortion Rates: A Comparison of State Policy Tools," *Social Science Quarterly* 91 (2010): 266–283; Laura S. Hussey, "Is Welfare Pro-Life? Assistance Programs, Abortion, and the Moderating Role of States," *Social Service Review* 85 (2011): 75–107.

92. Anne H. Gauthier, "The Impact of Family Policies on Fertility in Industrialized Countries: A Review of the Literature," *Population Research and Policy Review* 26 (2007): 323–346.

93. Tomas Frejka and Sergei Zakharov, "The Apparent Failure of Russia's Pronatalist Family Policies," *Population and Development Review* 39, no. 4 (2013): 635–647.

94. Jan M. Hoem, "The Impact of Public Policies on European Fertility," *Demographic Research* 19, Special Collection 7 (July 2008): 249–260, http: //www.demographic-research.org/special/7.

95. I thank an anonymous reviewer for this insight.

96. Geraldine Faria, Elwin Barrett, and Linnea Meany Goodman, "Women and Abortion: Attitudes, Social Networks, Decision-Making," *Social Work in Health Care* 11, no. 1 (1985): 85–99; Gloria Feldt, *Behind Every Choice Is a Story* (Denton: University of North Texas Press, 2002); Lawrence B. Finer et al., "Reasons U.S. Women Have Abortions: Quantitative and Qualitative Perspectives," *Perspectives on Sexual and Reproductive Health* 37, no. 3 (2005): 110–118; Maggie Kirkman et al., "Reasons Women Give for Abortion: A Review of the Literature," *Archives of Women's Mental Health* 12 (2009): 365–378; Aida Torres and Jacqueline Darroch Forrest, "Why Do Women Have Abortions?," *Family Planning Perspectives* 20 (1988): 169–176.

97. Faria, Barrett, and Goodman, "Women and Abortion"; Torres and Forrest, "Why Do Women Have Abortions?"

98. Katha Pollitt, *Pro: Reclaiming Abortion Rights* (New York: Picador, 2014).

99. Nina Eliasoph, *The Politics of Volunteering* (Cambridge, UK: Polity, 2013), 125; David S. Gutterman, *Prophetic Politics: Christian Social Movements and American Democracy* (Ithaca, NY: Cornell University Press, 2005); Nancy D. Wadsworth, *Ambivalent Miracles: Evangelicals and the Politics of Racial Healing* (Charlottesville: University of Virginia Press, 2014).

CHAPTER 8. CONCLUSIONS: TARGETS, TRESPASS, SERVICE, AND FOUNDATIONS IN FAITH

1. Daniel K. Williams, "The Partisan Trajectory of the American Pro-Life Movement: How a Liberal Catholic Campaign Became a Conservative Evangelical Cause," *Religions* 6, no. 2 (2015): 451–475.

2. Edward G. Carmines and James Woods, "The Role of Party Activists in the Evolution of the Abortion Issue," *Political Behavior* 24, no. 4, *Special Issue: Parties and Partisanship, Part 3* (2002): 361–377; Geoffrey Layman, *The Great Divide: Religious and Cultural Conflict in American Party Politics* (New York: Columbia University Press, 2001); Christina Wolbrecht, *The Politics of Women's Rights: Parties, Positions, and Change* (Princeton, NJ: Princeton University Press, 2000); Geoffrey C. Layman et al., "Activists and Conflict Extension in American Party Politics," *American Political Science Review* 104, no. 2 (2010): 324–346.

3. David S. Meyer and Suzanne Staggenborg, "Movements, Countermovements, and the Structure of Political Opportunity," *American Journal of Sociology* 101 (1996): 1628–1660.

4. Louise Summerhill, *The Story of Birthright: The Alternative to Abortion* (Libertyville, IL: Prow/Franciscan Marytown, 1973/1984).

5. Nina Eliasoph, *The Politics of Volunteering* (Cambridge, UK: Polity, 2013), 63.

6. Heartbeat International, *The LOVE Approach Training Manual*, 3rd ed. (Columbus, OH: Heartbeat International, 2011), 25.

7. Care Net, *Serving with Care and Integrity: A Training Resource for Pregnancy Center Volunteers* (Lansdowne, VA: Care Net, 2003), 53.

8. Summerhill, *Story of Birthright*, 9.

9. Heartbeat International, *LOVE Approach*, 22.

10. Heartbeat International, *LOVE Approach*, 23, 29.

11. Care Net, *Serving with Care and Integrity*, 6.

12. Care Net, *Serving with Care and Integrity*, 187.

13. Summerhill, *Story of Birthright*, 11.

14. Care Net, *Serving with Care and Integrity*, 48.

15. Heartbeat International, *LOVE Approach*, 29.

16. Heartbeat International, *LOVE Approach*, 14. Care Net, *Serving with Care and Integrity*, 48.

17. Summerhill, *Story of Birthright*, 122.

18. Margaret H. Hartshorn, "Keynote Speech to the March for Life Rose Dinner," January 25, 2013, Heartbeat International, https://www.heartbeatinternational.org /component/k2/item/277-rose-dinner.

19. *Beautiful Everyday Holy Bible,* New Living Translation, 2nd ed. (Carol Stream, IL: Tyndale House, 2007), A7.

20. Care Net, *Serving with Care and Integrity,* 96.

21. Care Net, *Serving with Care and Integrity,* 96.

22. Care Net, *Serving with Care and Integrity,* 102.

23. Margaret H. Hartshorn, *Foot Soldiers Armed with Love: Heartbeat International's First Forty Years* (Virginia Beach, VA: Donning, 2011), 41.

24. Heartbeat International, *LOVE Approach,* 13.

25. Heartbeat International, *LOVE Approach,* 14.

26. See also Heartbeat International, *LOVE Approach,* 88.

27. Care Net, *Serving with Care and Integrity,* 6.

28. Care Net, *Serving with Care and Integrity,* 187.

29. Heartbeat International, *LOVE Approach,* 4.

30. Mary Cunningham Agee, *A Call to Effective Action: When Being Right Is Not Enough* (Washington, DC: Respect Life Program, 2004).

31. See also Meaghan Winter, "'Save the Mother, Save the Baby': An Inside Look at a Pregnancy Center Conference," *Cosmopolitan,* April 6, 2015, http://www.cosmopolitan .com/politics/a38642/heartbeat-international-conference-crisis-pregnancy-centers -abortion/.

32. Hartshorn, *Foot Soldiers.*

33. Heartbeat International, *LOVE Approach,* 25.

34. Hartshorn, *Foot Soldiers.*

35. Hartshorn, *Foot Soldiers.*

36. Carol Clews, "A History of the Center for Pregnancy Concerns" (speech, n.d.).

37. Hartshorn, in discussion with the author, August 23, 2012.

38. Hartshorn, *Foot Soldiers,* 14.

39. Care Net, *Serving with Care and Integrity;* Heartbeat International, *LOVE Approach;* Summerhill, *Story of Birthright,* 74.

40. Care Net, *Serving with Care and Integrity,* 46.

41. 40 Days for Life, "Mission," accessed August 4, 2016, https://40daysforlife.com /mission/.

42. Heartbeat International, "40 Years after *Roe,* God Reigns," accessed December 8, 2014, http://www.heartbeatinternational.org/40-years-after-roe-god-reigns.

43. Hartshorn, "Keynote Speech to the March for Life Rose Dinner."

44. Summerhill, *Story of Birthright,* 73.

45. Hartshorn, *Foot Soldiers,* 65.

46. Hartshorn, "Keynote Speech to the March for Life Rose Dinner."

47. See also Ziad Munson, *The Making of Pro-Life Activists: How Social Movement Mobilization Works* (Chicago: University of Chicago Press, 2008). Winter, "'Save the Mother, Save the Baby.'"

48. Laura Gauer, "A Christian Perspective on Poverty and Social Justice: Sin Is More Than Just Flawed Character," *Social Work and Christianity* 32, no. 4 (2005): 354–365; David P. Gushee, *The Future of Faith in American Politics: The Public Witness of the Evangelical Center* (Waco, TX: Baylor University Press, 2008); Gregory Allen Smith, *Politics in the Parish: The Political Influence of Catholic Priests* (Washington, DC: Georgetown University Perss, 2008).

49. Hartshorn, *Foot Soldiers,* 113 [italics in original].

50. Nancy D. Wadsworth, *Ambivalent Miracles: Evangelicals and the Politics of Racial Healing* (Charlottesville: University of Virginia Press, 2014).

51. Wadsworth, *Ambivalent Miracles,* 263.

52. Wadsworth, *Ambivalent Miracles.*

53. Terry Ianora, *Crisis Pregnancy Centers: The Birth of a Grassroots Movement* (Bloomington, IN: AuthorHouse, 2009).

54. See also Kimberly Kelly, "In the Name of the Mother: Gender and Religion in the Crisis Pregnancy Center Movement," PhD diss., University of Georgia Press, 2009), 241.

55. E. J. Dionne Jr., "Centrist Courage on Abortion," *Washington Post,* May 17, 2005, A21; Kurt Eichenwald, "America's Abortion Wars (and How to End Them)," *Newsweek,* December 17, 2015, https://www.newsweek.com/2015/12/25/abortion-war-overif-you-want-it-be-406137.html; James R. Kelly, "Truth, Not Truce: 'Common Ground' on Abortion, a Movement within Both Movements," *Virginia Review of Sociology* 2, no. 2 (1995): 213–241; Laurence Tribe, *Abortion: The Clash of Absolutes* (New York: Norton, 1990).

56. Kelly, "Truth, Not Truce."

57. Deborah B. Gould, *Moving Politics: Emotion and ACT UP's Fight against AIDS* (Chicago: University of Chicago Press, 2009); Verta Taylor and Nellie Van Dyke, "'Get Up, Stand Up': Tactical Repertoires of Social Movements," in *The Blackwell Companion to Social Movements,* ed. David A. Snow, Sarah A. Soule, and Hanspeter Kriesi (Malden, MA: Blackwell, 2004), 262–293; Ziad Munson, *The Making of Pro-Life Activists: How Social Movement Mobilization Works* (Chicago: University of Chicago Press, 2008).

58. Anthony M. Orum and John G. Dale, *Introduction to Political Sociology: Power and Participation in the Modern World,* 5th ed. (Oxford, UK: Oxford University Press, 2009), 291–292.

59. Ruth Braunstein, *Prophets and Patriots: Faith in Democracy across the Political Divide* (Berkeley: University of California Press, 2017), 183.

60. Munson, *Making of Pro-Life Activists.*

61. Nancy J. Davis and Robert V. Robinson, *Claiming Society for God: Religious Movements and Social Welfare in Egypt, Israel, Italy, and the United States* (Bloomington: Indiana University Press, 2012); Paul Lichterman, *Elusive Togetherness: Church Groups Trying to Bridge America's Divisions* (Princeton, NJ: Princeton University Press, 2005); Brian Steensland and Philip Goff, eds., *The New Evangelical Social Engagement* (Oxford, UK: Oxford University Press, 2014); Wadsworth, *Ambivalent Miracles.*

62. Stanley Feldman and Marco R. Steenbergen, "The Humanitarian Foundation of Public Support for Social Welfare," *American Journal of Political Science* 45, no. 3 (2001): 658–677; Ariel Malka et al., "Religiosity and Social Welfare: Competing Influences of

Cultural Conservatism and Prosocial Value Orientation," *Journal of Personality* 79, no. 4 (2011): 763–792; Joseph W. Ciarrocchi, Ralph L. Piedmont, and Joseph E. G. Williams, "Love Thy Neighbor: Spirituality and Personality as Predictors of Prosocial Behavior in Men and Women," *Research on the Social Scientific Study of Religion* 14 (2003): 61–75; Robert D. Putnam and David E. Campbell, *American Grace: How Religion Divides and Unites Us* (New York: Simon and Schuster, 2010); Markus H. Schafer, "Religiously Traditional, Unusually Supportive? Examining Who Gives, Helps, and Advises in Americans' Close Networks," *Social Currents* 2, no. 1 (2015): 81–104; Brandon Vaidyanathan, Jonathan P. Hill, and Christian Smith, "Religion and Charitable Financial Giving to Religious and Secular Causes: Does Political Ideology Matter?," *Journal for the Scientific Study of Religion* 50, no. 3 (2011): 450–469; James D. Unnever, Francis T. Cullen, and John P. Bartkowski, "Images of God and Public Support for Capital Punishment: Does a Close Relationship with a Loving God Matter?," *Criminology* 44, no. 4 (2006): 835–866; Davis and Robinson, *Claiming Society for God*; Paul Perl and Jamie S. McClintock, "The Catholic 'Consistent Life Ethic' and Attitudes toward Capital Punishment and Welfare Reform," *Sociology of Religion* 62, no. 3 (2001): 275–299.

63. Mayer N. Zald and John D. McCarthy, "Religious Groups as Crucibles of Social Movements," in *Social Movements in an Organizational Society*, ed. Mayer N. Zald and John D. McCarthy (New Brunswick, NJ: Transaction, 1987), 67–96; Putnam and Campbell, *American Grace*.

64. Schafer, "Religiously Traditional, Unusually Supportive?"

65. Unnever, Cullen, and Bartkowski, "Images of God and Public Support for Capital Punishment."

66. Elizabeth Weiss Ozorak, "Love of God and Neighbor: Religion and Volunteer Service among College Students," *Review of Religious Research* 44, no. 3 (2003): 285–299.

67. Munson, *Making of Pro-Life Activists*.

68. Samuel L. Perry, "Conservative Christians and Support for Transracial Adoption as an Alternative to Abortion," *Social Science Quarterly* 95, no. 2 (2014): 380–392.

69. Daniel M. Shea, "Young Voters, Declining Trust and the Limits of 'Service Politics,'" *Forum* 13, no. 3 (2015): 459–479; Cliff Zukin et al., *A New Engagement: Political Participation, Civic Life, and the Changing American Citizen* (Oxford, UK: Oxford University Press, 2006); Adriane Bilous, "'We Need a Revival": Young Evangelical Women Redefine Activism in New York City," in *The New Evangelical Social Engagement*, ed. Brian Steensland and Philip Goff (Oxford, UK: Oxford University Press, 2014), 109–128.

70. Craig A. Rimmerman, *The New Citizenship: Unconventional Politics, Activism, and Service*, 3rd ed. (Boulder, CO: Westview, 2005); Russell J. Dalton, *The Good Citizen: How a Younger Generation Is Reshaping American Politics*, rev. ed. (Washington, DC: Congressional Quarterly Press, 2009); Patricia Strach, "Political Participation in a Consumer Era: Why Americans Choose Politics," paper presented at the Annual Meeting of the Midwest Political Science Association, Chicago, IL, April 12–14, 2012.

71. "Last Five Years Account for More Than One-Quarter of All Abortion Restrictions Enacted since *Roe*," Guttmacher Institute, January 13, 2016, https://www.guttmacher.org/article/2016/01/last-five-years-account-more-one-quarter-all-abortion

-restrictions-enacted-roe; Elizabeth Nash et al., *Laws Affecting Reproductive Health and Rights: State Trends at Midyear, 2016* (New York: Guttmacher Institute, 2016), https://www.guttmacher.org/article/2016/07/laws-affecting-reproductive-health-and-rights-state-trends-midyear-2016.

72. Ellen M. Dran and James R. Bowers, "What If Abortion Were Illegal? Policy Alternatives Won't Be Easy," in *Understanding the New Politics of Abortion*, ed. Malcolm L. Goggin (Thousand Oaks, CA: Sage, 1993), 102.

73. Davis and Robinson, *Claiming Society for God*.

74. Kerry N. Jacoby, *Souls, Bodies, Spirits: The Drive to Abolish Abortion since 1973* (Westport, CT: Praeger, 1999).

75. For example, Helen Alvaré et al., "The Lazy Slander of the Pro-Life Cause," *Public Discourse*, January 17, 2011, https://www.thepublicdiscourse.com/2011/01/2380/.

76. For example, Micaiah Bilger, "Former Planned Parenthood Abortion Clinic Re-Opens as a Pro-Life Pregnancy Center," LifeNews.com, November 9, 2015, http://www.lifenews.com/2015/11/09/former-planned-parenthood-abortion-clinic-re-opens-as-a-pro-life-pregnancy-center/; Jay Hobbs, "Heartbeat of Miami Converting Second Ex-Abortion Mill into Pro-Life Help Clinic," *Pregnancy Help News*, November 19, 2015, https://pregnancyhelpnews.com/heartbeat-of-miami-converting-second-ex-abortion-mill-into-pro-life-help-clinic; Jay Hobbs, "Pregnancy Center That Helps Women Takes Over Former Planned Parenthood Abortion Clinic," LifeNews.com, February 15, 2016, http://www.lifenews.com/2016/02/15/pregnancy-center-that-helps-women-takes-over-former-planned-parenthood-abortion-clinic/.

77. Hartshorn, *Foot Soldiers*, 106.

78. Heartbeat International, "Worldwide Directory of Pregnancy Help," accessed October 8, 2018, https://www.heartbeatinternational.org/worldwide-directory.

79. Heartbeat International, *Life Trends Report 2015* (Columbus, OH: Heartbeat International, 2016).

80. Hartshorn, *Foot Soldiers*.

81. Gould, *Moving Politics;* Taylor and Van Dyke, "'Get Up, Stand Up.'"

82. James Davison Hunter, *Before the Shooting Begins: Searching for Democracy in America's Culture War* (New York: Free Press, 1994); Jonathan Haidt, *The Righteous Mind: Why Good People Are Divided by Politics and Religion* (New York: Vintage, 2012); John R. Petrocik, "Issue Ownership in Presidential Elections, with a 1980 Case Study," *American Journal of Political Science* 40, no. 3 (1996): 825–850.

83. Haidt, *Righteous Mind*.

84. Daniel K. Williams, *Defenders of the Unborn: The Pro-Life Movement before Roe v. Wade* (New York: Oxford University Press, 2016); Mary Ziegler, *After Roe: The Lost History of the Abortion Debate* (Cambridge, MA: Harvard University Press, 2015); Hunter, *Before the Shooting Begins;* Munson, *Making of Pro-Life Activists;* Clyde Wilcox and Carin Larson, *Onward Christian Soldiers? The Religious Right in American Politics*, 3rd ed. (Boulder, CO: Westview, 2006).

85. Andrew R. Lewis, *The Rights Turn in Conservative Christian Politics* (Cambridge, UK: Cambridge University Press, 2017).

86. Rose Ernst, *The Price of Progressive Politics: The Welfare Rights Movement in an Era of Colorblind Racism* (New York: New York University Press, 2010).

87. Adam Kahane, *Power and Love: A Theory and Practice of Social Change* (San Francisco: Berrett-Koehler, 2010).

88. Jennifer Nelson, *Women of Color and the Reproductive Rights Movement* (New York: New York University Press, 2003); Dorothy Roberts, "Reproductive Justice, Not Just Rights," *Dissent* 62, no. 4 (2015): 79–82; Kathy Rudy, *Beyond Pro-Life and Pro-Choice: Moral Diversity in the Abortion Debate* (Boston: Beacon, 1996); Rickie Solinger, *Beggars and Choosers: How the Politics of Choice Shapes Adoption, Abortion, and Welfare in the United States* (New York: Hill and Wang, 2001).

89. Sandy Christiansen, in discussion with the author, July 9, 2012.

Selected Bibliography

Bilous, Adriane. "'We Need a Revival': Young Evangelical Women Redefine Activism in New York City." In *The New Evangelical Social Engagement*, edited by Brian Steensland and Philip Goff, 109–128. Oxford, UK: Oxford University Press, 2014.

Blackstone, Amy. "'It's Just about Being Fair': Activism and the Politics of Volunteering in the Breast Cancer Movement." *Gender and Society* 18, no. 3 (2004): 350–368.

Blanchard, Dallas A. *The Anti-Abortion Movement and the Rise of the Religious Right: From Polite to Fiery Protest.* New York: Twayne, 1994.

Bryant, Amy G., and Erika E. Levi. "Abortion Misinformation from Crisis Pregnancy Centers in North Carolina." *Contraception* 86, no. 6 (2012): 752–756.

Bryant, Amy G., Subasri Narasimhan, Katelyn Bryant-Comstock, and Erika E. Levi. "Crisis Pregnancy Center Websites: Information, Misinformation, and Disinformation." *Contraception* 90, no. 6 (2014): 601–605.

Bryant, Amy G., and Jonas J. Swartz. "Why Crisis Pregnancy Centers Are Legal but Unethical." *AMA Journal of Ethics* 20, no. 3 (2018): 269–277.

Burns, Gene. *The Moral Veto: Framing Contraception, Abortion, and Cultural Pluralism in the United States.* New York: Cambridge University Press, 2005.

Collins, Barbara G., and Mary B. Whalen. "The Rape Crisis Movement: Radical or Reformist?" *Social Work* 34, no. 1 (1989): 61–63.

Conger, Kimberly H. *The Christian Right in Republican State Politics.* New York: Palgrave Macmillan, 2009.

Cress, Daniel M. "Nonprofit Incorporation among Movements of the Poor." *Sociological Quarterly* 38, no. 2 (1997): 343–360.

Davis, Nancy J., and Robert V. Robinson. *Claiming Society for God: Religious Movements and Social Welfare in Egypt, Israel, Italy, and the United States.* Bloomington: Indiana University Press, 2012.

Deines, Helen. "The Catholic Worker Movement: Communities of Personal Hospitality and Justice." *Social Work and Christianity* 35, no. 4 (2008): 429–448.

Diamond, Sara. *Not by Politics Alone: The Enduring Influence of the Christian Right.* New York: Guilford, 1998.

Doan, Alesha. *Opposition and Intimidation: The Abortion Wars and Strategies of Political Harassment.* Ann Arbor: University of Michigan Press, 2007.

Eliasoph, Nina. *Avoiding Politics: How Americans Produce Apathy in Everyday Life.* New York: Cambridge University Press, 1998.

———. *The Politics of Volunteering.* Cambridge, UK: Polity Press, 2013.

Ferree, Myra Marx, William Anthony Gamson, Jurgen Gerhards, and Dieter Rucht. *Shaping Abortion Discourse: Democracy and the Public Sphere in Germany and the United States.* Cambridge, UK: Cambridge University Press, 2002.

Freedman, Lori, and Tracy A. Weitz. "The Politics of Motherhood Meets the Politics of Poverty." *Contemporary Sociology* 41, no. 1 (2012): 36–42.

Ginsburg, Faye D. *Contested Lives: The Abortion Debate in an American Community.* Updated ed. Berkeley: University of California Press, 1998.

Glessner, Thomas. *The Emerging Brave New World.* Crane, MO: HighWay, 2008.

Gould, Deborah B. *Moving Politics: Emotion and Act Up's Fight against Aids.* Chicago: University of Chicago Press, 2009.

Hartshorn, Margaret H. *Foot Soldiers Armed with Love: Heartbeat International's First Forty Years.* Virginia Beach, VA: Donning, 2011.

———. "Pregnancy Help Centers, Abstinence, STDs, and Healing: Putting It All Together." In *Back to the Drawing Board: The Future of the Pro-Life Movement,* edited by Teresa R. Wagner, 106–120. South Bend, IN: St. Augustine's, 2003.

Heise, Kia. Interactive Framing Dynamics and Ideological Boundaries in the American Abortion Debate. PhD diss., University of Minnesota, 2015. https://conservancy .umn.edu/bitstream/handle/11299/175461/Heise_umn_0130E_16389.pdf.

Hunter, James Davison. *Before the Shooting Begins: Searching for Democracy in America's Culture War.* New York: Free Press, 1994.

Hussey, Laura S. "Crisis Pregnancy Centers, Poverty, and the Expanding Frontiers of American Abortion Politics." *Politics & Policy* 41 (2013): 985–1011.

———. "Political Action versus Personal Action: Understanding Social Movements' Pursuit of Change through Nongovernmental Channels." *American Politics Research* 42, no. 3 (2014): 409–440.

Ianora, Terry. *Crisis Pregnancy Centers: The Birth of a Grassroots Movement.* Bloomington, IN: AuthorHouse, 2009.

Jacoby, Kerry N. *Souls, Bodies, Spirits: The Drive to Abolish Abortion since 1973.* Westport, CT: Praeger, 1999.

Kelly, James R. "Pro-Life Politics: From Counter-Movement to Transforming Movement." In *Consistently Opposing Killing: From Abortion to Assisted Suicide, the Death Penalty, and War,* edited by Rachel M. MacNair and Stephen Zunes, 159–172. Westport, CT: Praeger, 2008.

———. "Truth, Not Truce: 'Common Ground' on Abortion, a Movement within Both Movements." *Virginia Review of Sociology* 2, no. 2 (1995): 213–241.

Kelly, Kimberly. "Evangelical Underdogs: Intrinsic Success, Organizational Solidarity, and Marginalized Identities as Religious Movement Resources." *Journal of Contemporary Ethnography* 43, no. 4 (2014): 419–455.

———. "In the Name of the Mother: Gender and Religion in the Crisis Pregnancy Center Movement." PhD diss., University of Georgia, 2009.

———. "In the Name of the Mother: Renegotiating Conservative Women's Authority in the Crisis Pregnancy Center Movement." *Signs* 38, no. 1 (2012): 203–230.

Kelly, Kimberly, and Amanda Gochanour. "Racial Reconciliation or Spiritual Smokescreens? Blackwashing the Crisis Pregnancy Center Movement." *Qualitative Sociology* 41, no. 3 (2018): 423–443.

Kimport, Katrina, Rebecca Kriz, and Sarah C. M. Roberts. "The Prevalence and Impacts of Crisis Pregnancy Center Visits among a Population of Pregnant Women." *Contraception* 98, no. 1 (2018): 69–73.

Kunzel, Regina G. "The Professionalization of Benevolence: Evangelicals and Social Workers in the Florence Crittenton Homes, 1915 to 1945." *Journal of Social History* 22, no. 1 (1988): 21–43.

Luker, Kristin. *Abortion and the Politics of Motherhood.* Berkeley: University of California Press, 1984.

Majic, Samantha. "Serving Sex Workers and Promoting Democratic Engagement: Rethinking Nonprofits' Role in American Civic and Political Life." *Perspectives on Politics* 9, no. 4 (2011): 821–839.

Mathewes-Green, Frederica. *Real Choices: Listening to Women; Looking for Alternatives to Abortion.* Ben Lomond, CA: Conciliar, 1997.

Maxwell, Carol J. C. *Pro-Life Activists in America: Meaning, Motivation, and Direct Action.* Cambridge, UK: Cambridge University Press, 2002.

McVeigh, Rory, Bryant Crubaugh, and Kevin Estep. "Plausibility Structures, Status Threats, and the Establishment of Anti-Abortion Pregnancy Centers." *American Journal of Sociology* 122, no. 5 (2017): 1533–1571.

Minkoff, Debra C. "The Emergence of Hybrid Organizational Forms: Combining Identity-Based Service Provision and Political Action." *Nonprofit and Voluntary Sector Quarterly* 31 (2002): 377–400.

———. *Organizing for Equality: The Evolution of Women's and Racial-Ethnic Organizations in America, 1955–1985.* New Brunswick, NJ: Rutgers University Press, 1995.

Morton, Marian J. "Fallen Women, Federated Charities, and Maternity Homes, 1913–1973." *Social Service Review* 62, no. 1 (1988): 61–82.

Munson, Ziad. *The Making of Pro-Life Activists: How Social Movement Mobilization Works.* Chicago: University of Chicago Press, 2008.

Olasky, Marvin N. "Abortion Rights: Anatomy of a Negative Campaign." *Public Relations Review* 13, no. 3 (1987): 12–23.

Rimmerman, Craig A. *The New Citizenship: Unconventional Politics, Activism, and Service.* 3rd ed. Boulder, CO: Westview, 2005.

Risen, James, and Judy L. Thomas. *Wrath of Angels: The American Abortion War.* New York: Basic Books, 1998.

Rose, Melody. "Pro-Life, Pro-Woman? Frame Extension in the American Antiabortion Movement." *Journal of Women, Politics, and Policy* 32, no. 1 (2011): 1–27.

———. *Safe, Legal, and Unavailable? Abortion Politics in the United States.* Washington, DC: Congressional Quarterly Press, 2007.

Rudy, Kathy. *Beyond Pro-Life and Pro-Choice: Moral Diversity in the Abortion Debate.* Boston: Beacon, 1996.

Shea, Daniel M. "Young Voters, Declining Trust and the Limits of 'Service Politics.'" *Forum* 13, no. 3 (2015): 459–479.

Shepard, Benjamin. "From Community Organization to Direct Services: The Street Trans Action Revolutionaries to Sylvia Rivera Law Project." *Journal of Social Service Research* 39, no. 1 (2013): 95–114.

Shields, Jon A. *The Democratic Virtues of the Christian Right.* Princeton, NJ: Princeton University Press, 2009.

Siegel, Reva B. "The Right's Reasons: Constitutional Conflict and the Spread of Woman-Protective Antiabortion Argument." *Duke Law Journal* 57 (2008): 1641–1692.

Summerhill, Louise. *The Story of Birthright: The Alternative to Abortion.* Libertyville, IL: Prow/Franciscan Marytown, 1973/1984.

Wharton, Carol S. "Establishing Shelters for Battered Women: Local Manifestations of a Social Movement." *Qualitative Sociology* 10, no. 2 (1987): 146–163.

Wilcox, Clyde, and Carin Larson. *Onward Christian Soldiers? The Religious Right in American Politics.* 3rd ed. Boulder, CO: Westview, 2006.

Williams, Daniel K. *Defenders of the Unborn: The Pro-Life Movement before* Roe v. Wade. New York: Oxford University Press, 2016.

———. *God's Own Party: The Making of the Christian Right.* Oxford, UK: Oxford University Press, 2010.

———. "The Partisan Trajectory of the American Pro-Life Movement: How a Liberal Catholic Campaign Became a Conservative Evangelical Cause." *Religions* 6 (2015): 451–475.

Willke, Dr. and Mrs. John C. *Abortion and the Pro-Life Movement: An Inside View.* West Conshohocken, PA: Infinity, 2014.

Wilson, Joshua. *The Street Politics of Abortion: Speech, Violence, and America's Culture Wars.* Palo Alto, CA: Stanford University, 2013.

Yuengert, Andrew, and Joel Fetzer. "Location Decisions of Abortion Clinics and Crisis Pregnancy Centers in California." *Catholic Social Science Review* 15 (2010): 211–235.

Ziegler, Mary. *After* Roe: *The Lost History of the Abortion Debate.* Cambridge, MA: Harvard University Press, 2015.

Zukin, Cliff, Scott Keeter, Molly Andolina, Krista Jenkins, and Michael X. Delli Carpini. *A New Engagement: Political Participation, Civic Life, and the Changing American Citizen.* Oxford, UK: Oxford University Press, 2006.

Index

AAI, 77, 78, 81, 84, 85, 86, 87, 104; founding of, 75; pregnancy centers and, 88. *See also* Heartbeat International

abortion: access to, 5, 43, 67, 187, 197, 234; changing mind about, 183, 183 (fig.), 204, 205 (table); choosing, 24, 33, 34, 38, 50, 73, 77, 89, 112, 123, 145, 200, 207, 215; common ground on, 230–231; conflict over, 210, 235; considering, 34, 55, 59, 65, 109, 117, 118, 144, 188, 192, 199, 203; decline in, 107, 161; demand for, 13, 99, 209, 232; ending, 4, 7, 9, 11, 12, 23, 25, 27, 72, 86–87, 90, 118, 119, 122, 124, 138, 142, 147, 154, 160, 167, 168, 169, 182, 197, 211, 214, 216, 228; fighting, 8, 15, 16, 25, 36, 45, 67, 71, 76, 84, 91, 144, 148, 175–176; harmful effects of, 43, 44, 189–190, 208; illegal, 72, 99; impact of, 43–44, 182–186, 187, 203; incidence of, 3, 24, 104–105, 106, 132, 182, 185, 195, 208, 213; increase in, 91, 98, 101, 107; legalization of, 20, 27, 42, 67, 69, 70, 71, 72, 73, 75, 87, 91, 92, 132, 147, 151, 162; obtaining, 133, 208; opposition to, 2–3, 12, 13, 41, 65, 87, 97, 104, 123, 169; preventing, 39, 60, 62, 182, 185, 198; problem of, 33–47, 115, 118–119; reducing, 3, 115, 164, 178, 182, 206, 207, 208; referral for, 187, 191; regretting, 30, 60–61, 190, 217; regulating, 71, 125–126, 234; at risk for, 36, 104, 108, 111, 184–185, 194, 195; risks of, 43, 185 (fig.), 189–190, 208; seeking, 36, 84, 109, 146; theory of, 33–38, 93, 200; understanding, 36–37; unwanted, 61, 213

abortion clinics, 44, 89, 103, 116, 121, 123, 124, 132, 140, 200, 202, 230; bombings of, 273n78; client characteristics of, 254–255 (table); client surveys for, 253–256; closing, 6, 9; community characteristics of, 134, 135, 135 (table); criticism of, 42; location of, 22, 134, 279n25; poverty rates and, 134; pregnancy centers and, 95, 116, 133, 215–216; shadowing, 133; working at, 230; ZCTA-level locations of, 246–248

abortion issue, 98, 236, 282n18; approach to, 224; magnitude of, 137; political discourse and, 2

abortion laws, 12, 165, 227, 230; changes in, 7, 13, 77, 90, 106, 147, 182; fighting, 71

abortion-minded women, 66, 86, 104, 109, 111, 112, 113, 138, 184, 185, 193, 228–229, 237; reaching, 107, 200; sympathy for, 213

abortion providers, 7, 42, 116, 123, 215, 229, 230; clinic-based, 133; metropolitan areas and, 134; number of, 13, 126–127, 131; pregnancy centers and, 138; strategies of, 216

abortion rates, 98, 126, 138, 212; pregnancy centers and, 128–129

abortion recovery, 60–61, 97

abortion rights, 11, 12, 81, 152, 156, 201, 215

"Abortion: What Can I Do?" (CAC), 93

abstinence, 57, 62, 65, 98, 100, 127, 202, 211; promoting, 100; talking about, 63

ACS. *See* American Community Survey

activism, 13, 44, 81; antiabortion, 12, 42, 43, 65–66, 147–148, 166, 167, 178, 210, 232; anti-AIDS, 115; contemporary, 175; cultural, 203; grassroots, 83, 150; lifestyle and, 231; political, 175; prior, 151–154; probability of, 170–171;